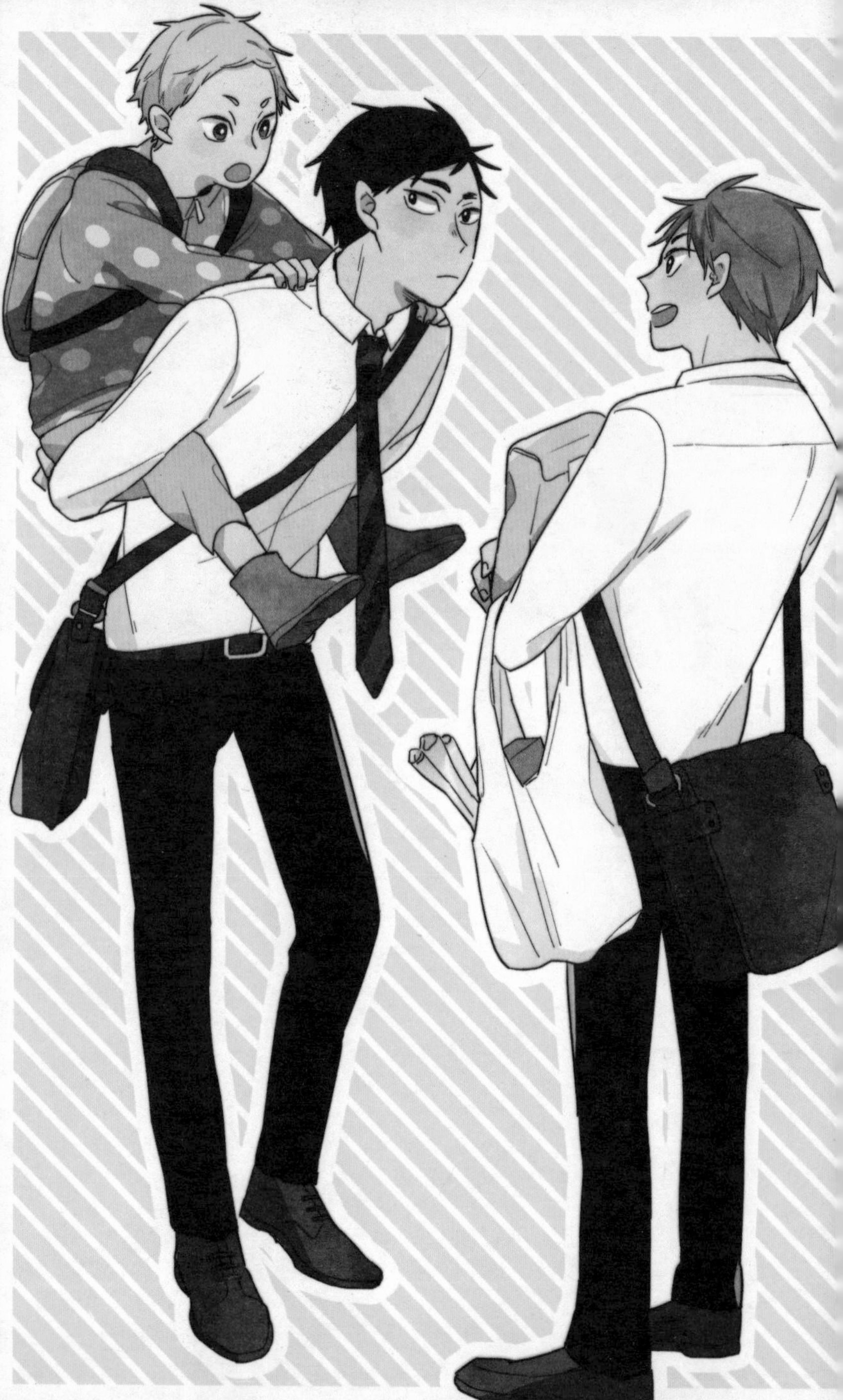

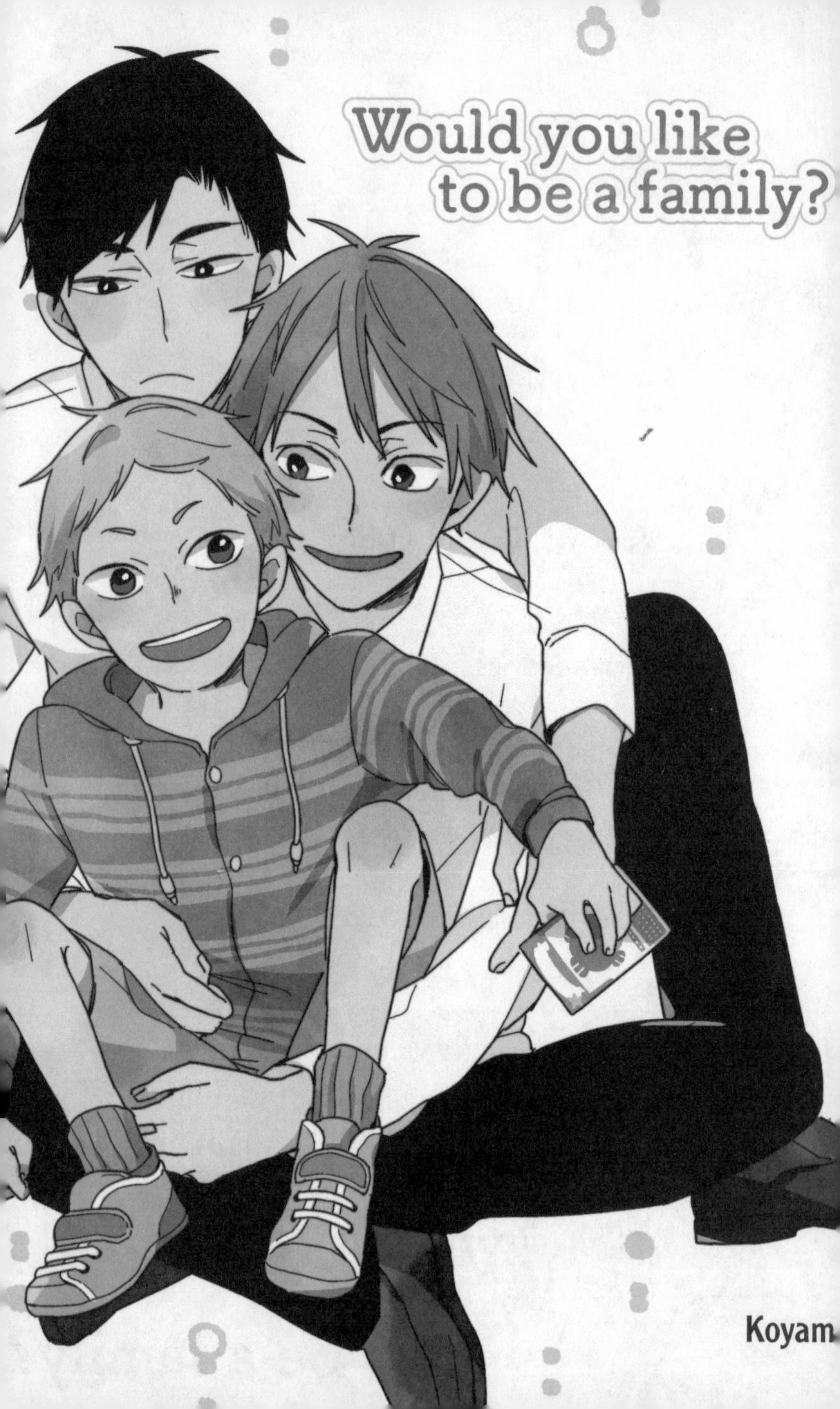
Would you like
to be a family?
Koyam

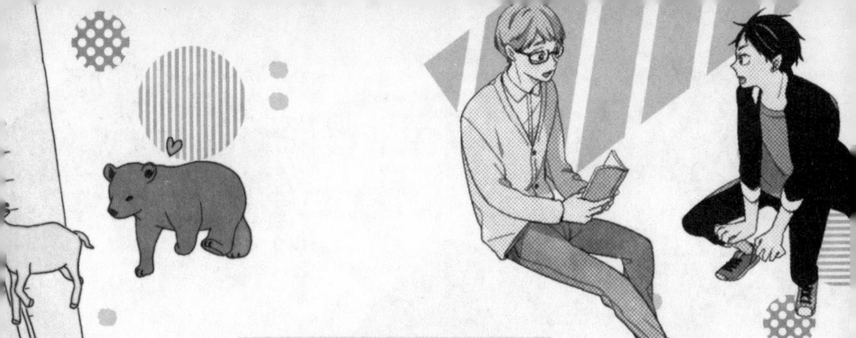

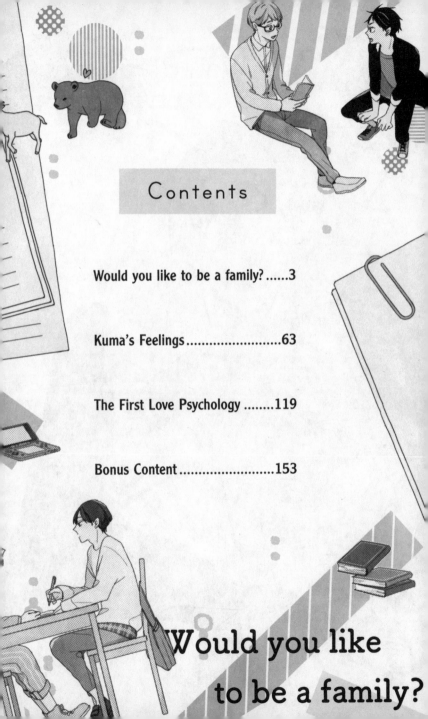

Contents

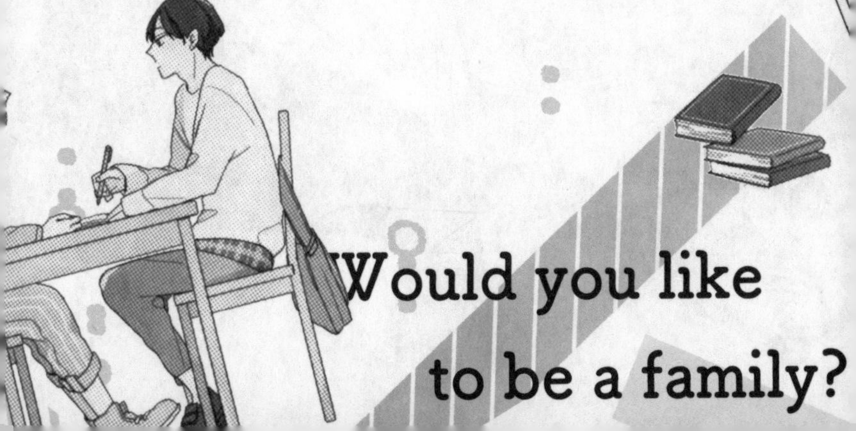

Would you like
to be a family?

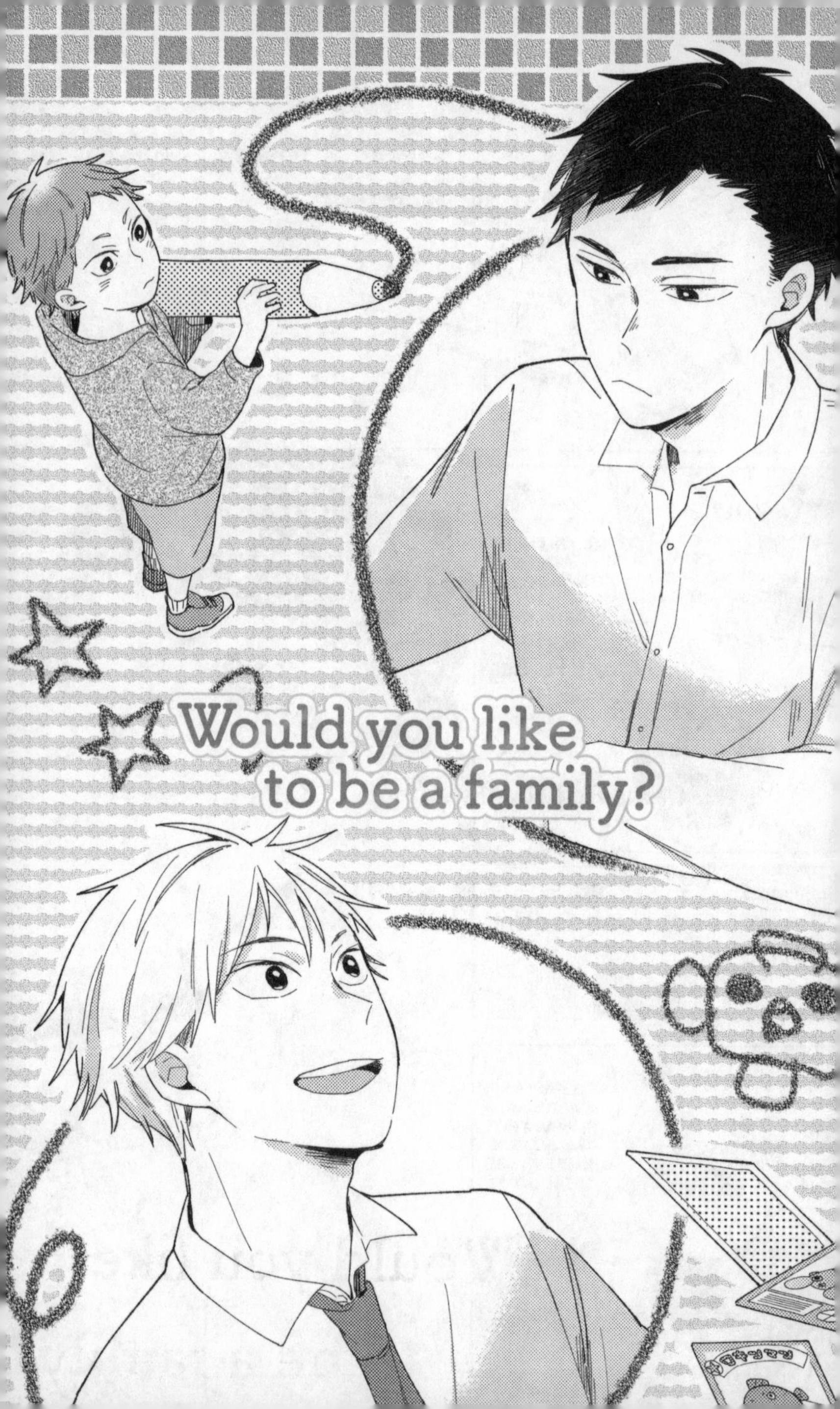
Would you like
to be a family?

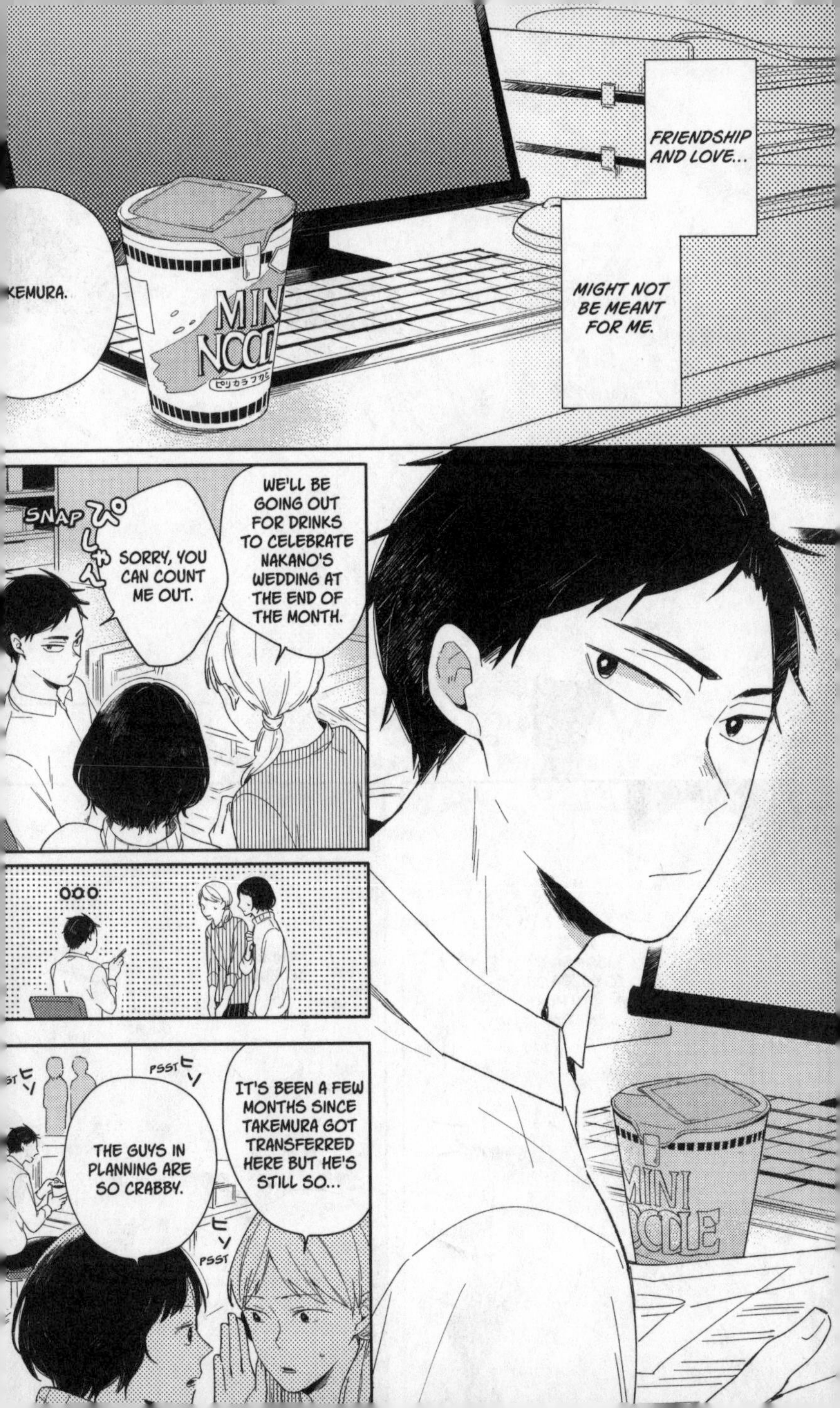
FRIENDSHIP AND LOVE...
MIGHT NOT BE MEANT FOR ME.
KEMURA.
WE'LL BE GOING OUT FOR DRINKS TO CELEBRATE NAKANO'S WEDDING AT THE END OF THE MONTH.
ぴしゃん SNAP
SORRY, YOU CAN COUNT ME OUT.
...
IT'S BEEN A FEW MONTHS SINCE TAKEMURA GOT TRANSFERRED HERE BUT HE'S STILL SO...
ヒソ PSST
ヒソ PSST
THE GUYS IN PLANNING ARE SO CRABBY.
MINI NOODLE

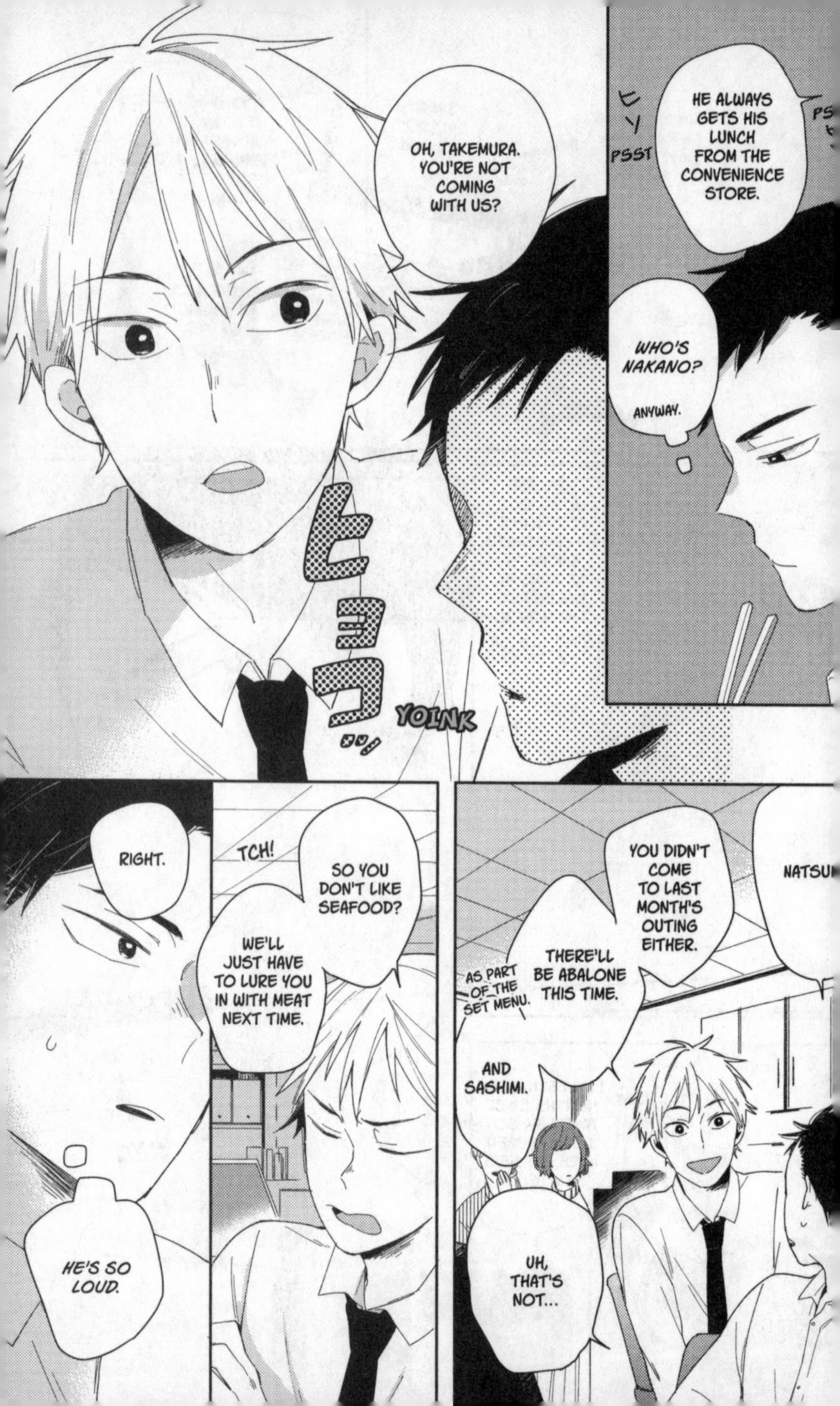
ヒソ PSST
HE ALWAYS GETS HIS LUNCH FROM THE CONVENIENCE STORE.
WHO'S NAKANO? ANYWAY.
OH, TAKEMURA. YOU'RE NOT COMING WITH US?
ヒョコッ YOINK
NATSU
YOU DIDN'T COME TO LAST MONTH'S OUTING EITHER.
THERE'LL BE ABALONE THIS TIME.
AS PART OF THE SET MENU.
AND SASHIMI.
UH, THAT'S NOT...
TCH!
SO YOU DON'T LIKE SEAFOOD?
WE'LL JUST HAVE TO LURE YOU IN WITH MEAT NEXT TIME.
RIGHT.
HE'S SO LOUD.

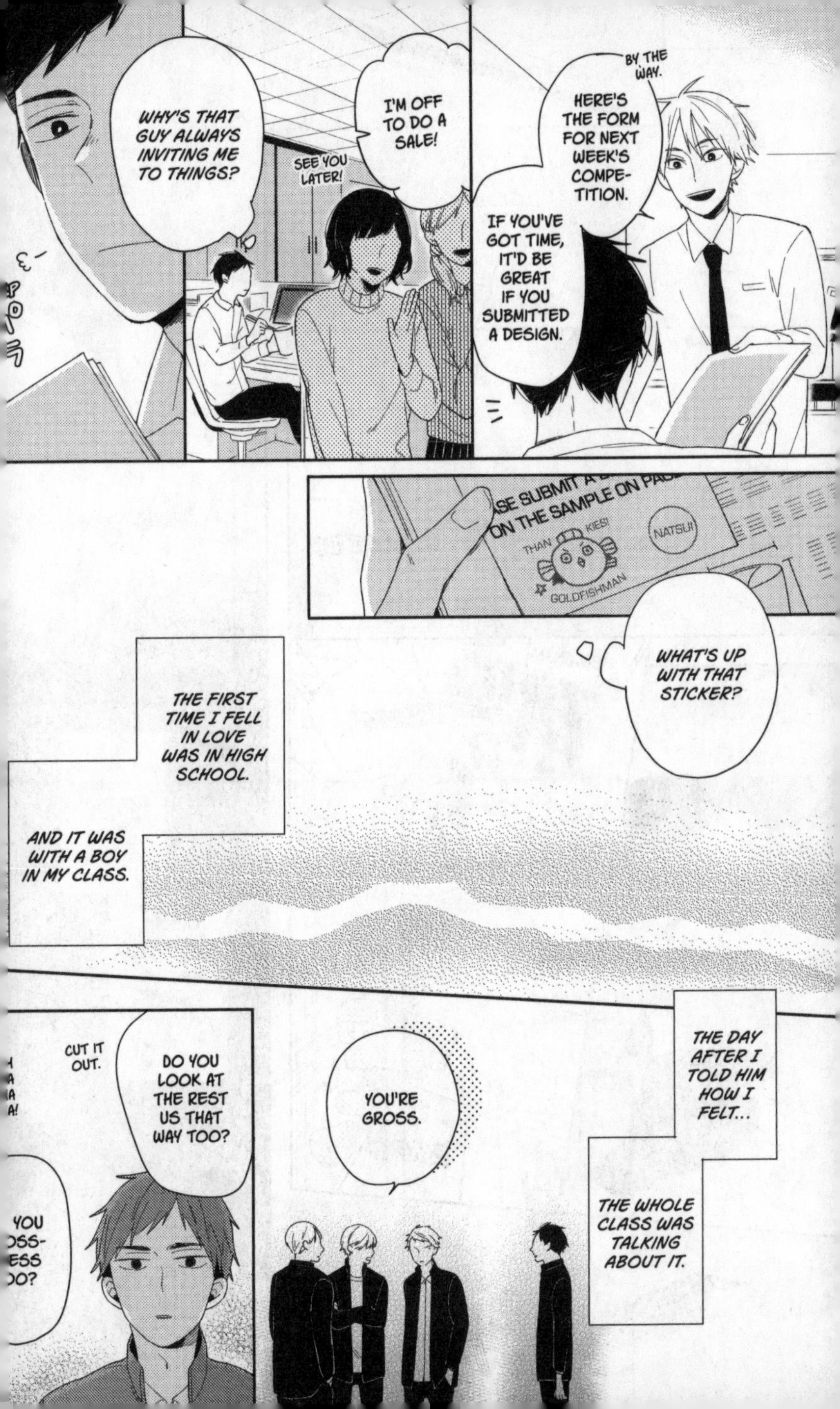
BY THE WAY.
HERE'S THE FORM FOR NEXT WEEK'S COMPE-TITION.
IF YOU'VE GOT TIME, IT'D BE GREAT IF YOU SUBMITTED A DESIGN.
I'M OFF TO DO A SALE!
SEE YOU LATER!
WHY'S THAT GUY ALWAYS INVITING ME TO THINGS?
NATSUI
GOLDFISHMAN
WHAT'S UP WITH THAT STICKER?
THE FIRST TIME I FELL IN LOVE WAS IN HIGH SCHOOL.
AND IT WAS WITH A BOY IN MY CLASS.
THE DAY AFTER I TOLD HIM HOW I FELT...
THE WHOLE CLASS WAS TALKING ABOUT IT.
YOU'RE GROSS.
DO YOU LOOK AT THE REST US THAT WAY TOO?
CUT IT OUT.

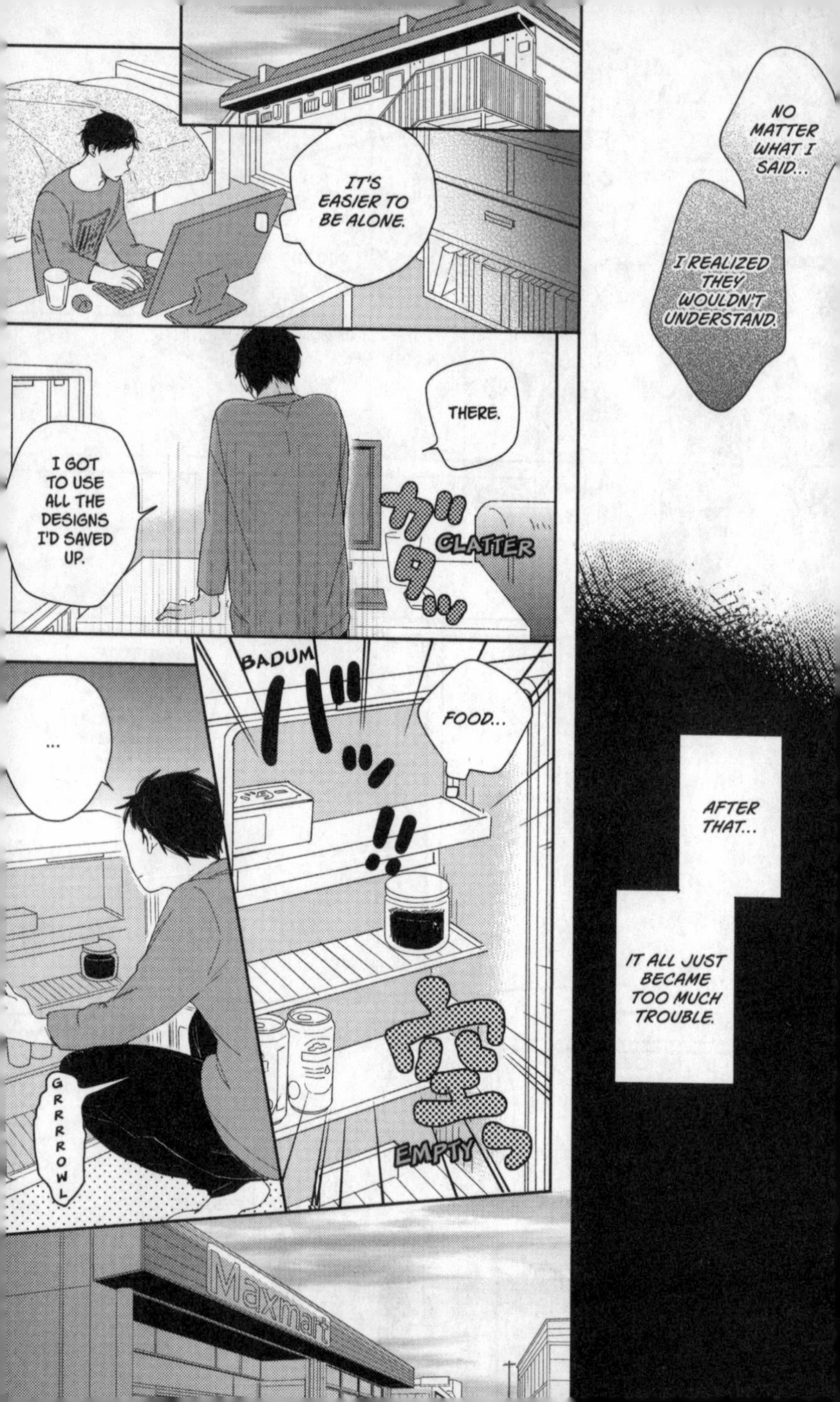

NO MATTER WHAT I SAID...
I REALIZED THEY WOULDN'T UNDERSTAND.
AFTER THAT...
IT ALL JUST BECAME TOO MUCH TROUBLE.
IT'S EASIER TO BE ALONE.
THERE.
CLATTER
I GOT TO USE ALL THE DESIGNS I'D SAVED UP.
BADUM
FOOD...
EMPTY
...
GRRRROWL
Maxmart

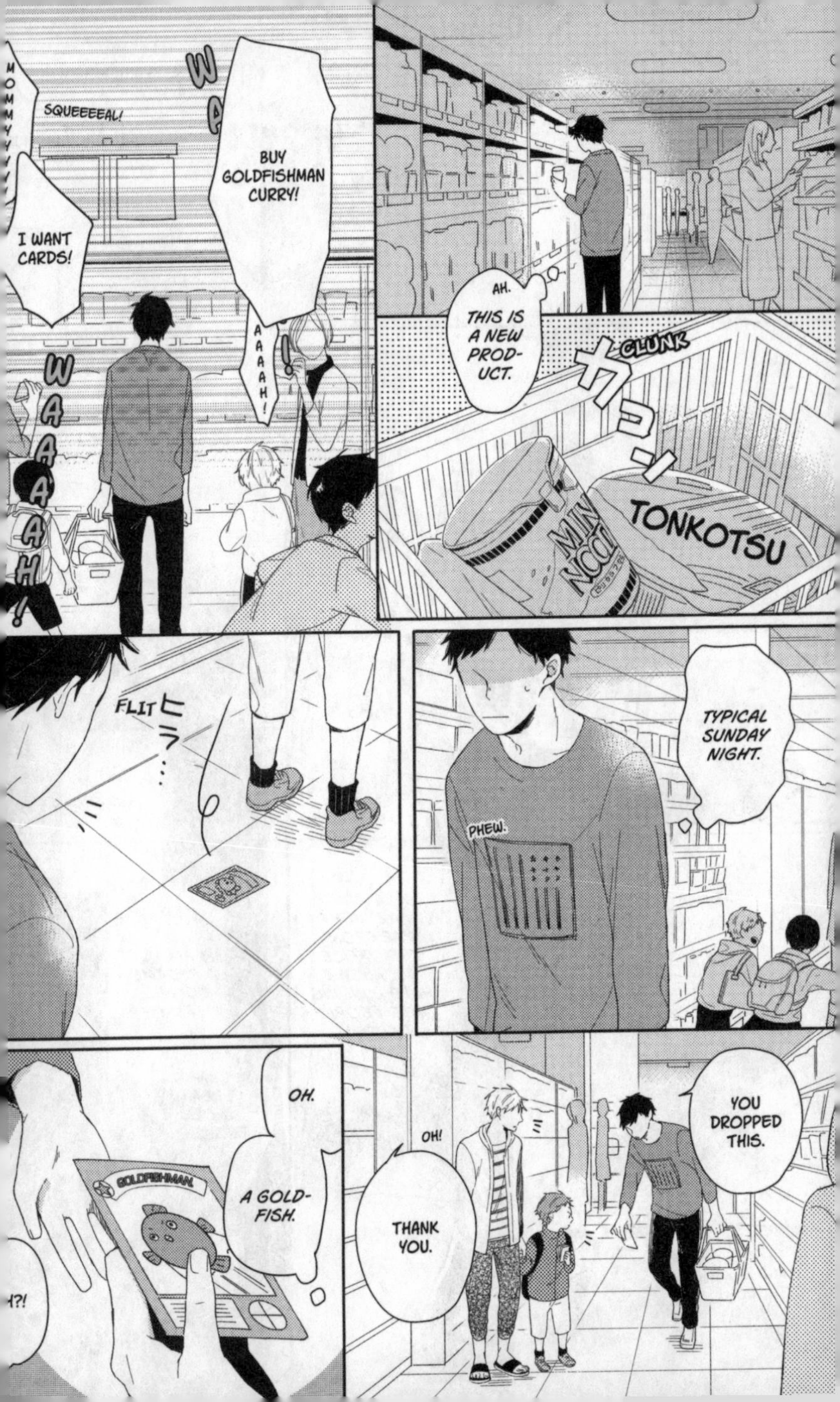
AH.
THIS IS A NEW PROD-UCT.
CLUNK
TONKOTSU
WAAAH
MOMMYYYYY
SQUEEEEAL!
BUY GOLDFISHMAN CURRY!
I WANT CARDS!
AAAAAH!
WAAAAAAH!
TYPICAL SUNDAY NIGHT.
PHEW.
FLIT
YOU DROPPED THIS.
OH!
THANK YOU.
OH.
A GOLD-FISH.
GOLDFISHMAN

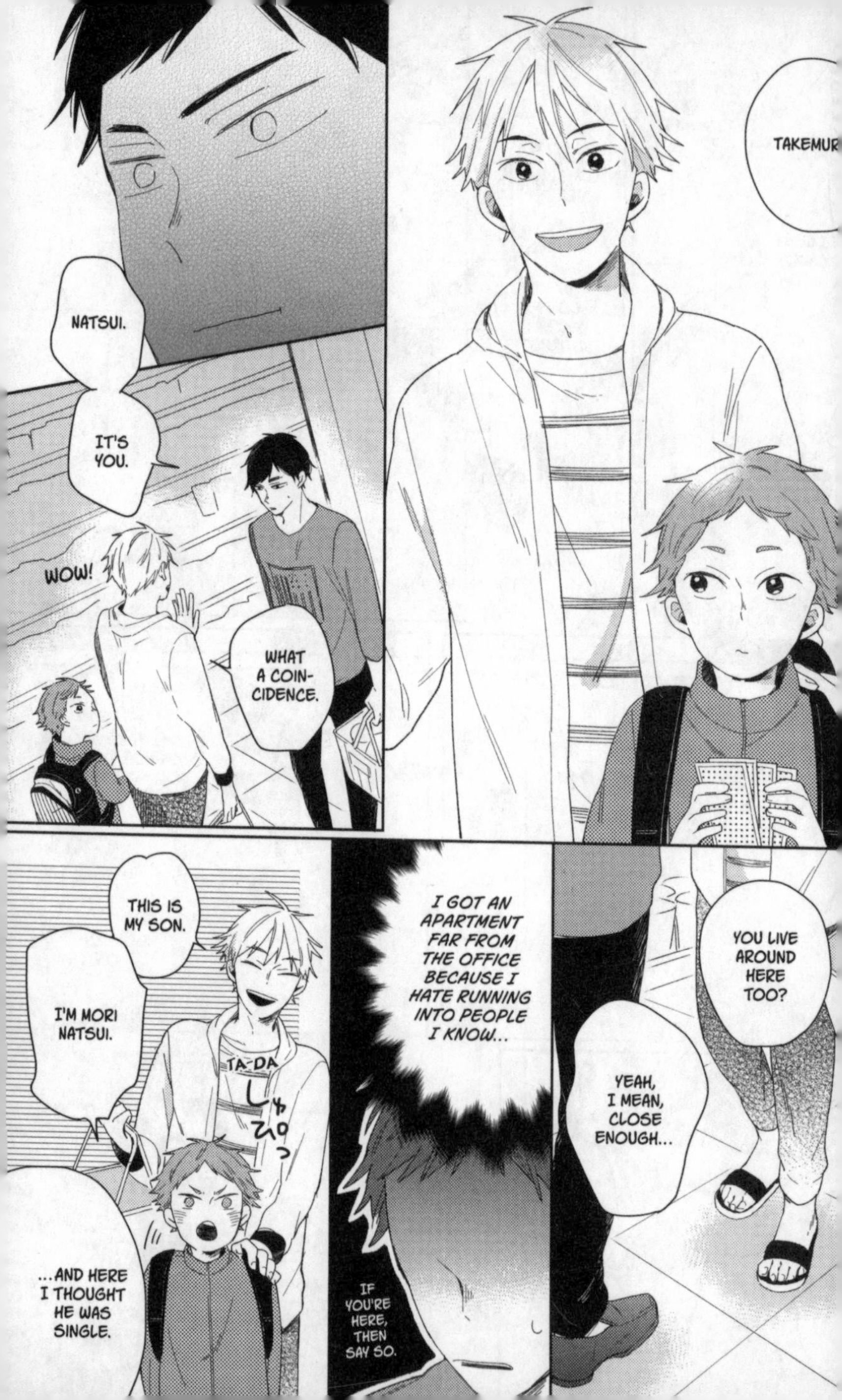
TAKEMUR
NATSUI.
IT'S YOU.
WOW!
WHAT A COINCIDENCE.
YOU LIVE AROUND HERE TOO?
YEAH, I MEAN, CLOSE ENOUGH...
I GOT AN APARTMENT FAR FROM THE OFFICE BECAUSE I HATE RUNNING INTO PEOPLE I KNOW...
IF YOU'RE HERE, THEN SAY SO.
THIS IS MY SON.
TA-DA
I'M MORI NATSUI.
...AND HERE I THOUGHT HE WAS SINGLE.

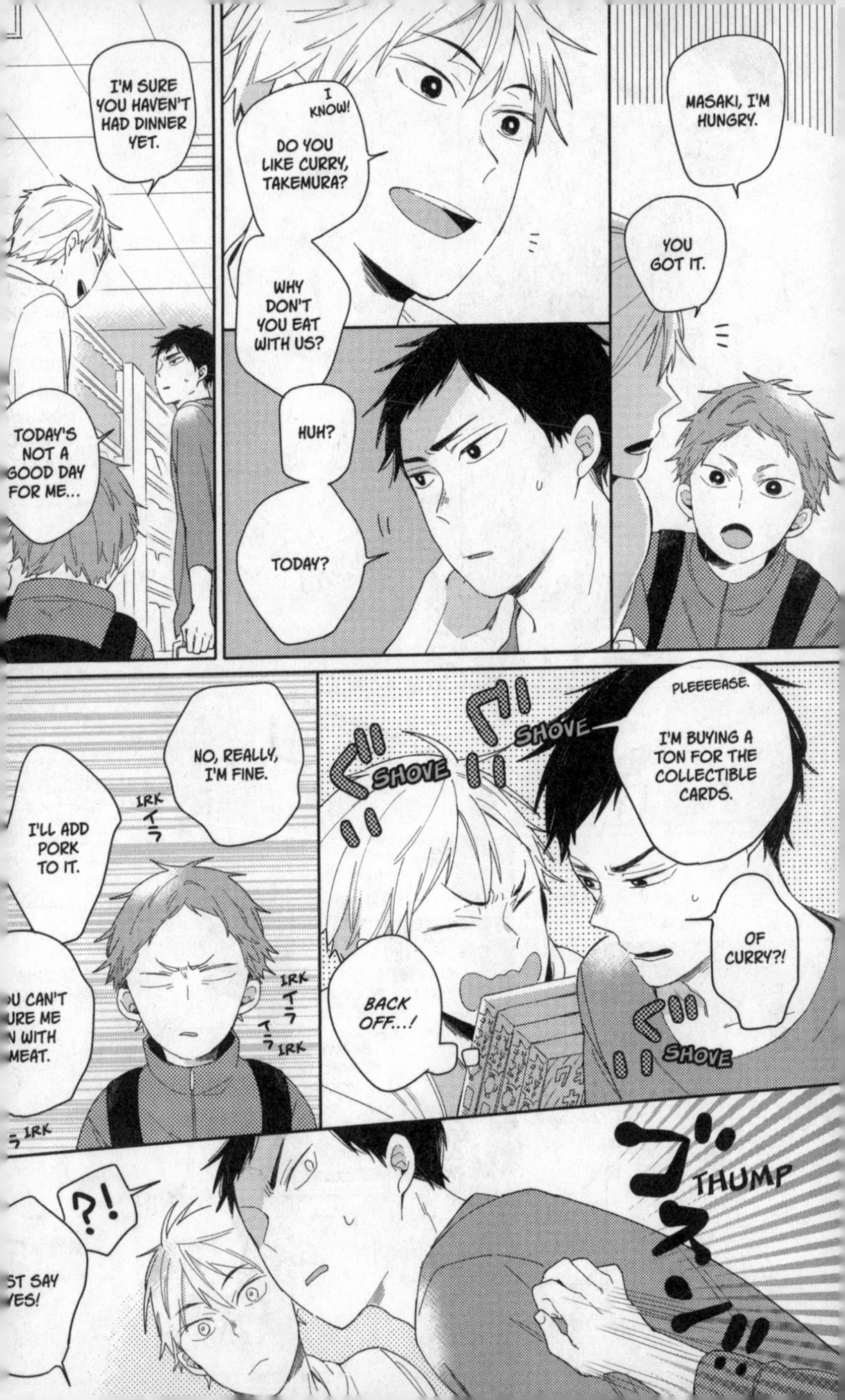
MASAKI, I'M HUNGRY.
YOU GOT IT.
I KNOW!
DO YOU LIKE CURRY, TAKEMURA?
WHY DON'T YOU EAT WITH US?
HUH?
TODAY?
I'M SURE YOU HAVEN'T HAD DINNER YET.
TODAY'S NOT A GOOD DAY FOR ME...
PLEEEEASE.
I'M BUYING A TON FOR THE COLLECTIBLE CARDS.
SHOVE
SHOVE
OF CURRY?!
BACK OFF...!
SHOVE
NO, REALLY, I'M FINE.
IRK
I'LL ADD PORK TO IT.
IRK
IRK
OU CAN'T URE ME N WITH MEAT.
IRK
THUMP
?!
ST SAY YES!

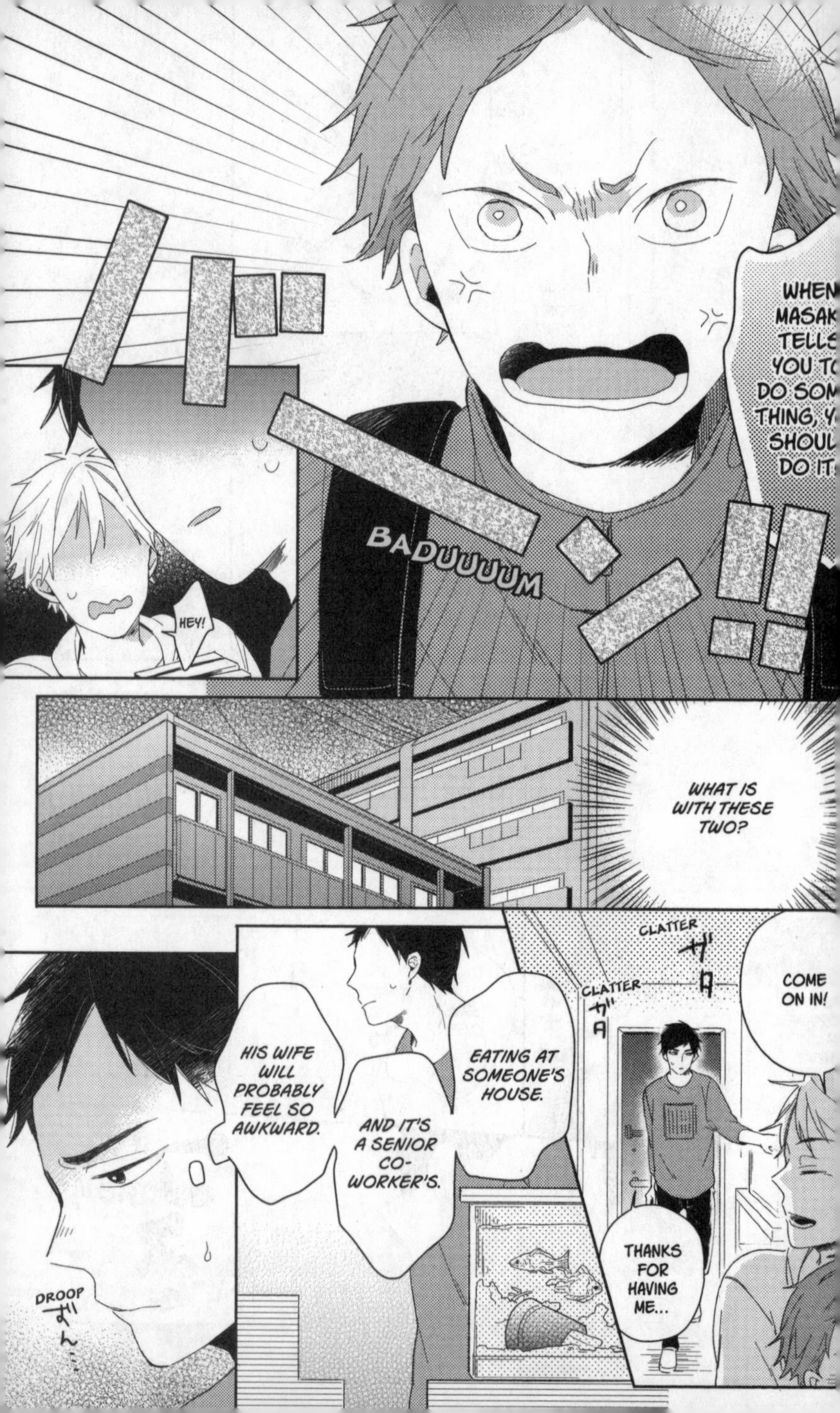
WHEN MASAK TELLS YOU TO DO SOM THING, Y SHOUL DO IT
BADUUUUM
HEY!
WHAT IS WITH THESE TWO?
COME ON IN!
CLATTER
CLATTER
THANKS FOR HAVING ME...
EATING AT SOMEONE'S HOUSE.
AND IT'S A SENIOR CO-WORKER'S.
HIS WIFE WILL PROBABLY FEEL SO AWKWARD.
DROOP

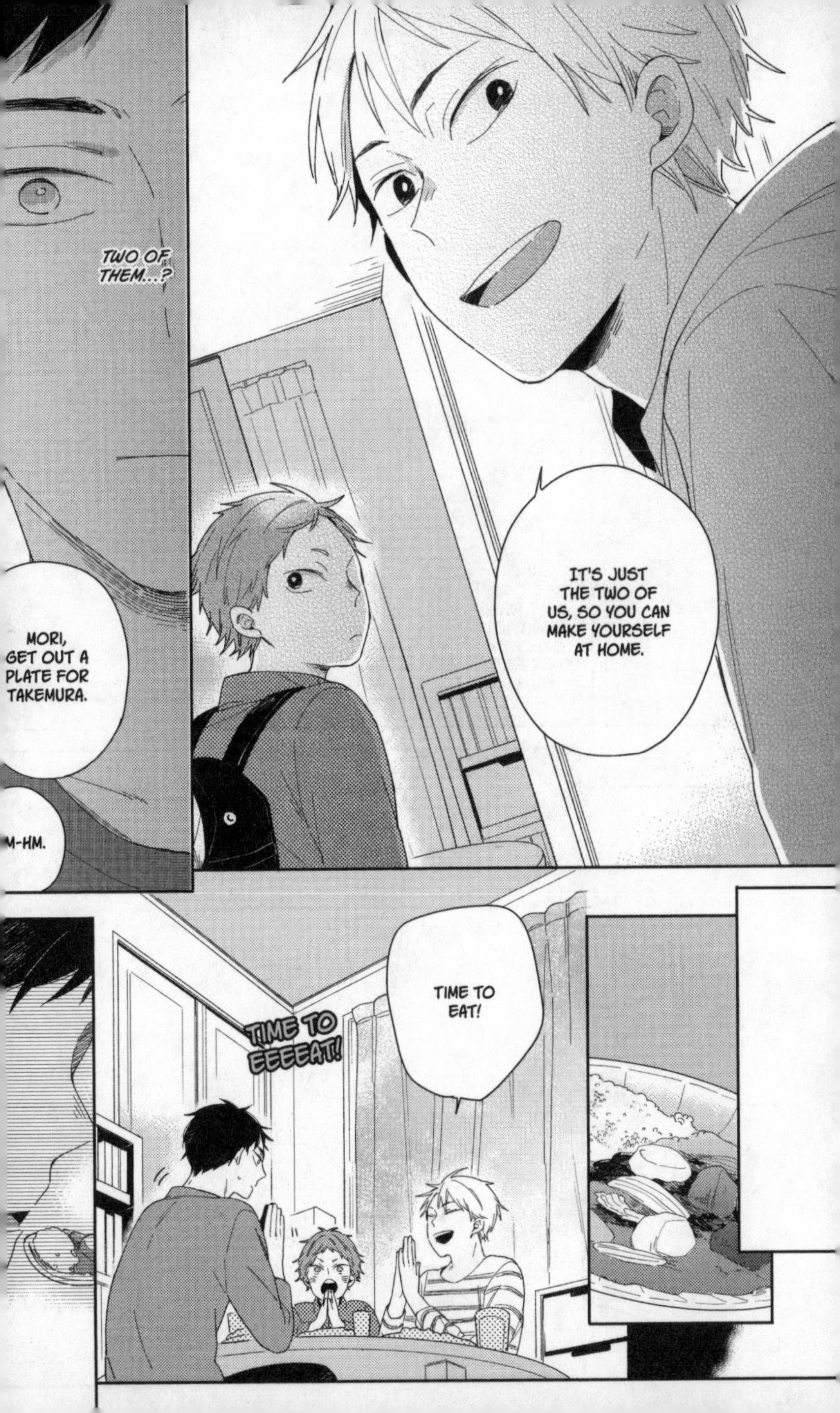
IT'S JUST THE TWO OF US, SO YOU CAN MAKE YOURSELF AT HOME.
TWO OF THEM...?
MORI, GET OUT A PLATE FOR TAKEMURA.
M-HM.
TIME TO EAT!
TIME TO EEEEAT!

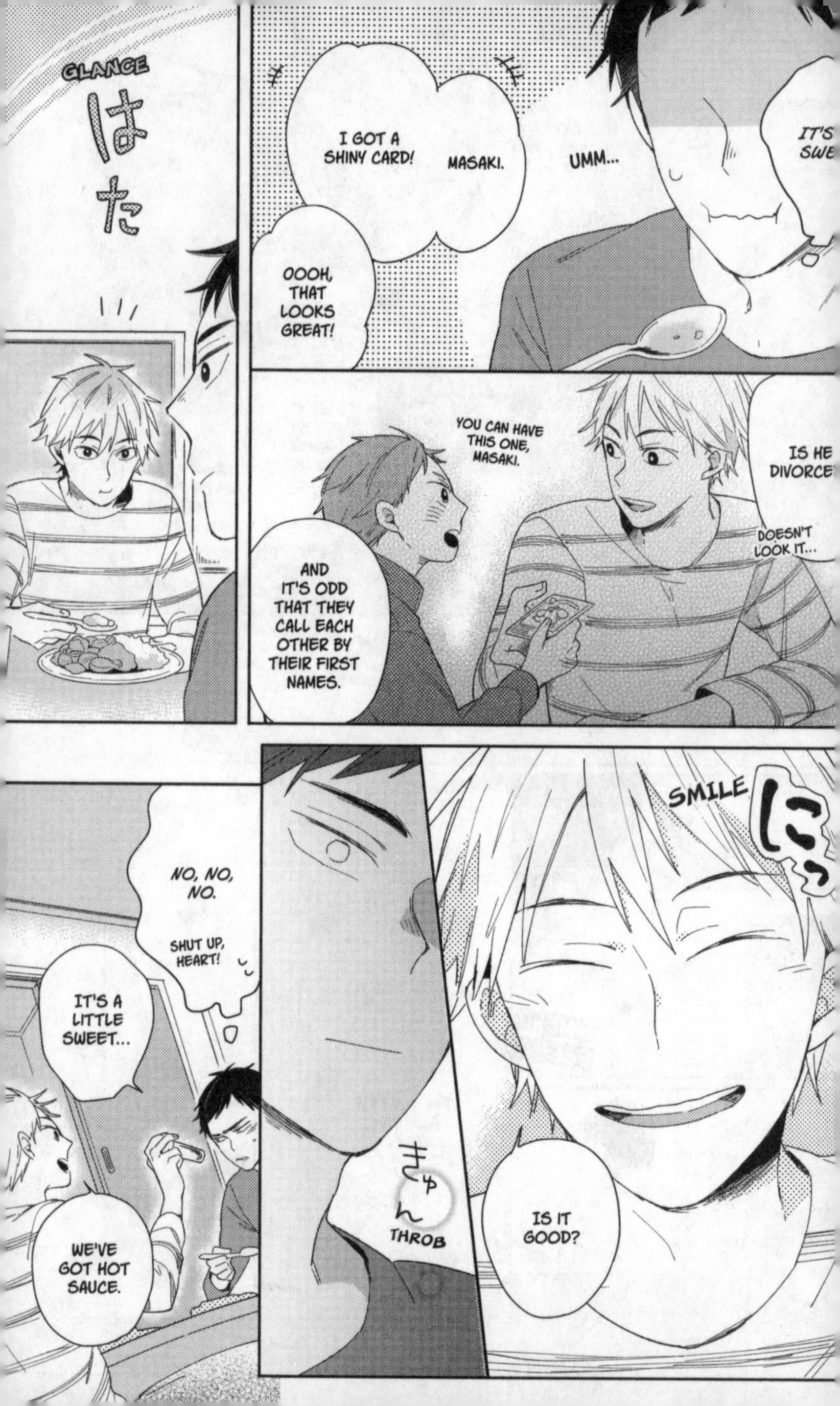
IT'S SWE
UMM...
MASAKI.
I GOT A SHINY CARD!
OOOH, THAT LOOKS GREAT!
IS HE DIVORCE
DOESN'T LOOK IT...
YOU CAN HAVE THIS ONE, MASAKI.
AND IT'S ODD THAT THEY CALL EACH OTHER BY THEIR FIRST NAMES.
GLANCE
はた
SMILE
にこ
IS IT GOOD?
きゅん
THROB
NO, NO, NO.
SHUT UP, HEART!
IT'S A LITTLE SWEET...
WE'VE GOT HOT SAUCE.

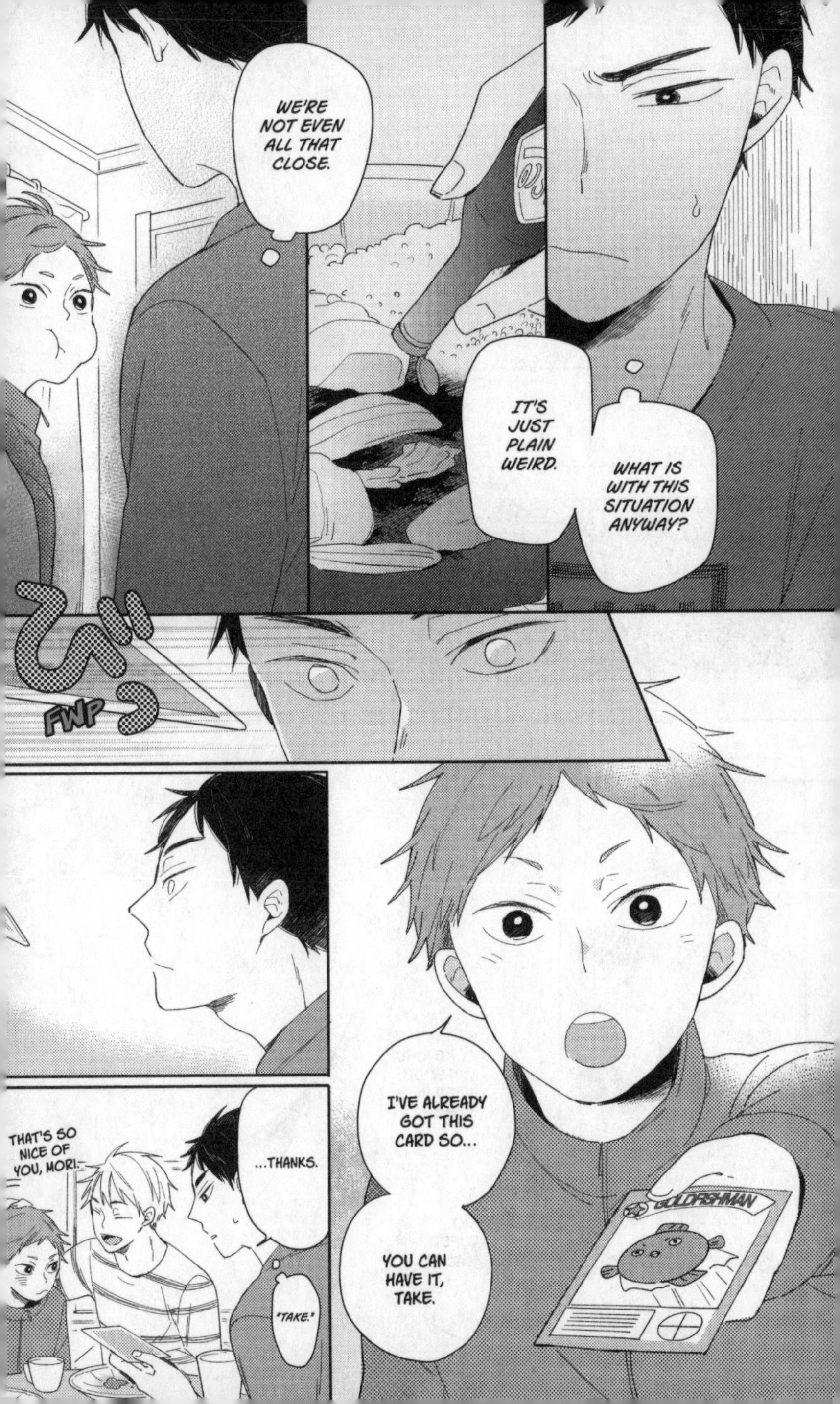
WHAT IS WITH THIS SITUATION ANYWAY?
IT'S JUST PLAIN WEIRD.
WE'RE NOT EVEN ALL THAT CLOSE.
FWP
I'VE ALREADY GOT THIS CARD SO...
YOU CAN HAVE IT, TAKE.
GOLDFISHMAN
...THANKS.
"TAKE."
THAT'S SO NICE OF YOU, MORI.

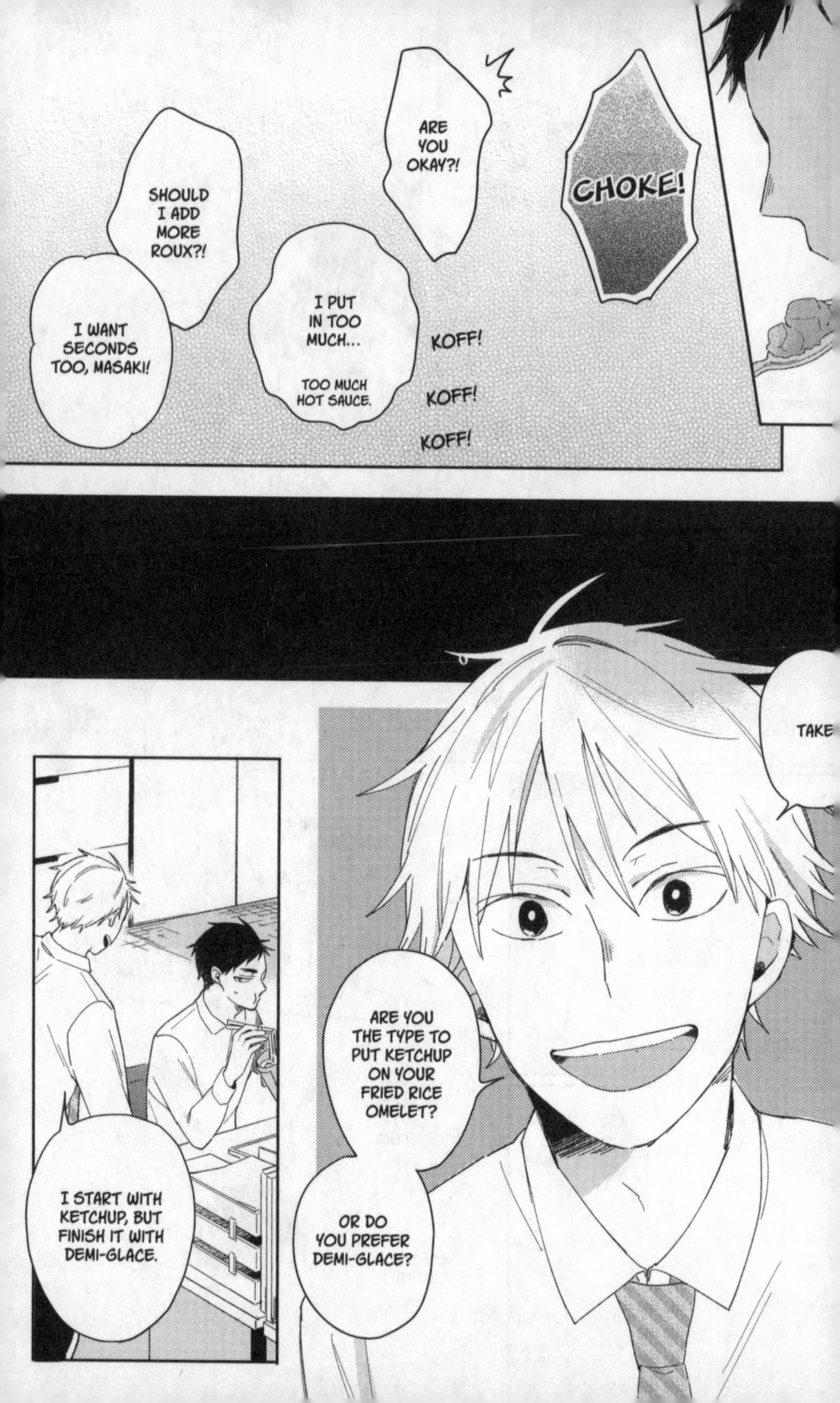
CHOKE!
ARE YOU OKAY?!
KOFF!
KOFF!
KOFF!
I PUT IN TOO MUCH...
TOO MUCH HOT SAUCE.
SHOULD I ADD MORE ROUX?!
I WANT SECONDS TOO, MASAKI!
TAKE
ARE YOU THE TYPE TO PUT KETCHUP ON YOUR FRIED RICE OMELET?
OR DO YOU PREFER DEMI-GLACE?
I START WITH KETCHUP, BUT FINISH IT WITH DEMI-GLACE.

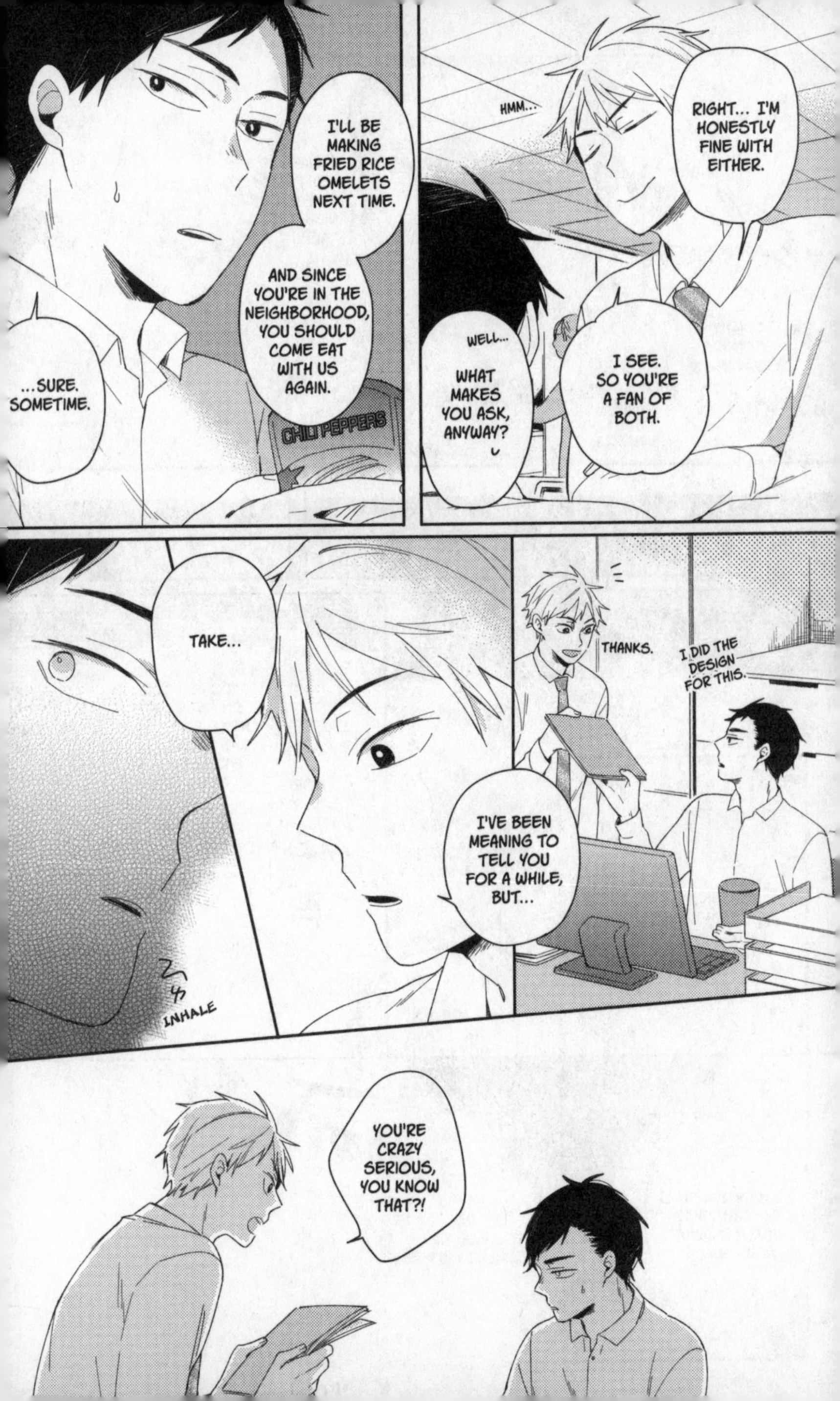
RIGHT... I'M HONESTLY FINE WITH EITHER.
HMM...
I SEE. SO YOU'RE A FAN OF BOTH.
WELL... WHAT MAKES YOU ASK, ANYWAY?
I'LL BE MAKING FRIED RICE OMELETS NEXT TIME.
AND SINCE YOU'RE IN THE NEIGHBORHOOD, YOU SHOULD COME EAT WITH US AGAIN.
CHILI PEPPERS
...SURE. SOMETIME.
I DID THE DESIGN FOR THIS.
THANKS.
I'VE BEEN MEANING TO TELL YOU FOR A WHILE, BUT...
TAKE...
INHALE
YOU'RE CRAZY SERIOUS, YOU KNOW THAT?!

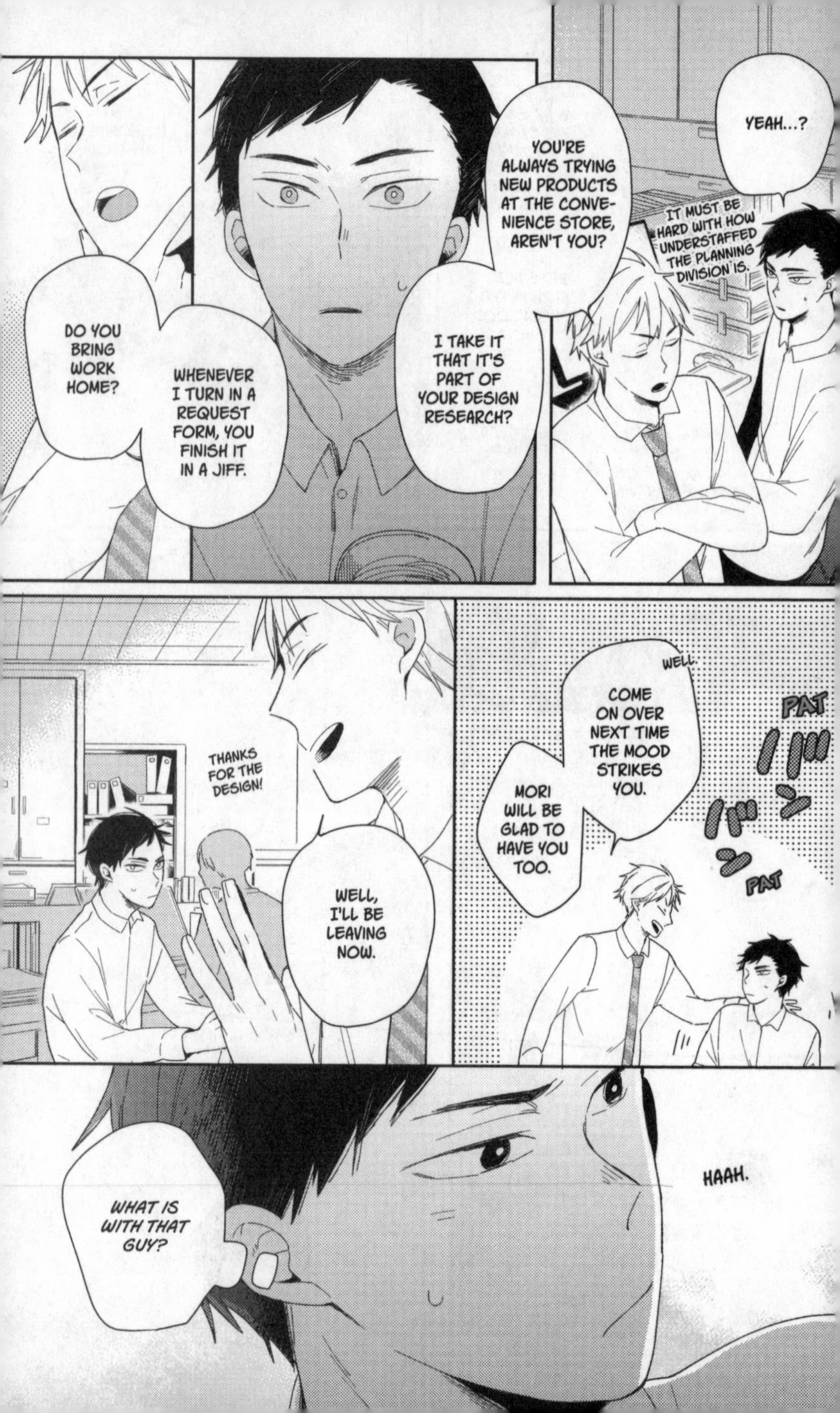
YEAH...?
IT MUST BE HARD WITH HOW UNDERSTAFFED THE PLANNING DIVISION IS.
YOU'RE ALWAYS TRYING NEW PRODUCTS AT THE CONVE-NIENCE STORE, AREN'T YOU?
I TAKE IT THAT IT'S PART OF YOUR DESIGN RESEARCH?
WHENEVER I TURN IN A REQUEST FORM, YOU FINISH IT IN A JIFF.
DO YOU BRING WORK HOME?
WELL.
COME ON OVER NEXT TIME THE MOOD STRIKES YOU.
MORI WILL BE GLAD TO HAVE YOU TOO.
PAT
PAT
THANKS FOR THE DESIGN!
WELL, I'LL BE LEAVING NOW.
HAAH.
WHAT IS WITH THAT GUY?

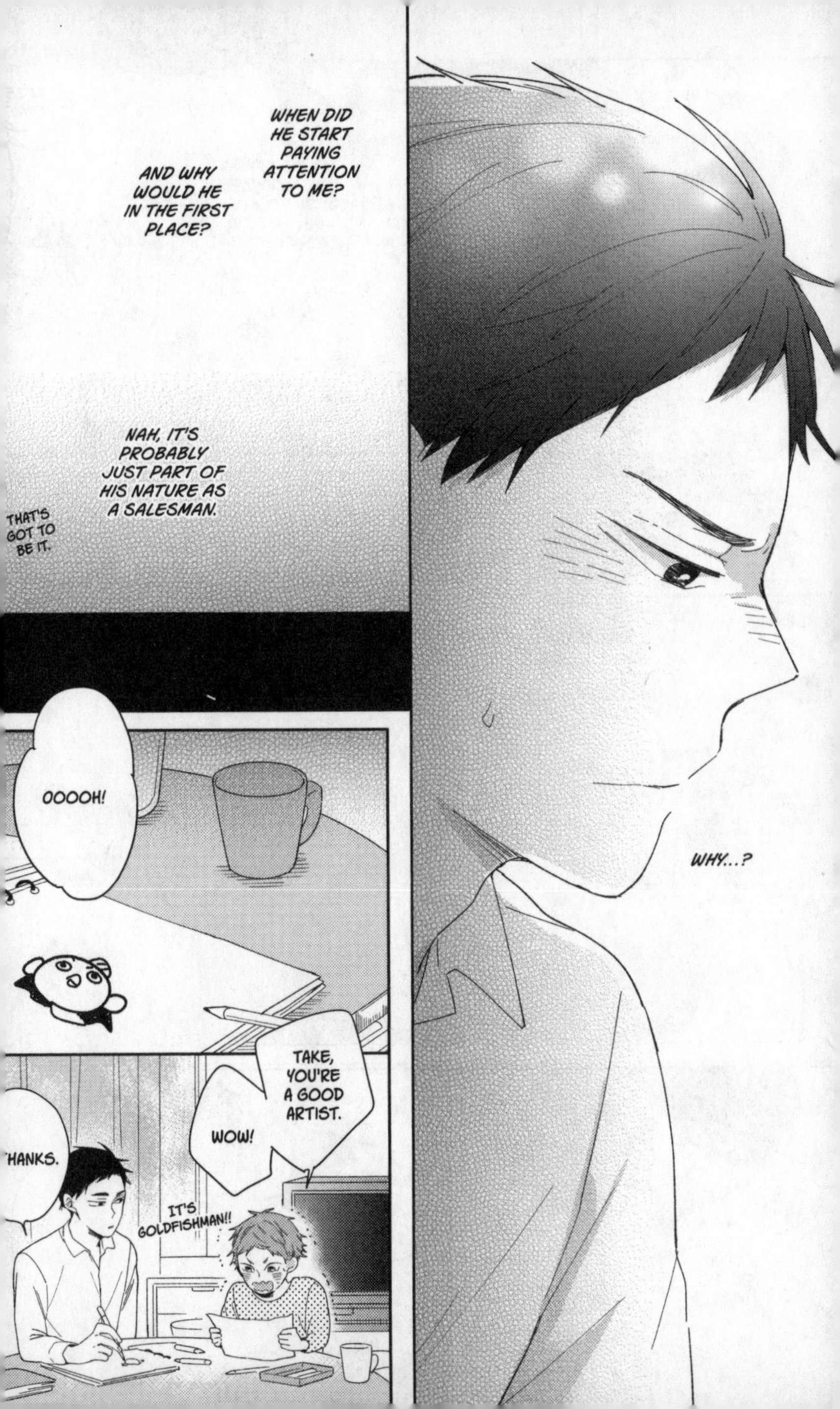
WHY...?
WHEN DID HE START PAYING ATTENTION TO ME?
AND WHY WOULD HE IN THE FIRST PLACE?
NAH, IT'S PROBABLY JUST PART OF HIS NATURE AS A SALESMAN.
THAT'S GOT TO BE IT.
OOOOH!
TAKE, YOU'RE A GOOD ARTIST.
WOW!
IT'S GOLDFISHMAN!!
THANKS.

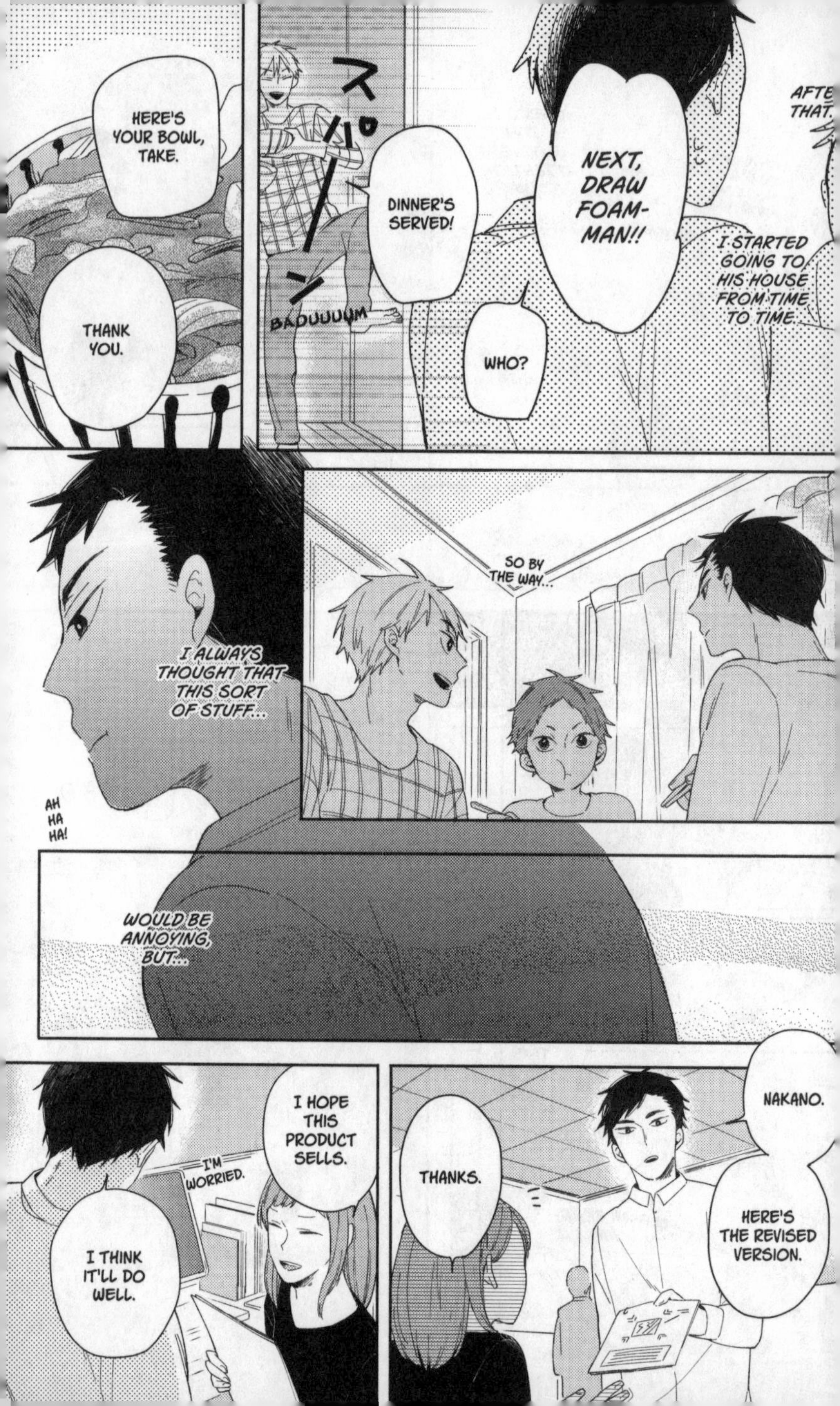

AFTE THAT.
NEXT, DRAW FOAM-MAN!!
I STARTED GOING TO HIS HOUSE FROM TIME TO TIME.
WHO?
DINNER'S SERVED!
BADUUUUM
HERE'S YOUR BOWL, TAKE.
THANK YOU.
SO BY THE WAY...
I ALWAYS THOUGHT THAT THIS SORT OF STUFF...
AH HA HA!
WOULD BE ANNOYING, BUT...
NAKANO.
HERE'S THE REVISED VERSION.
THANKS.
I HOPE THIS PRODUCT SELLS.
I'M WORRIED.
I THINK IT'LL DO WELL.

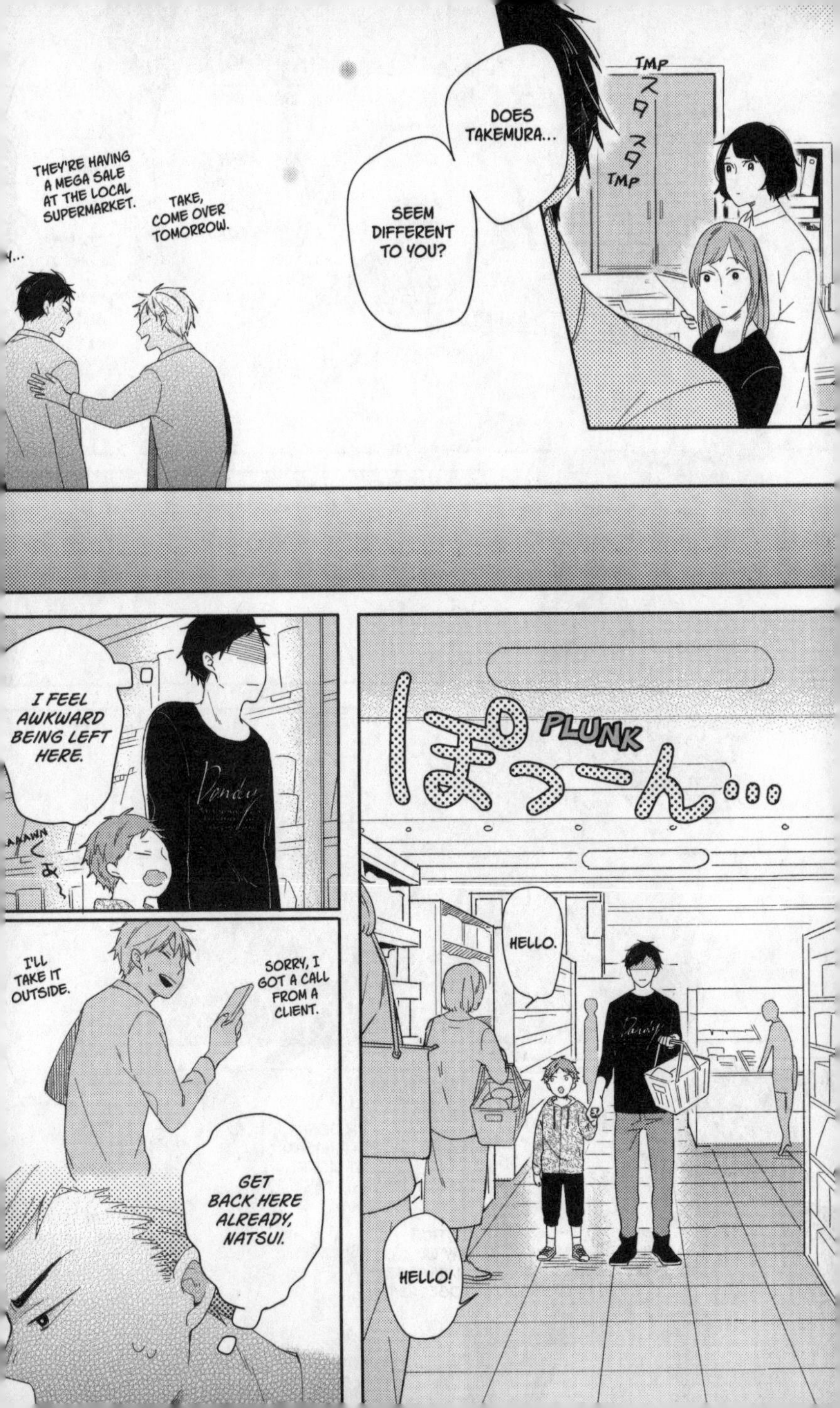
DOES TAKEMURA...
SEEM DIFFERENT TO YOU?
TMP
スタ
スタ
TMP
TAKE, COME OVER TOMORROW.
THEY'RE HAVING A MEGA SALE AT THE LOCAL SUPERMARKET.
ぽつ〜ん…
PLUNK
HELLO.
HELLO!
I FEEL AWKWARD BEING LEFT HERE.
SORRY, I GOT A CALL FROM A CLIENT.
I'LL TAKE IT OUTSIDE.
GET BACK HERE ALREADY, NATSUI.

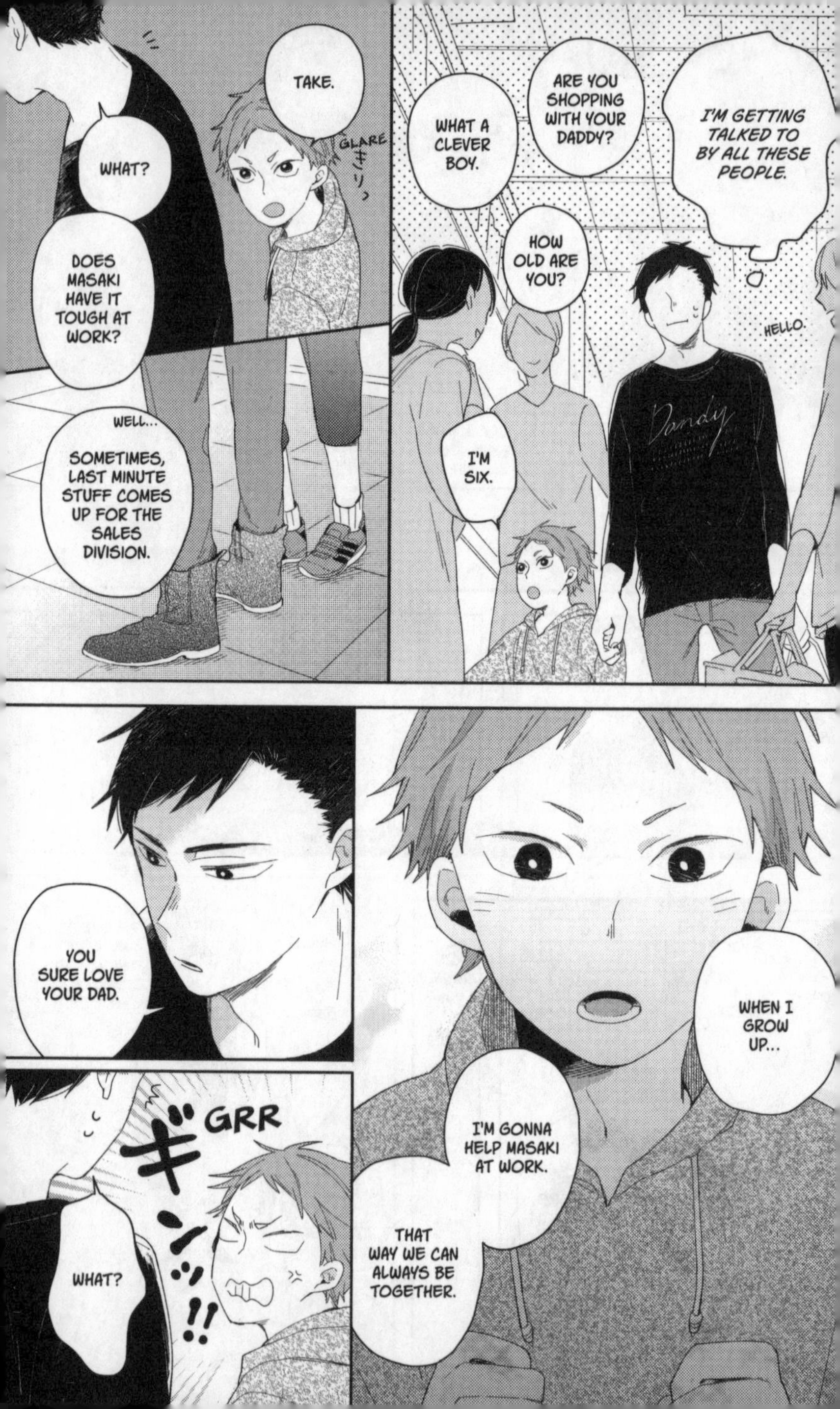
I'M GETTING TALKED TO BY ALL THESE PEOPLE.
ARE YOU SHOPPING WITH YOUR DADDY?
WHAT A CLEVER BOY.
HOW OLD ARE YOU?
HELLO.
I'M SIX.
TAKE.
GLARE
WHAT?
DOES MASAKI HAVE IT TOUGH AT WORK?
WELL...
SOMETIMES, LAST MINUTE STUFF COMES UP FOR THE SALES DIVISION.
WHEN I GROW UP...
I'M GONNA HELP MASAKI AT WORK.
THAT WAY WE CAN ALWAYS BE TOGETHER.
YOU SURE LOVE YOUR DAD.
GRR
WHAT?

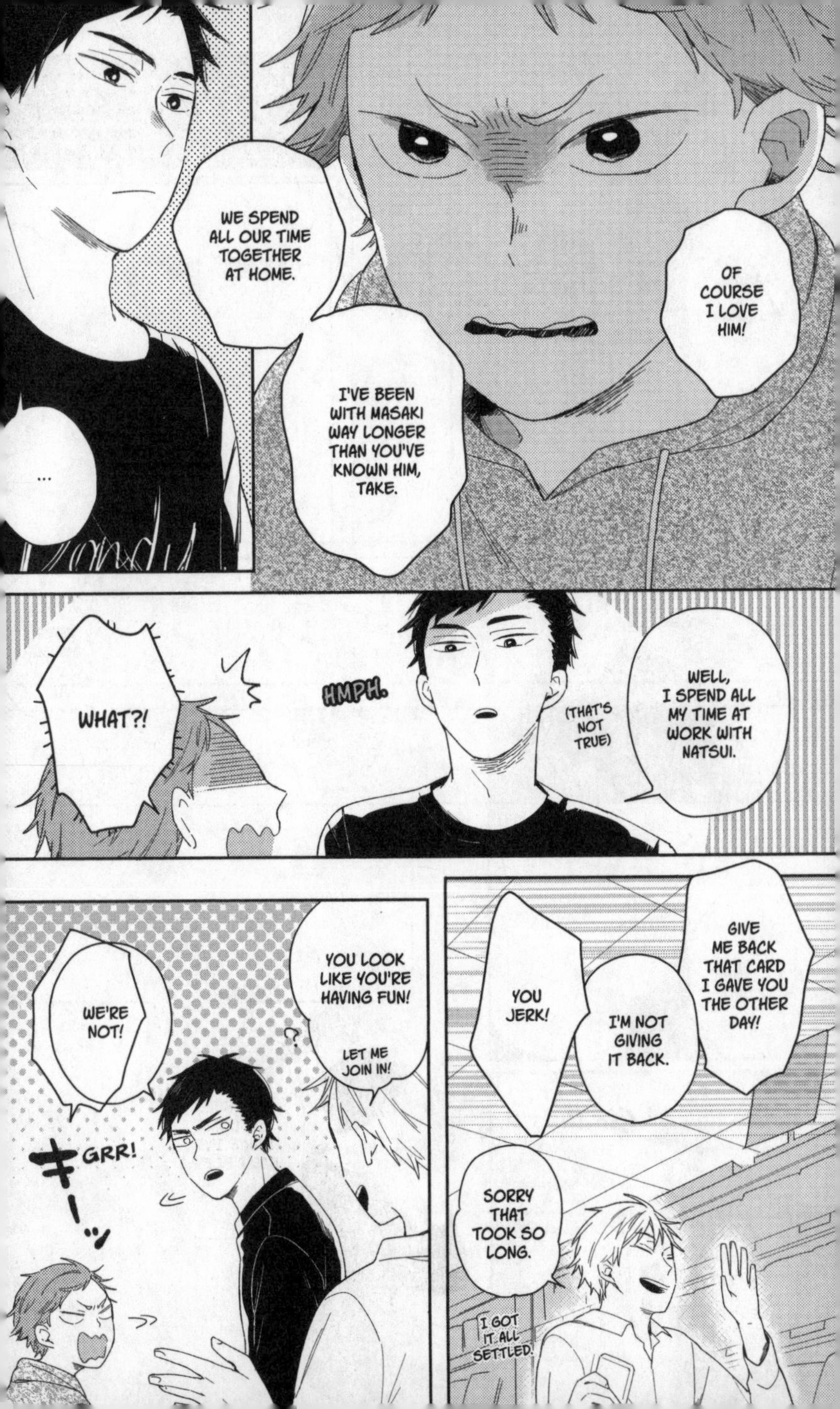
OF COURSE I LOVE HIM!
WE SPEND ALL OUR TIME TOGETHER AT HOME.
I'VE BEEN WITH MASAKI WAY LONGER THAN YOU'VE KNOWN HIM, TAKE.
...
WELL, I SPEND ALL MY TIME AT WORK WITH NATSUI.
(THAT'S NOT TRUE)
HMPH.
WHAT?!
GIVE ME BACK THAT CARD I GAVE YOU THE OTHER DAY!
I'M NOT GIVING IT BACK.
YOU JERK!
SORRY THAT TOOK SO LONG.
I GOT IT ALL SETTLED.
YOU LOOK LIKE YOU'RE HAVING FUN!
LET ME JOIN IN!
?
WE'RE NOT!
GRR!
キーッ

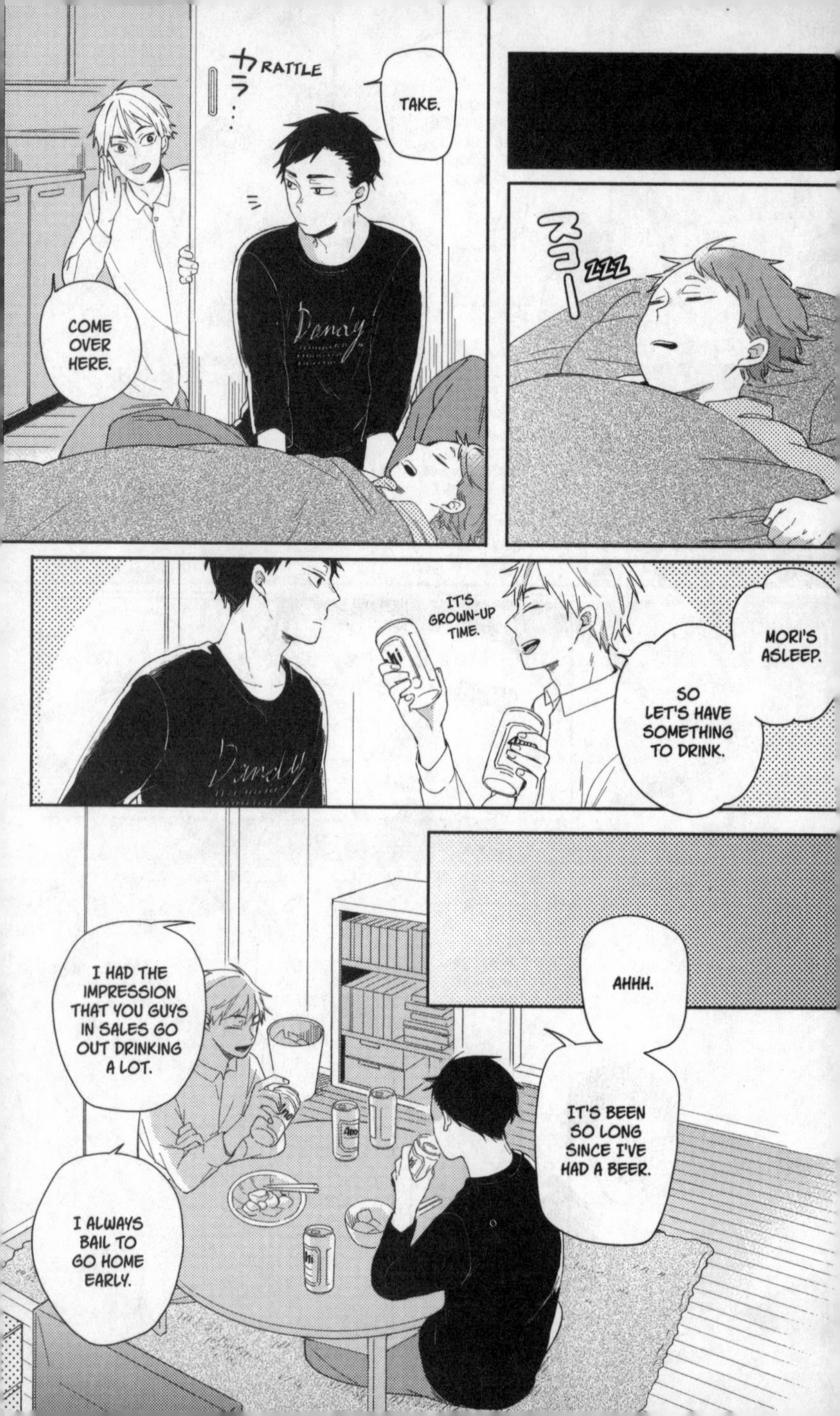

スコー
ZZZ
TAKE.
カラ RATTLE
COME OVER HERE.
MORI'S ASLEEP.
SO LET'S HAVE SOMETHING TO DRINK.
IT'S GROWN-UP TIME.
AHHH.
IT'S BEEN SO LONG SINCE I'VE HAD A BEER.
I HAD THE IMPRESSION THAT YOU GUYS IN SALES GO OUT DRINKING A LOT.
I ALWAYS BAIL TO GO HOME EARLY.

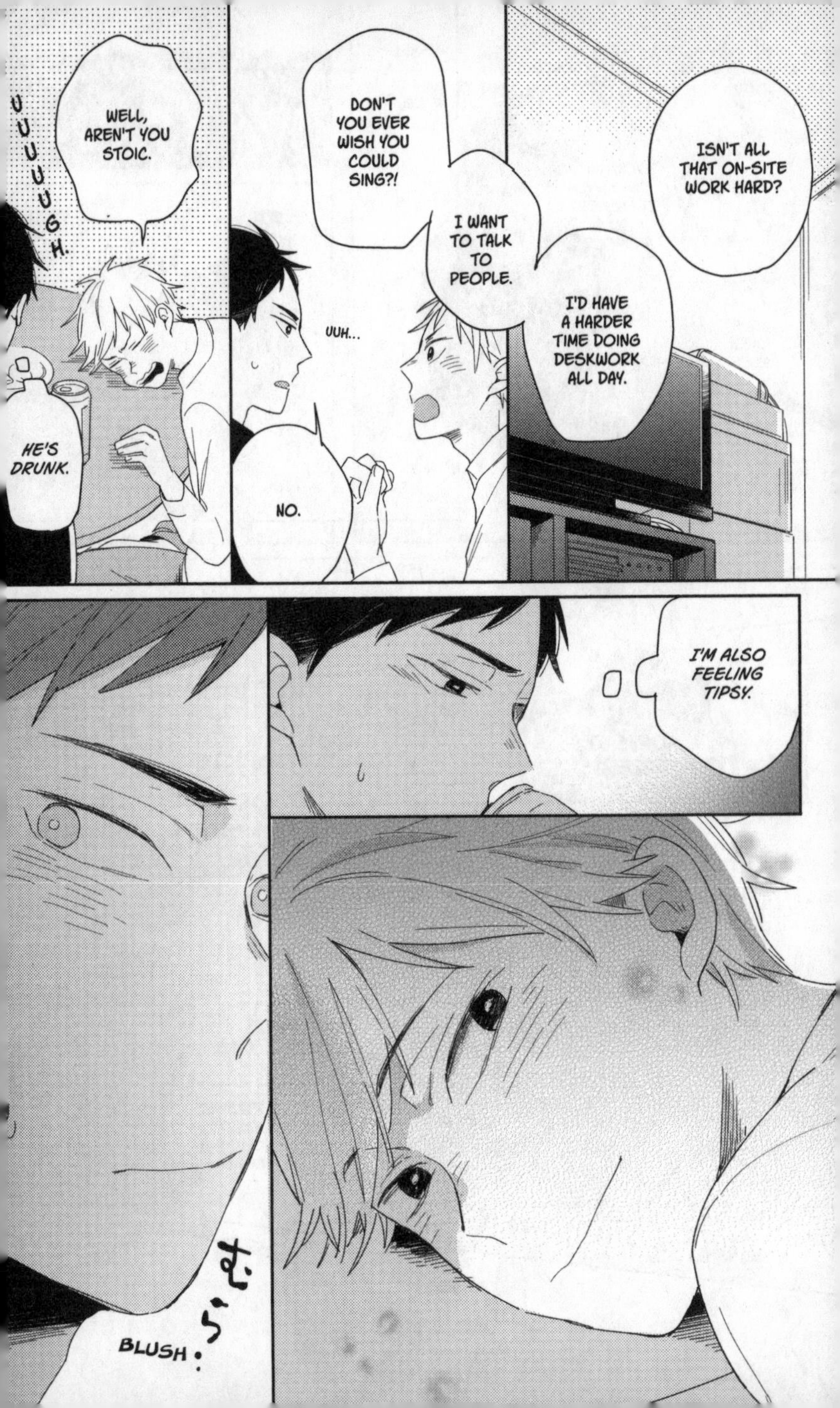
ISN'T ALL THAT ON-SITE WORK HARD?
I'D HAVE A HARDER TIME DOING DESKWORK ALL DAY.
I WANT TO TALK TO PEOPLE.
DON'T YOU EVER WISH YOU COULD SING?!
UUH...
NO.
WELL, AREN'T YOU STOIC.
UUUUUUGH.
HE'S DRUNK.
I'M ALSO FEELING TIPSY.
BLUSH

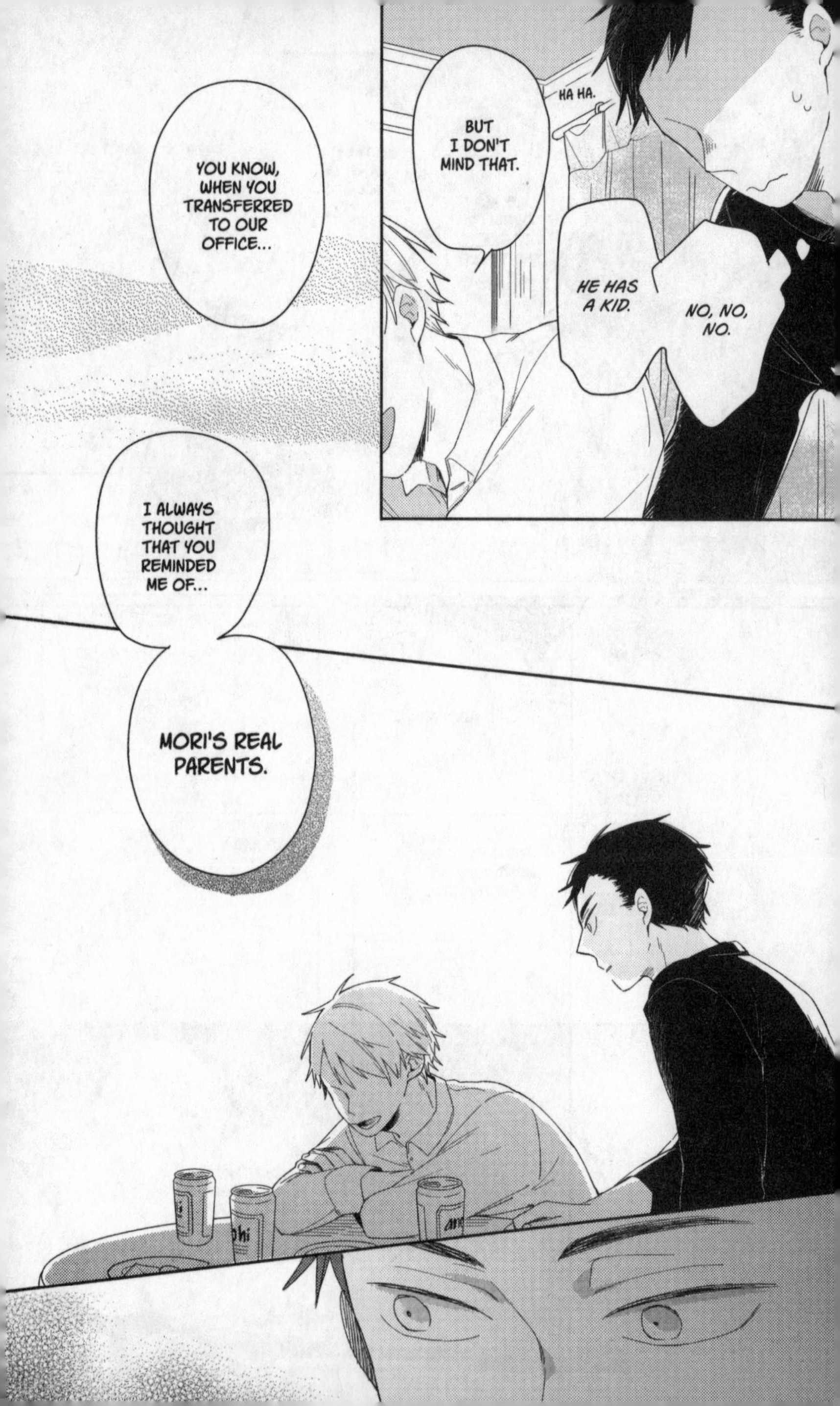

BUT I DON'T MIND THAT.
HA HA.
HE HAS A KID.
NO, NO, NO.
YOU KNOW, WHEN YOU TRANSFERRED TO OUR OFFICE...
I ALWAYS THOUGHT THAT YOU REMINDED ME OF...
MORI'S REAL PARENTS.

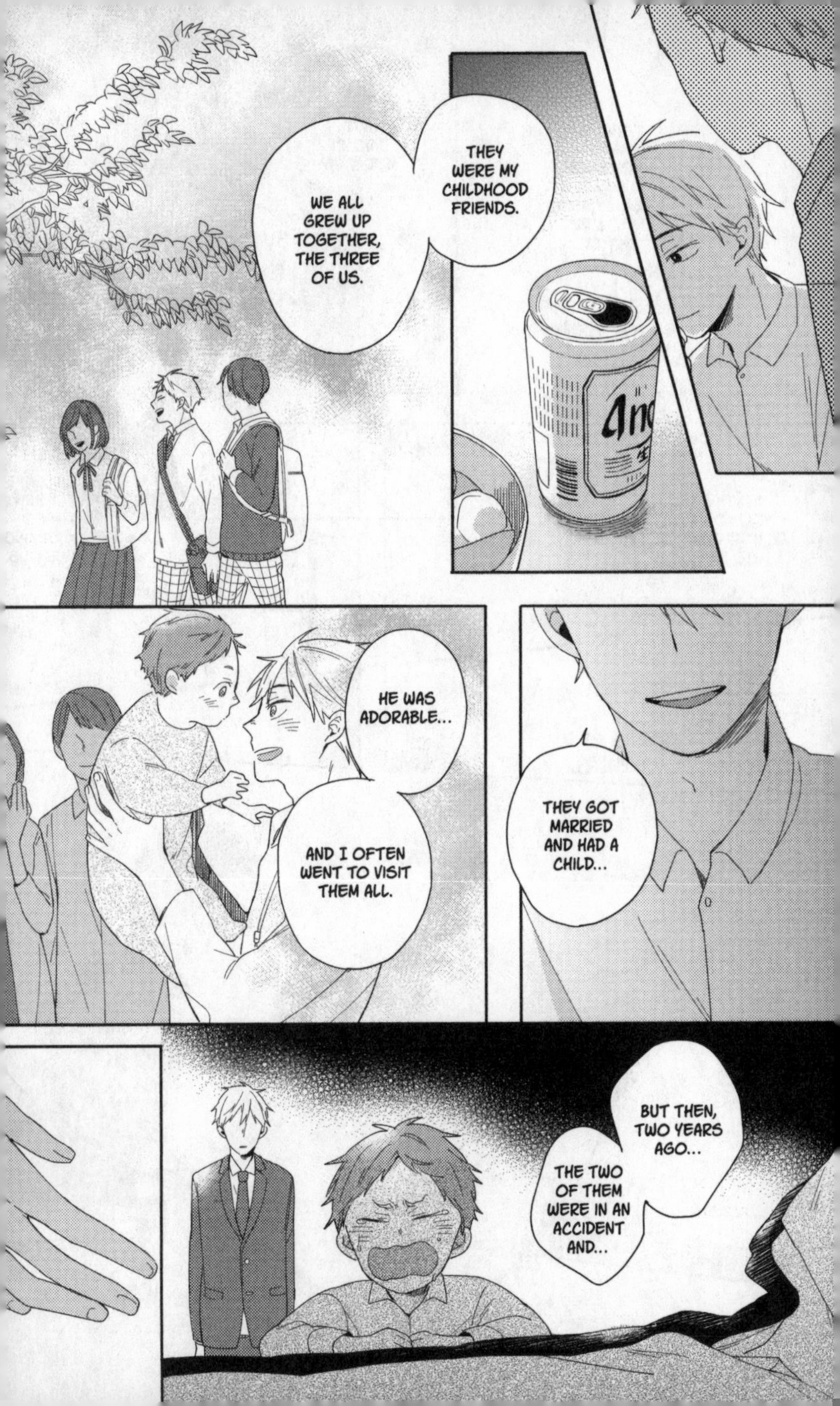
THEY WERE MY CHILDHOOD FRIENDS.
WE ALL GREW UP TOGETHER, THE THREE OF US.
THEY GOT MARRIED AND HAD A CHILD...
HE WAS ADORABLE...
AND I OFTEN WENT TO VISIT THEM ALL.
BUT THEN, TWO YEARS AGO...
THE TWO OF THEM WERE IN AN ACCIDENT AND...

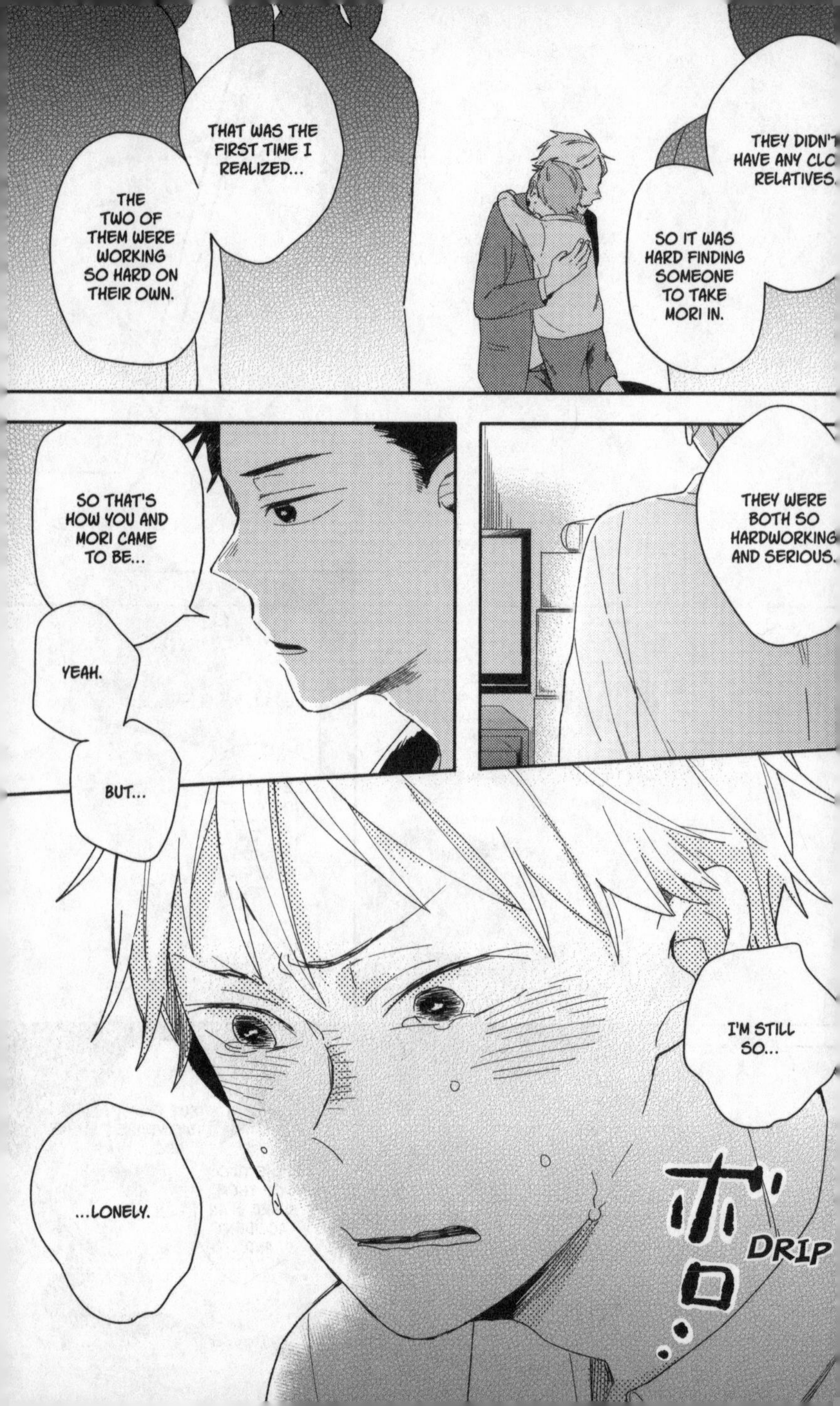
THEY DIDN'T HAVE ANY CLO RELATIVES.
SO IT WAS HARD FINDING SOMEONE TO TAKE MORI IN.
THAT WAS THE FIRST TIME I REALIZED...
THE TWO OF THEM WERE WORKING SO HARD ON THEIR OWN.
THEY WERE BOTH SO HARDWORKING AND SERIOUS.
SO THAT'S HOW YOU AND MORI CAME TO BE...
YEAH.
BUT...
I'M STILL SO...
ポロ…
DRIP
...LONELY.

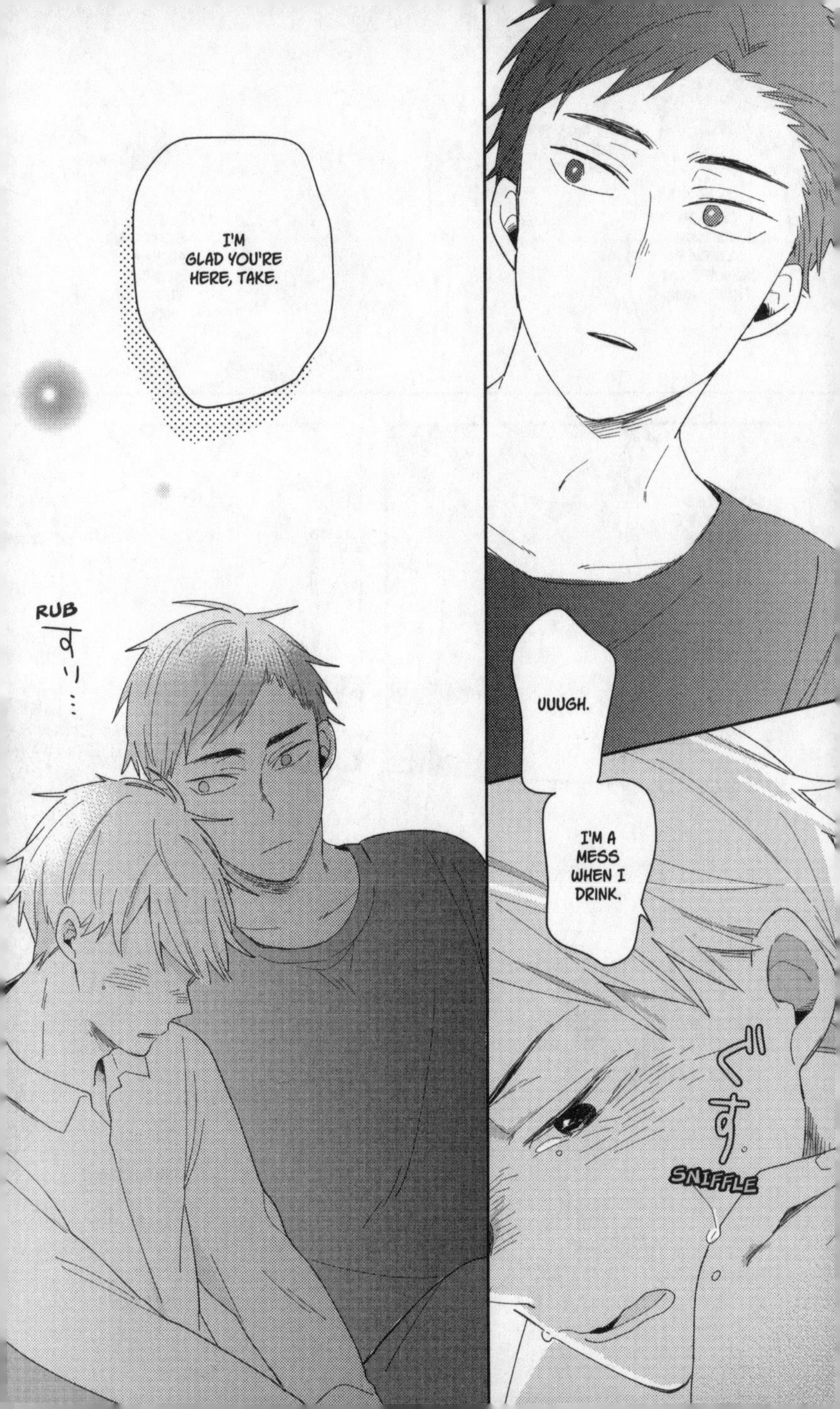
UUUGH.
I'M A MESS WHEN I DRINK.
ぐす
SNIFFLE
I'M GLAD YOU'RE HERE, TAKE.
RUB
すり…

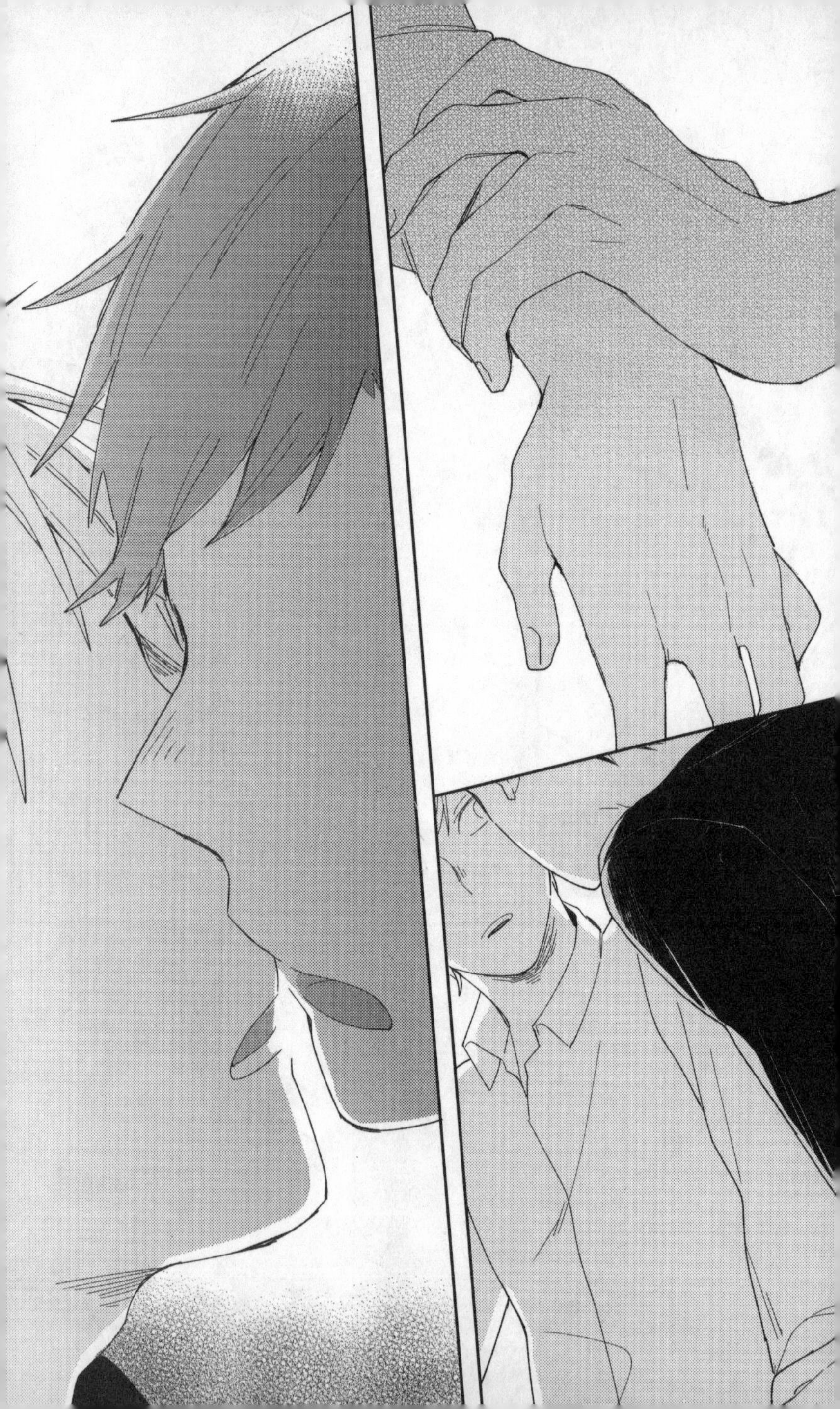

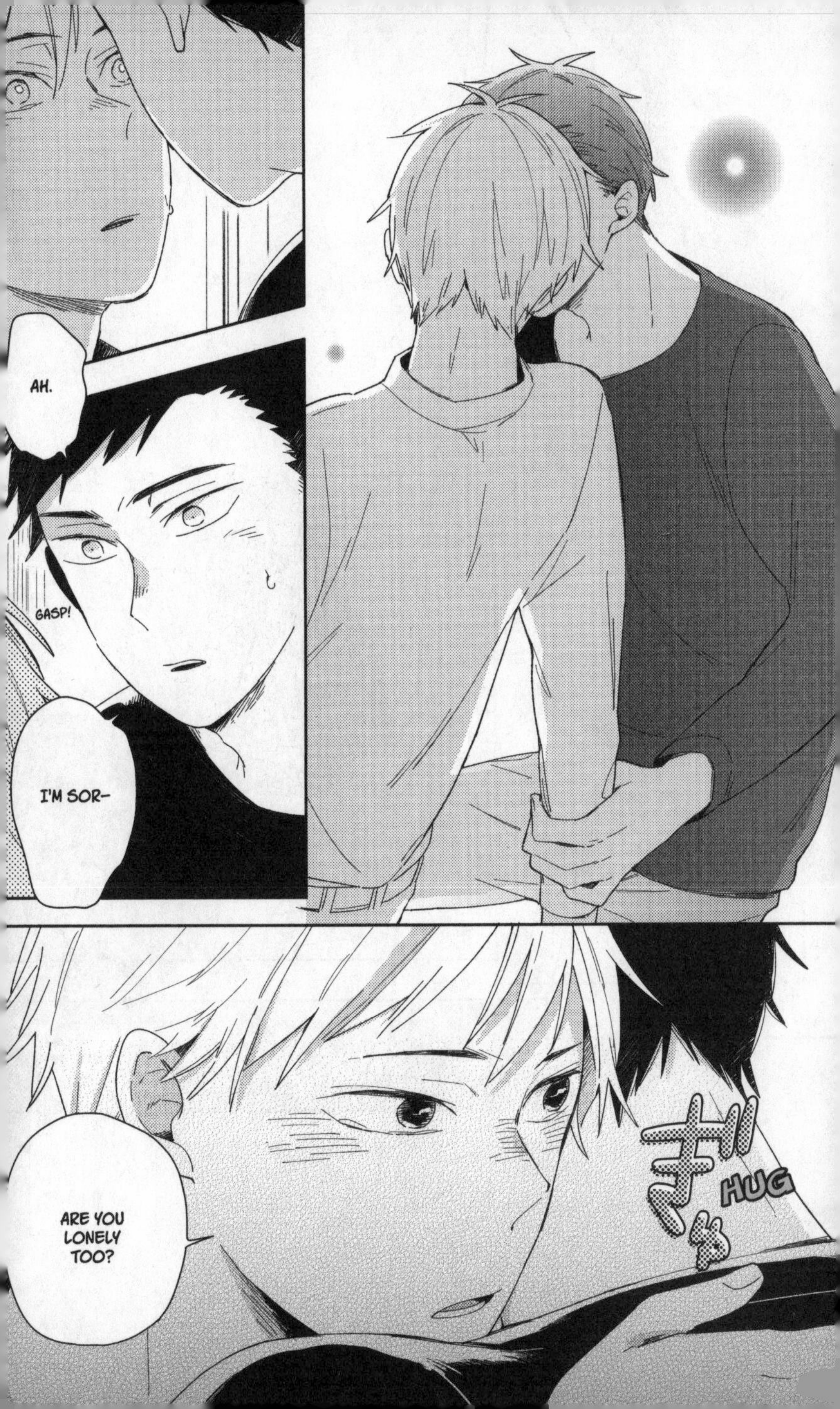
AH.
GASP!
I'M SOR-
HUG
ARE YOU LONELY TOO?

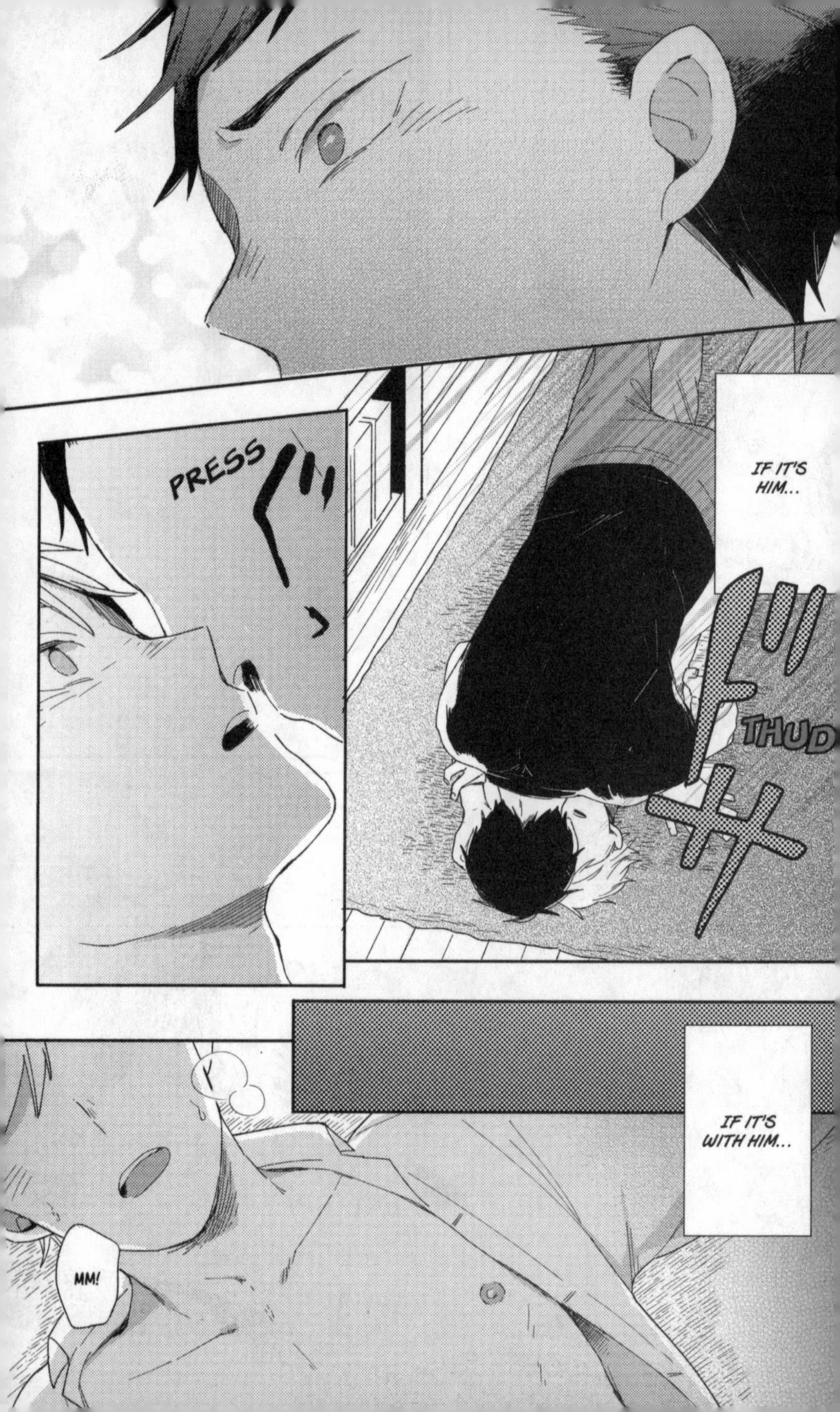
IF IT'S HIM...
THUD
PRESS
IF IT'S WITH HIM...
MM!

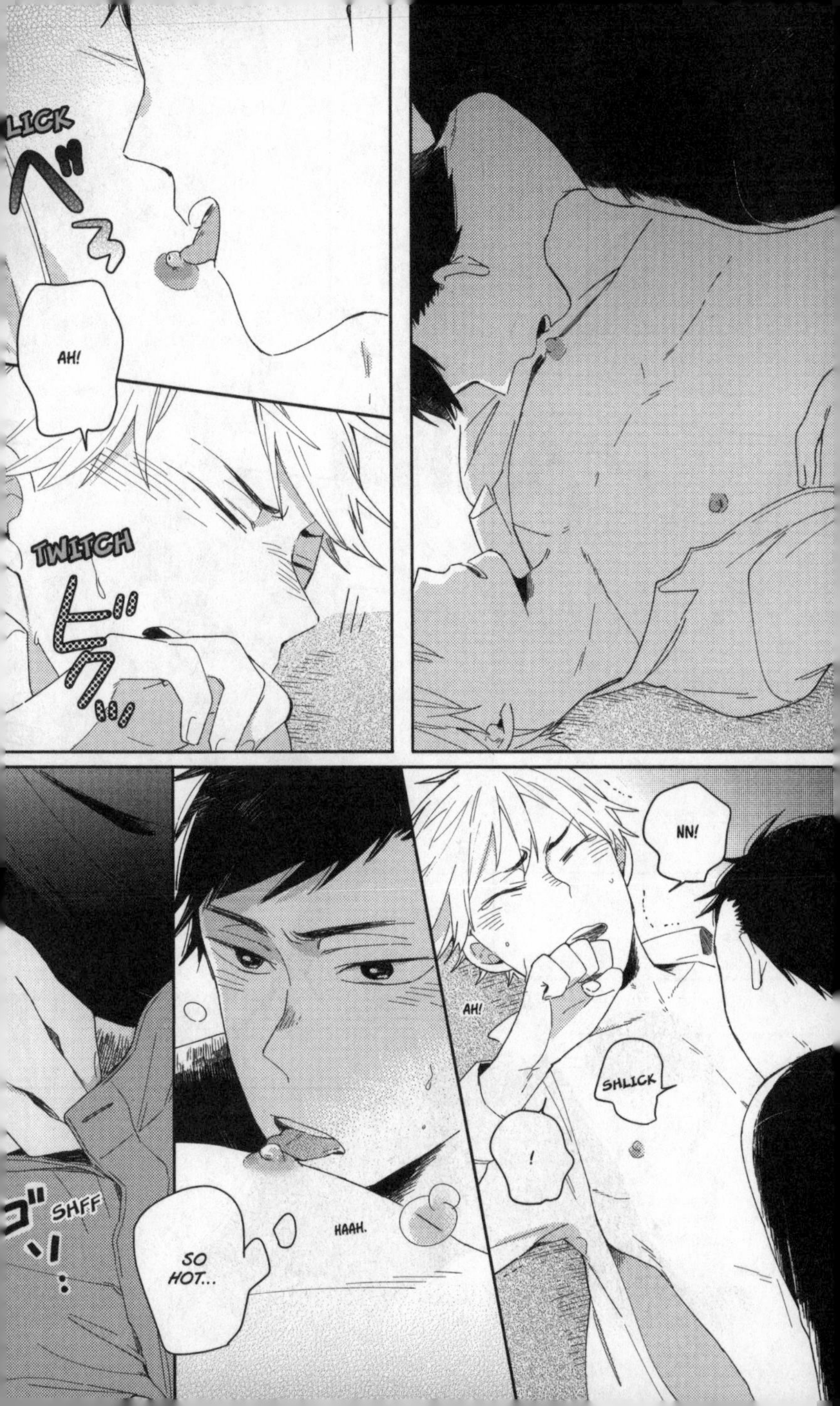
LICK
べろ
AH!
TWITCH
ビクッ
NN!
AH!
SHLICK
!
HAAH.
SO HOT...
SHFF
ゴソ

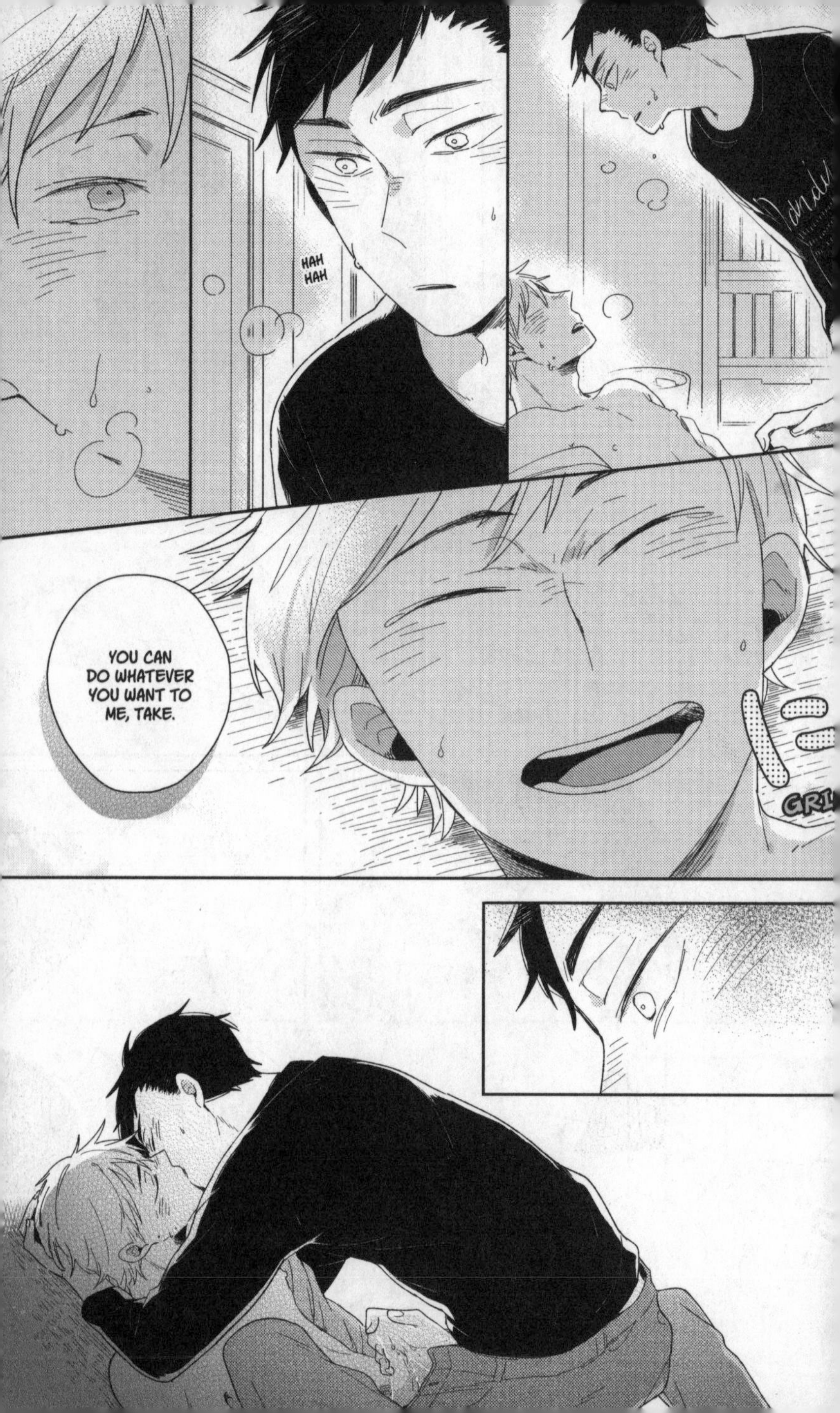
HAH HAH
YOU CAN DO WHATEVER YOU WANT TO ME, TAKE.
GRI

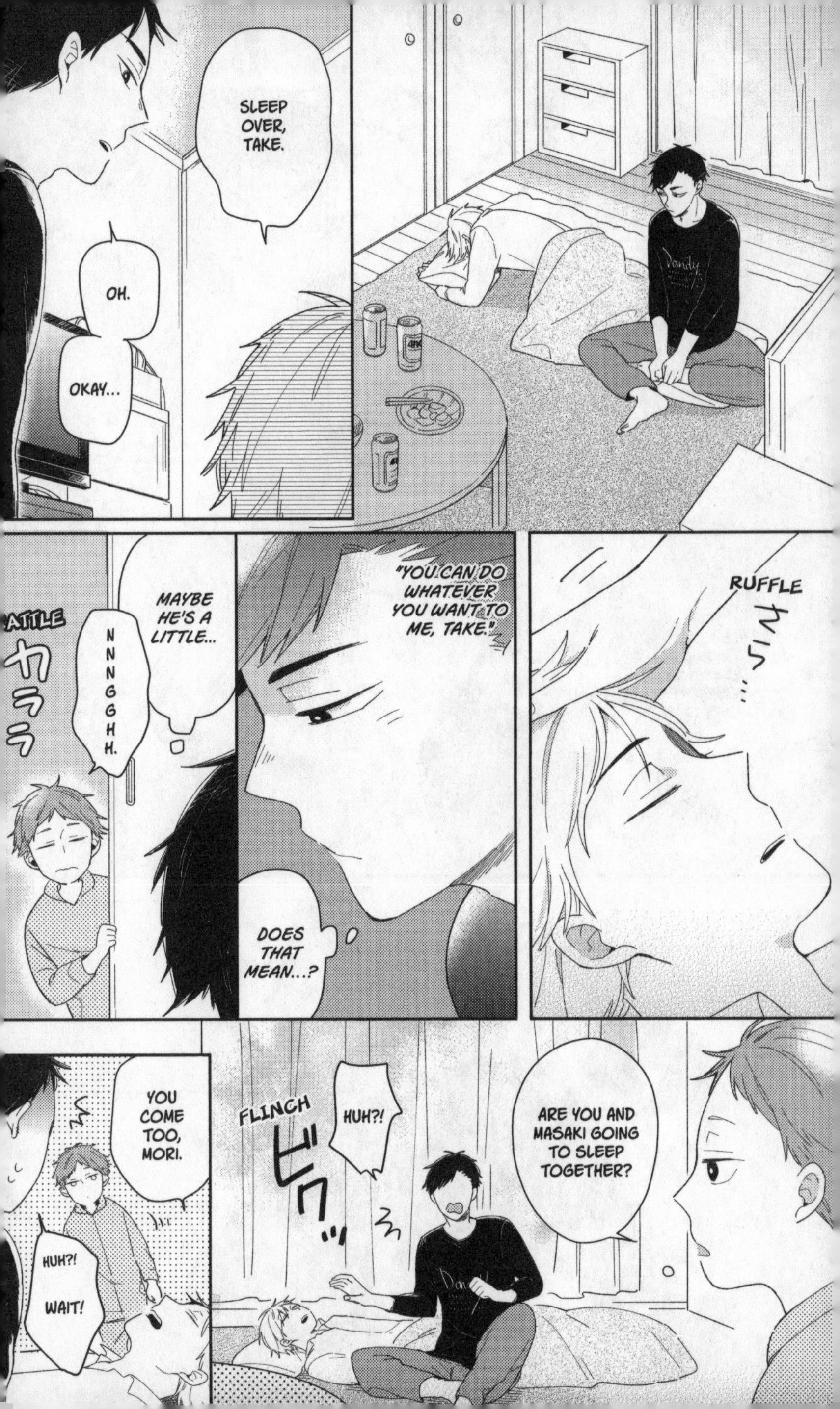
SLEEP OVER, TAKE.
OH.
OKAY...
RUFFLE
"YOU CAN DO WHATEVER YOU WANT TO ME, TAKE."
DOES THAT MEAN...?
MAYBE HE'S A LITTLE...
NNNGGHH.
ATTLE
ARE YOU AND MASAKI GOING TO SLEEP TOGETHER?
HUH?!
FLINCH
YOU COME TOO, MORI.
HUH?!
WAIT!

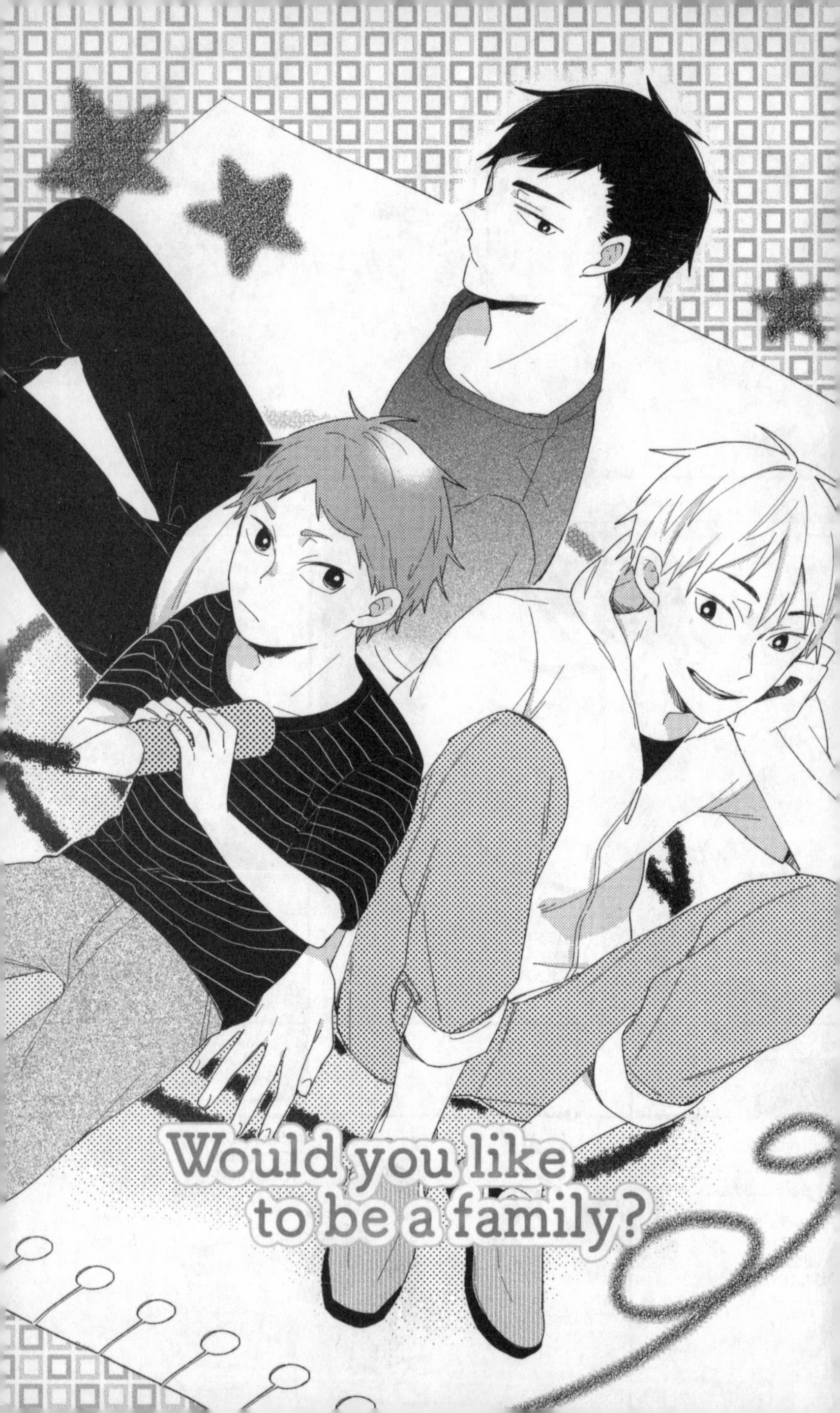
Would you like
to be a family?

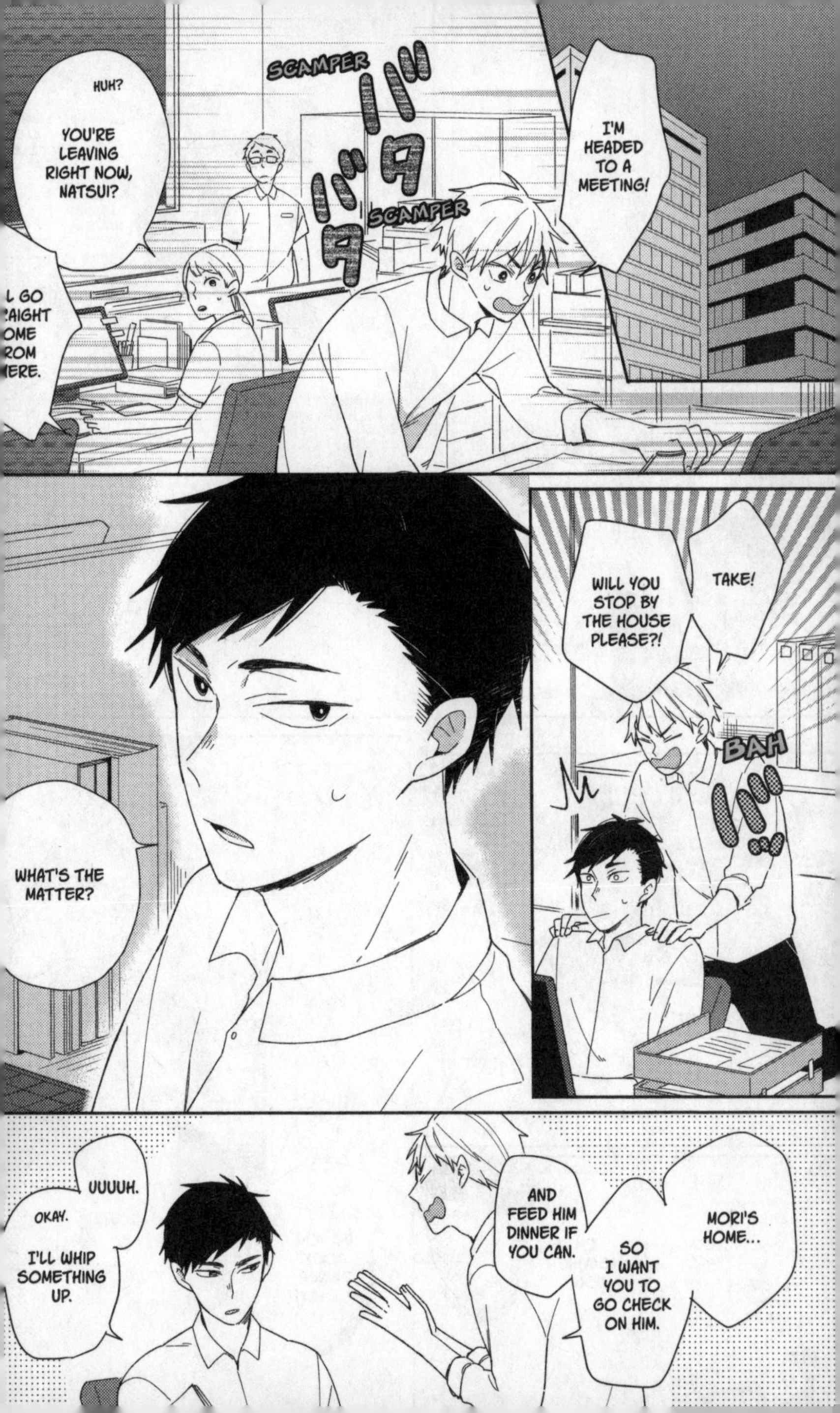
I'M HEADED TO A MEETING!
SCAMPER
SCAMPER
HUH?
YOU'RE LEAVING RIGHT NOW, NATSUI?
TAKE!
WILL YOU STOP BY THE HOUSE PLEASE?!
BAH
WHAT'S THE MATTER?
MORI'S HOME...
SO I WANT YOU TO GO CHECK ON HIM.
AND FEED HIM DINNER IF YOU CAN.
UUUUH.
OKAY.
I'LL WHIP SOMETHING UP.

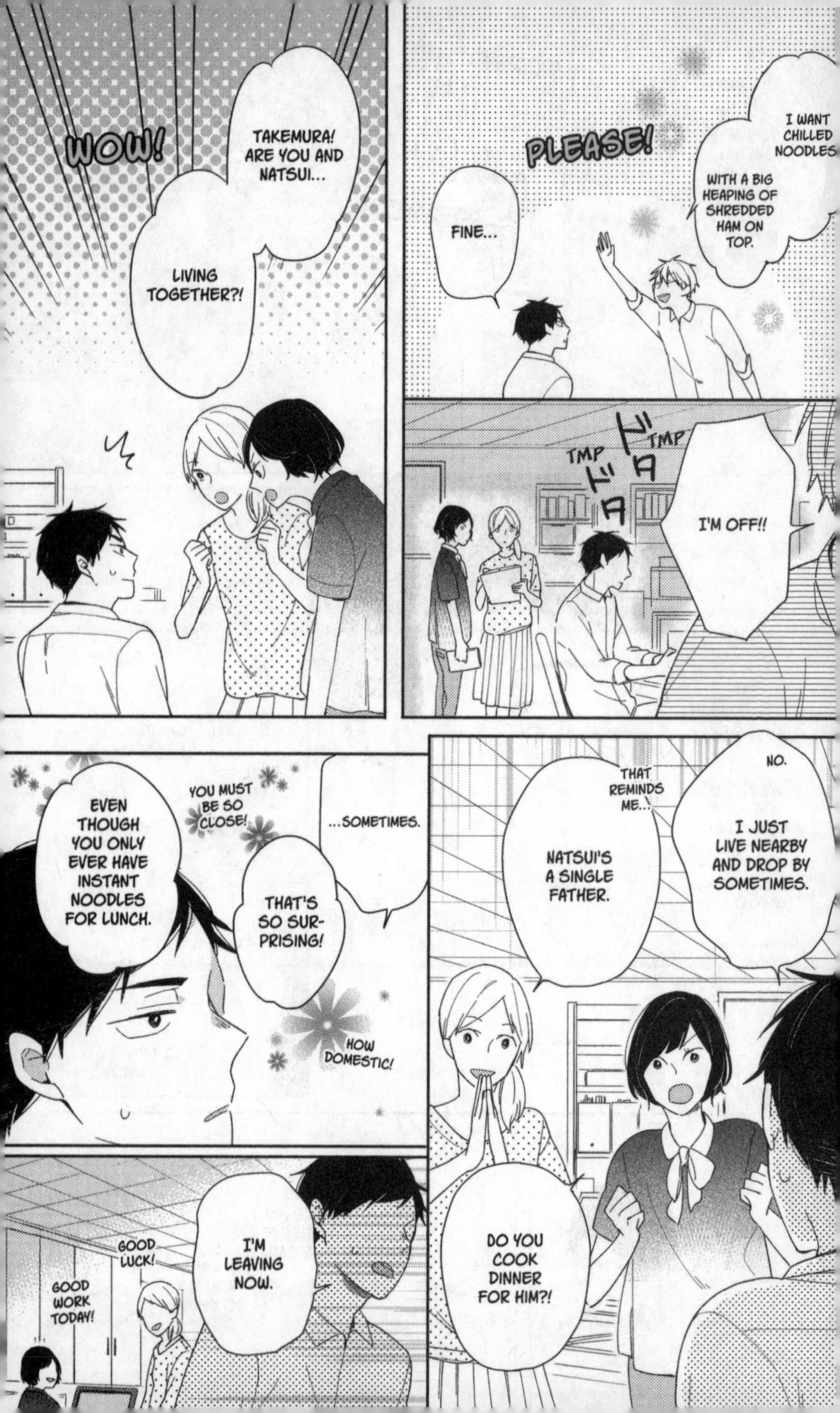
PLEASE!
I WANT CHILLED NOODLES
WITH A BIG HEAPING OF SHREDDED HAM ON TOP.
FINE...
TMP
TMP
ドタ
ドタ
I'M OFF!!
WOW!
TAKEMURA! ARE YOU AND NATSUI...
LIVING TOGETHER?!
NO.
I JUST LIVE NEARBY AND DROP BY SOMETIMES.
THAT REMINDS ME...
NATSUI'S A SINGLE FATHER.
DO YOU COOK DINNER FOR HIM?!
...SOMETIMES.
YOU MUST BE SO CLOSE!
THAT'S SO SUR-PRISING!
EVEN THOUGH YOU ONLY EVER HAVE INSTANT NOODLES FOR LUNCH.
HOW DOMESTIC!
I'M LEAVING NOW.
GOOD LUCK!
GOOD WORK TODAY!

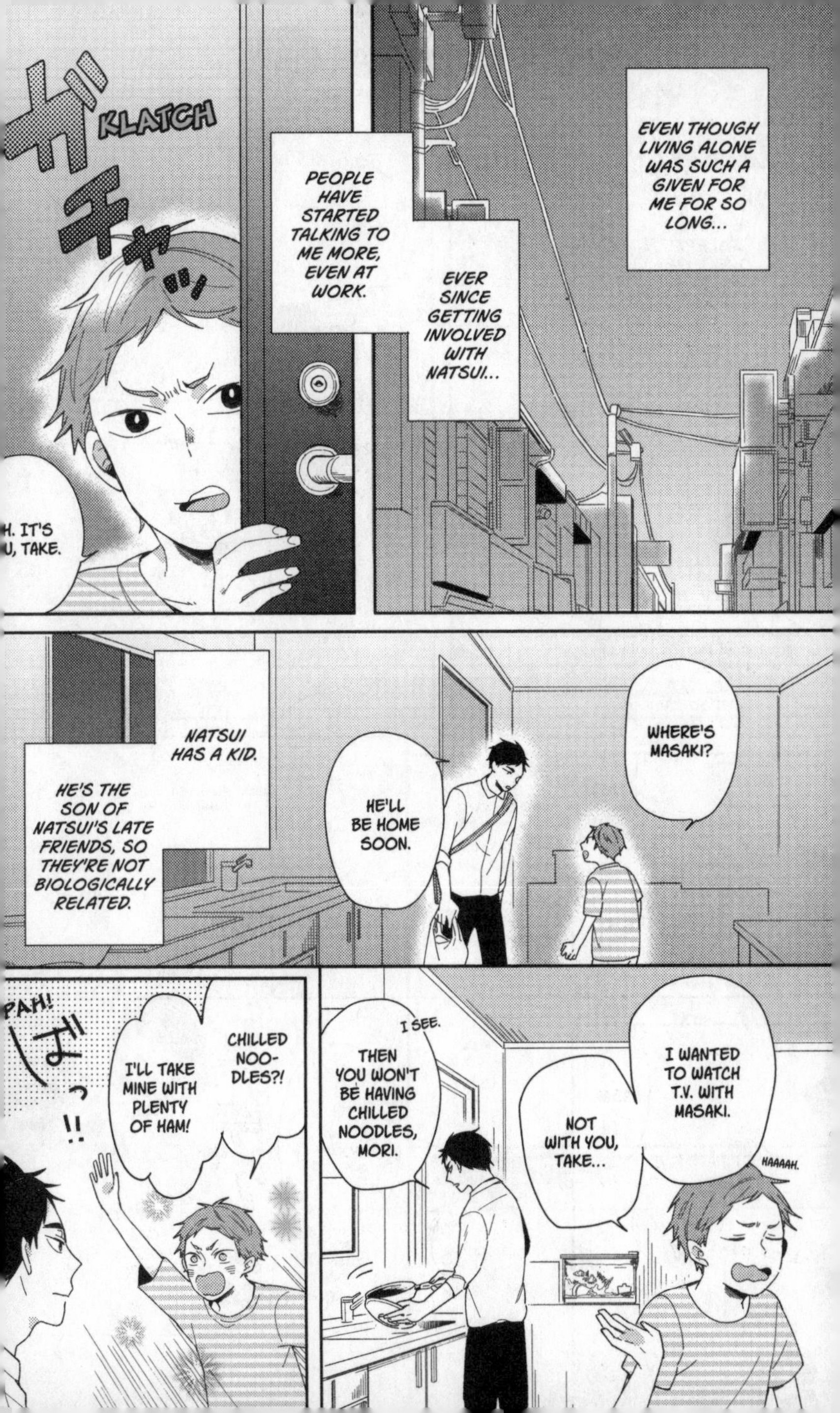

EVEN THOUGH LIVING ALONE WAS SUCH A GIVEN FOR ME FOR SO LONG...
EVER SINCE GETTING INVOLVED WITH NATSUI...
PEOPLE HAVE STARTED TALKING TO ME MORE, EVEN AT WORK.
KLATCH
H. IT'S
U, TAKE.
WHERE'S MASAKI?
HE'LL BE HOME SOON.
NATSUI HAS A KID.
HE'S THE SON OF NATSUI'S LATE FRIENDS, SO THEY'RE NOT BIOLOGICALLY RELATED.
I WANTED TO WATCH T.V. WITH MASAKI.
HAAAAH.
NOT WITH YOU, TAKE...
I SEE.
THEN YOU WON'T BE HAVING CHILLED NOODLES, MORI.
CHILLED NOODLES?!
I'LL TAKE MINE WITH PLENTY OF HAM!
PAH!
!!

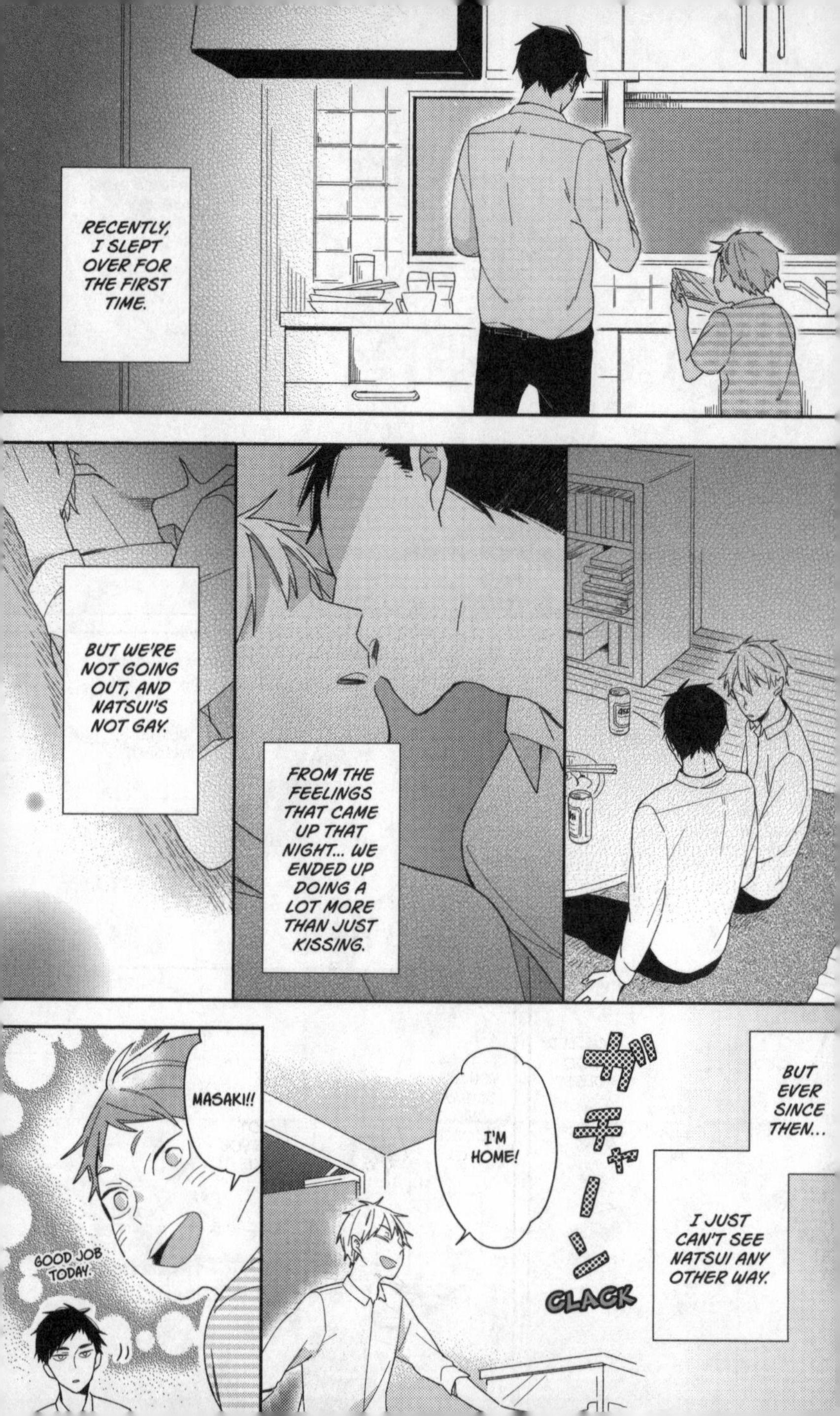

RECENTLY, I SLEPT OVER FOR THE FIRST TIME.
FROM THE FEELINGS THAT CAME UP THAT NIGHT... WE ENDED UP DOING A LOT MORE THAN JUST KISSING.
BUT WE'RE NOT GOING OUT, AND NATSUI'S NOT GAY.
BUT EVER SINCE THEN...
I JUST CAN'T SEE NATSUI ANY OTHER WAY.
CLACK
I'M HOME!
MASAKI!!
GOOD JOB TODAY.

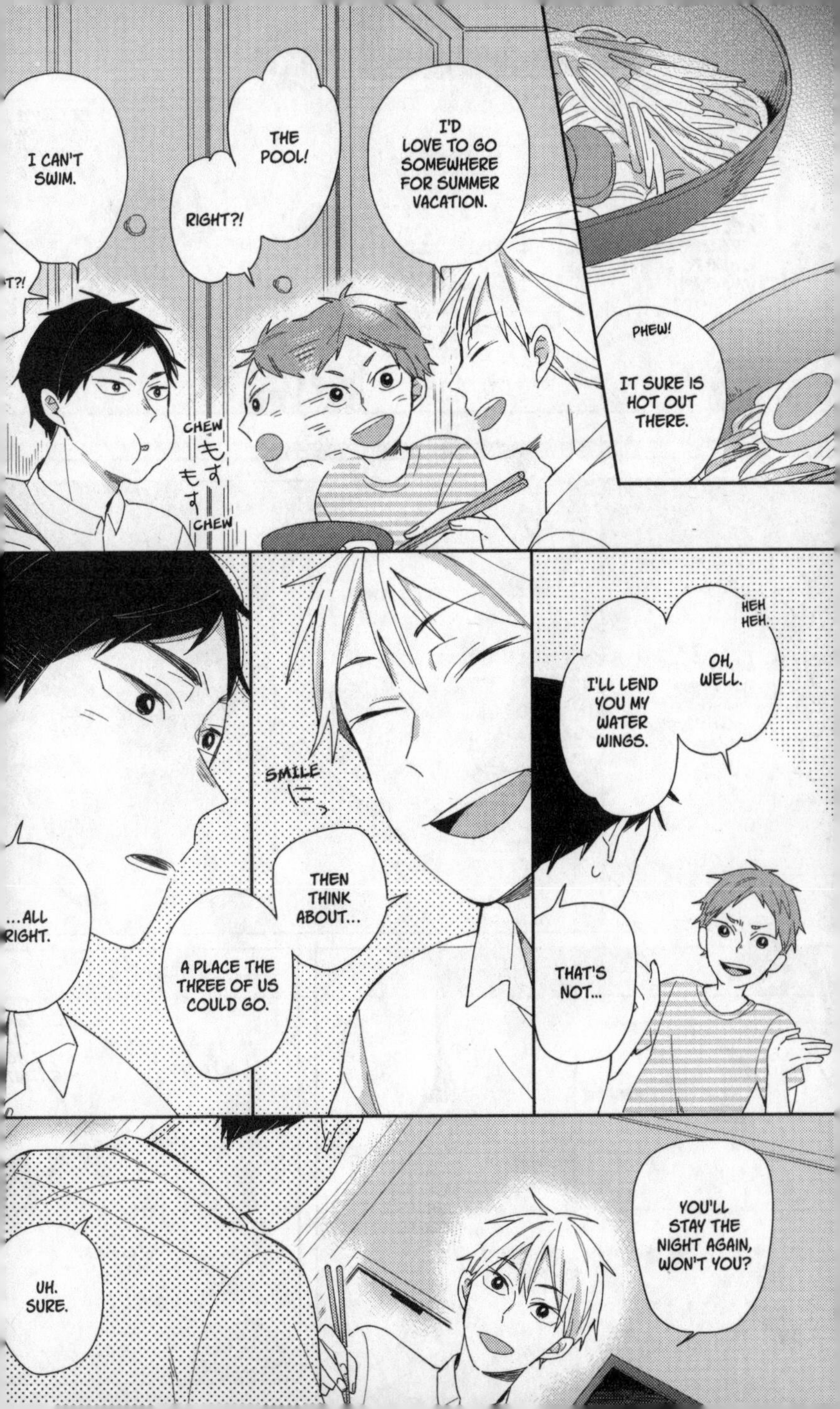
PHEW!
IT SURE IS HOT OUT THERE.
I'D LOVE TO GO SOMEWHERE FOR SUMMER VACATION.
THE POOL!
RIGHT?!
I CAN'T SWIM.
CHEW もす もす CHEW
HEH HEH.
OH, WELL.
I'LL LEND YOU MY WATER WINGS.
THAT'S NOT...
SMILE
THEN THINK ABOUT...
A PLACE THE THREE OF US COULD GO.
...ALL RIGHT.
YOU'LL STAY THE NIGHT AGAIN, WON'T YOU?
UH. SURE.

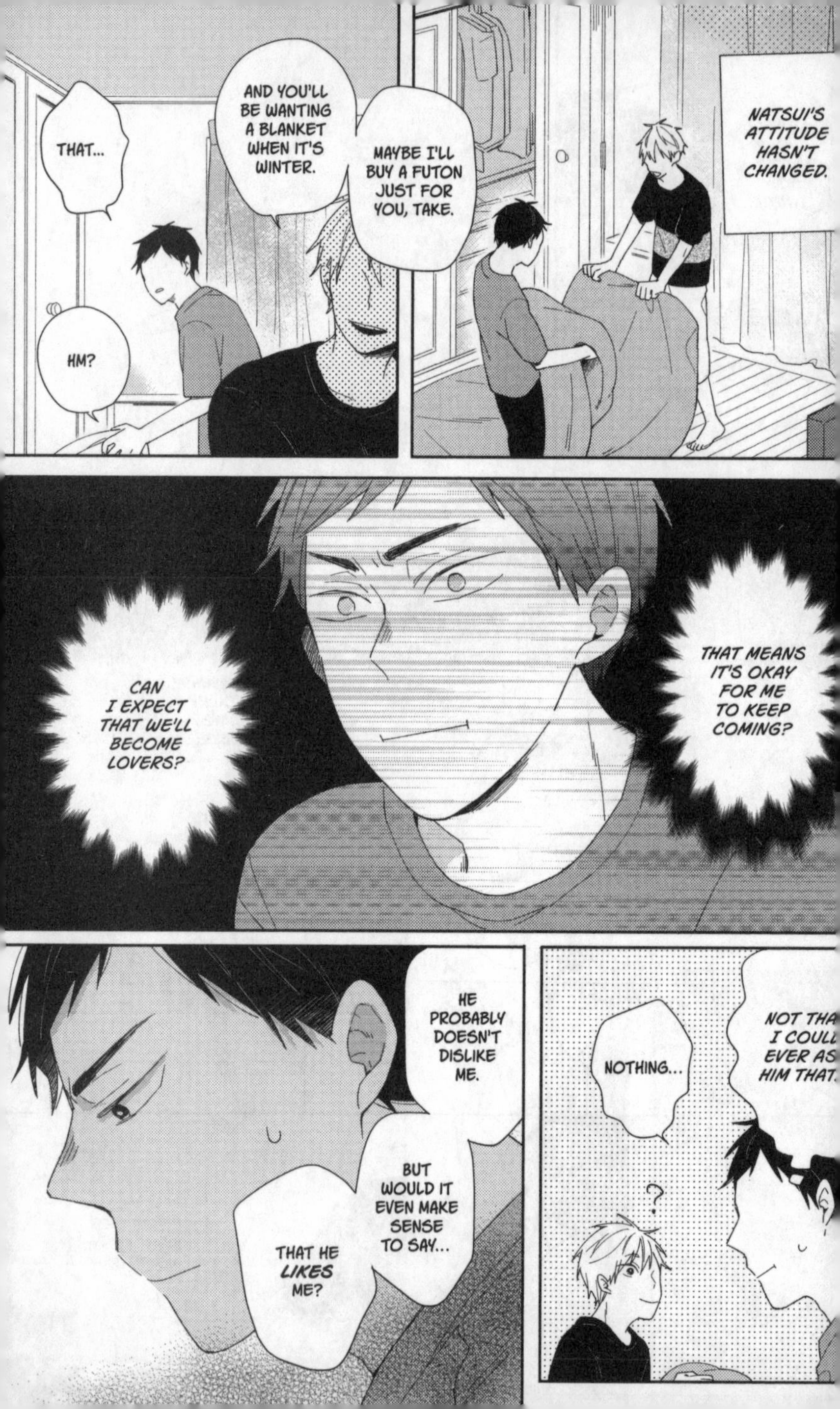

NATSUI'S ATTITUDE HASN'T CHANGED.
MAYBE I'LL BUY A FUTON JUST FOR YOU, TAKE.
AND YOU'LL BE WANTING A BLANKET WHEN IT'S WINTER.
THAT...
HM?
THAT MEANS IT'S OKAY FOR ME TO KEEP COMING?
CAN I EXPECT THAT WE'LL BECOME LOVERS?
NOT THA I COUL EVER AS HIM THAT.
NOTHING...
HE PROBABLY DOESN'T DISLIKE ME.
BUT WOULD IT EVEN MAKE SENSE TO SAY...
THAT HE *LIKES* ME?

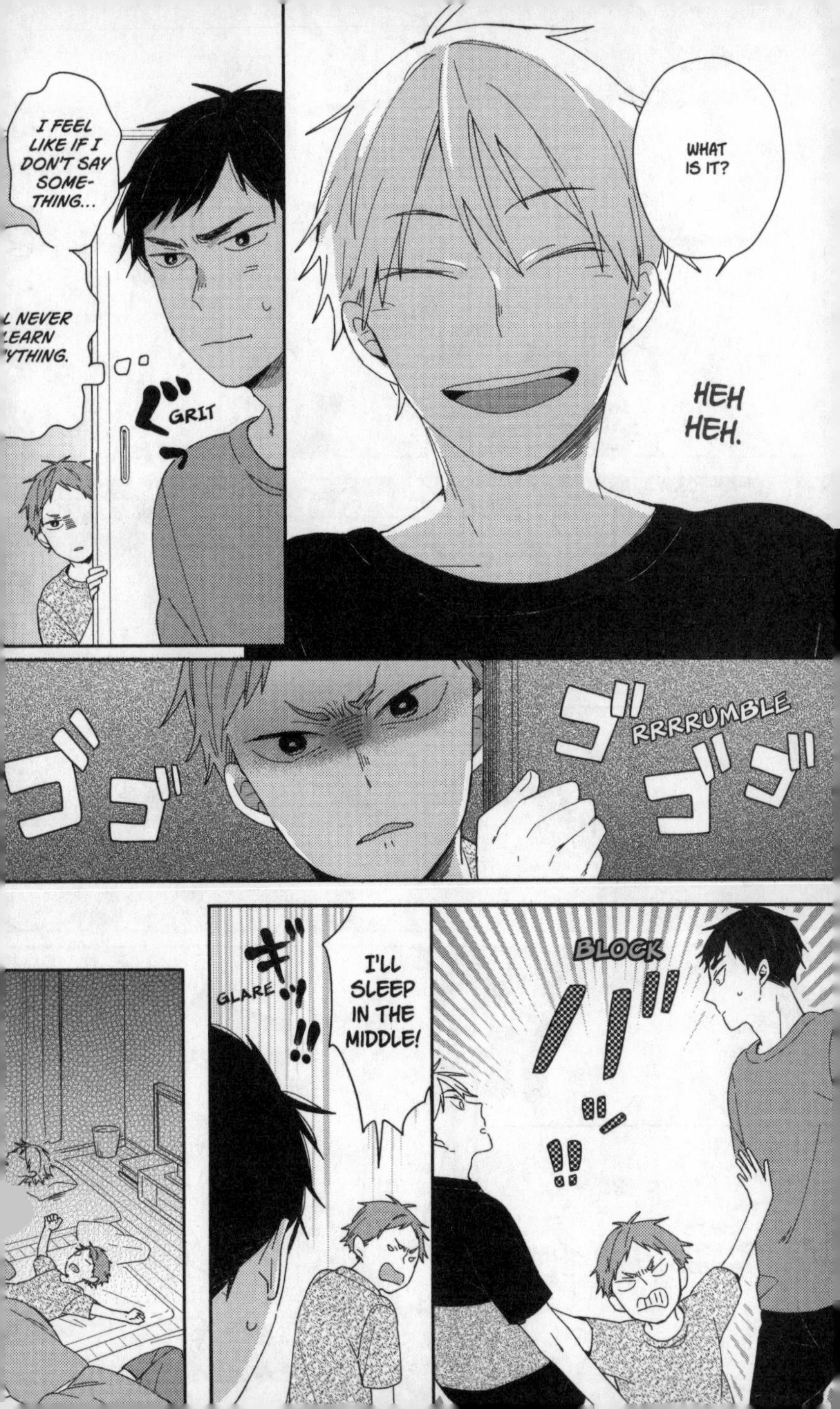
WHAT IS IT?
HEH HEH.
I FEEL LIKE IF I DON'T SAY SOME-THING...
L NEVER LEARN YTHING.
ぐっ
GRIT
ゴゴ
ゴゴゴ
RRRRUMBLE
バッ!!
BLOCK
I'LL SLEEP IN THE MIDDLE!
ギッ!!
GLARE

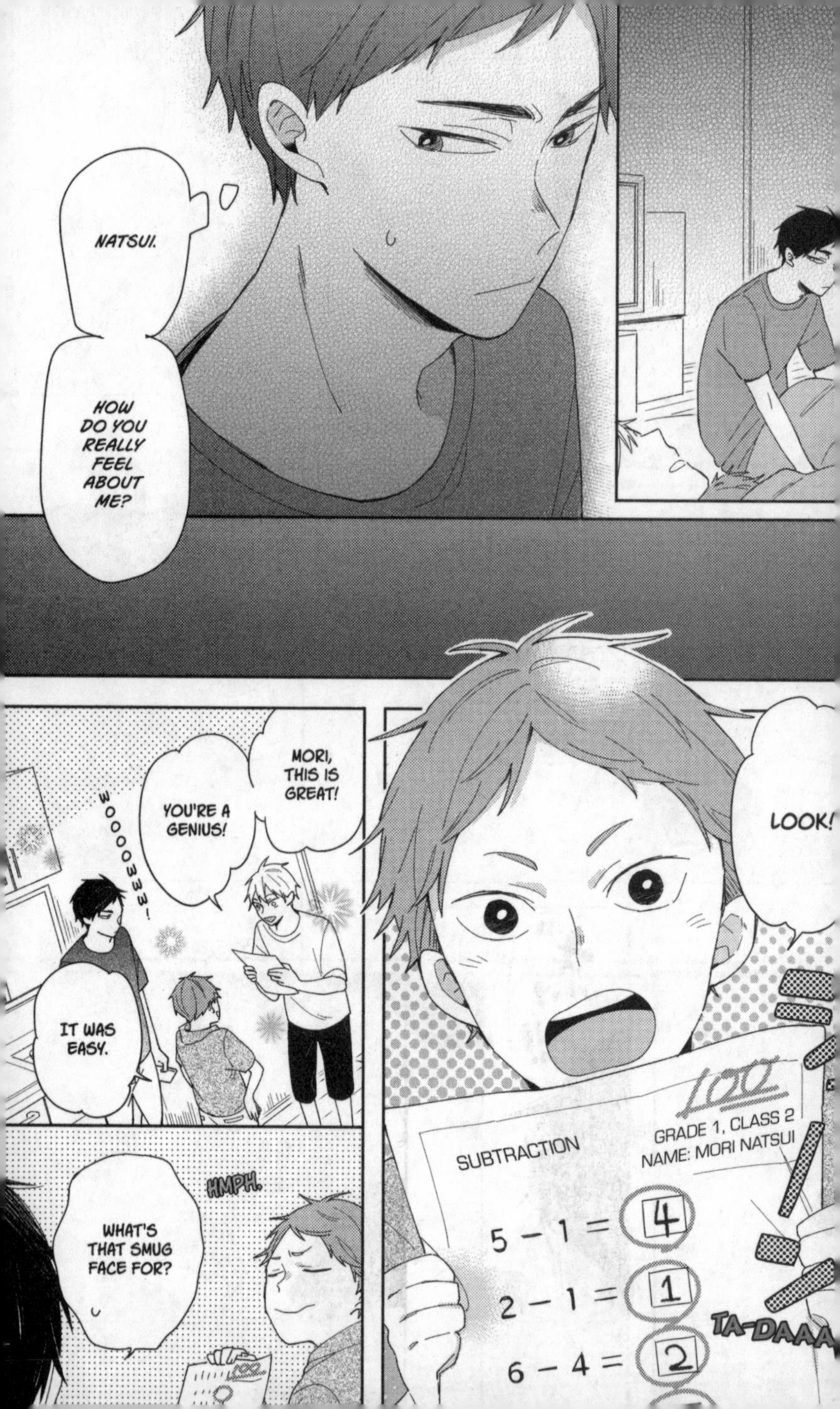
NATSUI.
HOW DO YOU REALLY FEEL ABOUT ME?
LOOK!
100
GRADE 1, CLASS 2
NAME: MORI NATSUI
SUBTRACTION
5 − 1 = 4
2 − 1 = 1
6 − 4 = 2
TA-DAAA
MORI, THIS IS GREAT!
YOU'RE A GENIUS!
WOOOOOWWW!
IT WAS EASY.
HMPH.
WHAT'S THAT SMUG FACE FOR?

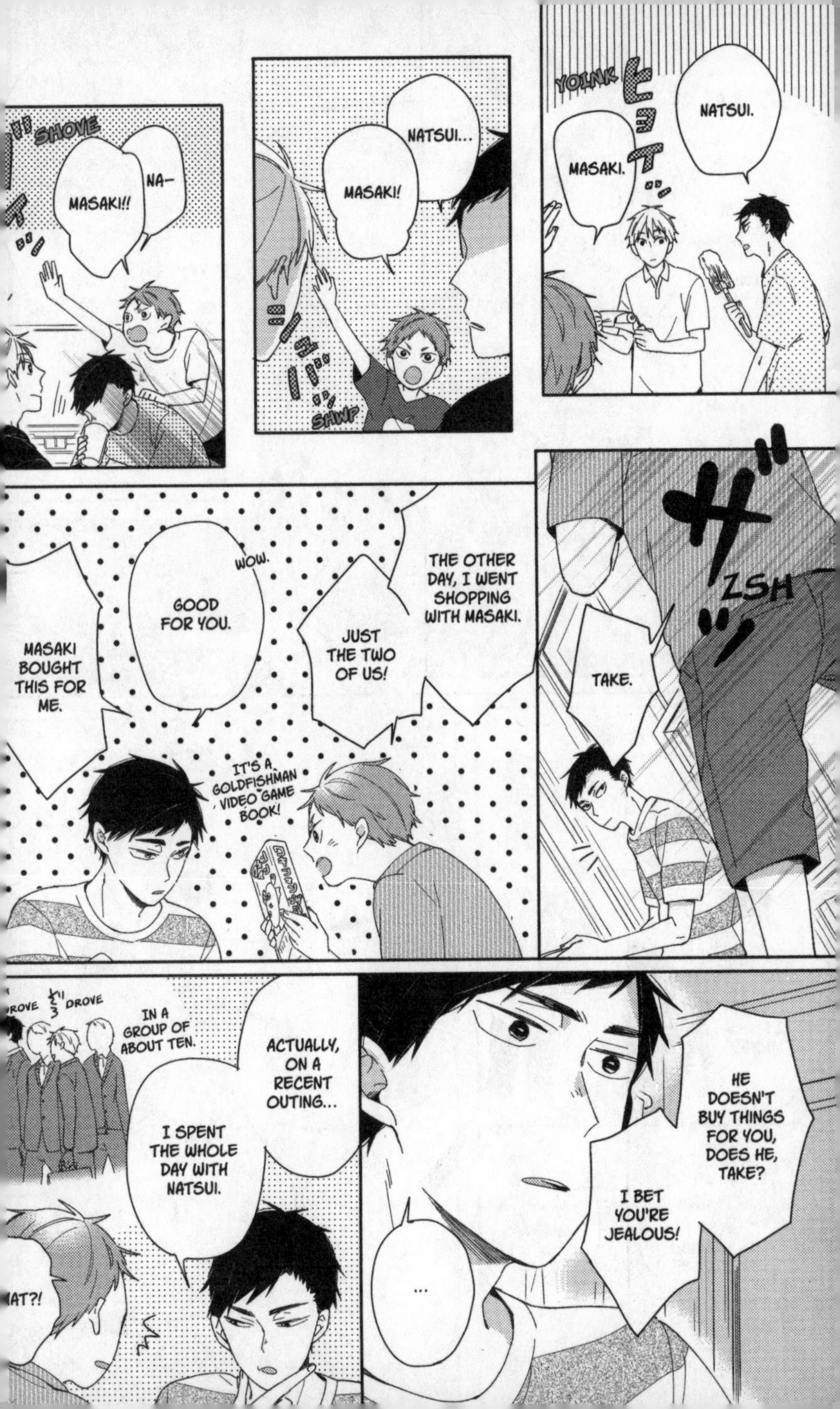
NATSUI.
YOINK
MASAKI.
NATSUI...
MASAKI!
SHWP
SHOVE
NA-
MASAKI!!
ZSH
TAKE.
THE OTHER DAY, I WENT SHOPPING WITH MASAKI.
JUST THE TWO OF US!
WOW.
GOOD FOR YOU.
MASAKI BOUGHT THIS FOR ME.
IT'S A GOLDFISHMAN VIDEO GAME BOOK!
HE DOESN'T BUY THINGS FOR YOU, DOES HE, TAKE?
I BET YOU'RE JEALOUS!
...
ACTUALLY, ON A RECENT OUTING...
I SPENT THE WHOLE DAY WITH NATSUI.
IN A GROUP OF ABOUT TEN.
DROVE
DROVE
AT?!

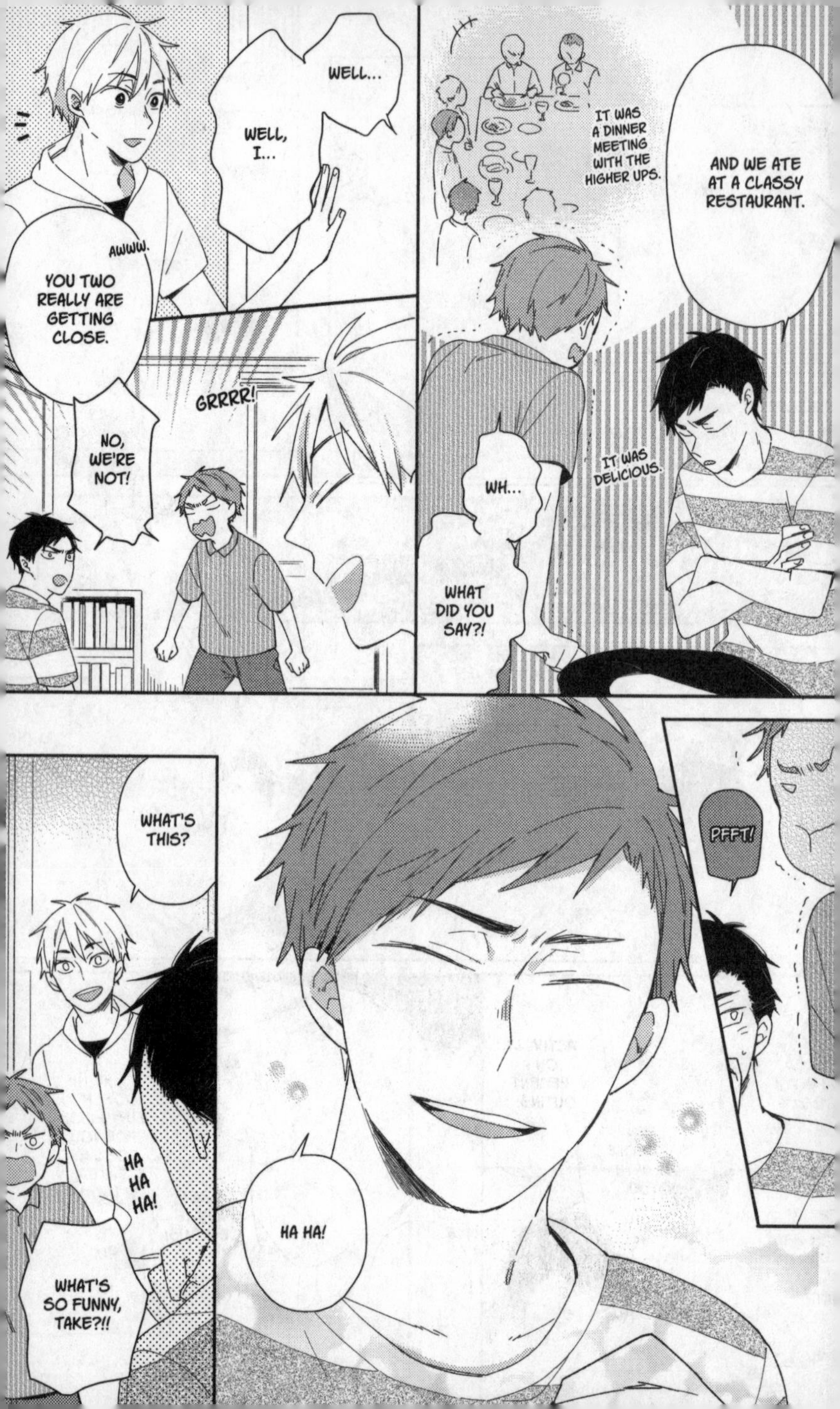
AND WE ATE AT A CLASSY RESTAURANT.
IT WAS A DINNER MEETING WITH THE HIGHER UPS.
IT WAS DELICIOUS.
WH...
WHAT DID YOU SAY?!
WELL...
WELL, I...
AWWW.
YOU TWO REALLY ARE GETTING CLOSE.
GRRRR!
NO, WE'RE NOT!
PFFT!
HA HA!
WHAT'S THIS?
HA HA HA!
WHAT'S SO FUNNY, TAKE?!!

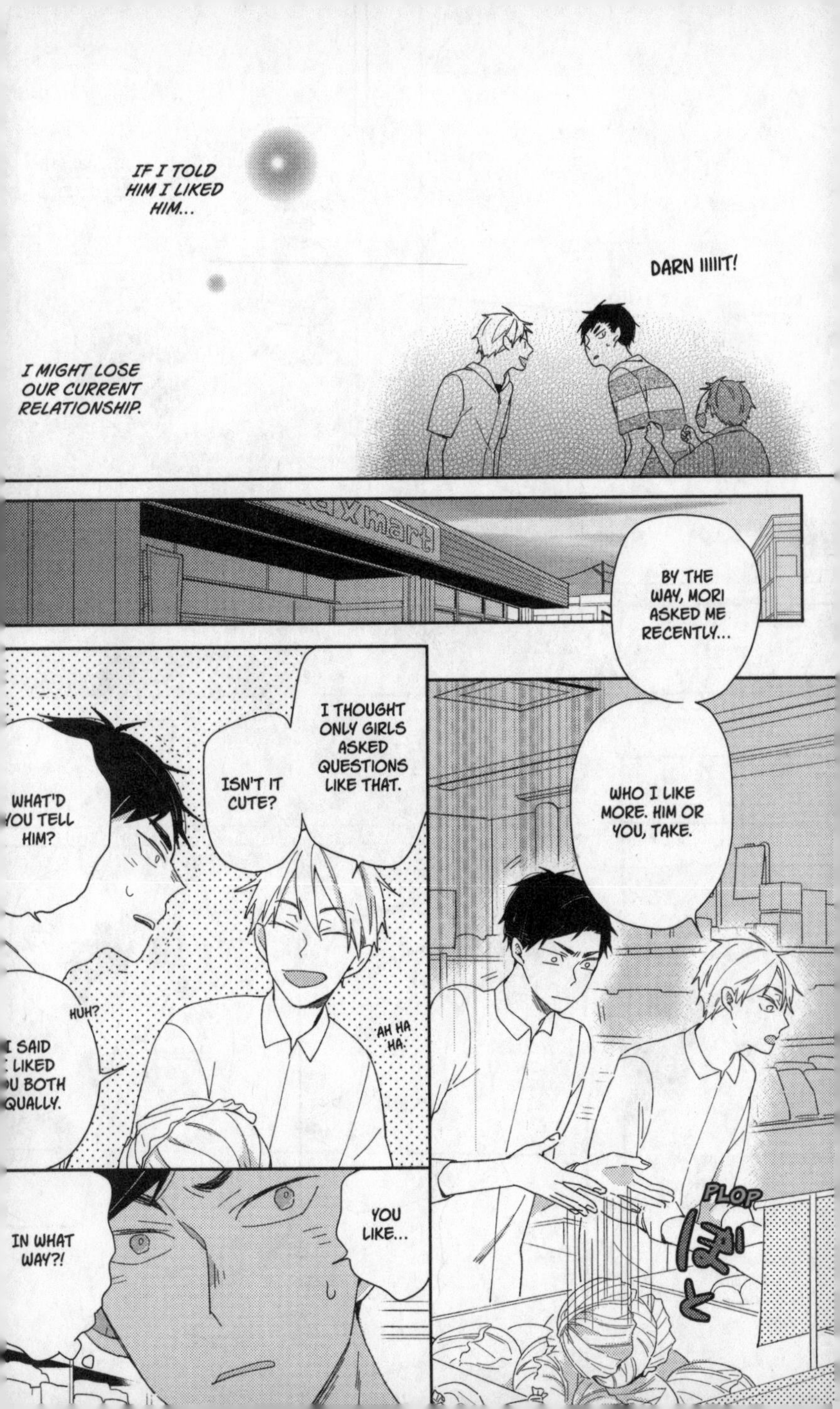
IF I TOLD HIM I LIKED HIM...
I MIGHT LOSE OUR CURRENT RELATIONSHIP.
DARN IIIIIT!
BY THE WAY, MORI ASKED ME RECENTLY...
WHO I LIKE MORE. HIM OR YOU, TAKE.
PLOP
ぽと
I THOUGHT ONLY GIRLS ASKED QUESTIONS LIKE THAT.
ISN'T IT CUTE?
AH HA HA.
WHAT'D YOU TELL HIM?
HUH?
I SAID I LIKED OU BOTH QUALLY.
YOU LIKE...
IN WHAT WAY?!

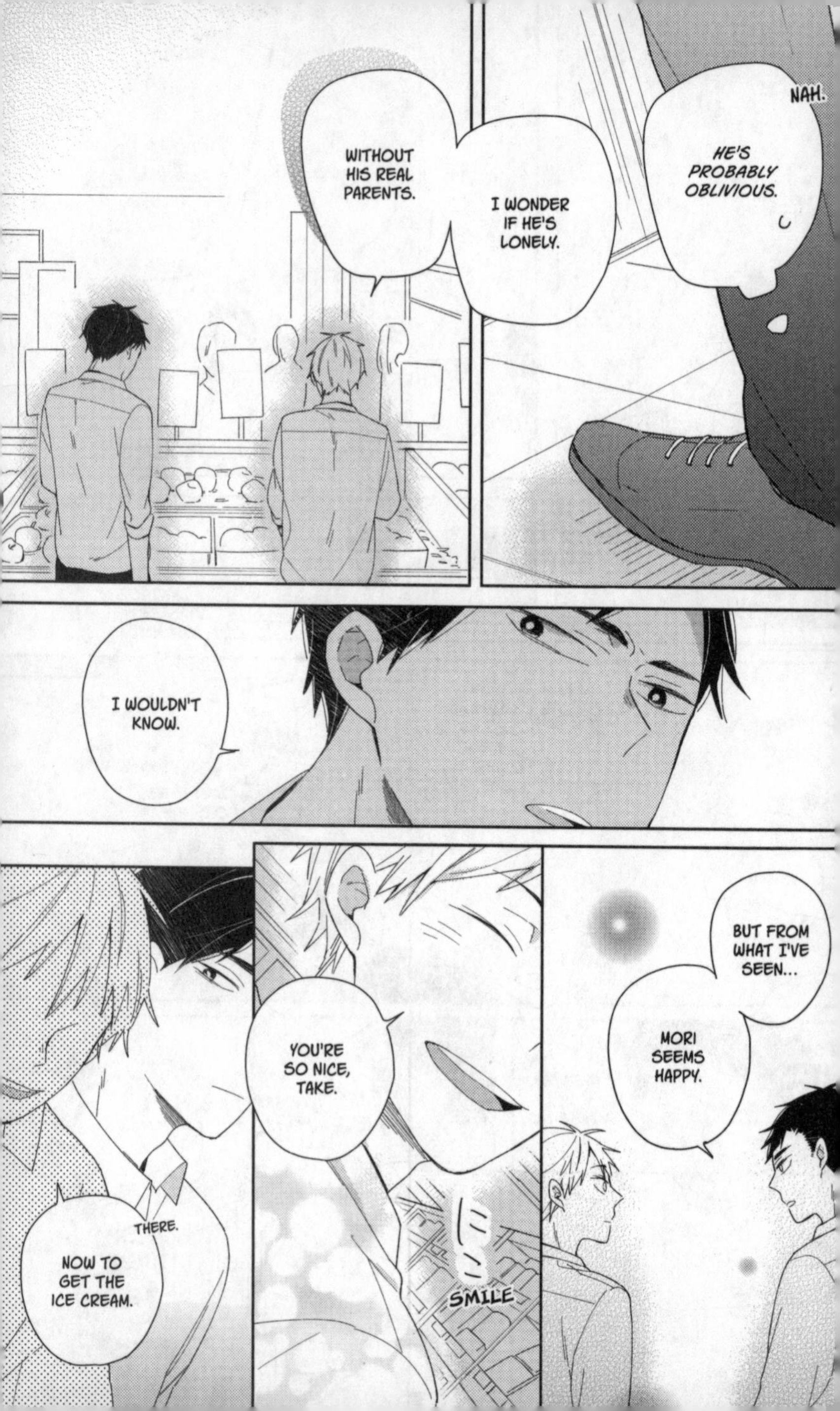
I WONDER IF HE'S LONELY.
WITHOUT HIS REAL PARENTS.
NAH.
HE'S PROBABLY OBLIVIOUS.
I WOULDN'T KNOW.
BUT FROM WHAT I'VE SEEN...
MORI SEEMS HAPPY.
YOU'RE SO NICE, TAKE.
SMILE
THERE.
NOW TO GET THE ICE CREAM.

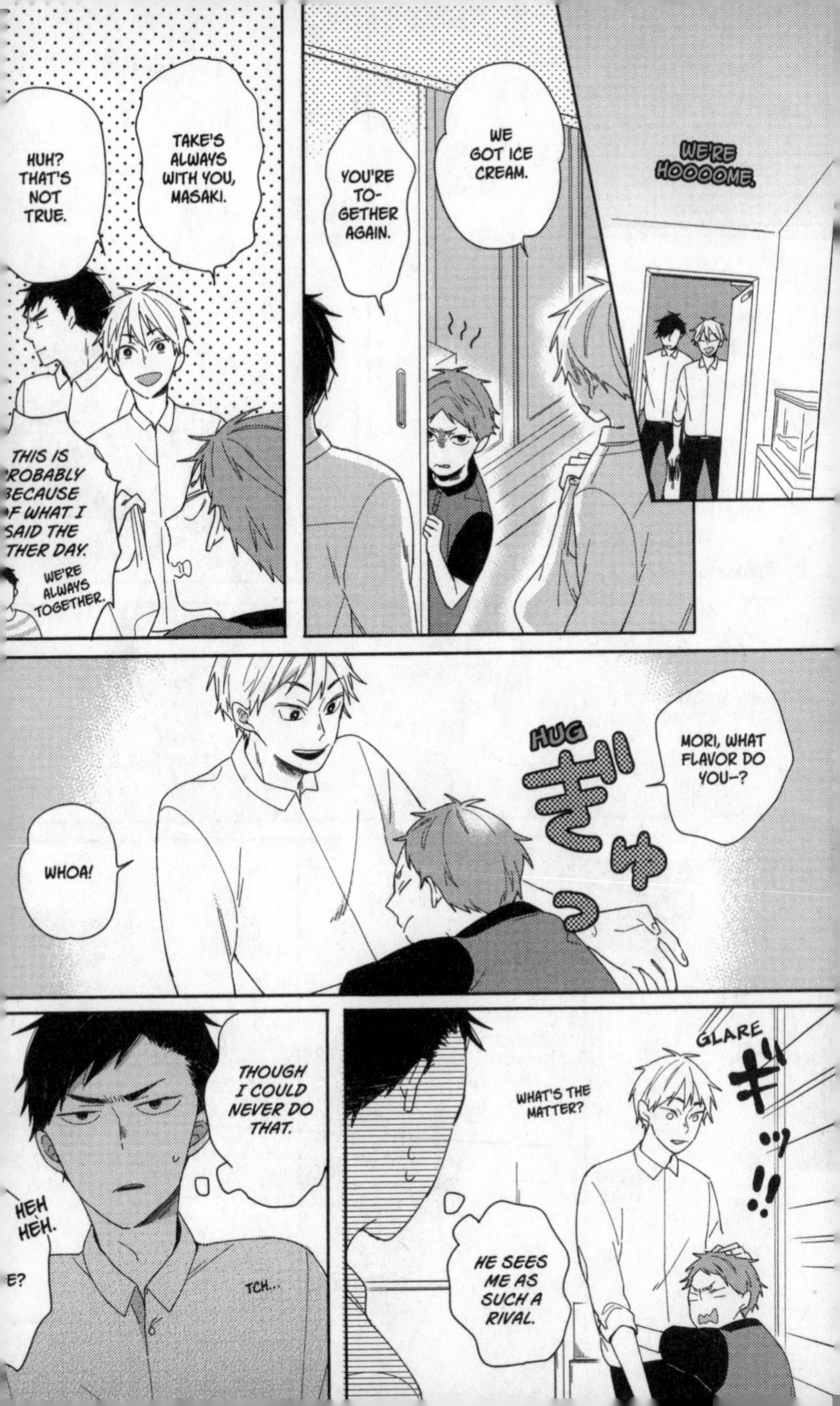
WE'RE HOOOOME.
WE GOT ICE CREAM.
YOU'RE TO-GETHER AGAIN.
TAKE'S ALWAYS WITH YOU, MASAKI.
HUH? THAT'S NOT TRUE.
THIS IS ROBABLY ECAUSE F WHAT I SAID THE THER DAY.
WE'RE ALWAYS TOGETHER.
MORI, WHAT FLAVOR DO YOU-?
HUG
ぎゅっ
WHOA!
GLARE
ギッ!!
WHAT'S THE MATTER?
HE SEES ME AS SUCH A RIVAL.
THOUGH I COULD NEVER DO THAT.
HEH HEH.
TCH...
E?

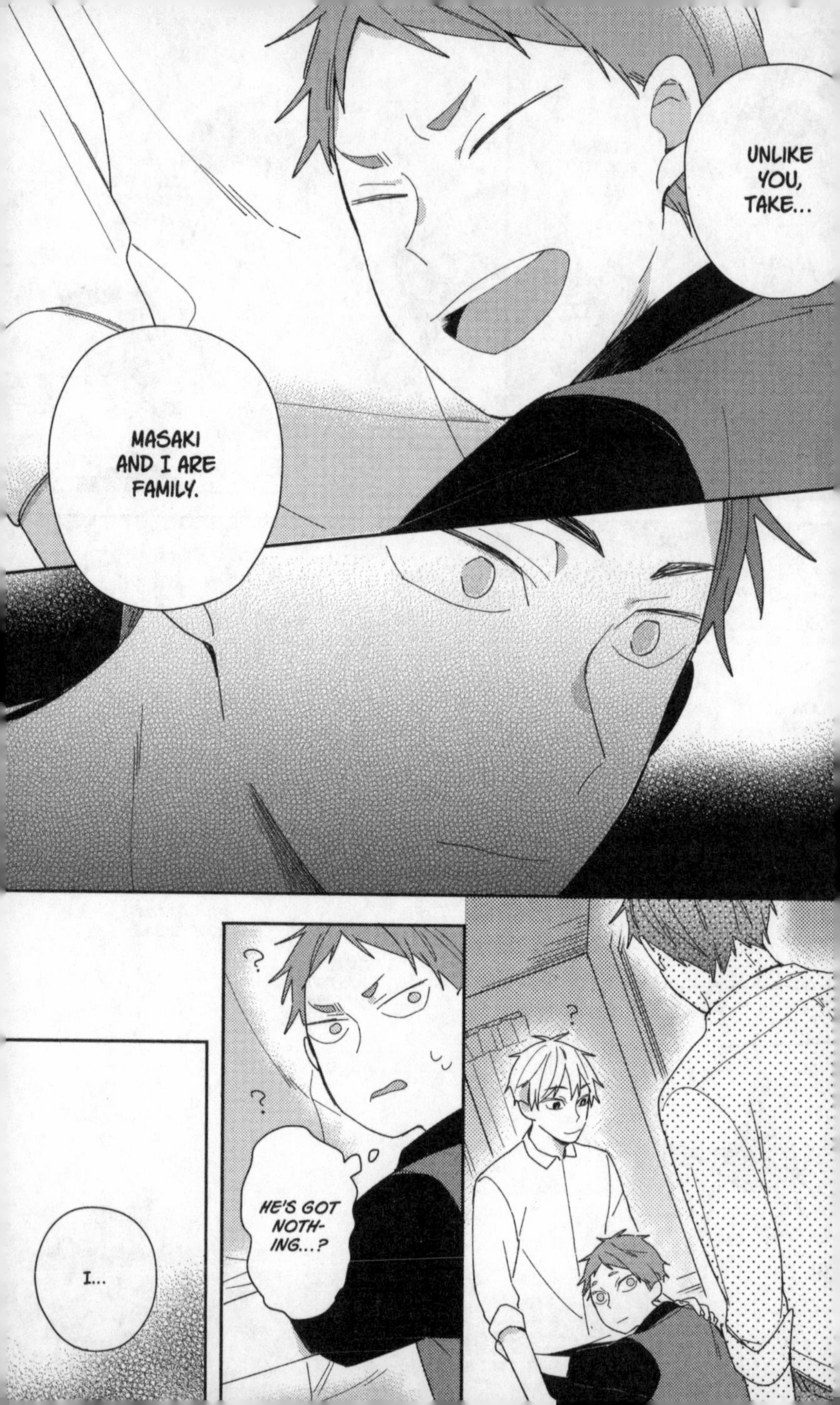
UNLIKE YOU, TAKE...
MASAKI AND I ARE FAMILY.
HE'S GOT NOTH-ING...?
I...

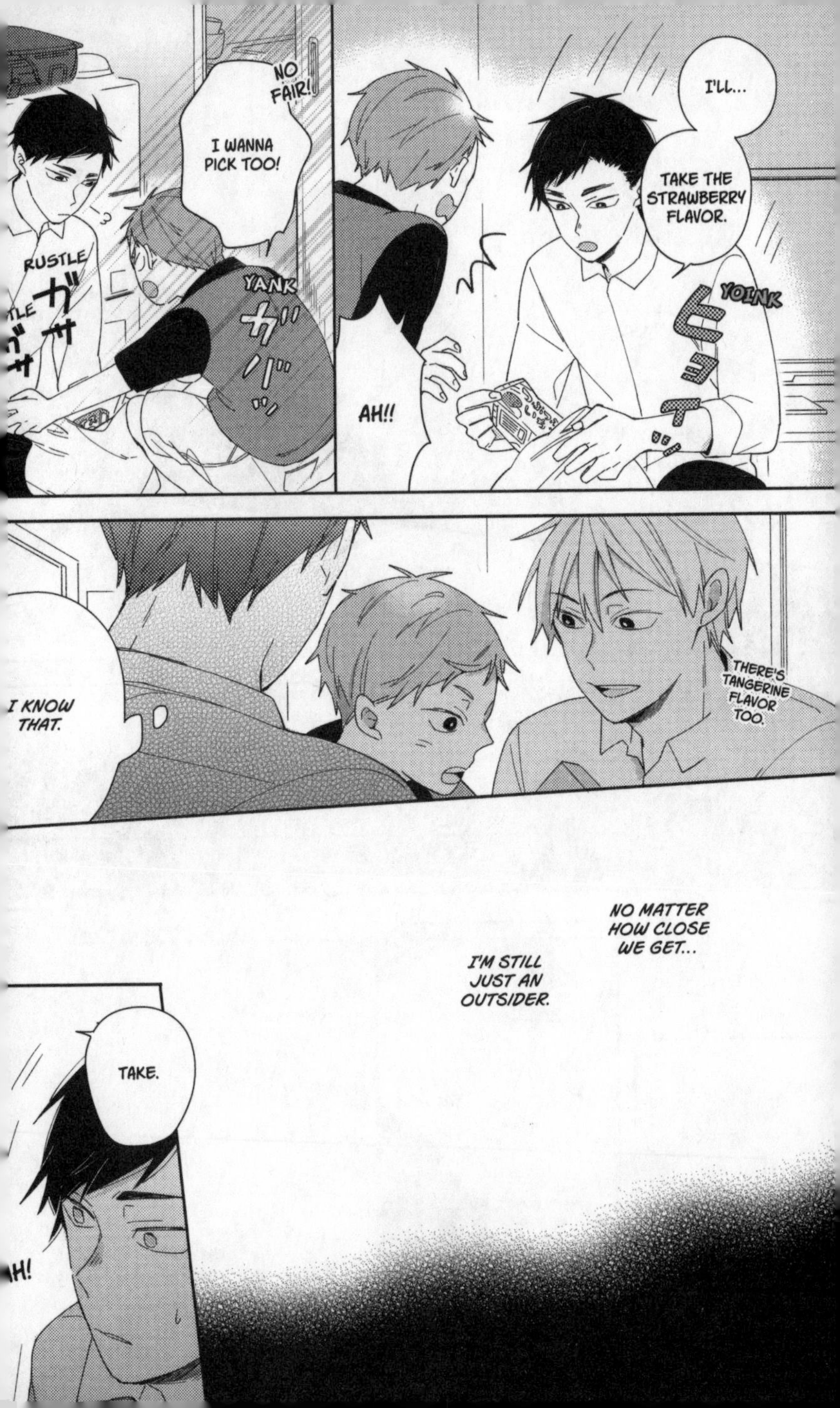
I'LL...
TAKE THE STRAWBERRY FLAVOR.
YOINK
AH!!
NO FAIR!
I WANNA PICK TOO!
YANK
RUSTLE
THERE'S TANGERINE FLAVOR TOO.
I KNOW THAT.
NO MATTER HOW CLOSE WE GET...
I'M STILL JUST AN OUTSIDER.
TAKE.

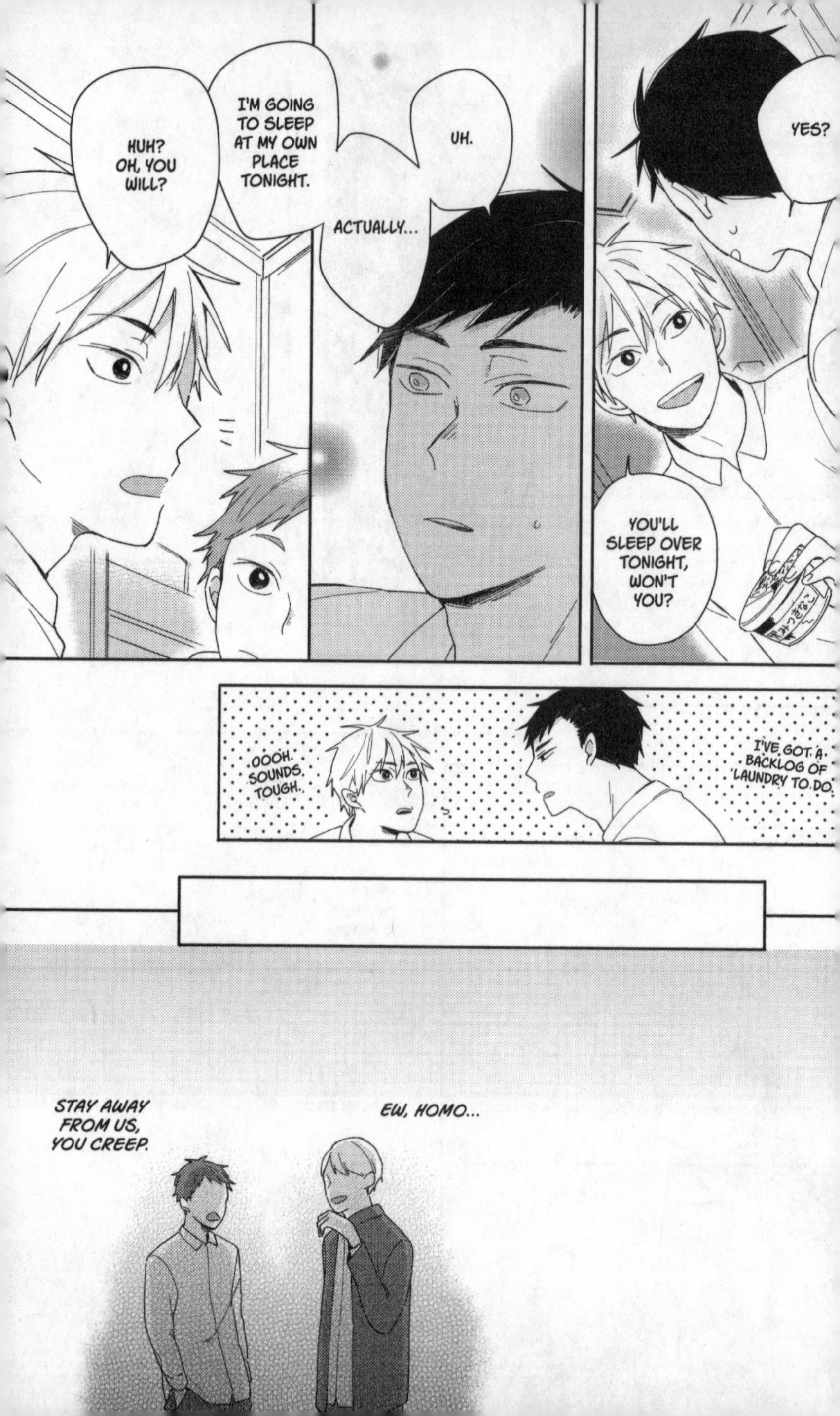
YES?
YOU'LL SLEEP OVER TONIGHT, WON'T YOU?
UH.
ACTUALLY...
I'M GOING TO SLEEP AT MY OWN PLACE TONIGHT.
HUH? OH, YOU WILL?
I'VE GOT A BACKLOG OF LAUNDRY TO DO.
OOOH. SOUNDS. TOUGH.
EW, HOMO...
STAY AWAY FROM US, YOU CREEP.

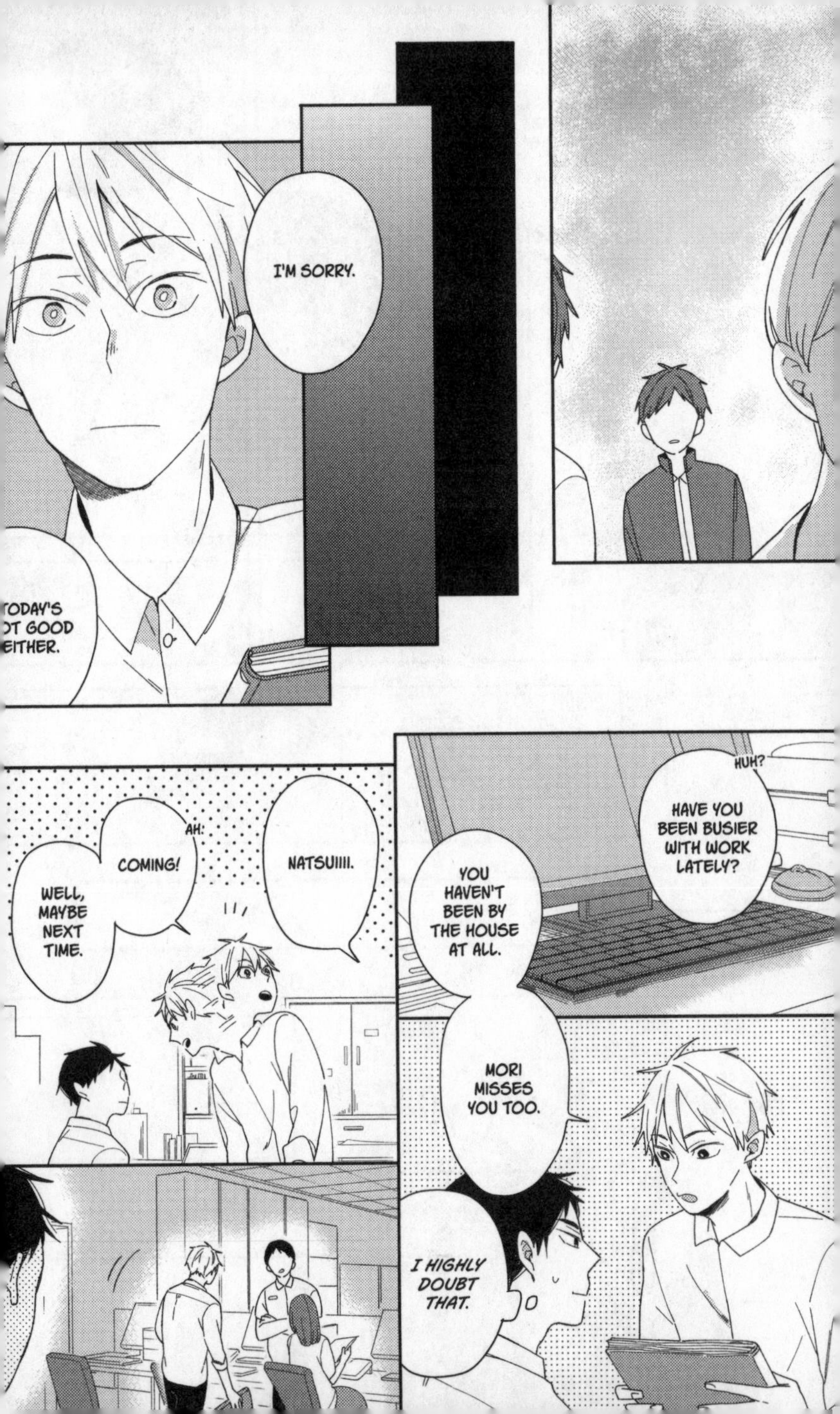
I'M SORRY.
TODAY'S
OT GOOD
EITHER.
HUH?
HAVE YOU BEEN BUSIER WITH WORK LATELY?
YOU HAVEN'T BEEN BY THE HOUSE AT ALL.
MORI MISSES YOU TOO.
I HIGHLY DOUBT THAT.
NATSUIIII.
AH:
COMING!
WELL, MAYBE NEXT TIME.

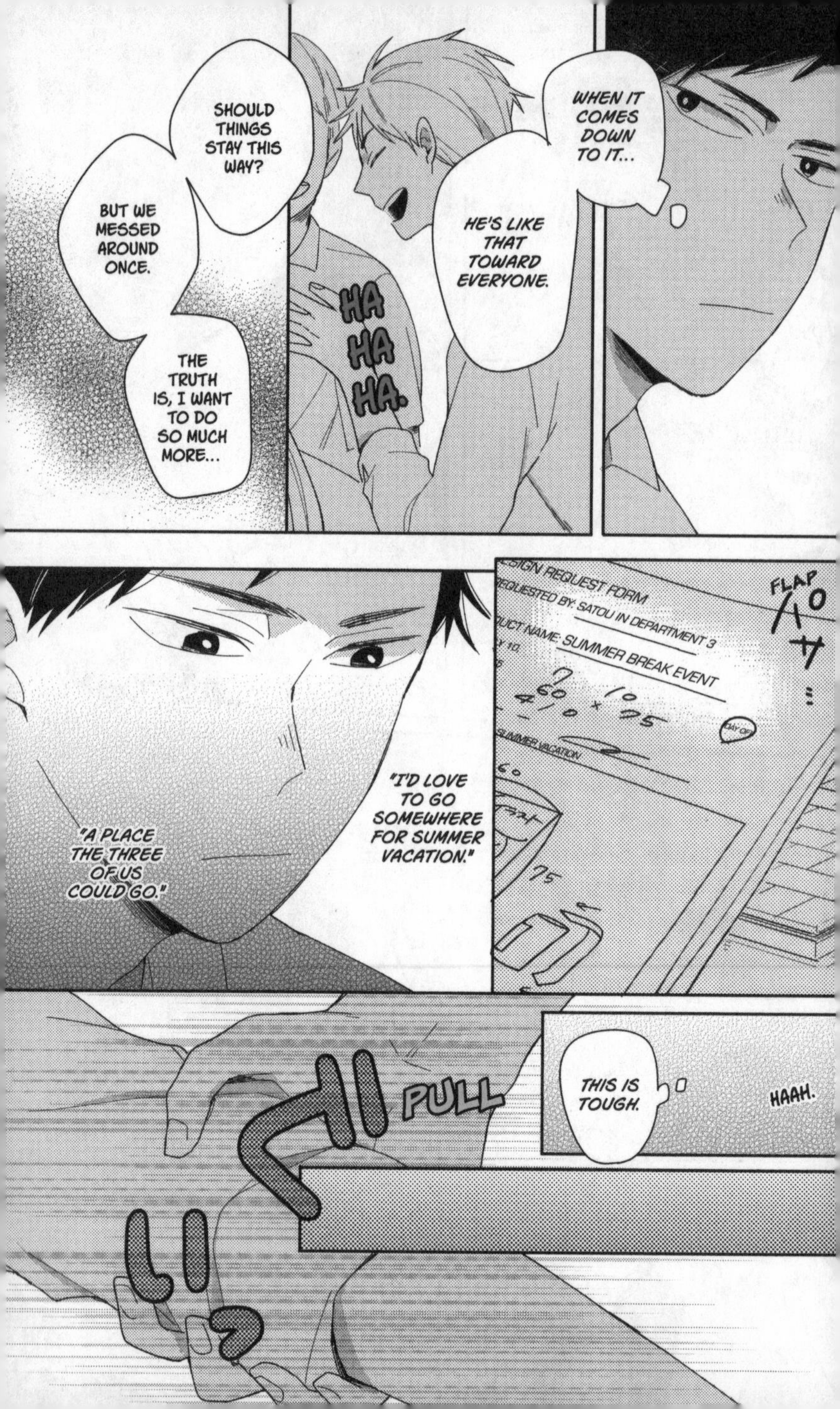
WHEN IT COMES DOWN TO IT...
HE'S LIKE THAT TOWARD EVERYONE.
HA HA HA.
SHOULD THINGS STAY THIS WAY?
BUT WE MESSED AROUND ONCE.
THE TRUTH IS, I WANT TO DO SO MUCH MORE...
FLAP
SIGN REQUEST FORM
REQUESTED BY: SATOU IN DEPARTMENT 3
UCT NAME: SUMMER BREAK EVENT
SUMMER VACATION
DAY OFF
"I'D LOVE TO GO SOMEWHERE FOR SUMMER VACATION."
"A PLACE THE THREE OF US COULD GO."
HAAH.
THIS IS TOUGH.
PULL

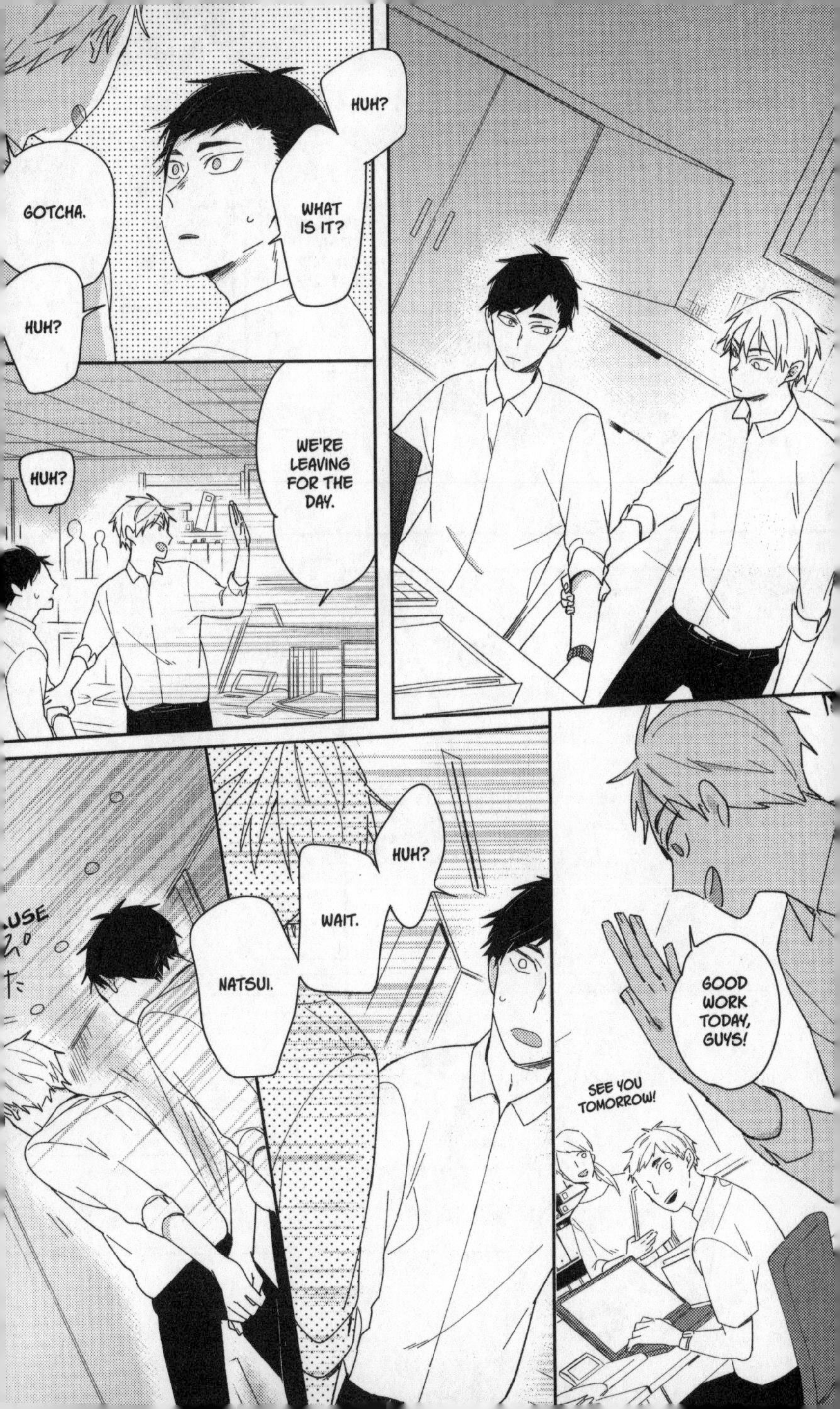
HUH?
WHAT IS IT?
GOTCHA.
HUH?
WE'RE LEAVING FOR THE DAY.
HUH?
GOOD WORK TODAY, GUYS!
SEE YOU TOMORROW!
HUH?
WAIT.
NATSUI.

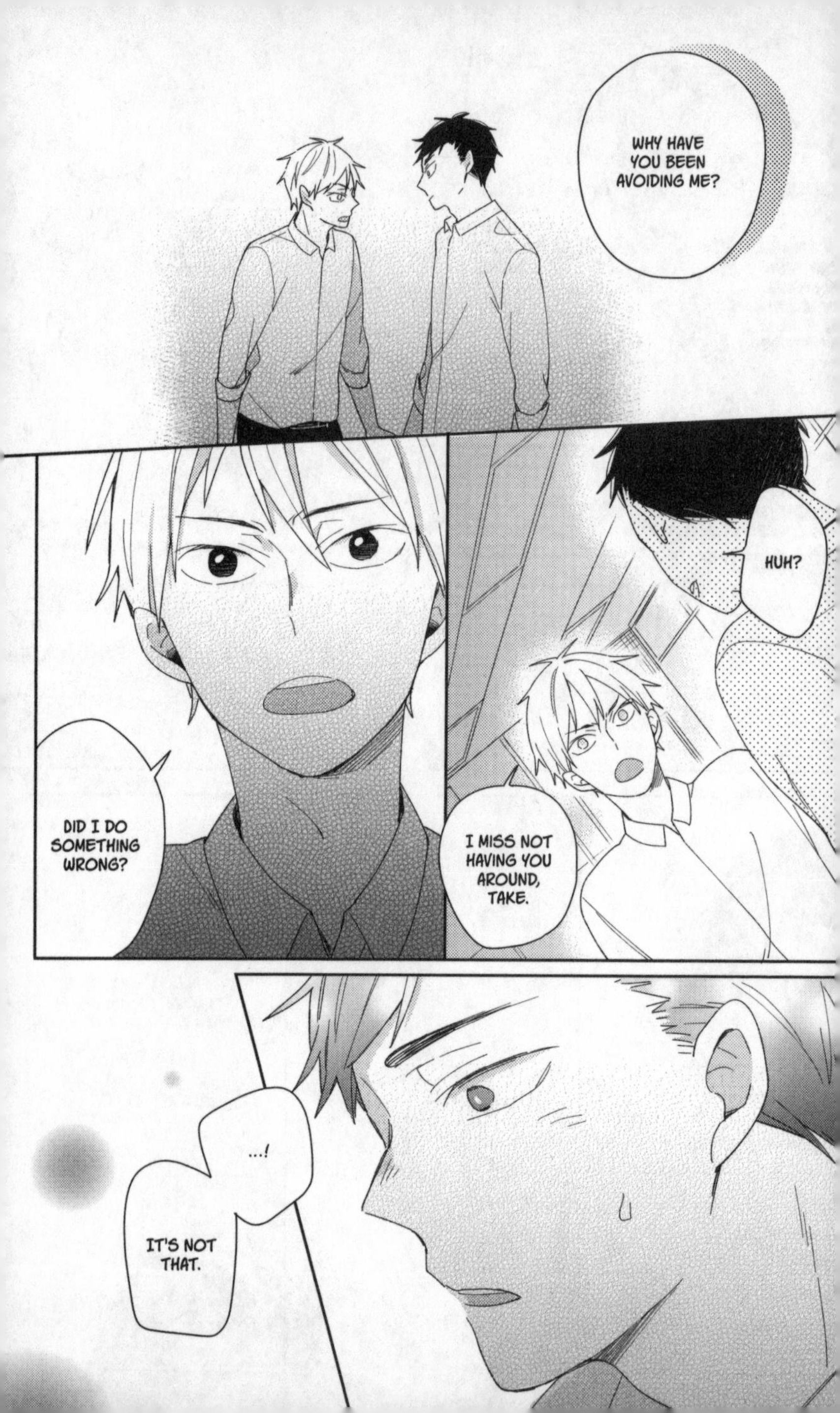
WHY HAVE YOU BEEN AVOIDING ME?
HUH?
I MISS NOT HAVING YOU AROUND, TAKE.
DID I DO SOMETHING WRONG?
...!
IT'S NOT THAT.

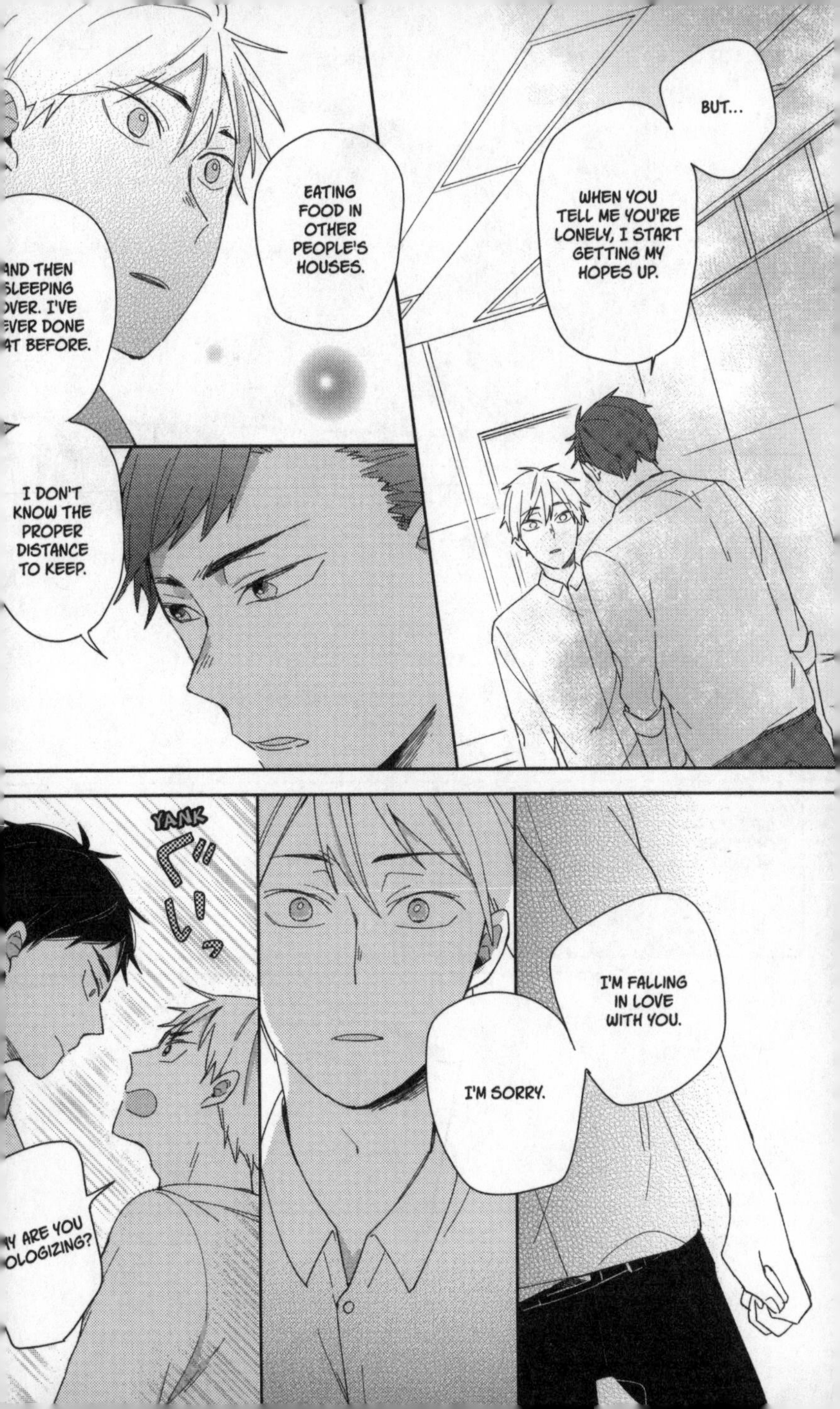
BUT...
WHEN YOU TELL ME YOU'RE LONELY, I START GETTING MY HOPES UP.
EATING FOOD IN OTHER PEOPLE'S HOUSES.
AND THEN SLEEPING OVER. I'VE EVER DONE AT BEFORE.
I DON'T KNOW THE PROPER DISTANCE TO KEEP.
I'M FALLING IN LOVE WITH YOU.
I'M SORRY.
YANK
Y ARE YOU OLOGIZING?

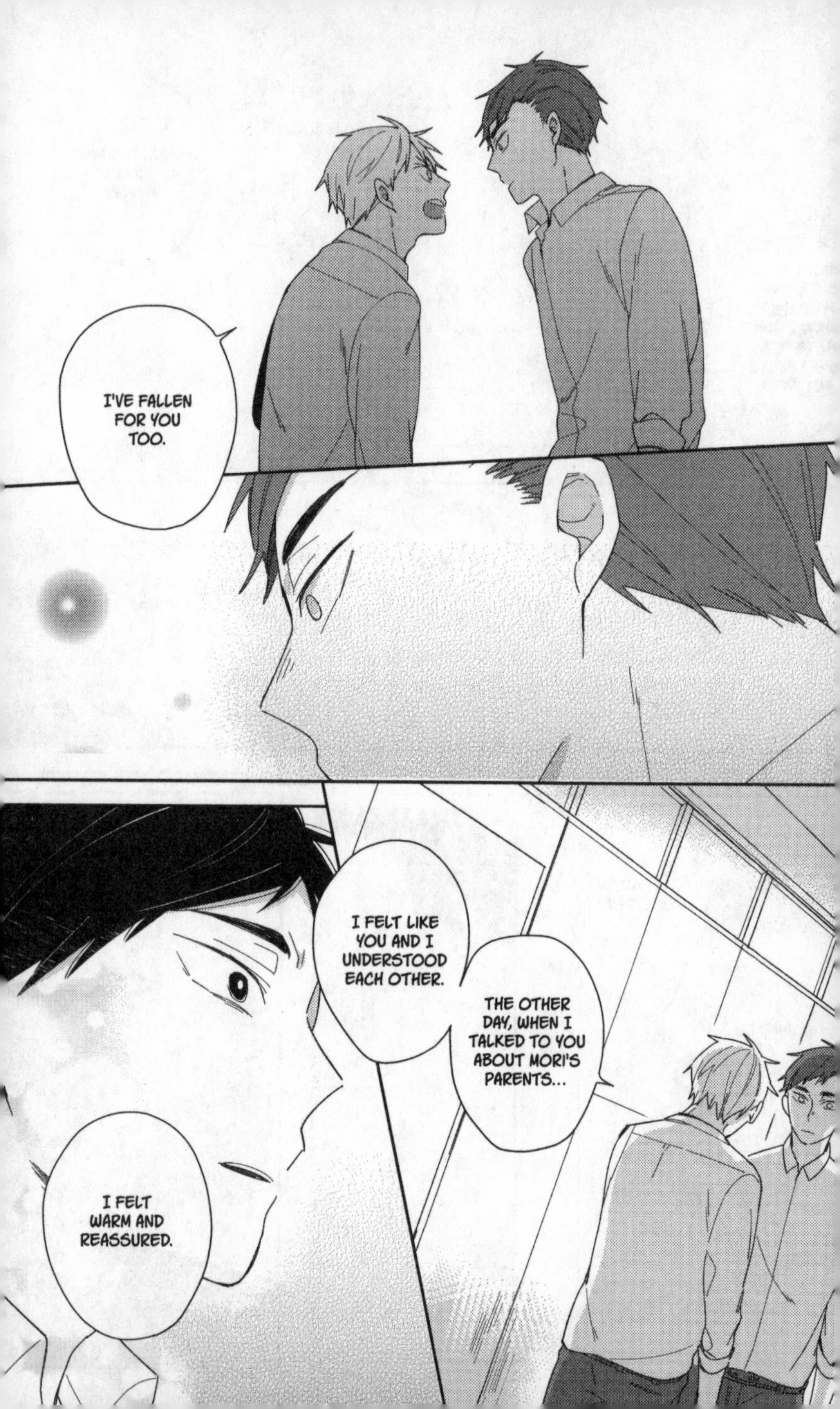
I'VE FALLEN FOR YOU TOO.
THE OTHER DAY, WHEN I TALKED TO YOU ABOUT MORI'S PARENTS...
I FELT LIKE YOU AND I UNDERSTOOD EACH OTHER.
I FELT WARM AND REASSURED.

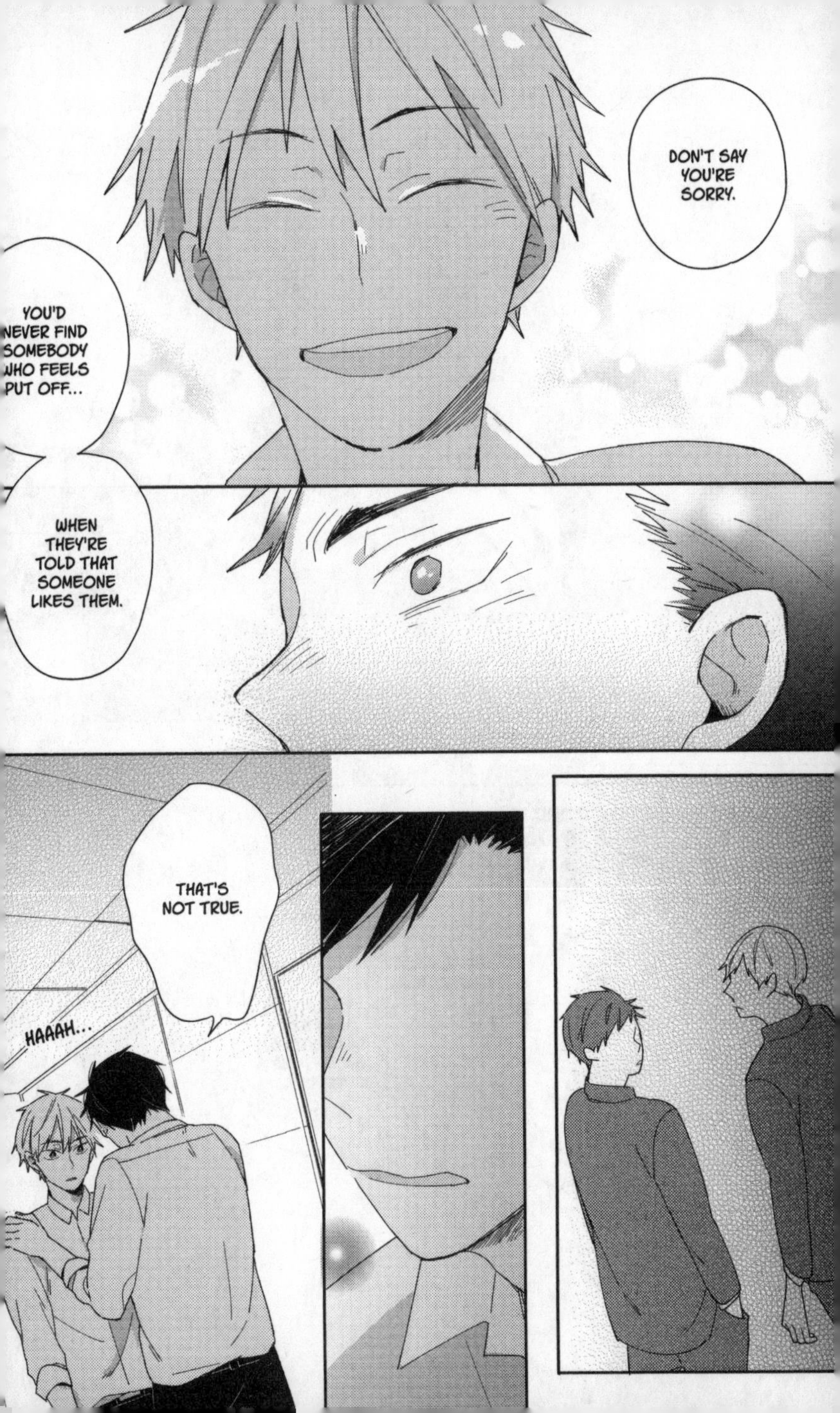
DON'T SAY YOU'RE SORRY.
YOU'D NEVER FIND SOMEBODY WHO FEELS PUT OFF...
WHEN THEY'RE TOLD THAT SOMEONE LIKES THEM.
THAT'S NOT TRUE.
HAAAH...

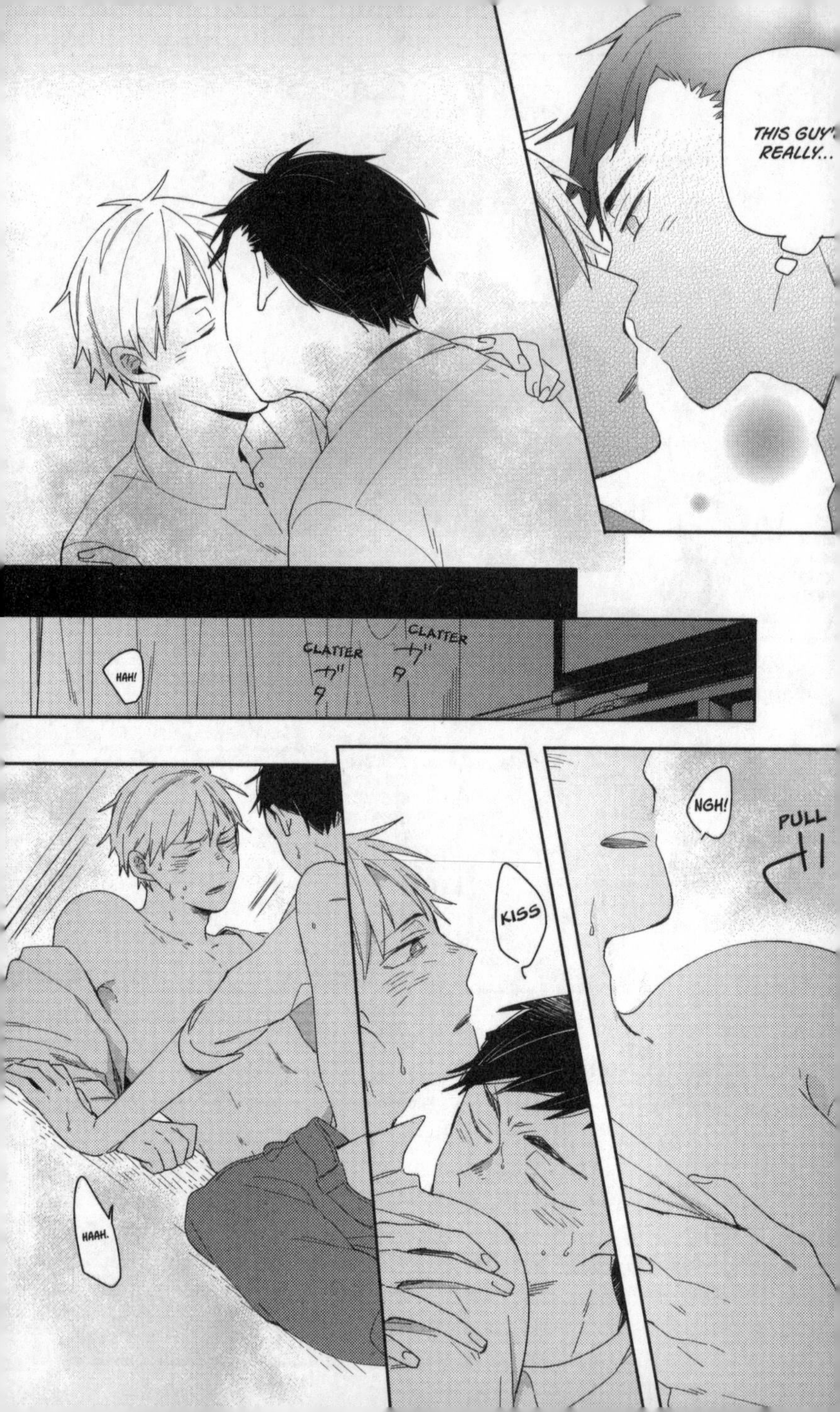
THIS GUY'S REALLY...
CLATTER
CLATTER
HAH!
NGH!
PULL
KISS
HAAH.

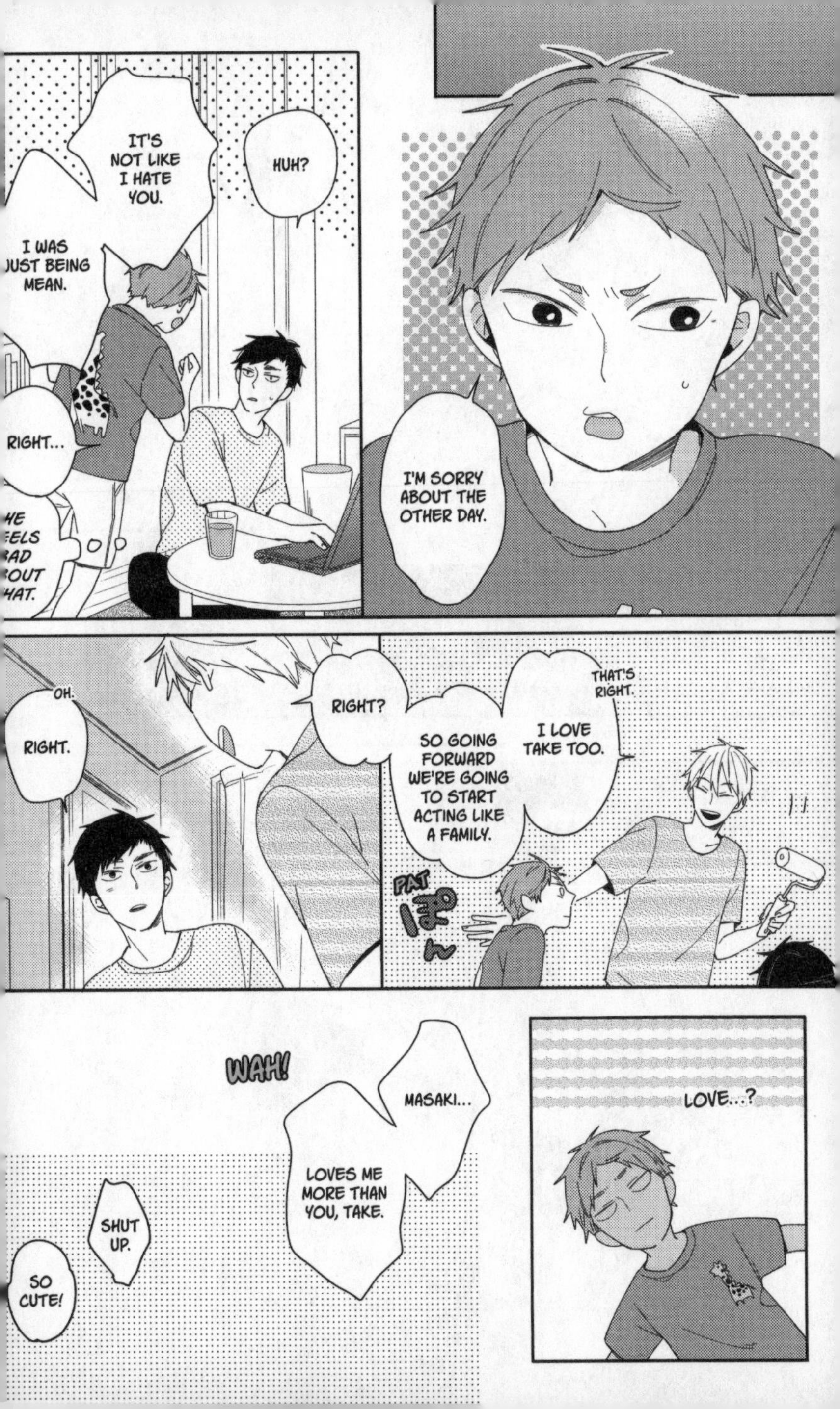
I'M SORRY ABOUT THE OTHER DAY.
HUH?
IT'S NOT LIKE I HATE YOU.
I WAS JUST BEING MEAN.
RIGHT...
THAT'S RIGHT.
I LOVE TAKE TOO.
SO GOING FORWARD WE'RE GOING TO START ACTING LIKE A FAMILY.
PAT
RIGHT?
OH.
RIGHT.
LOVE...?
MASAKI...
LOVES ME MORE THAN YOU, TAKE.
WAH!
SHUT UP.
SO CUTE!

Would you like

to be a family?

Would you like

to be a family?

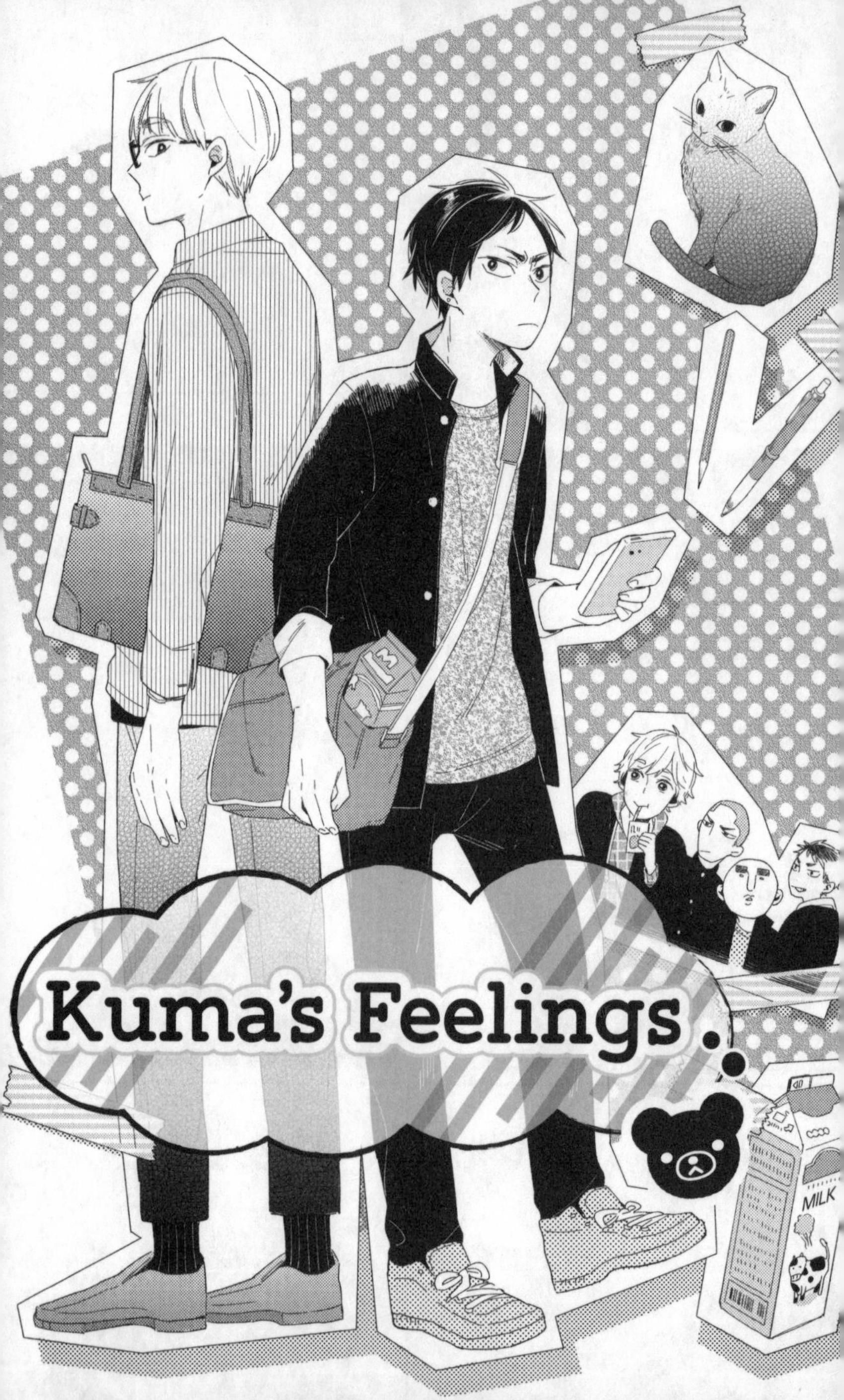
Kuma's Feelings
MILK

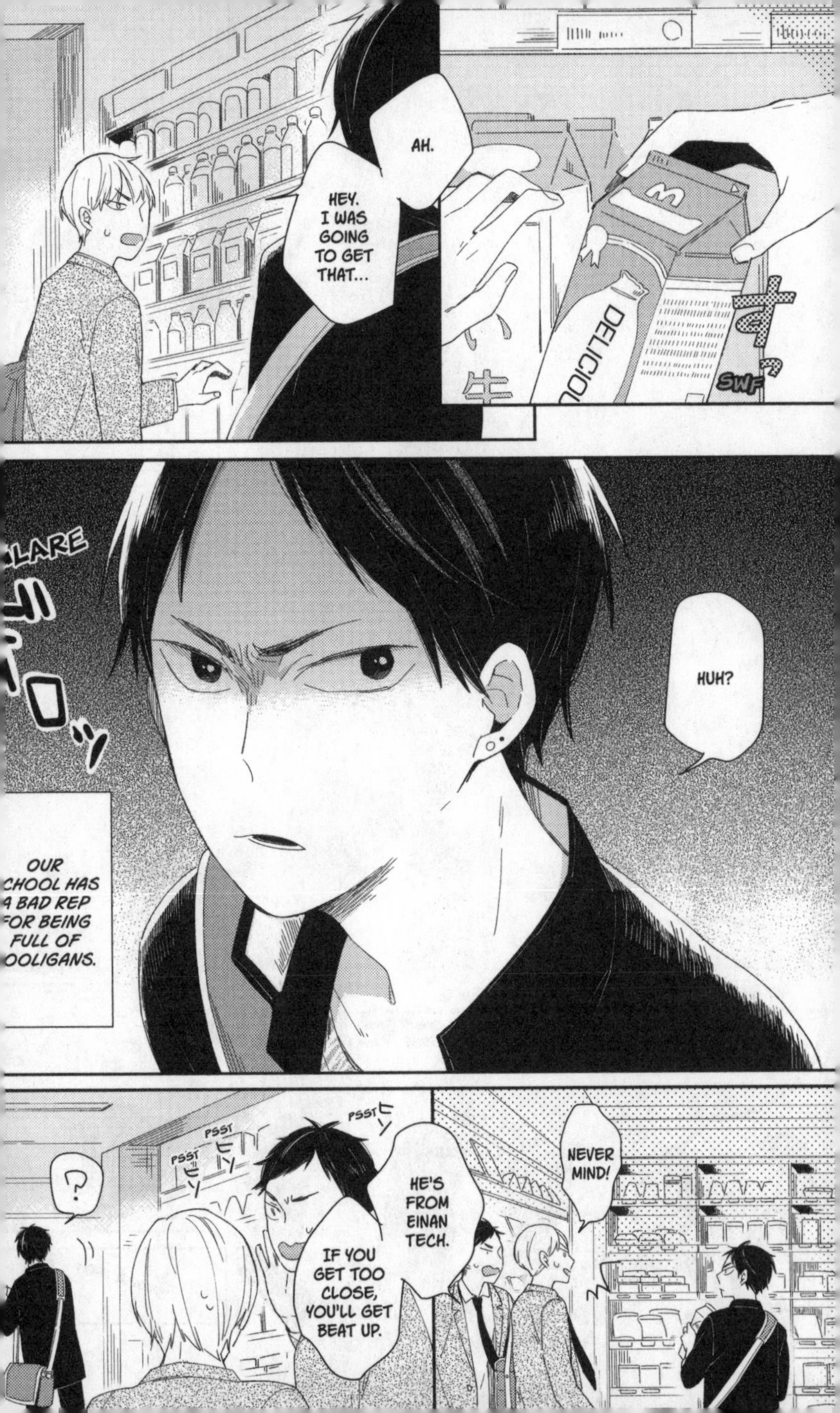
AH.
SWF
HEY. I WAS GOING TO GET THAT...
HUH?
LARE
OUR CHOOL HAS A BAD REP FOR BEING FULL OF OOLIGANS.
NEVER MIND!
PSST
HE'S FROM EINAN TECH.
IF YOU GET TOO CLOSE, YOU'LL GET BEAT UP.
PSST
PSST
?

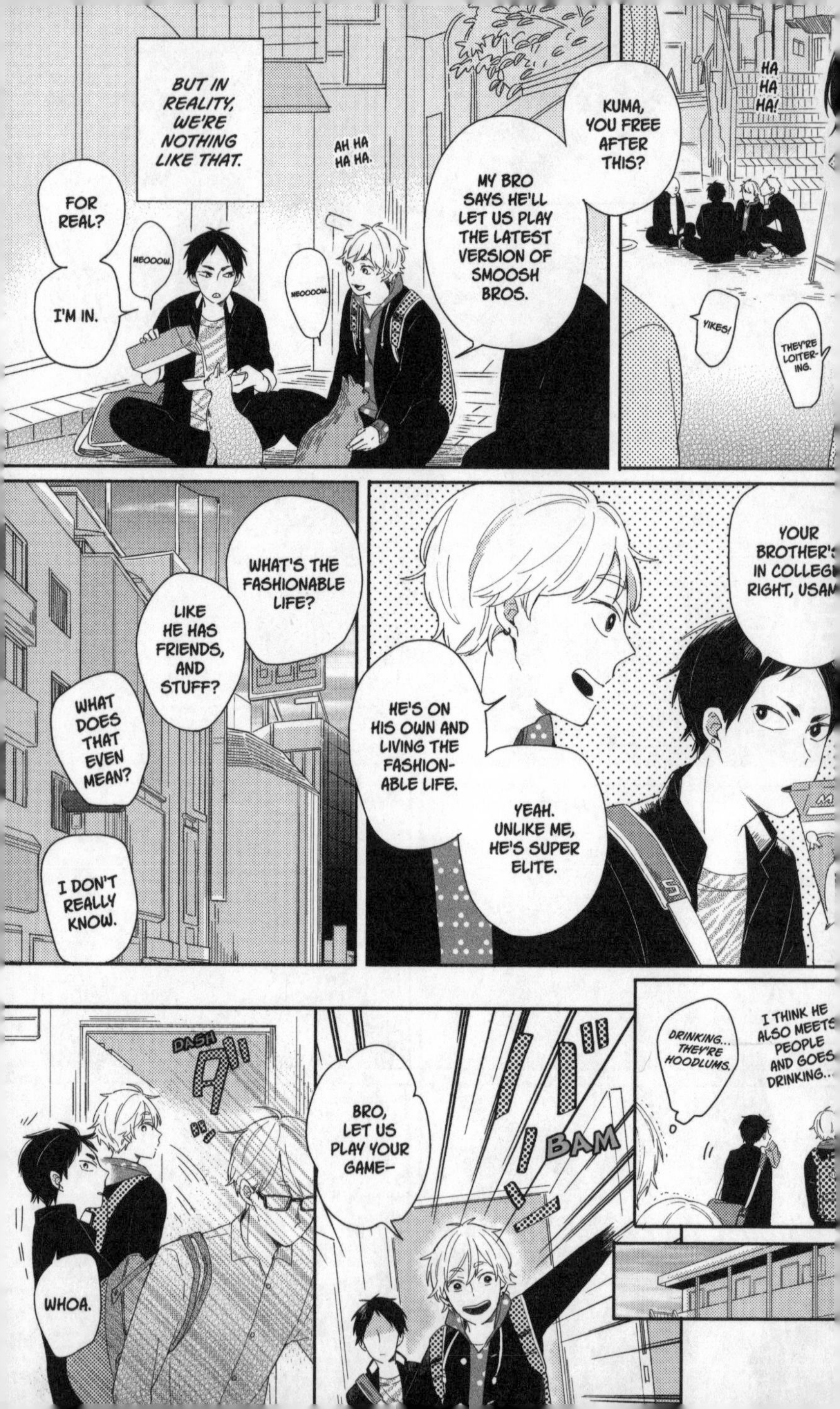
HA HA HA!
THEY'RE LOITER-ING.
YIKES!
KUMA, YOU FREE AFTER THIS?
MY BRO SAYS HE'LL LET US PLAY THE LATEST VERSION OF SMOOSH BROS.
AH HA HA HA.
BUT IN REALITY, WE'RE NOTHING LIKE THAT.
MEOOOW.
MEOOOW.
FOR REAL?
I'M IN.
YOUR BROTHER'S IN COLLEG RIGHT, USAM
HE'S ON HIS OWN AND LIVING THE FASHION-ABLE LIFE.
YEAH. UNLIKE ME, HE'S SUPER ELITE.
WHAT'S THE FASHIONABLE LIFE?
LIKE HE HAS FRIENDS, AND STUFF?
WHAT DOES THAT EVEN MEAN?
I DON'T REALLY KNOW.
I THINK HE ALSO MEETS PEOPLE AND GOES DRINKING...
DRINKING... THEY'RE HOODLUMS.
BAM
BRO, LET US PLAY YOUR GAME-
DASH
WHOA.

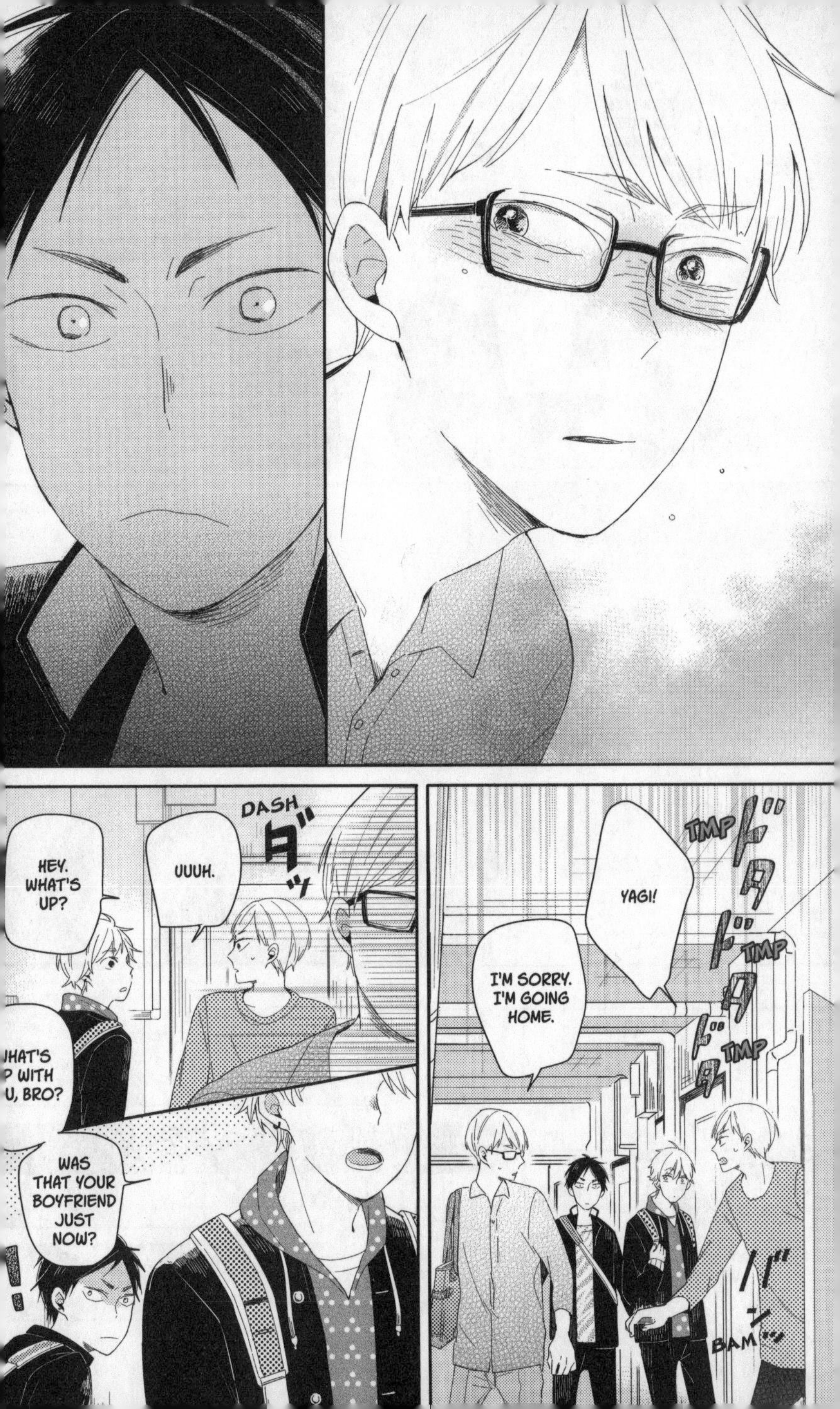
TMP
YAGI!
TMP
TMP
I'M SORRY. I'M GOING HOME.
BAM
DASH
UUUH.
HEY. WHAT'S UP?
HAT'S P WITH U, BRO?
WAS THAT YOUR BOYFRIEND JUST NOW?

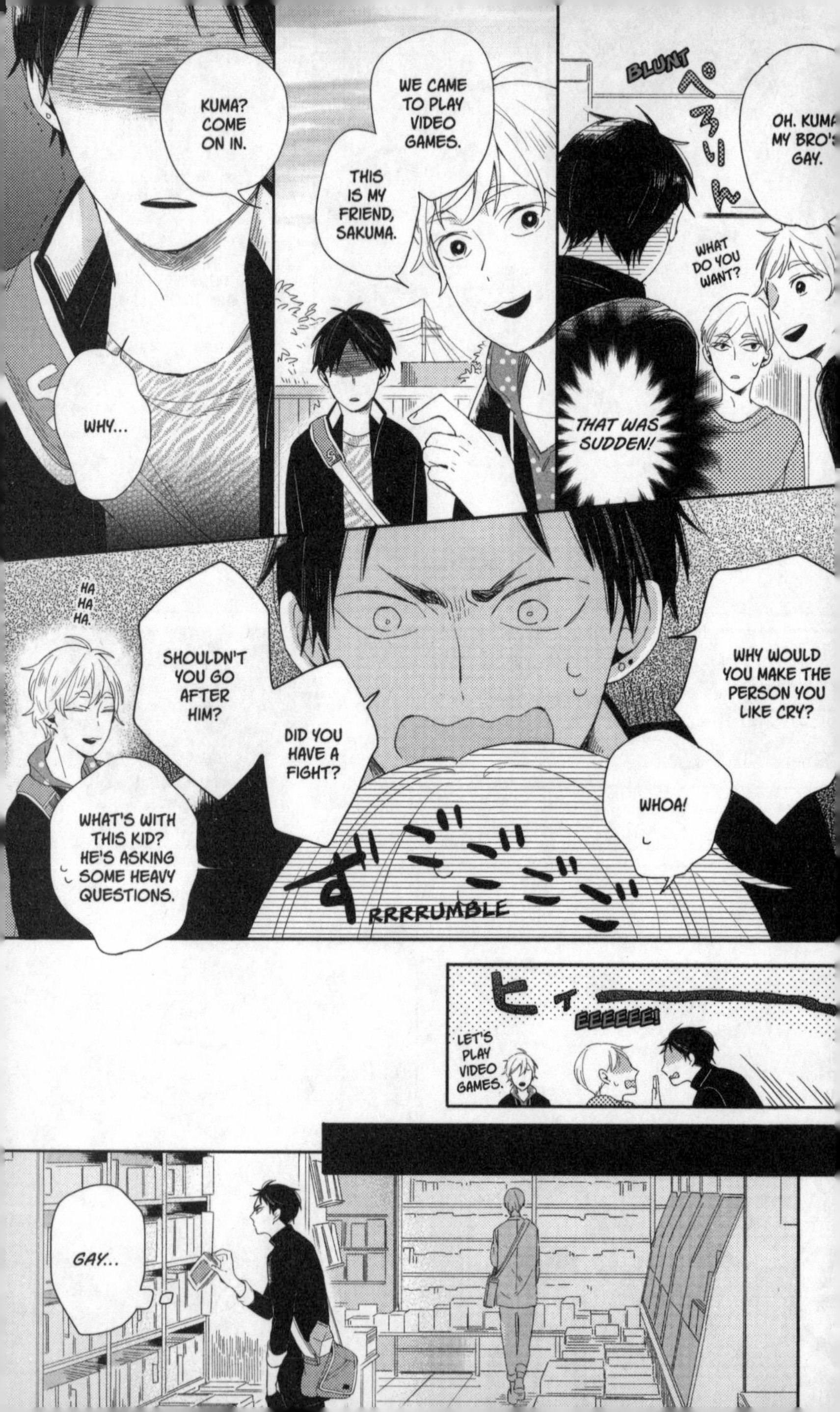
BLUNT
OH. KUMA MY BRO'S GAY.
WHAT DO YOU WANT?
THAT WAS SUDDEN!
WE CAME TO PLAY VIDEO GAMES.
THIS IS MY FRIEND, SAKUMA.
KUMA? COME ON IN.
WHY...
WHY WOULD YOU MAKE THE PERSON YOU LIKE CRY?
WHOA!
RRRRUMBLE
DID YOU HAVE A FIGHT?
SHOULDN'T YOU GO AFTER HIM?
HA HA HA.
WHAT'S WITH THIS KID? HE'S ASKING SOME HEAVY QUESTIONS.
EEEEEE!
LET'S PLAY VIDEO GAMES.
GAY...

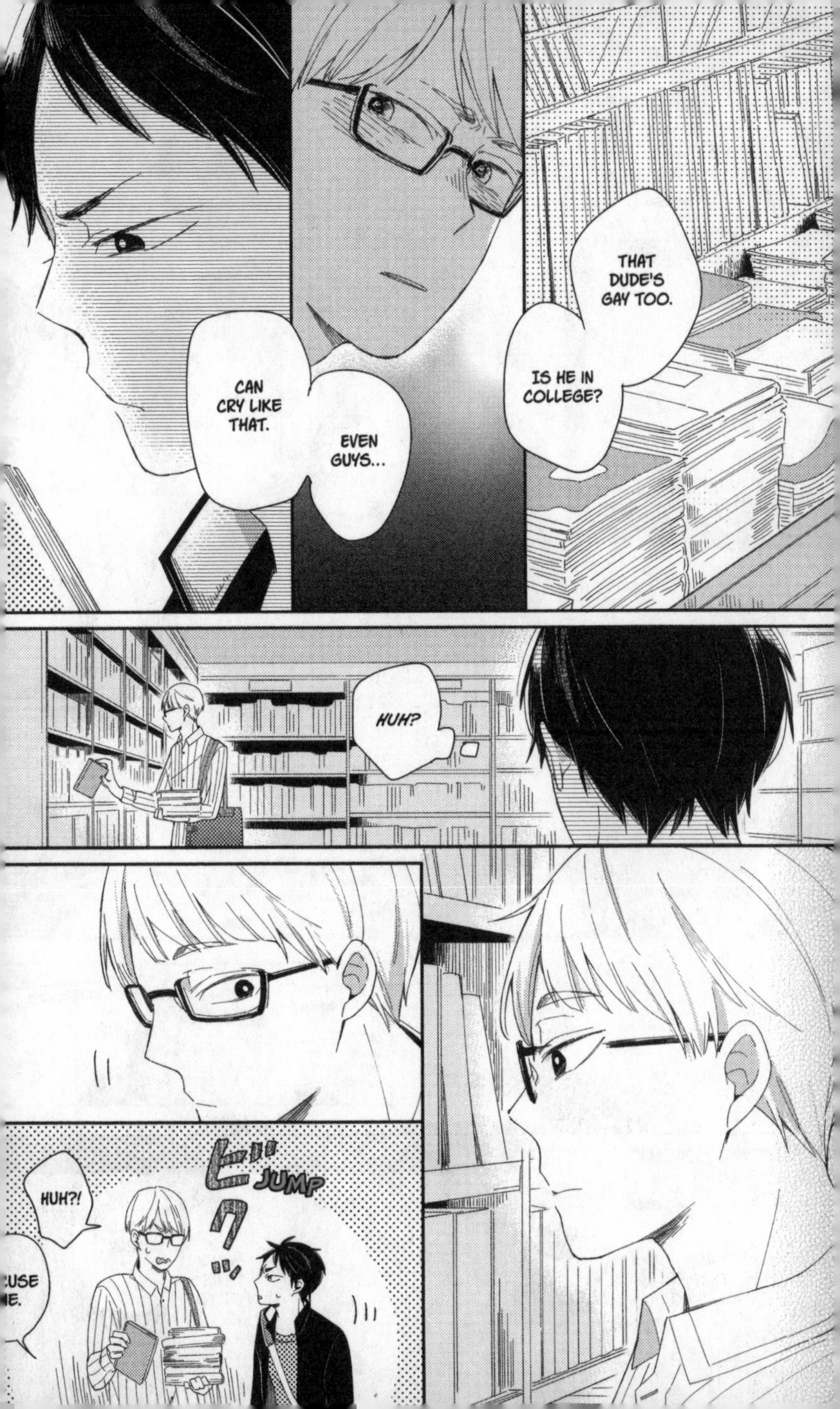
THAT DUDE'S GAY TOO.
IS HE IN COLLEGE?
EVEN GUYS...
CAN CRY LIKE THAT.
HUH?
JUMP
HUH?!

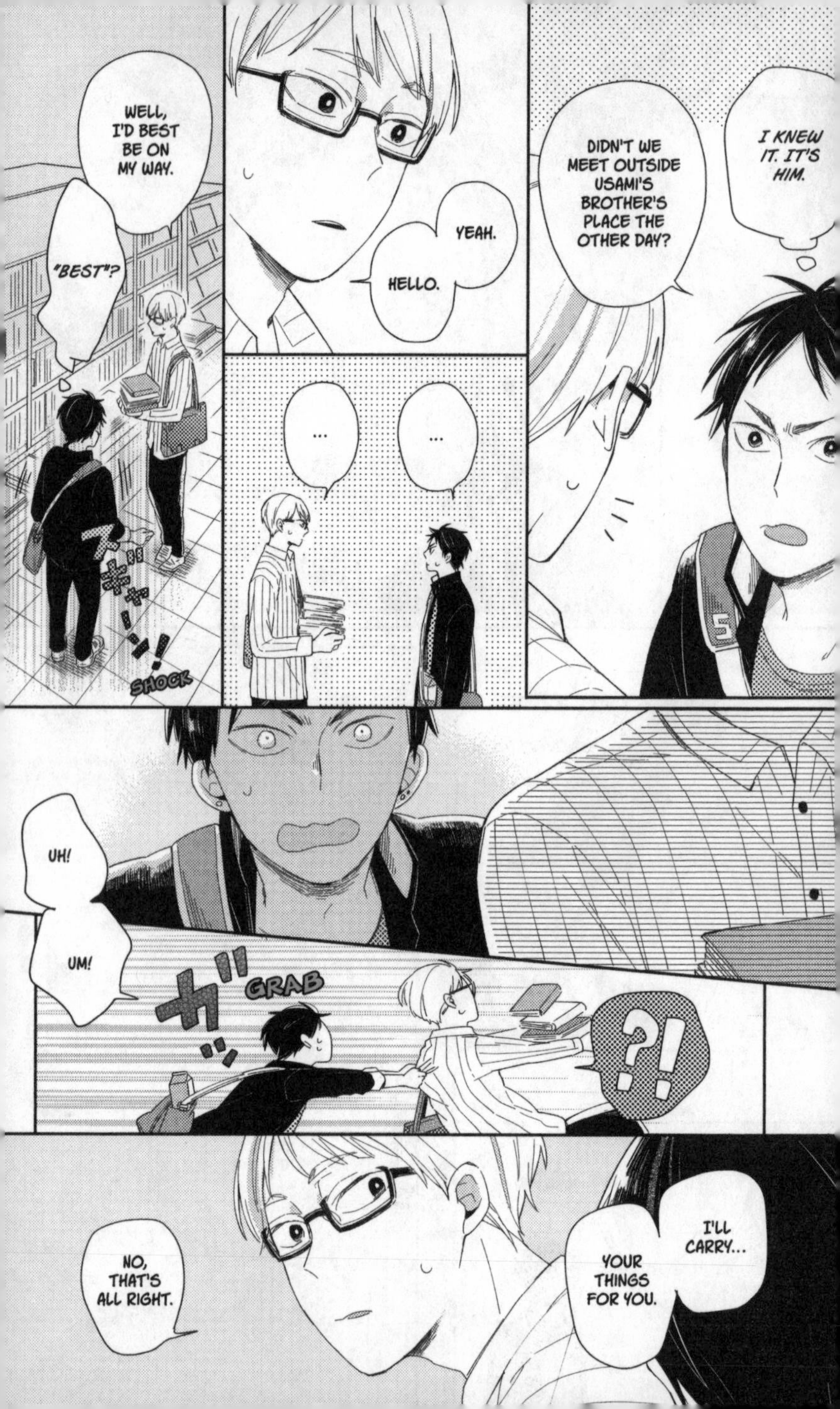
I KNEW IT. IT'S HIM.
DIDN'T WE MEET OUTSIDE USAMI'S BROTHER'S PLACE THE OTHER DAY?
YEAH.
HELLO.
...
...
WELL, I'D BEST BE ON MY WAY.
"BEST"?
SHOCK
UH!
UM!
GRAB
?!
I'LL CARRY...
YOUR THINGS FOR YOU.
NO, THAT'S ALL RIGHT.

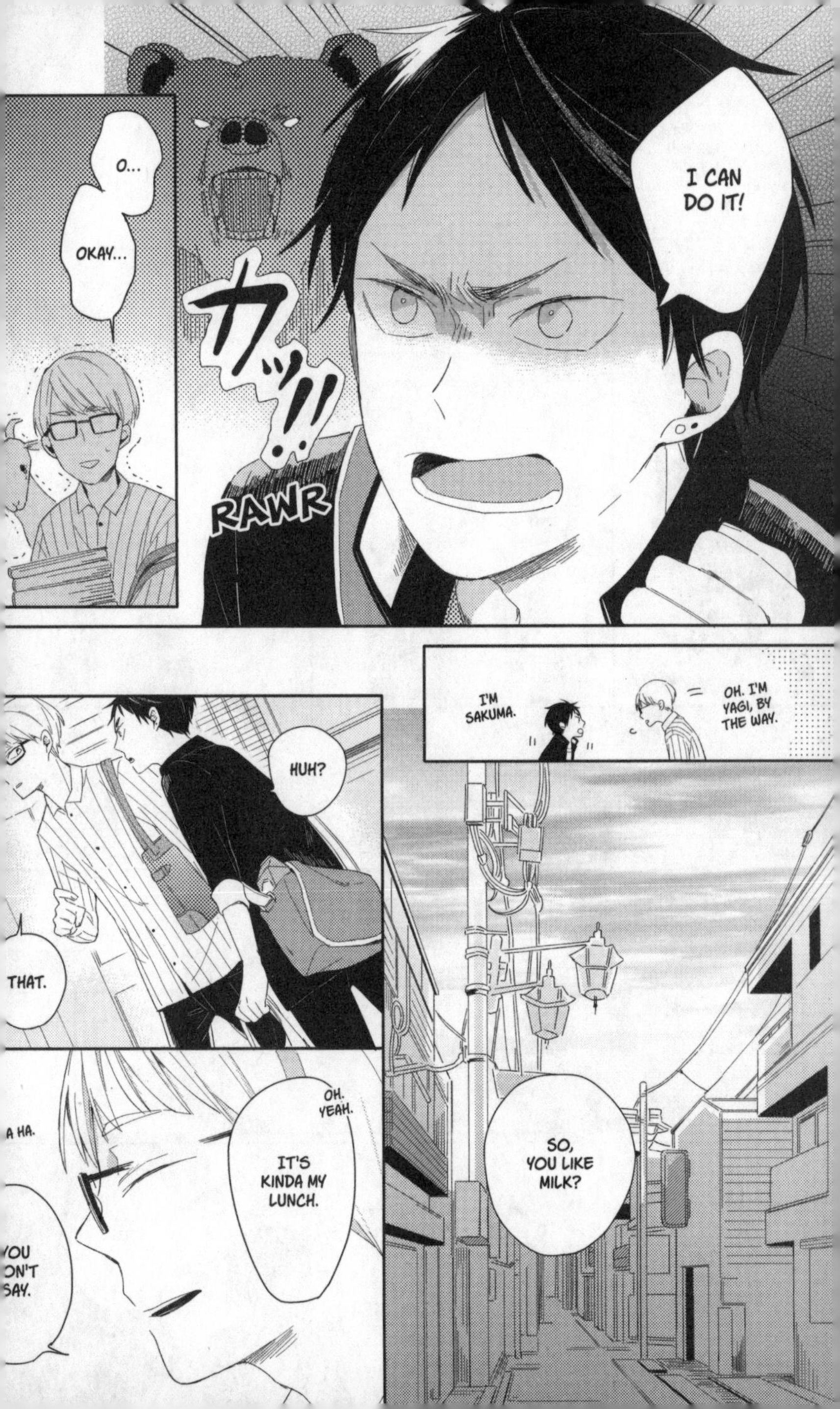
I CAN DO IT!
カッ!!
RAWR
O...
OKAY...
OH. I'M YAGI, BY THE WAY.
I'M SAKUMA.
SO, YOU LIKE MILK?
HUH?
THAT.
OH. YEAH.
IT'S KINDA MY LUNCH.
A HA.
YOU ON'T SAY.

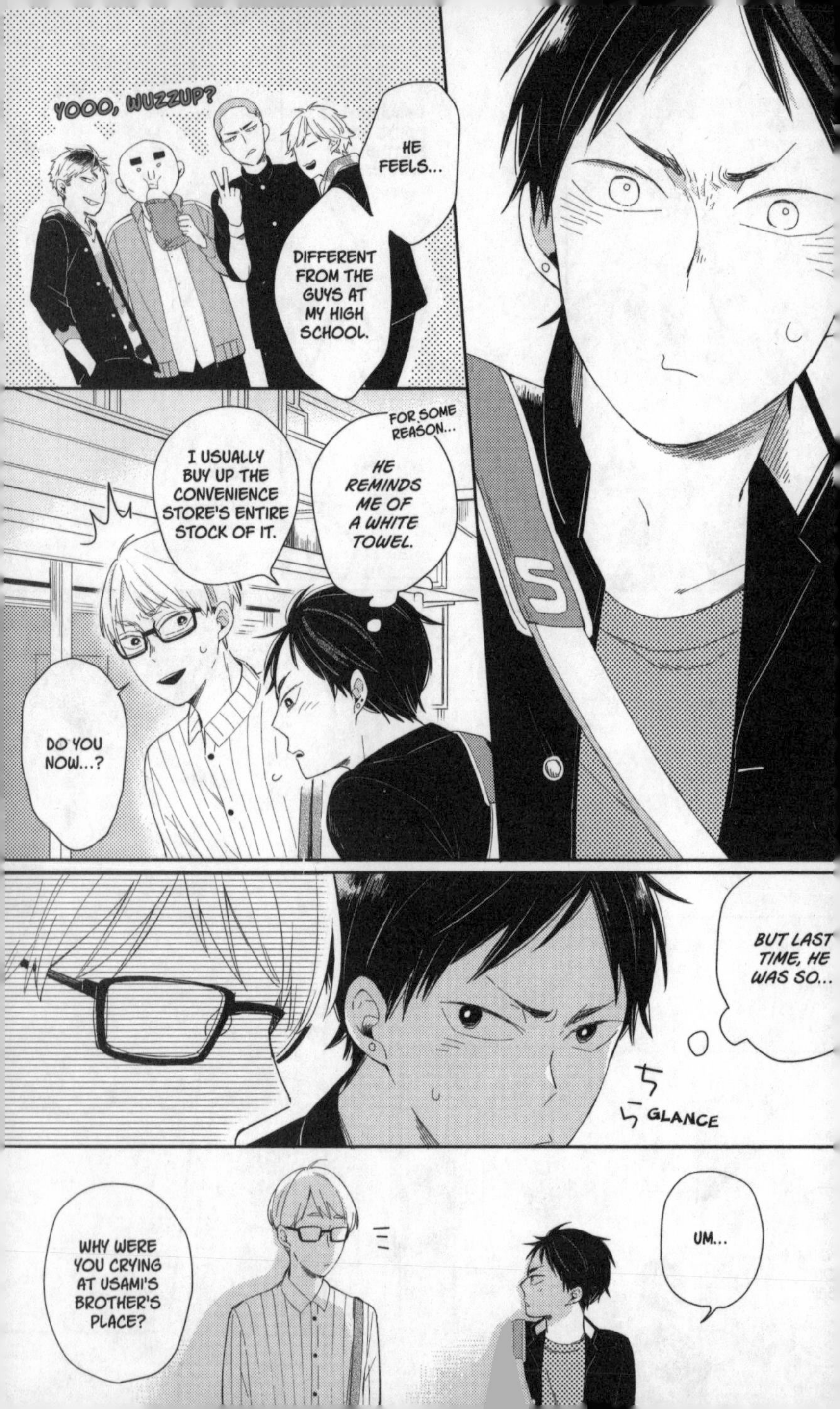
HE FEELS...
DIFFERENT FROM THE GUYS AT MY HIGH SCHOOL.
YOOO, WUZZUP?
FOR SOME REASON...
HE REMINDS ME OF A WHITE TOWEL.
I USUALLY BUY UP THE CONVENIENCE STORE'S ENTIRE STOCK OF IT.
DO YOU NOW...?
BUT LAST TIME, HE WAS SO...
GLANCE
UM...
WHY WERE YOU CRYING AT USAMI'S BROTHER'S PLACE?

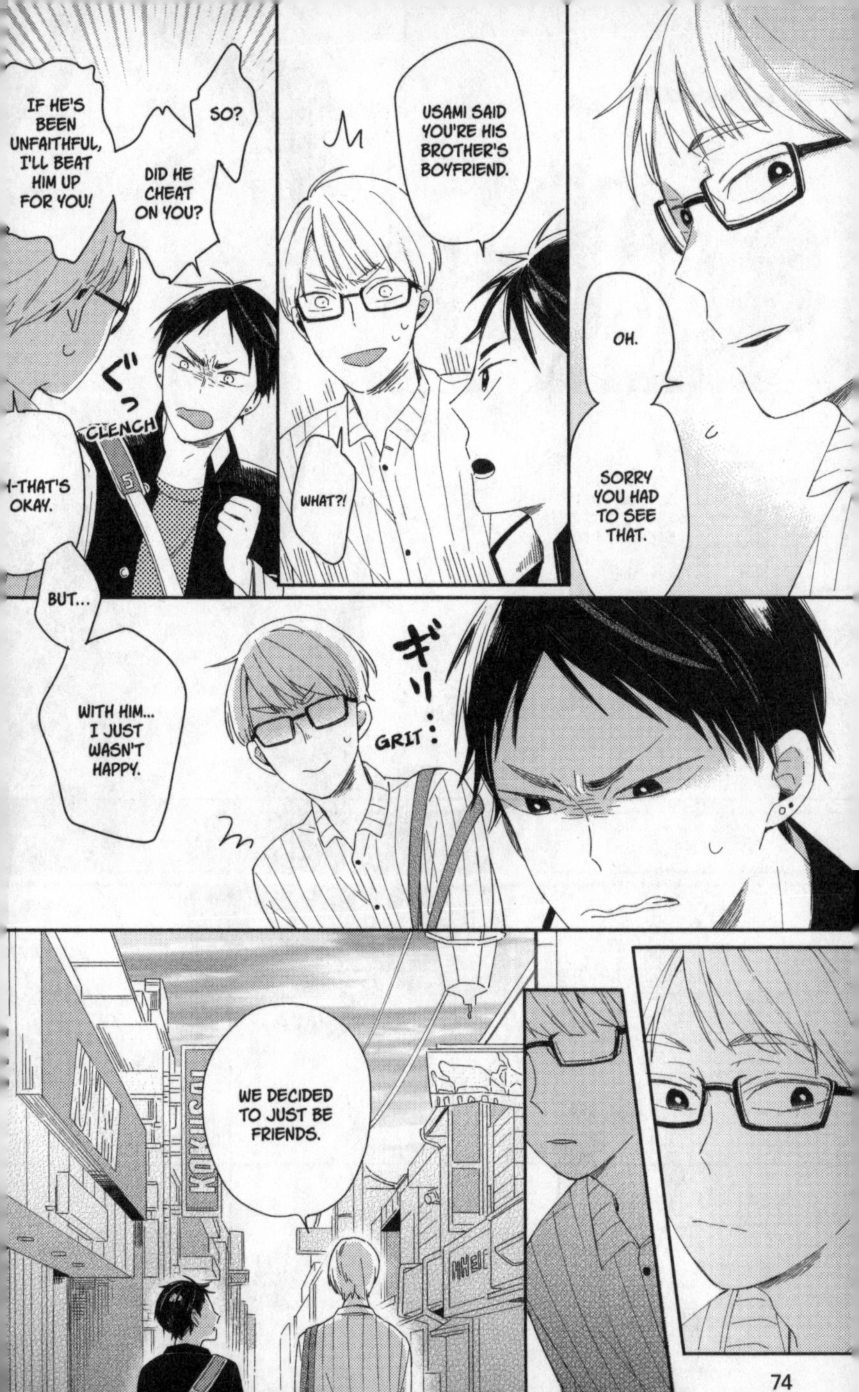
OH.
SORRY YOU HAD TO SEE THAT.
USAMI SAID YOU'RE HIS BROTHER'S BOYFRIEND.
WHAT?!
SO?
DID HE CHEAT ON YOU?
IF HE'S BEEN UNFAITHFUL, I'LL BEAT HIM UP FOR YOU!
ぐっ
CLENCH
H-THAT'S OKAY.
BUT...
WITH HIM... I JUST WASN'T HAPPY.
ギリ…
GRIT
WE DECIDED TO JUST BE FRIENDS.

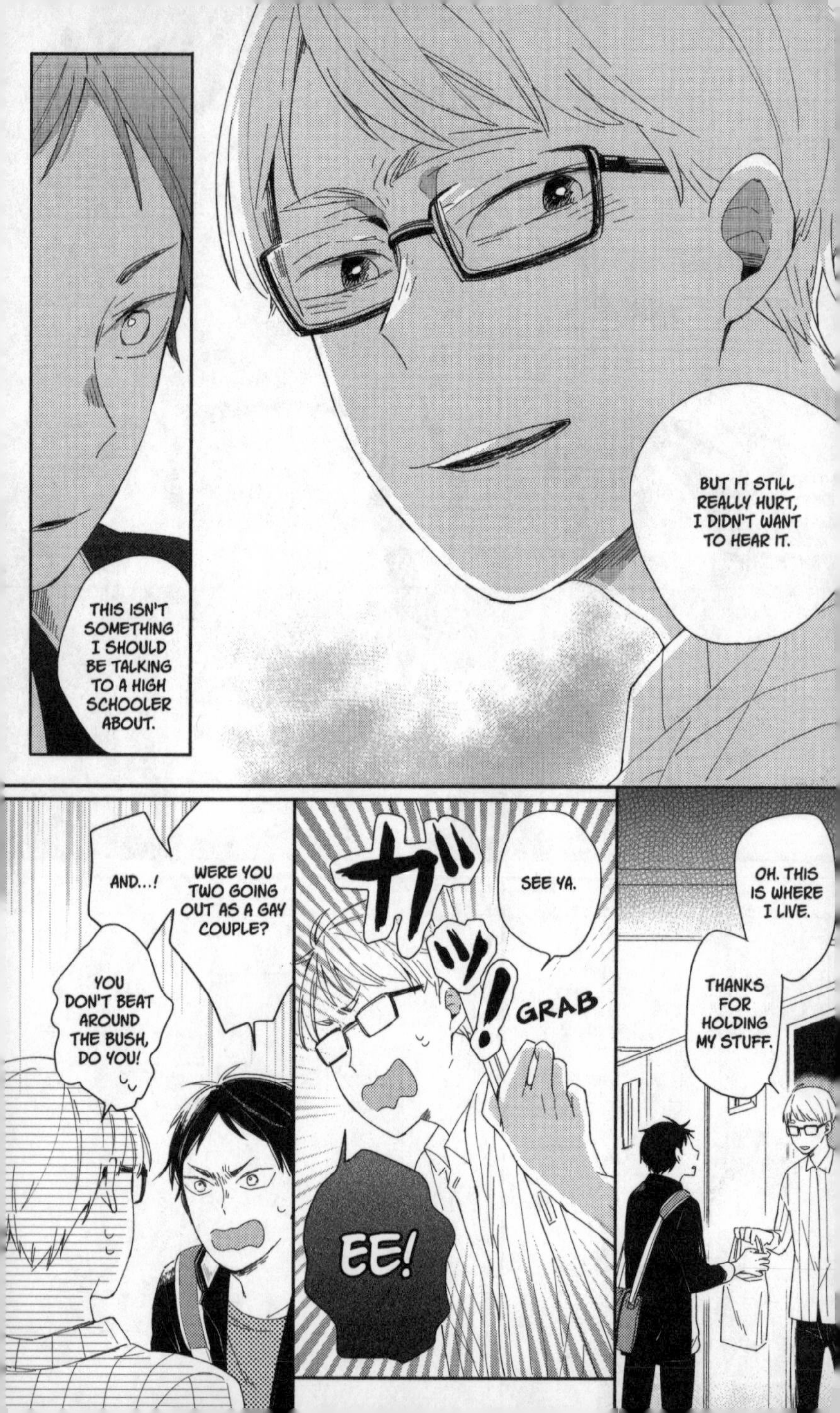
BUT IT STILL REALLY HURT, I DIDN'T WANT TO HEAR IT.
THIS ISN'T SOMETHING I SHOULD BE TALKING TO A HIGH SCHOOLER ABOUT.
OH. THIS IS WHERE I LIVE.
THANKS FOR HOLDING MY STUFF.
SEE YA.
GRAB
EE!
AND...!
WERE YOU TWO GOING OUT AS A GAY COUPLE?
YOU DON'T BEAT AROUND THE BUSH, DO YOU!

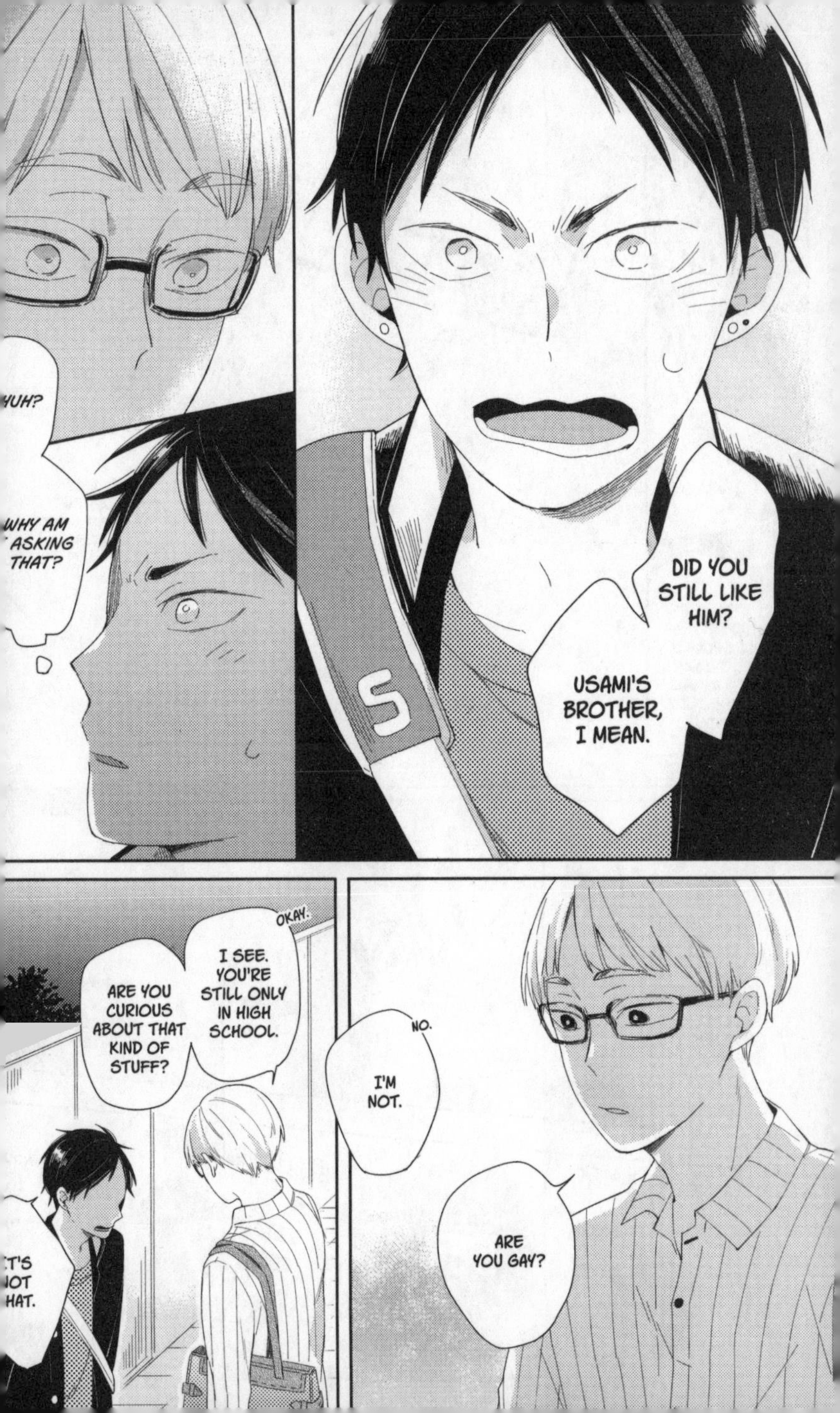

DID YOU STILL LIKE HIM?
USAMI'S BROTHER, I MEAN.
UH?
WHY AM ASKING THAT?
ARE YOU GAY?
NO.
I'M NOT.
OKAY.
I SEE. YOU'RE STILL ONLY IN HIGH SCHOOL.
ARE YOU CURIOUS ABOUT THAT KIND OF STUFF?
T'S OT HAT.

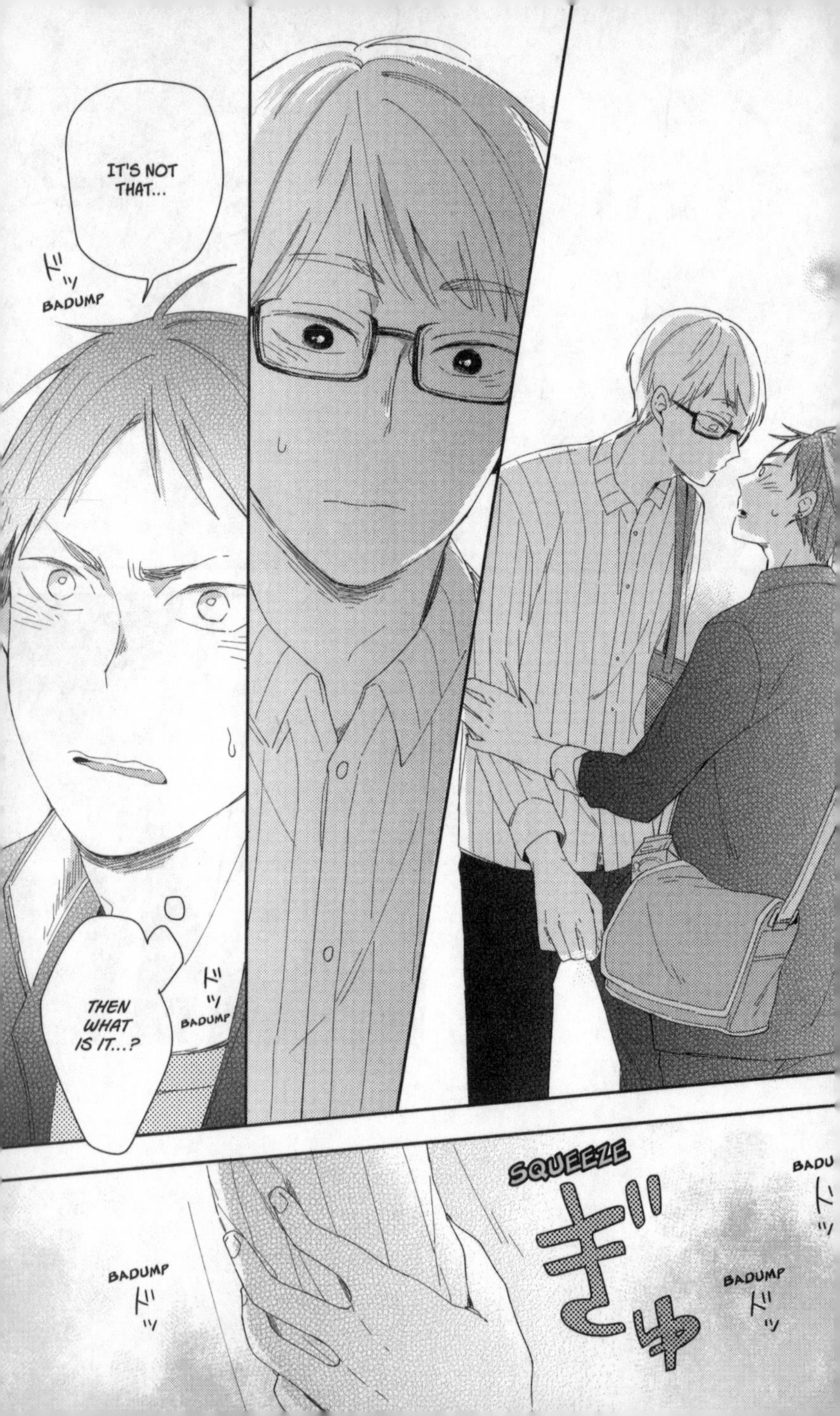
IT'S NOT THAT...
ドッ
BADUMP
THEN WHAT IS IT...?
ドッ
BADUMP
BADU
ドッ
BADUMP
ドッ
SQUEEZE
ぎゅ
BADUMP
ドッ

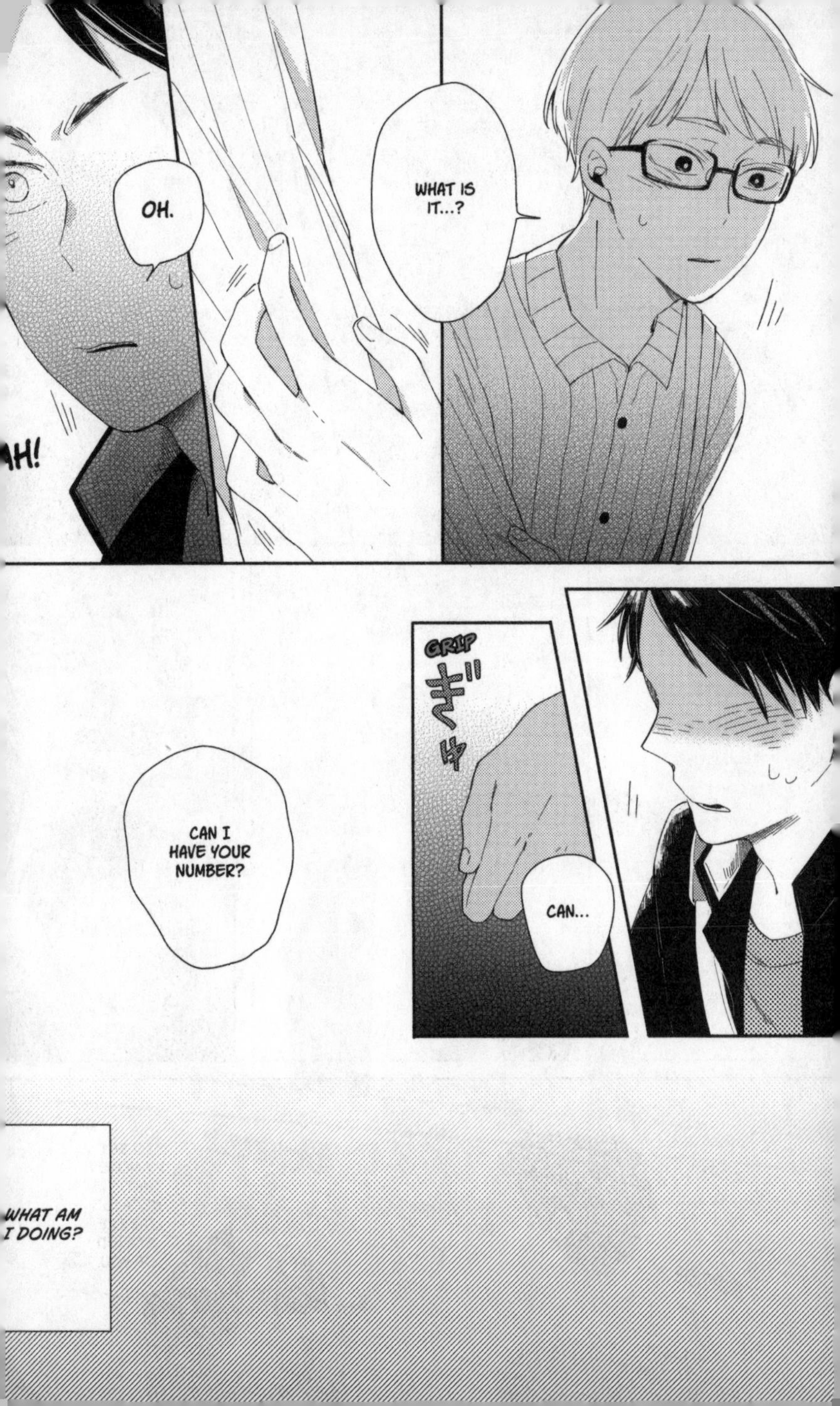
WHAT IS IT...?
OH.
AH!
CAN...
GRIP
CAN I HAVE YOUR NUMBER?
WHAT AM I DOING?

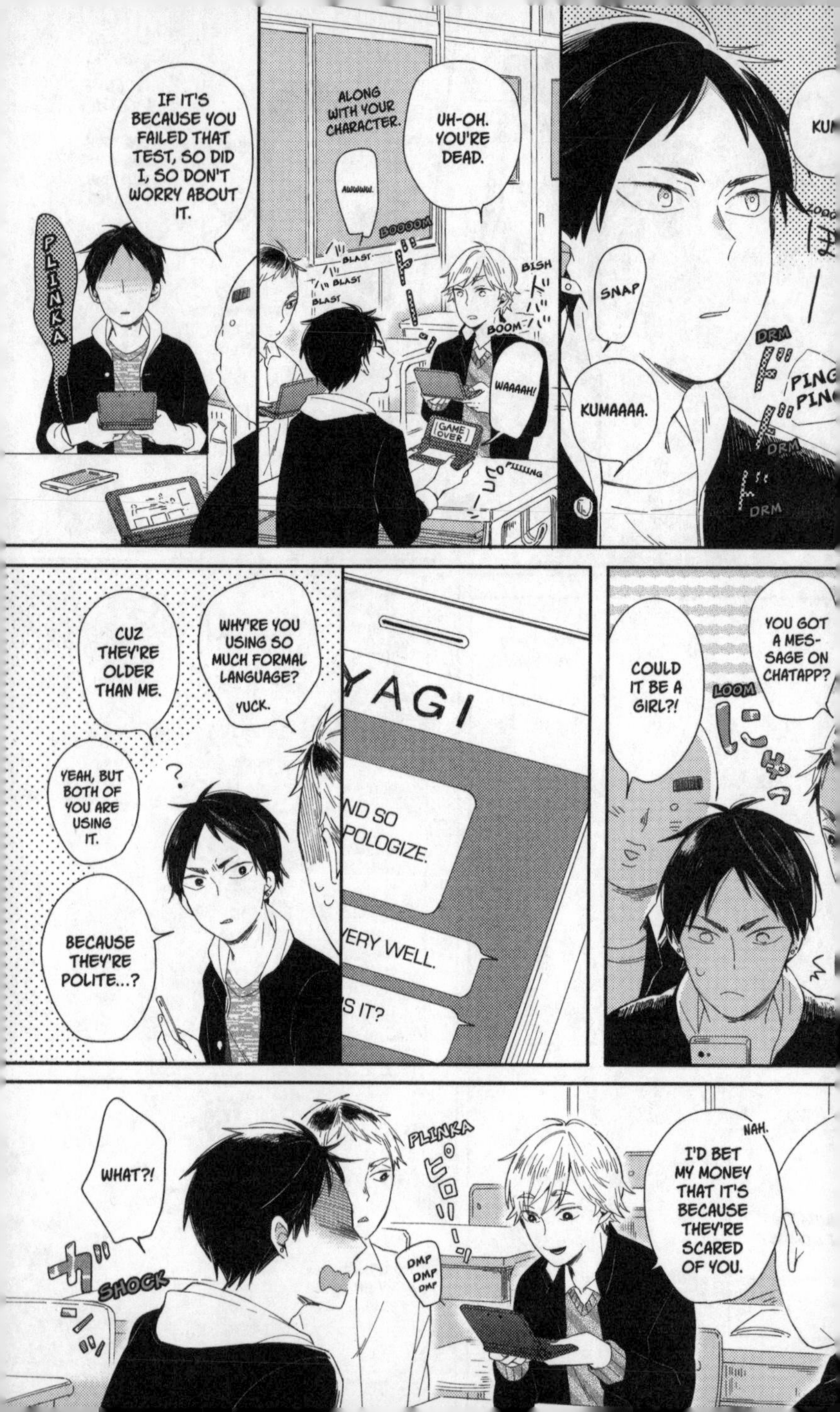

SNAP
KUMAAAA.
DRM
PING
DRM
DRM
UH-OH. YOU'RE DEAD.
ALONG WITH YOUR CHARACTER.
AWWWW.
BOOOOM
BISH
BLAST
BLAST
BLAST
BOOM
WAAAAH!
GAME OVER
PIIIING
IF IT'S BECAUSE YOU FAILED THAT TEST, SO DID I, SO DON'T WORRY ABOUT IT.
PLINKA
YOU GOT A MES-SAGE ON CHATAPP?
LOOM
COULD IT BE A GIRL?!
YAGI
ND SO
POLOGIZE.
VERY WELL.
WHY'RE YOU USING SO MUCH FORMAL LANGUAGE?
YUCK.
CUZ THEY'RE OLDER THAN ME.
?
YEAH, BUT BOTH OF YOU ARE USING IT.
BECAUSE THEY'RE POLITE...?
NAH.
I'D BET MY MONEY THAT IT'S BECAUSE THEY'RE SCARED OF YOU.
PLINKA
DMP DMP DMP
WHAT?!
SHOCK

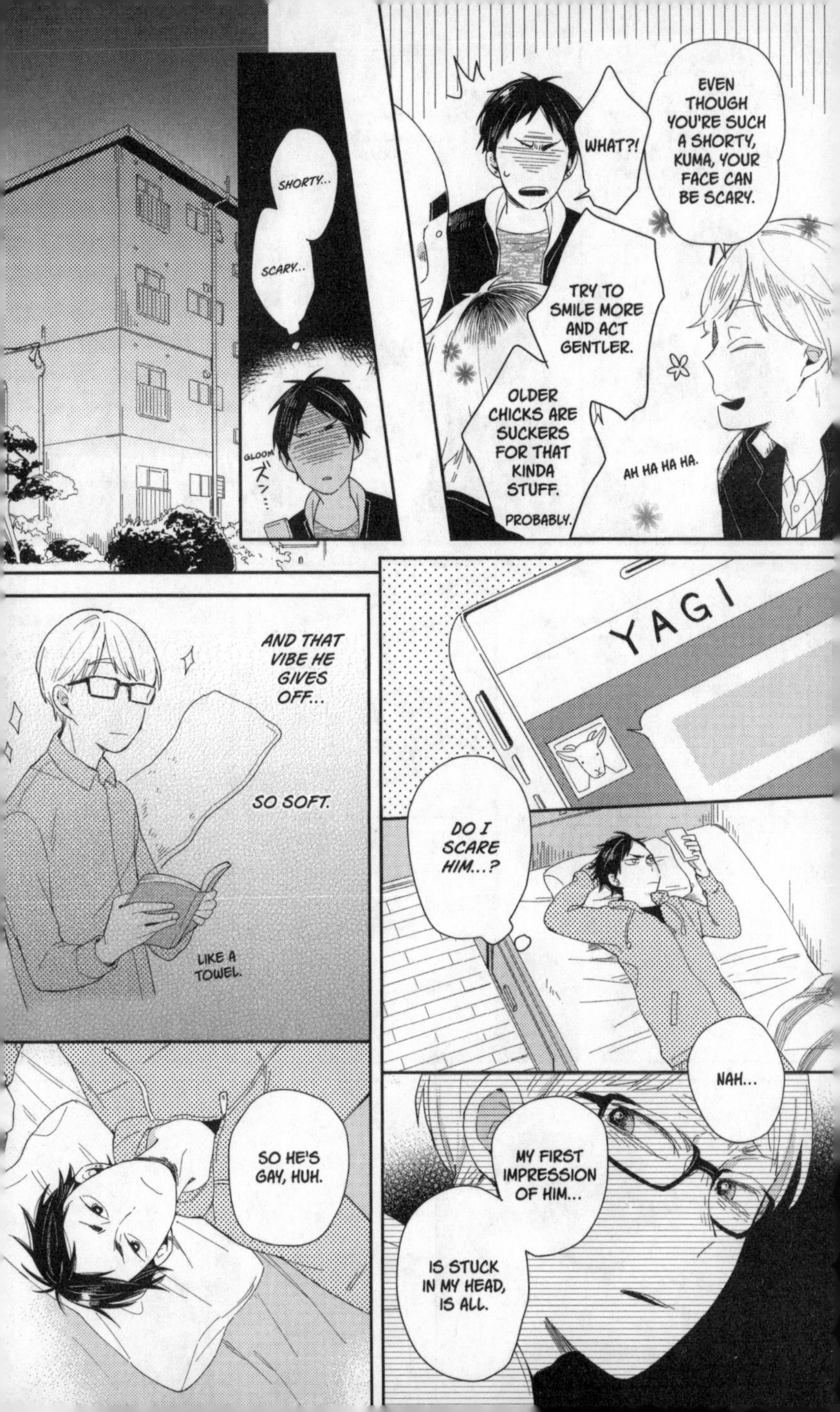
EVEN THOUGH YOU'RE SUCH A SHORTY, KUMA, YOUR FACE CAN BE SCARY.
WHAT?!
TRY TO SMILE MORE AND ACT GENTLER.
OLDER CHICKS ARE SUCKERS FOR THAT KINDA STUFF.
AH HA HA HA.
PROBABLY.
SHORTY...
SCARY...
GLOOM
ズン...
YAGI
DO I SCARE HIM...?
AND THAT VIBE HE GIVES OFF...
SO SOFT.
LIKE A TOWEL.
NAH...
MY FIRST IMPRESSION OF HIM...
IS STUCK IN MY HEAD, IS ALL.
SO HE'S GAY, HUH.

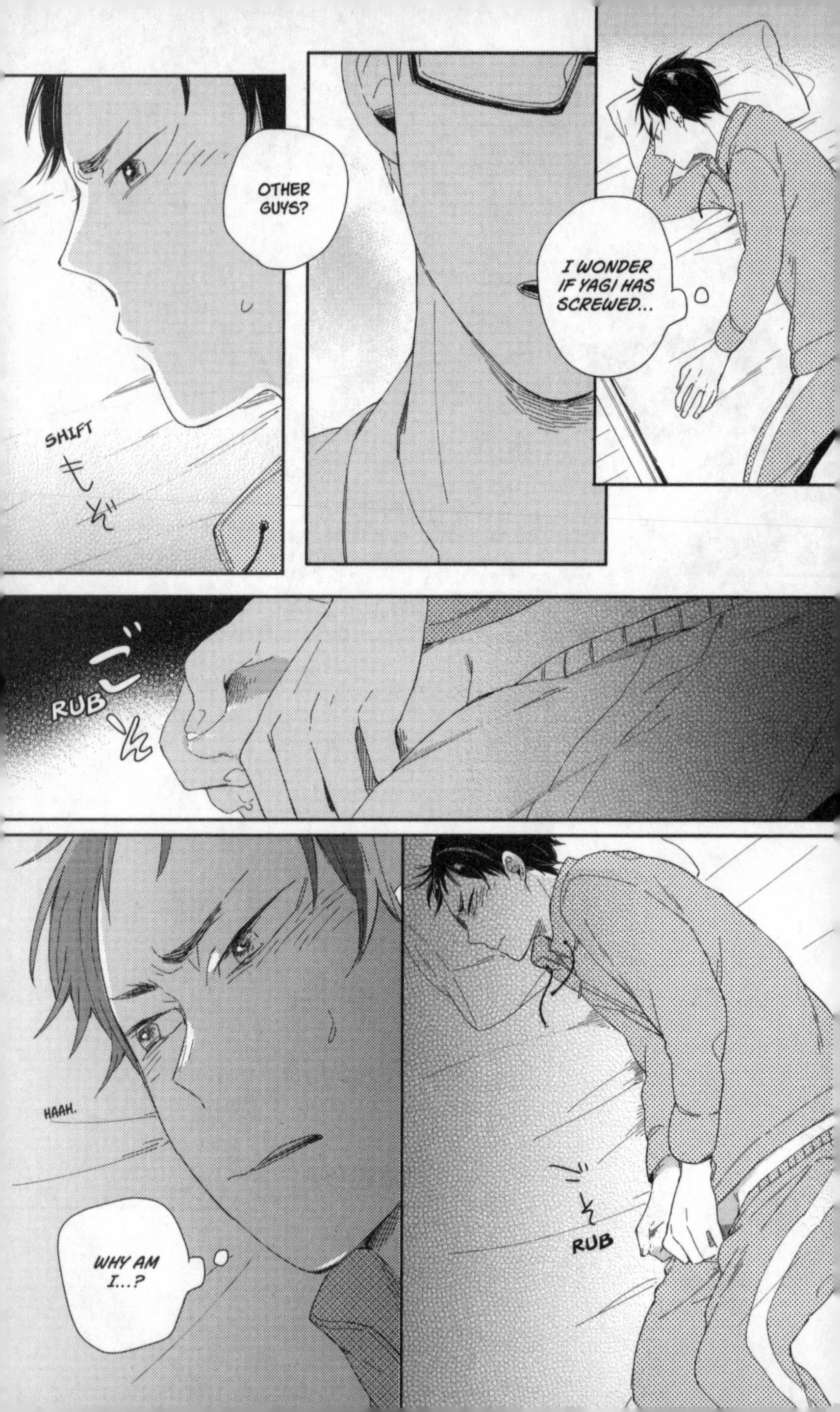
I WONDER IF YAGI HAS SCREWED...
OTHER GUYS?
SHIFT
もぞ
RUB
RUB
HAAH.
WHY AM I...?

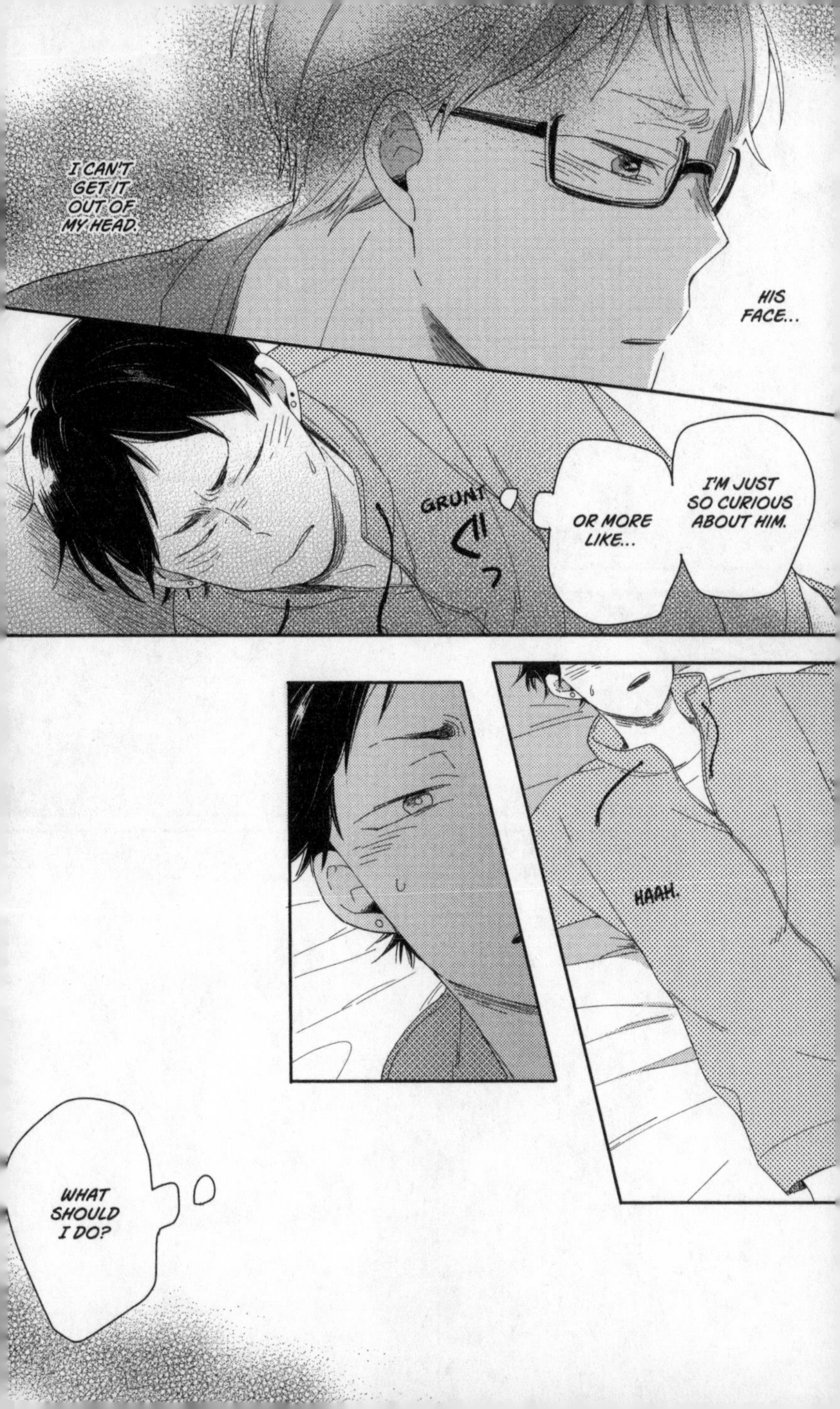
HIS FACE...
I CAN'T GET IT OUT OF MY HEAD.
I'M JUST SO CURIOUS ABOUT HIM.
OR MORE LIKE...
GRUNT
HAAH.
WHAT SHOULD I DO?

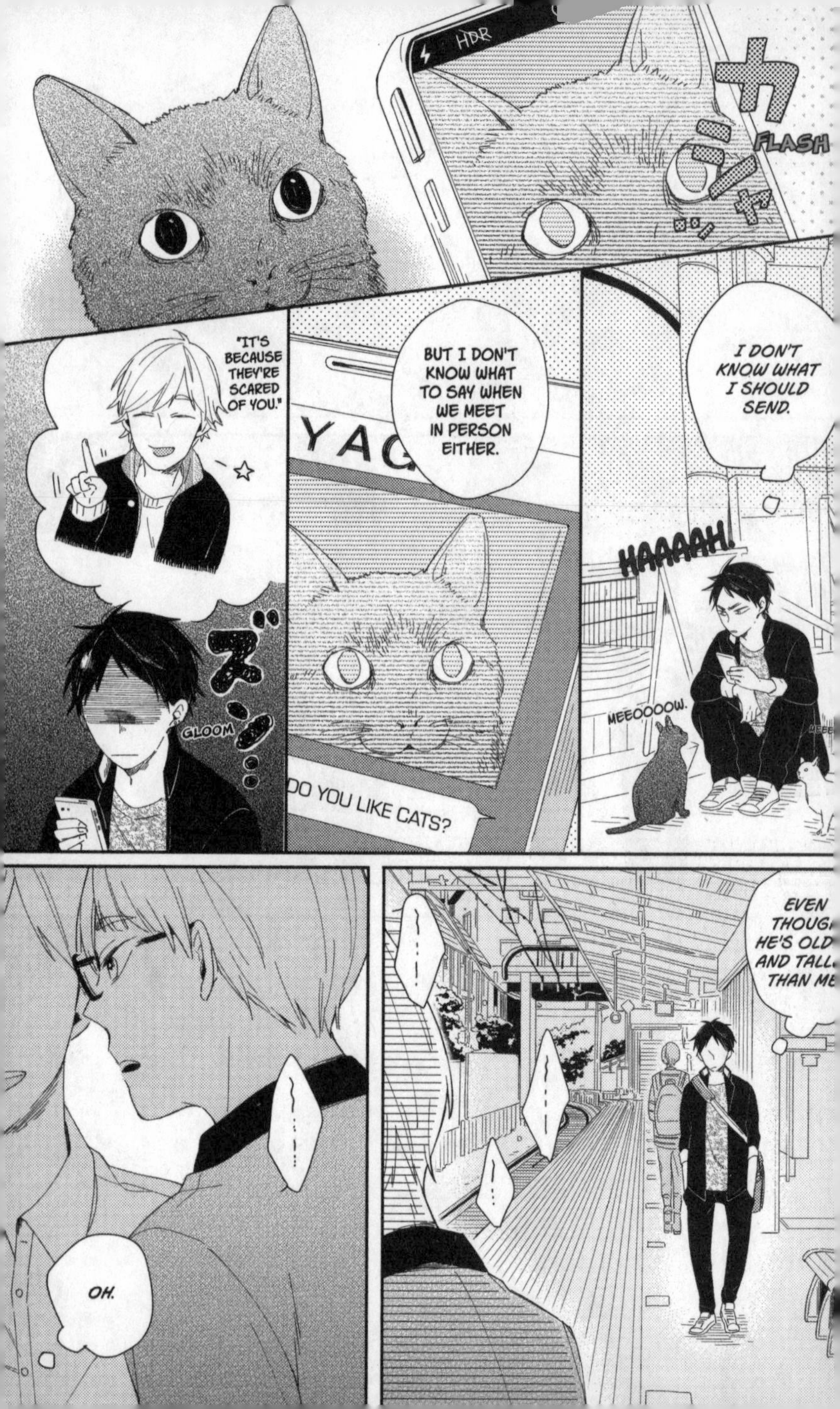

HDR
FLASH
I DON'T KNOW WHAT I SHOULD SEND.
HAAAAH!
MEEOOOOW.
BUT I DON'T KNOW WHAT TO SAY WHEN WE MEET IN PERSON EITHER.
YAG
DO YOU LIKE CATS?
"IT'S BECAUSE THEY'RE SCARED OF YOU."
GLOOM
EVEN THOUG HE'S OLD AND TALL THAN ME
......
......
......
......
OH.

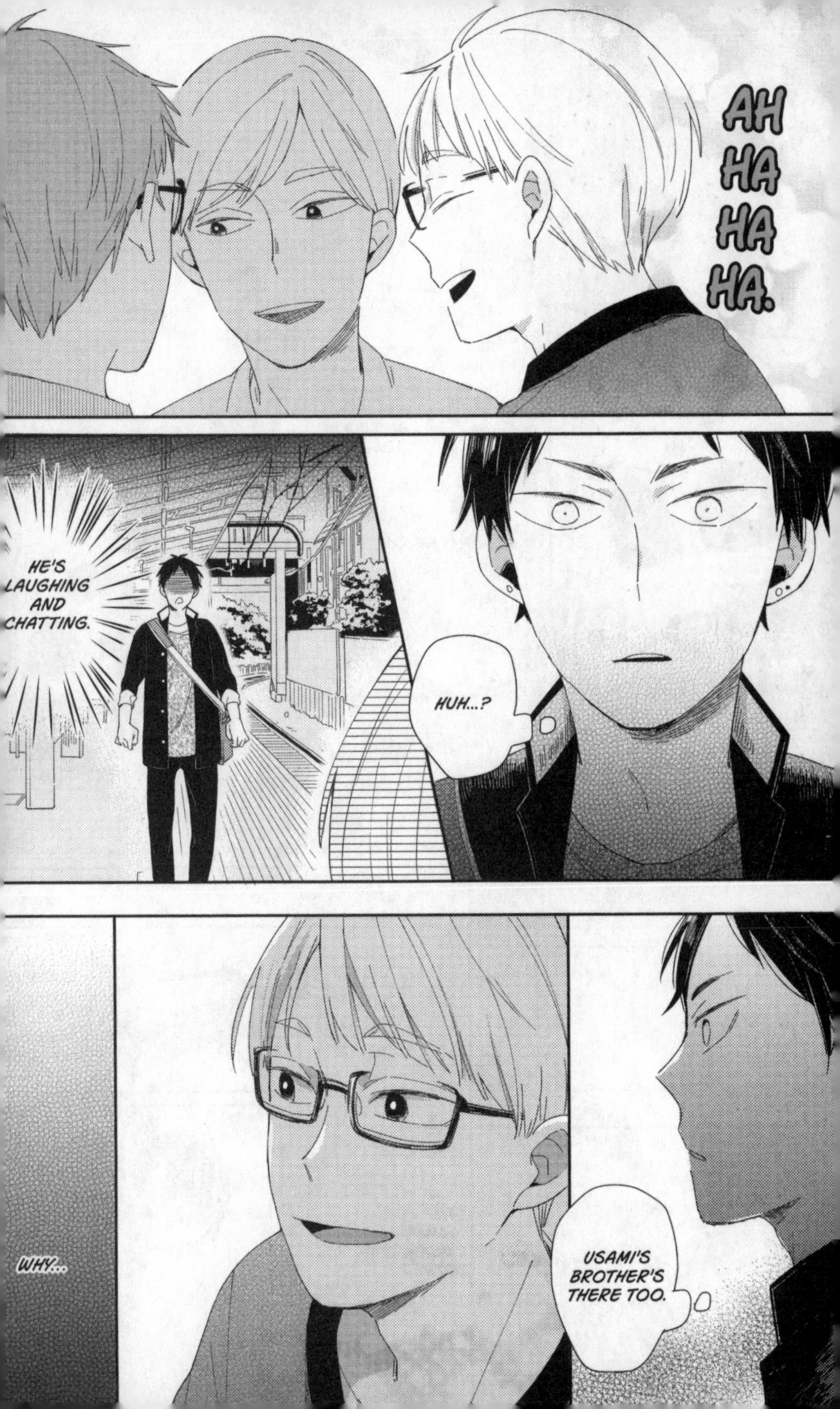
AH HA HA HA.
HUH...?
HE'S LAUGHING AND CHATTING.
USAMI'S BROTHER'S THERE TOO.
WHY...

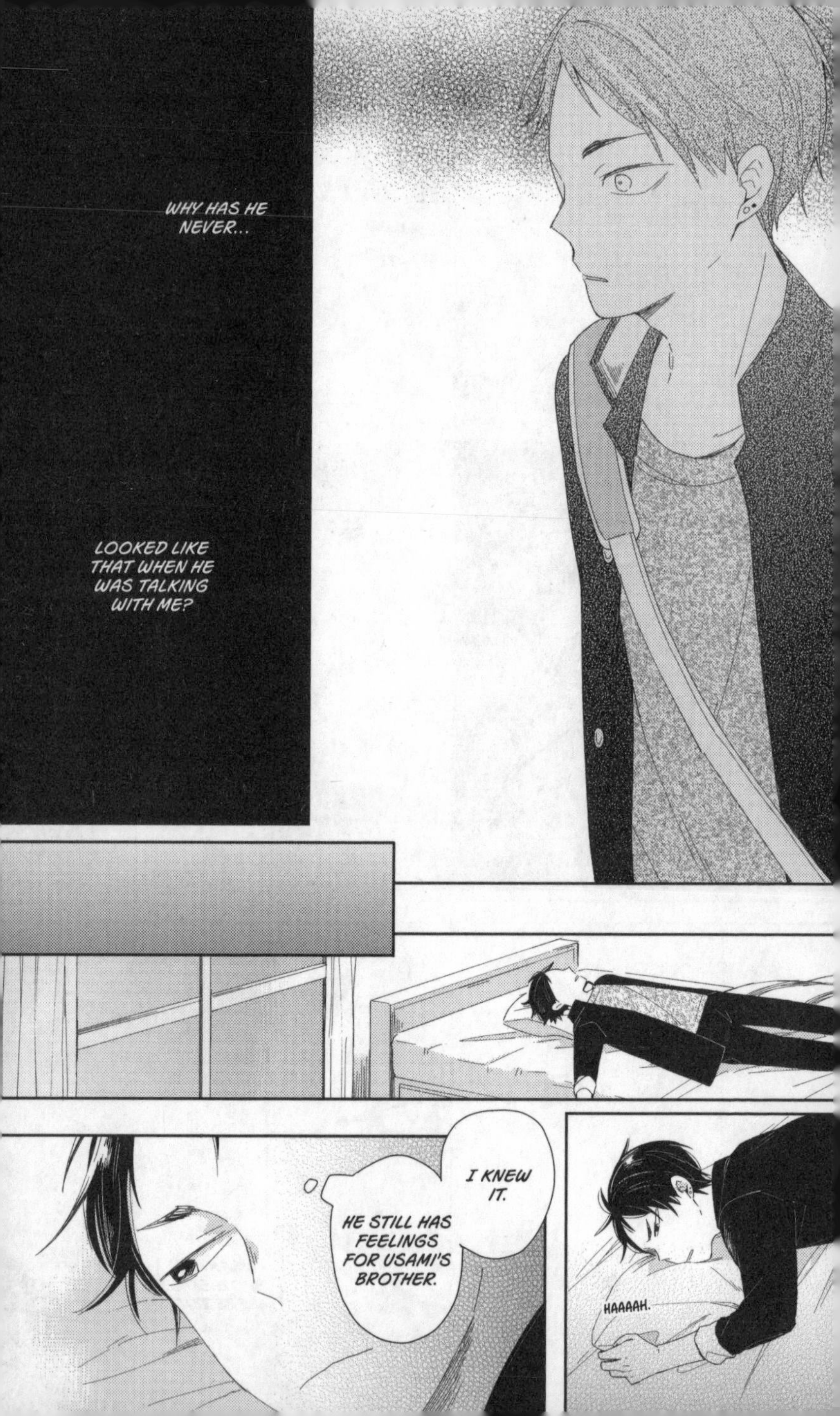
WHY HAS HE NEVER...
LOOKED LIKE THAT WHEN HE WAS TALKING WITH ME?
HAAAAH.
I KNEW IT.
HE STILL HAS FEELINGS FOR USAMI'S BROTHER.

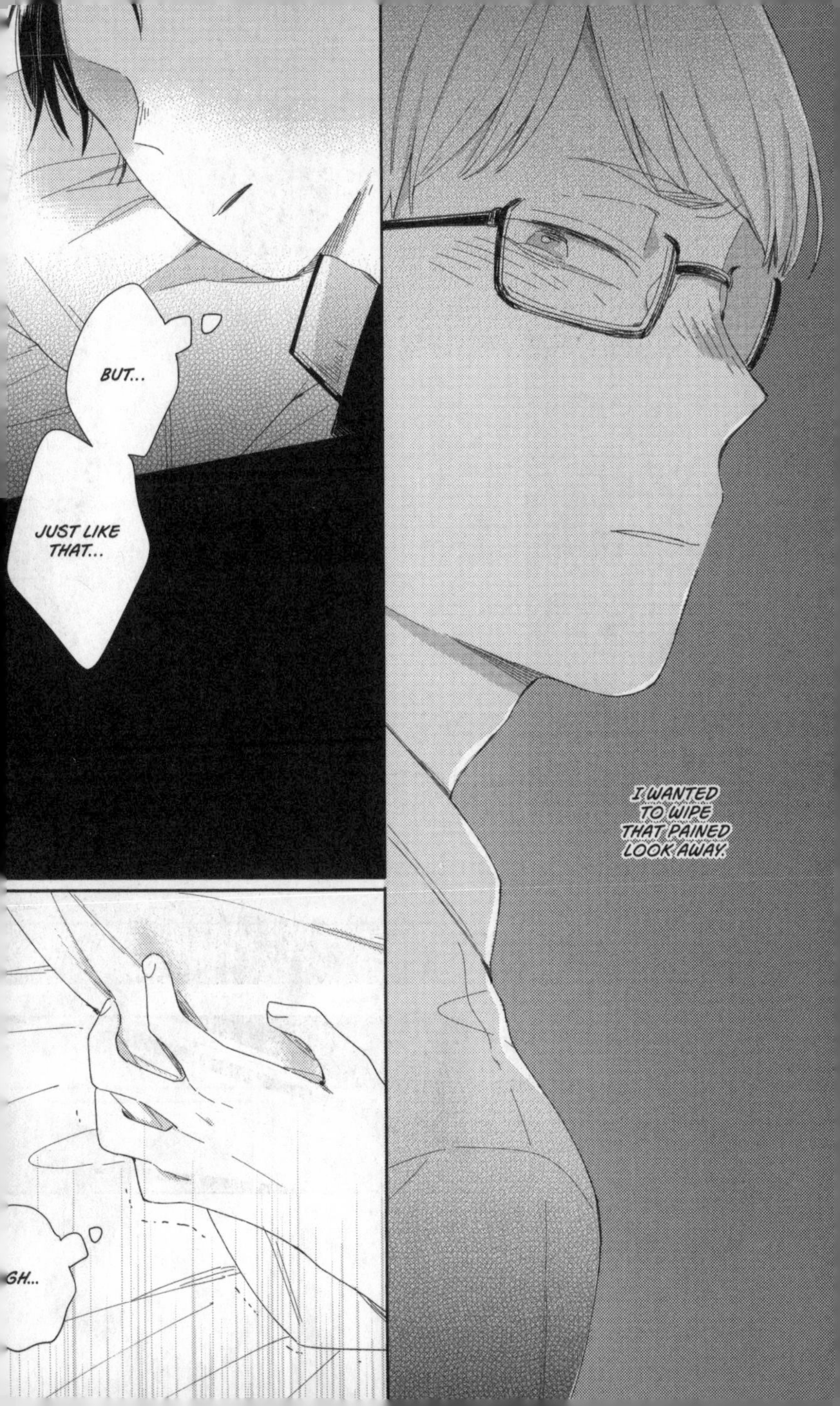
I WANTED TO WIPE THAT PAINED LOOK AWAY.
BUT...
JUST LIKE THAT...
GH...

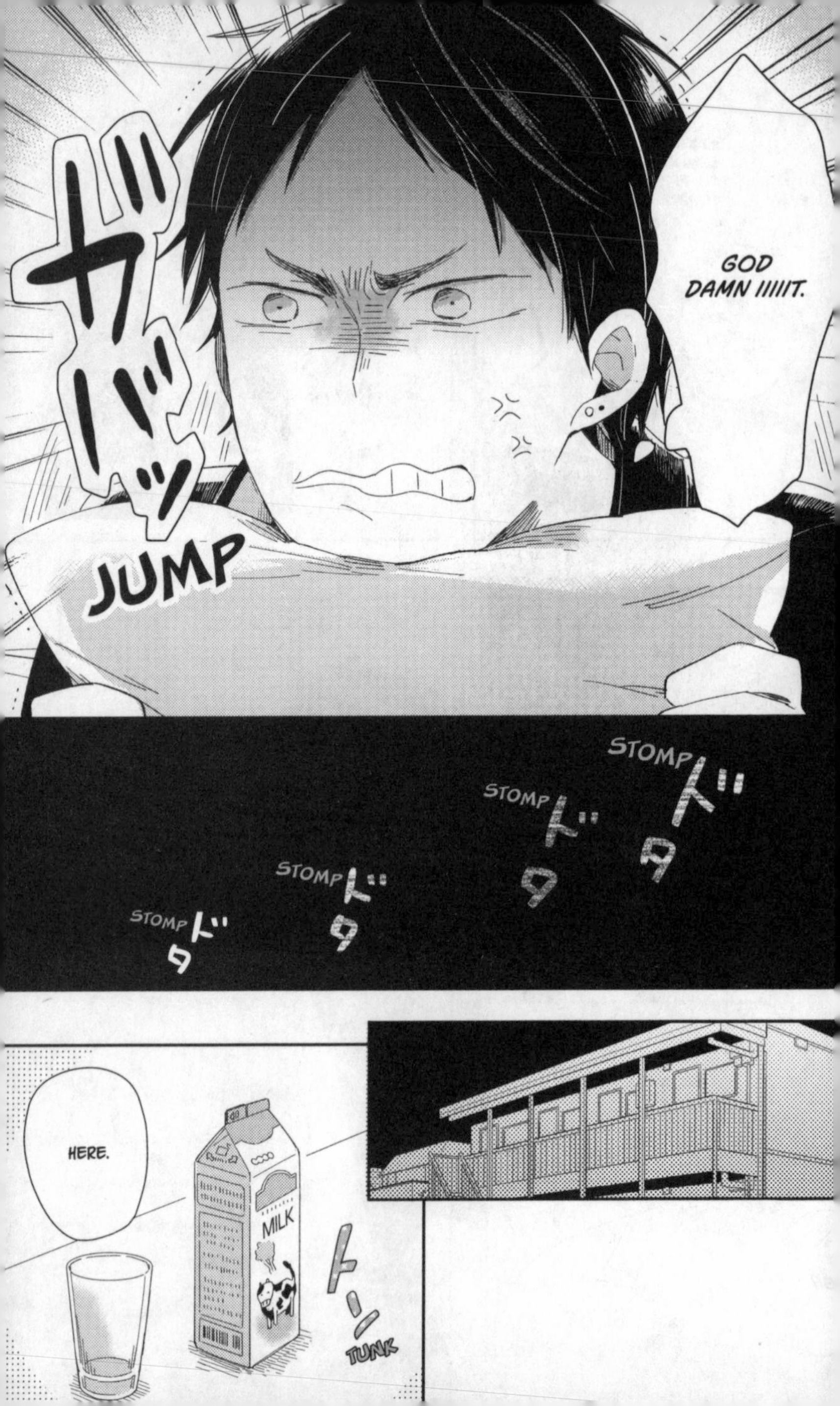
GOD DAMN IIIIIT.
JUMP
STOMP
STOMP
STOMP
STOMP
HERE.
TUNK

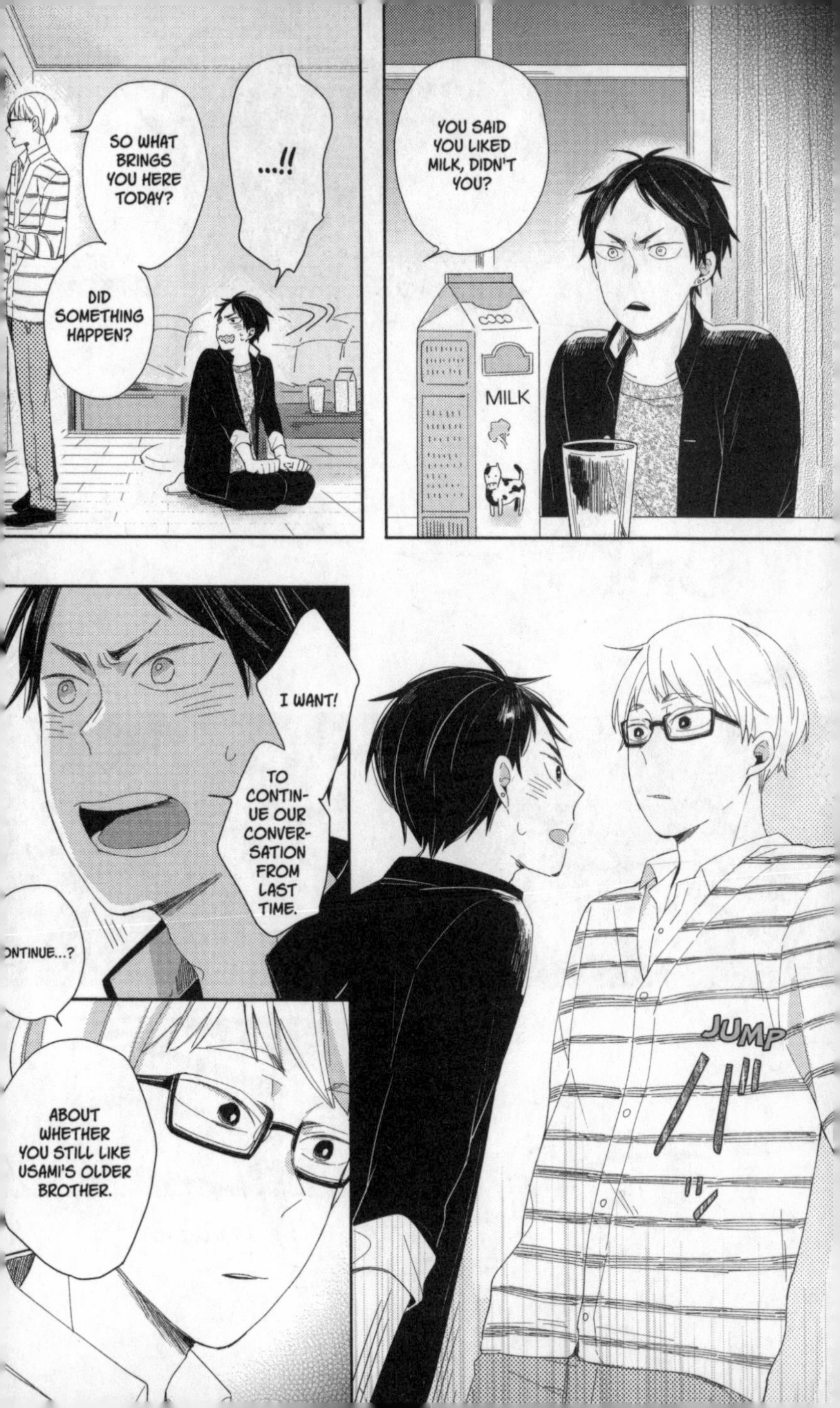
YOU SAID YOU LIKED MILK, DIDN'T YOU?
MILK
...!!
SO WHAT BRINGS YOU HERE TODAY?
DID SOMETHING HAPPEN?
JUMP
I WANT!
TO CONTIN-UE OUR CONVER-SATION FROM LAST TIME.
ONTINUE...?
ABOUT WHETHER YOU STILL LIKE USAMI'S OLDER BROTHER.

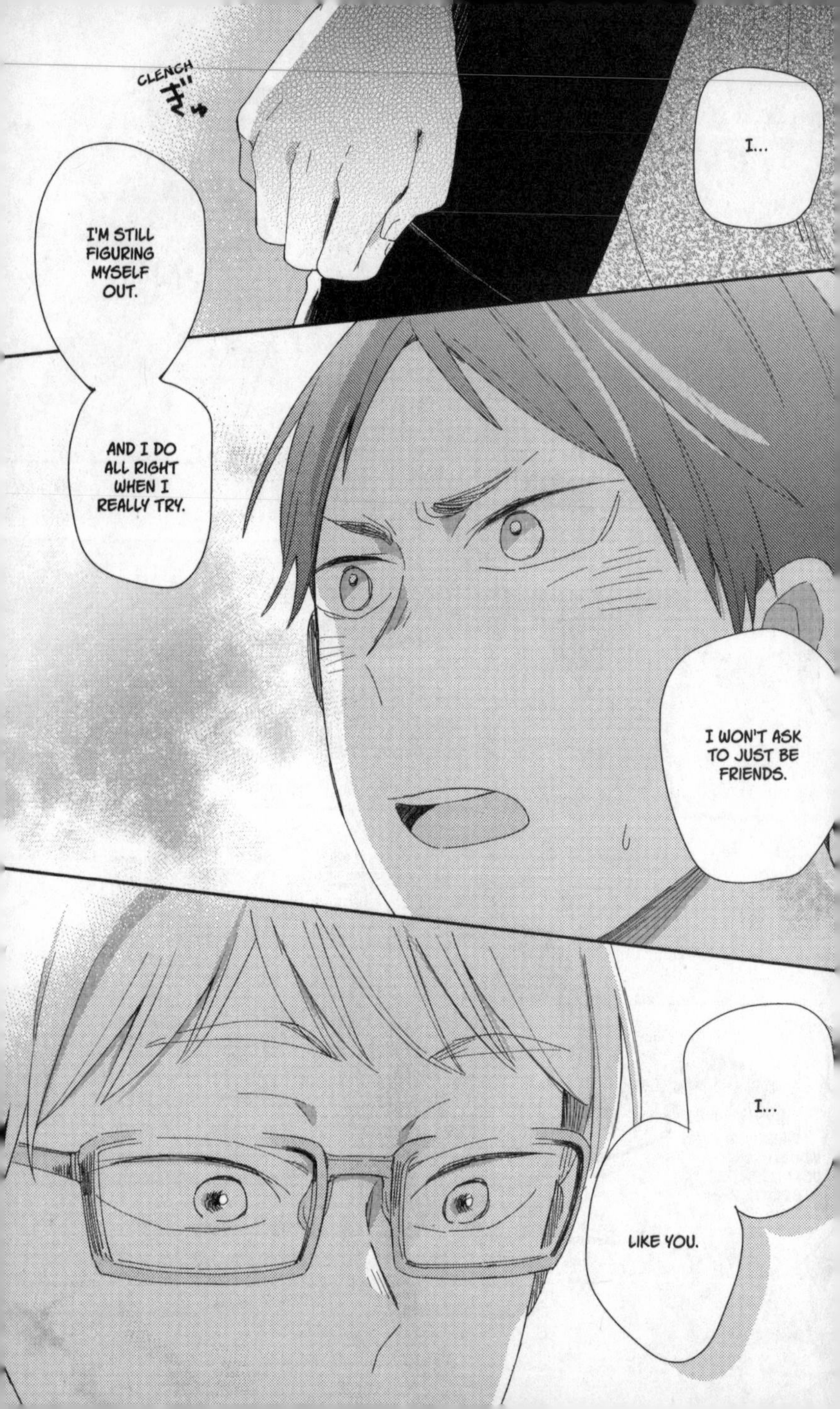
I...
CLENCH
ぎゅ
I'M STILL FIGURING MYSELF OUT.
AND I DO ALL RIGHT WHEN I REALLY TRY.
I WON'T ASK TO JUST BE FRIENDS.
I...
LIKE YOU.

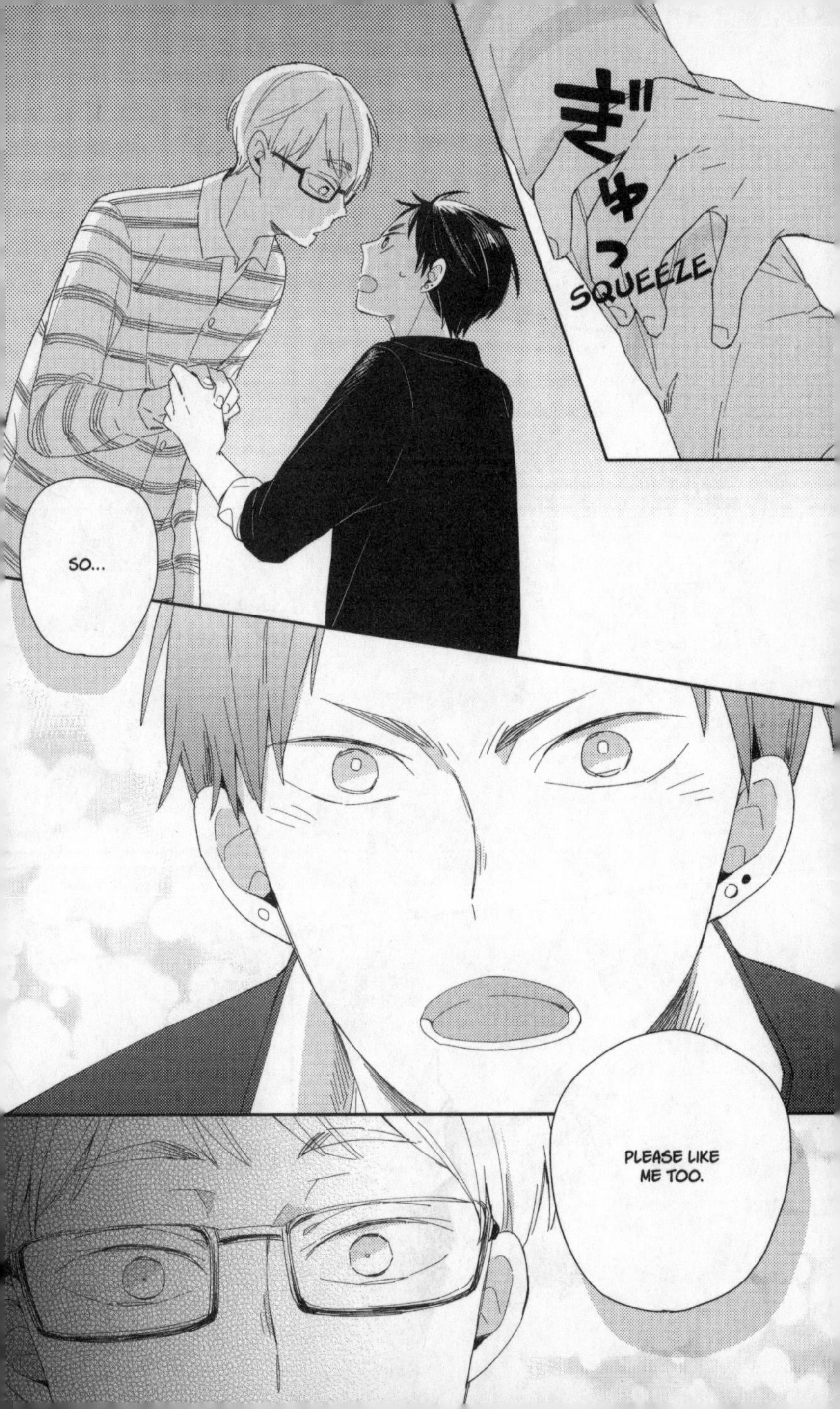
ぎゅっ
SQUEEZE
SO...
PLEASE LIKE ME TOO.

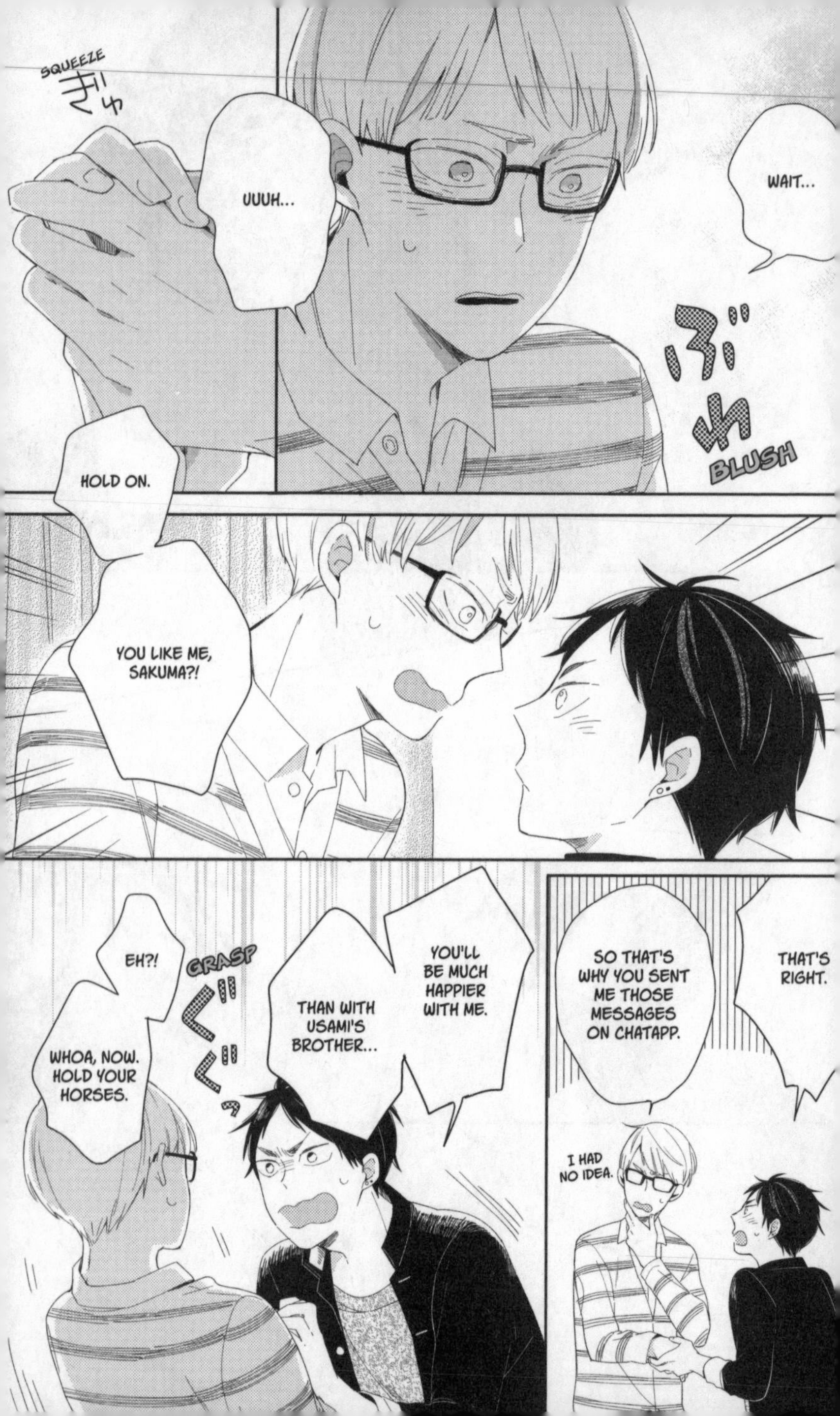
WAIT...
ぶわ
BLUSH
SQUEEZE
ぎゅ
UUUH...
HOLD ON.
YOU LIKE ME, SAKUMA?!
THAT'S RIGHT.
SO THAT'S WHY YOU SENT ME THOSE MESSAGES ON CHATAPP.
I HAD NO IDEA.
YOU'LL BE MUCH HAPPIER WITH ME.
THAN WITH USAMI'S BROTHER...
GRASP
ぐぐっ
EH?!
WHOA, NOW. HOLD YOUR HORSES.

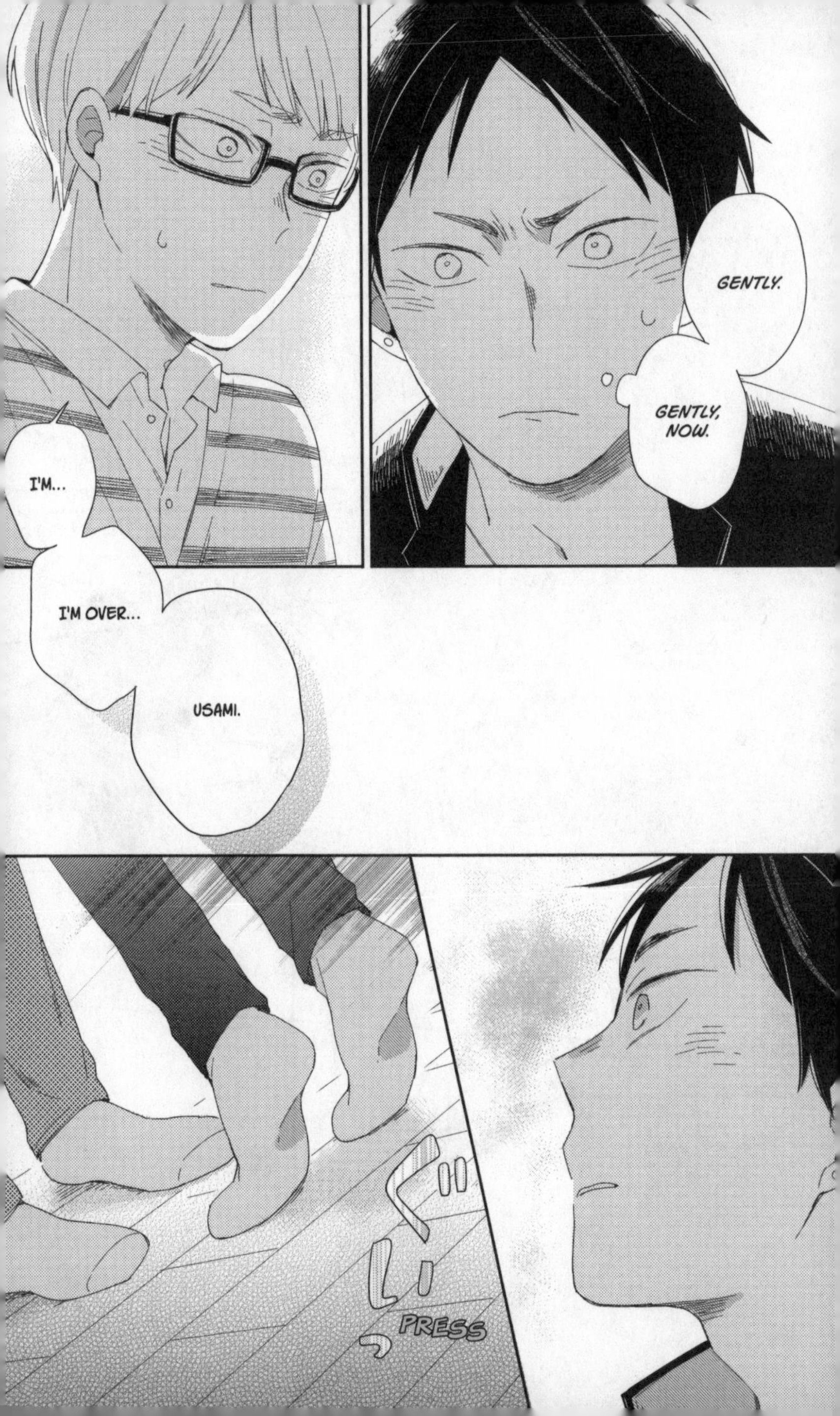
GENTLY.
GENTLY, NOW.
I'M...
I'M OVER...
USAMI.
PRESS

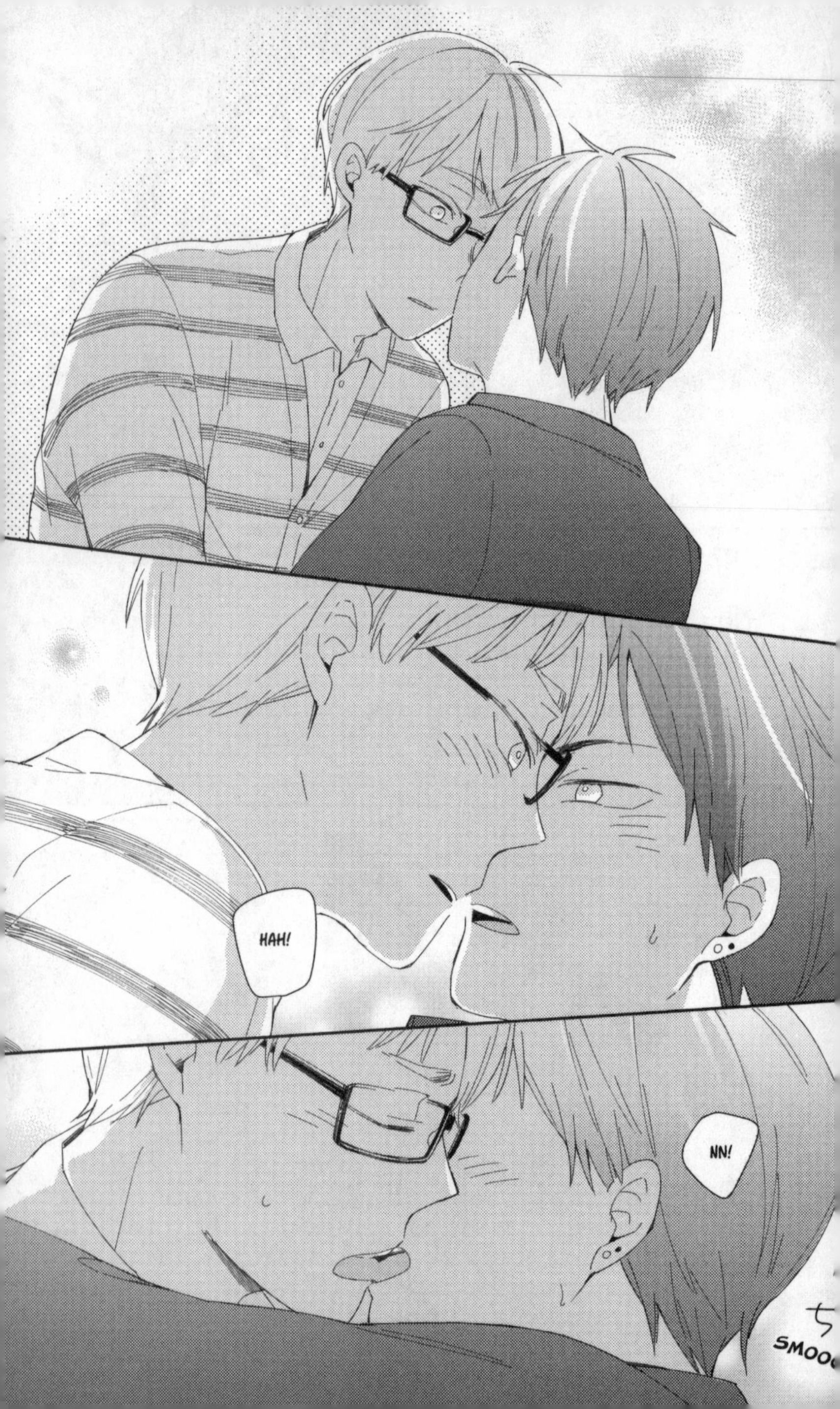
HAH!
NN!
SMOO

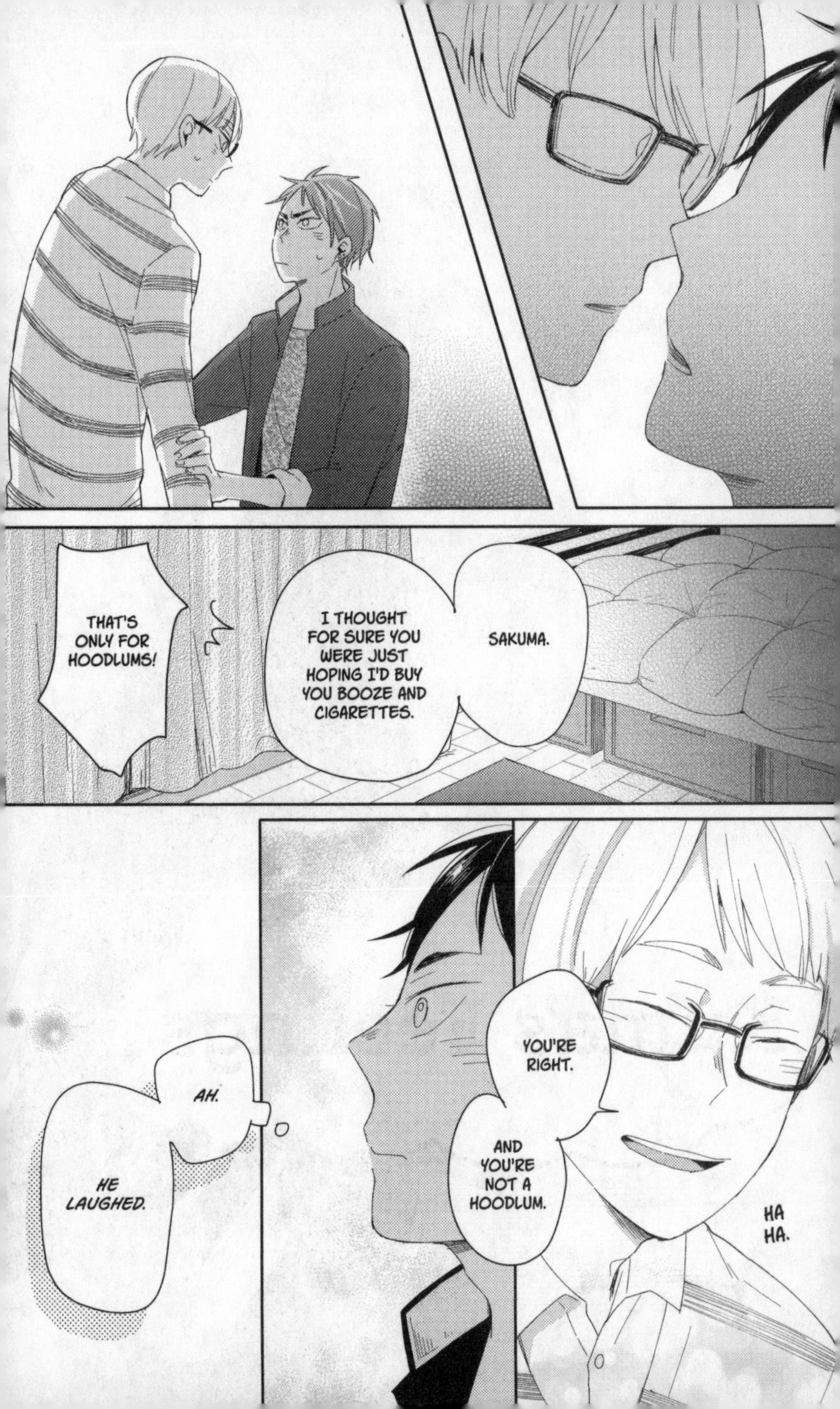
SAKUMA.
I THOUGHT FOR SURE YOU WERE JUST HOPING I'D BUY YOU BOOZE AND CIGARETTES.
THAT'S ONLY FOR HOODLUMS!
YOU'RE RIGHT.
AND YOU'RE NOT A HOODLUM.
HA HA.
AH.
HE LAUGHED.

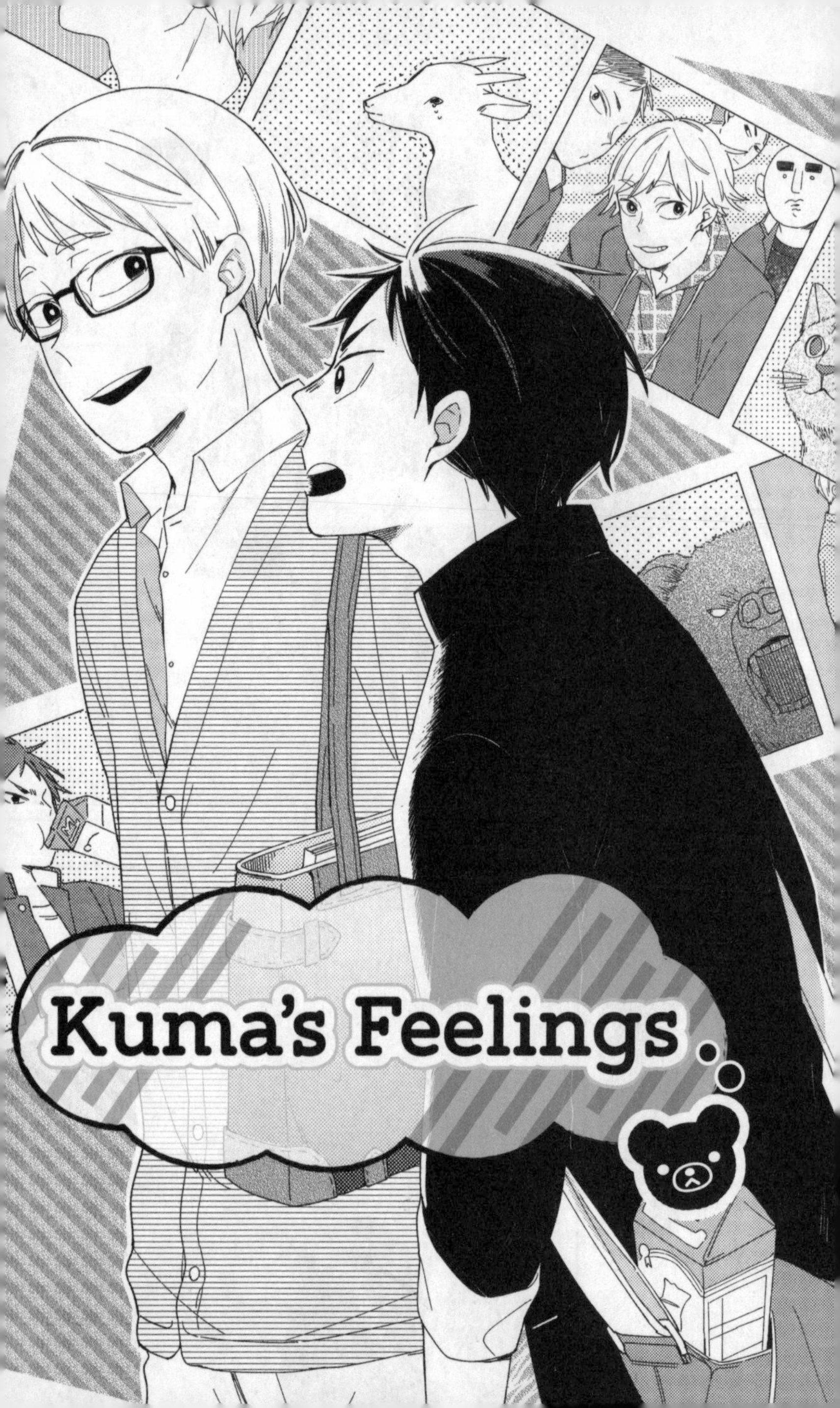
Kuma's Feelings

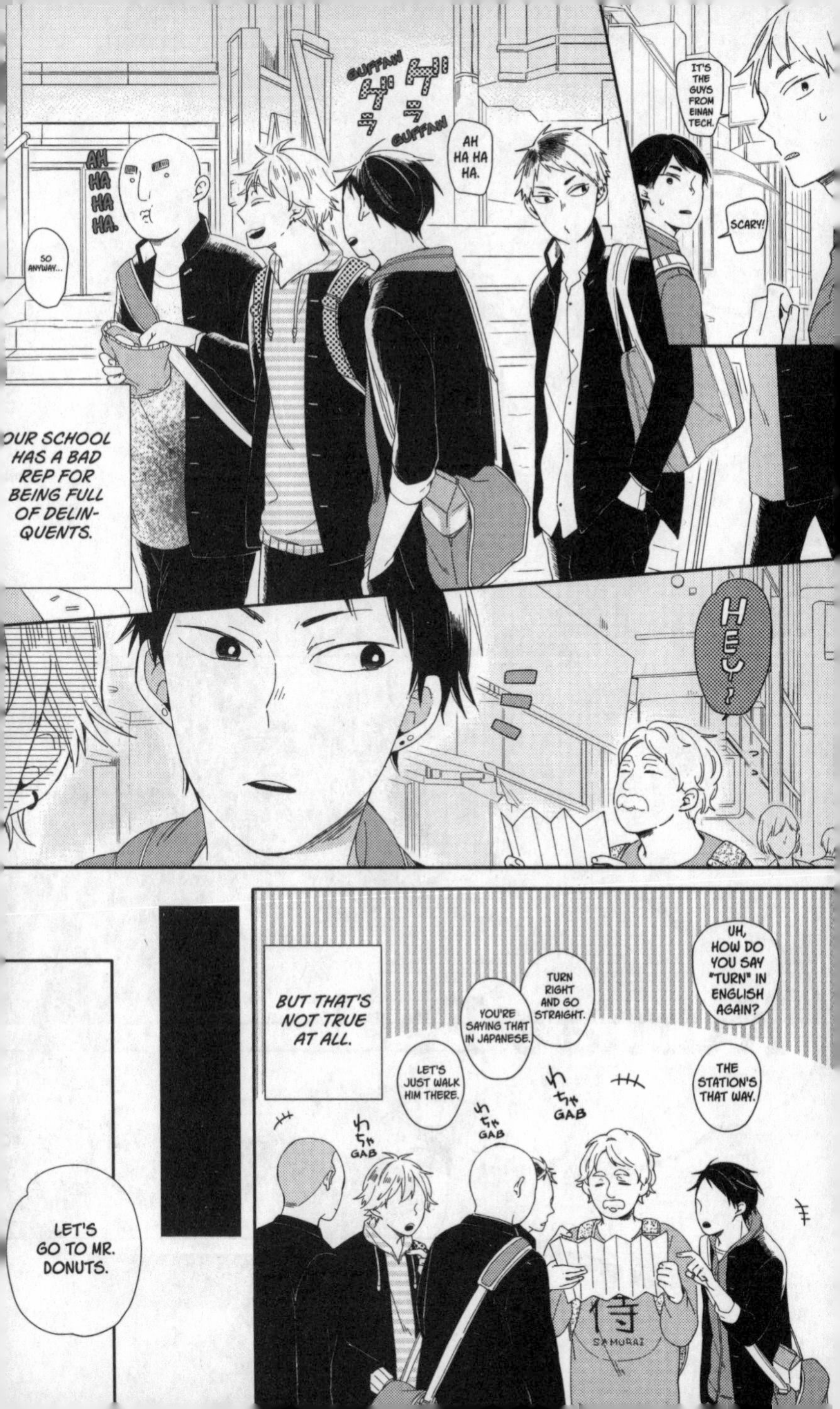

IT'S THE GUYS FROM EINAN TECH.
SCARY!
GUFFAW
GUFFAW
AH HA HA HA.
AH HA HA HA.
SO ANYWAY...
OUR SCHOOL HAS A BAD REP FOR BEING FULL OF DELIN-QUENTS.
HEY!
BUT THAT'S NOT TRUE AT ALL.
UH, HOW DO YOU SAY "TURN" IN ENGLISH AGAIN?
TURN RIGHT AND GO STRAIGHT.
YOU'RE SAYING THAT IN JAPANESE.
THE STATION'S THAT WAY.
GAB
LET'S JUST WALK HIM THERE.
GAB
GAB
SAMURAI
LET'S GO TO MR. DONUTS.

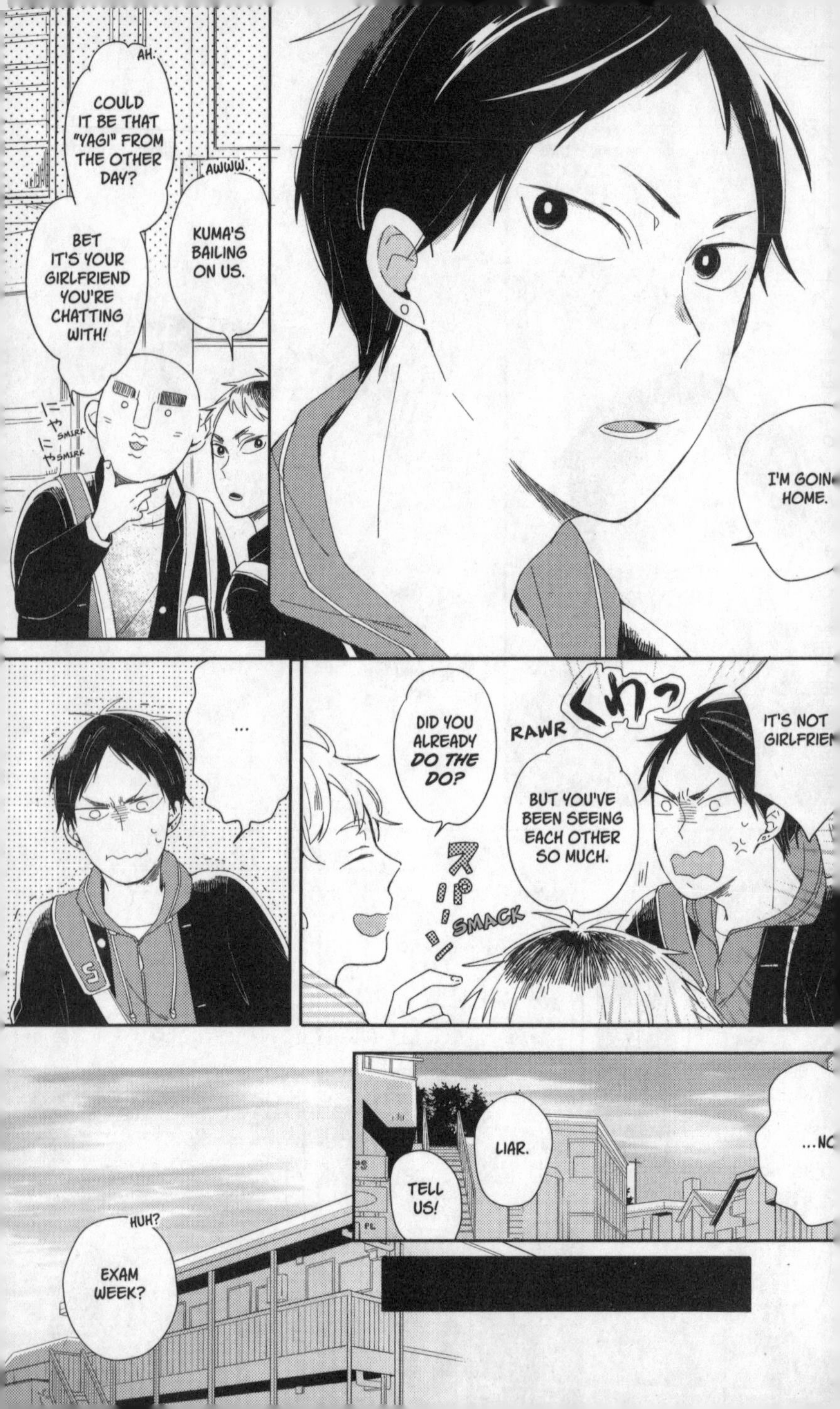
I'M GOIN
HOME.
AH.
COULD IT BE THAT "YAGI" FROM THE OTHER DAY?
AWWW.
KUMA'S BAILING ON US.
BET IT'S YOUR GIRLFRIEND YOU'RE CHATTING WITH!
にやにや
SMIRK SMIRK
IT'S NOT GIRLFRIEN
くわっ
RAWR
DID YOU ALREADY DO THE DO?
BUT YOU'VE BEEN SEEING EACH OTHER SO MUCH.
スパッ
SMACK
...
...N
LIAR.
TELL US!
HUH?
EXAM WEEK?

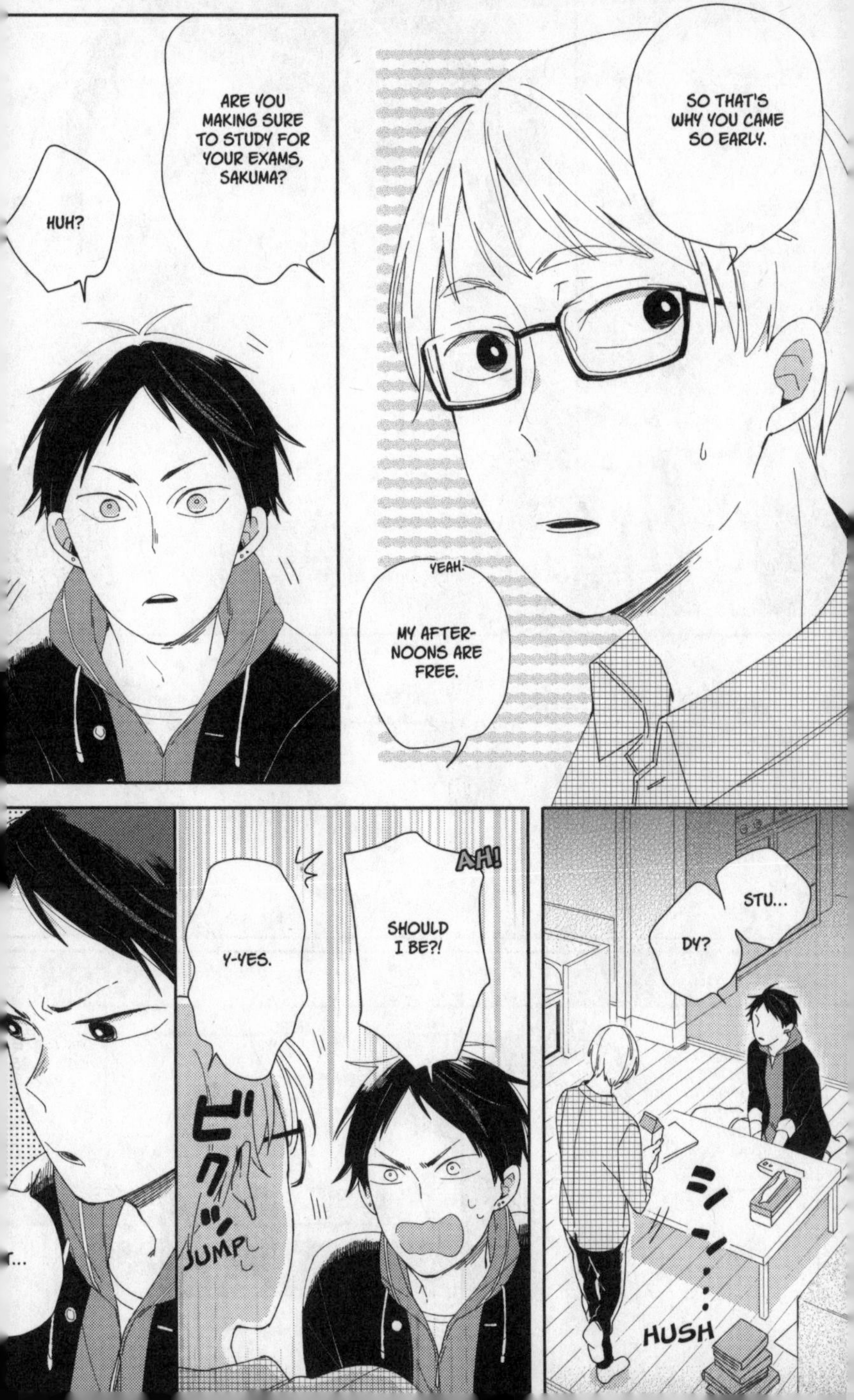
SO THAT'S WHY YOU CAME SO EARLY.
YEAH.
MY AFTER-NOONS ARE FREE.
ARE YOU MAKING SURE TO STUDY FOR YOUR EXAMS, SAKUMA?
HUH?
STU...
DY?
HUSH
AH!
SHOULD I BE?!
Y-YES.
JUMP

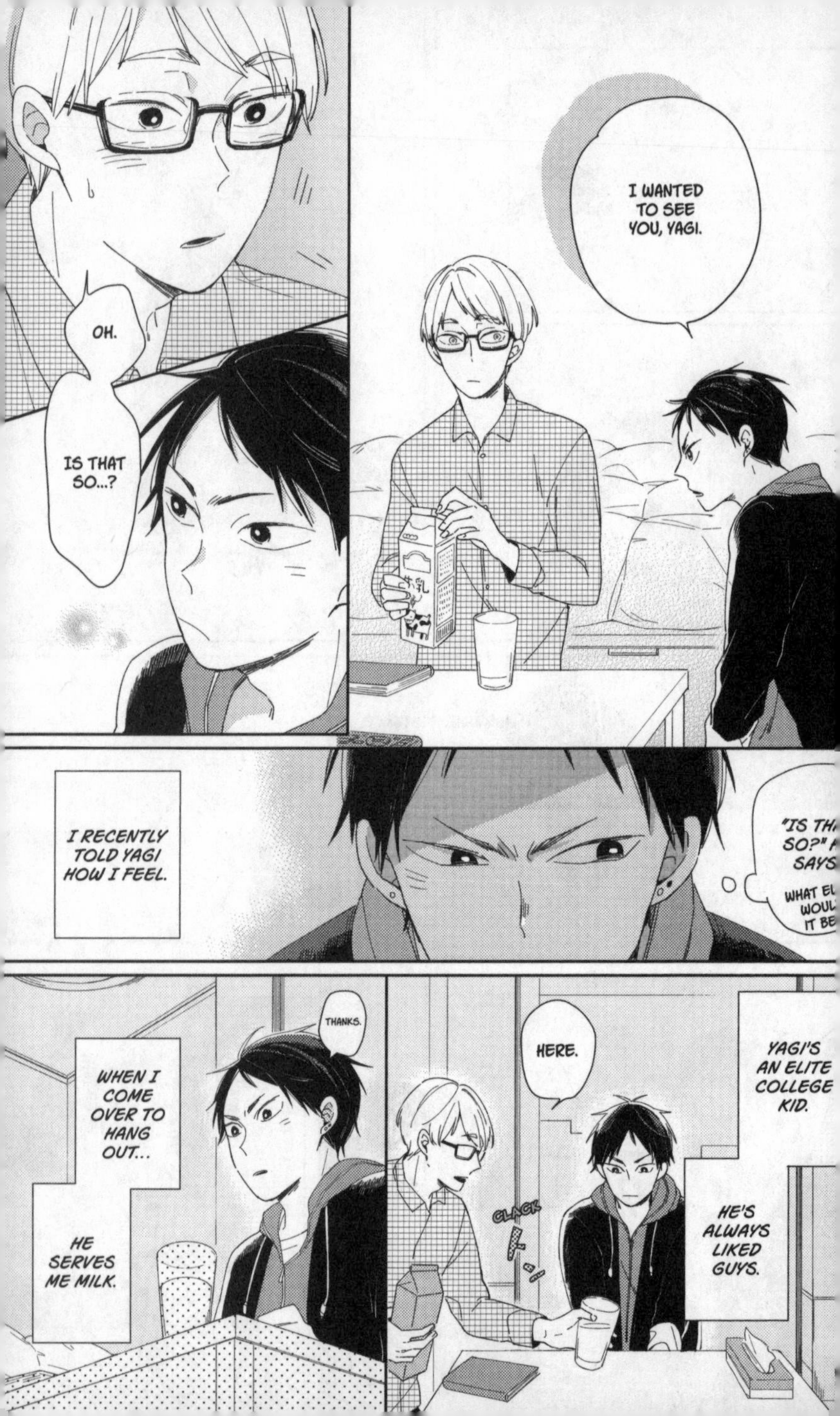
I WANTED TO SEE YOU, YAGI.
OH.
IS THAT SO...?
I RECENTLY TOLD YAGI HOW I FEEL.
YAGI'S AN ELITE COLLEGE KID.
HERE.
HE'S ALWAYS LIKED GUYS.
CLACK
THANKS.
WHEN I COME OVER TO HANG OUT...
HE SERVES ME MILK.

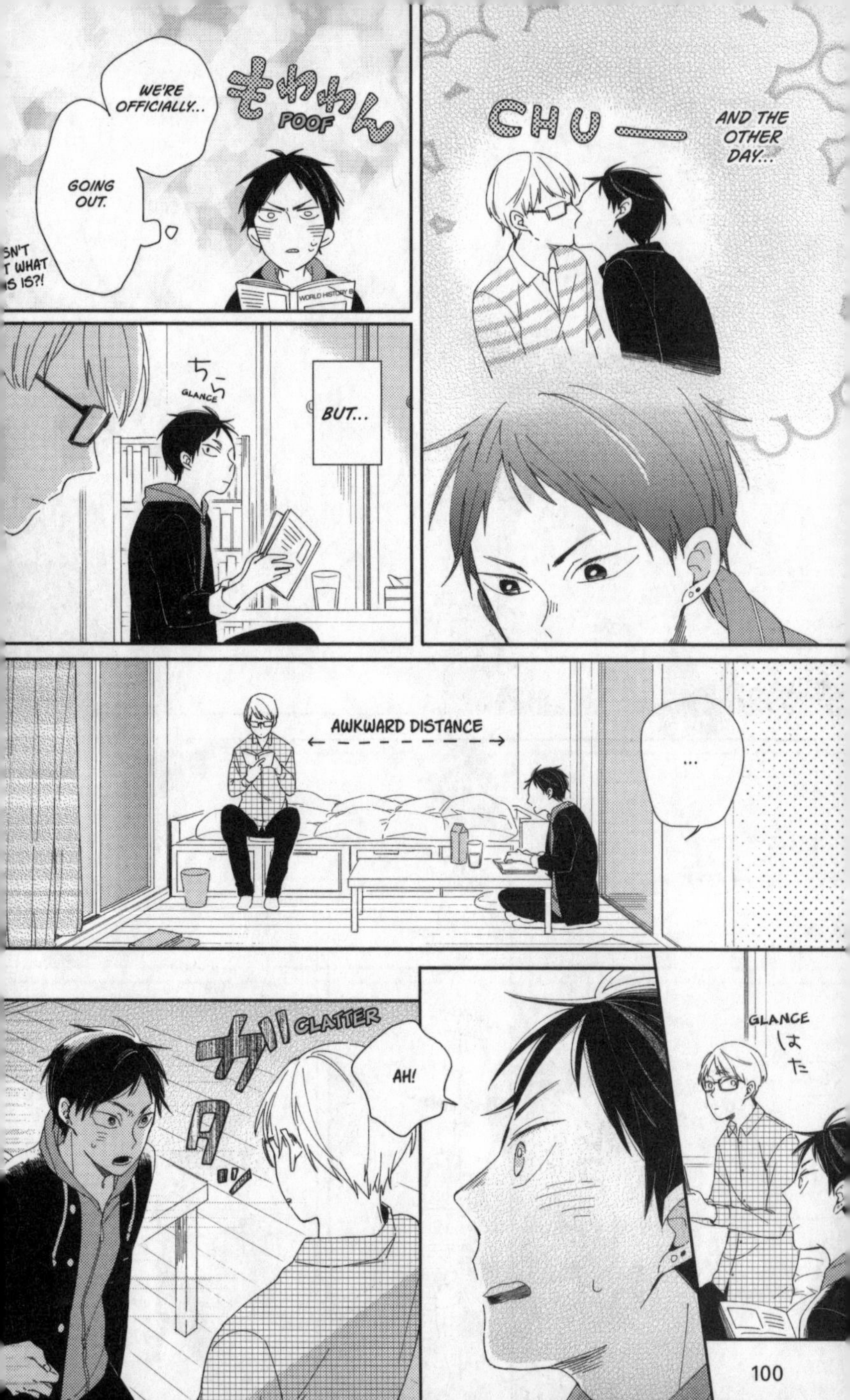
CHU—
AND THE OTHER DAY...
そわわん
POOF
WE'RE OFFICIALLY...
GOING OUT.
SN'T T WHAT S IS?!
WORLD HISTORY
ちら
GLANCE
BUT...
AWKWARD DISTANCE
...
はた
GLANCE
ガタ
CLATTER
AH!

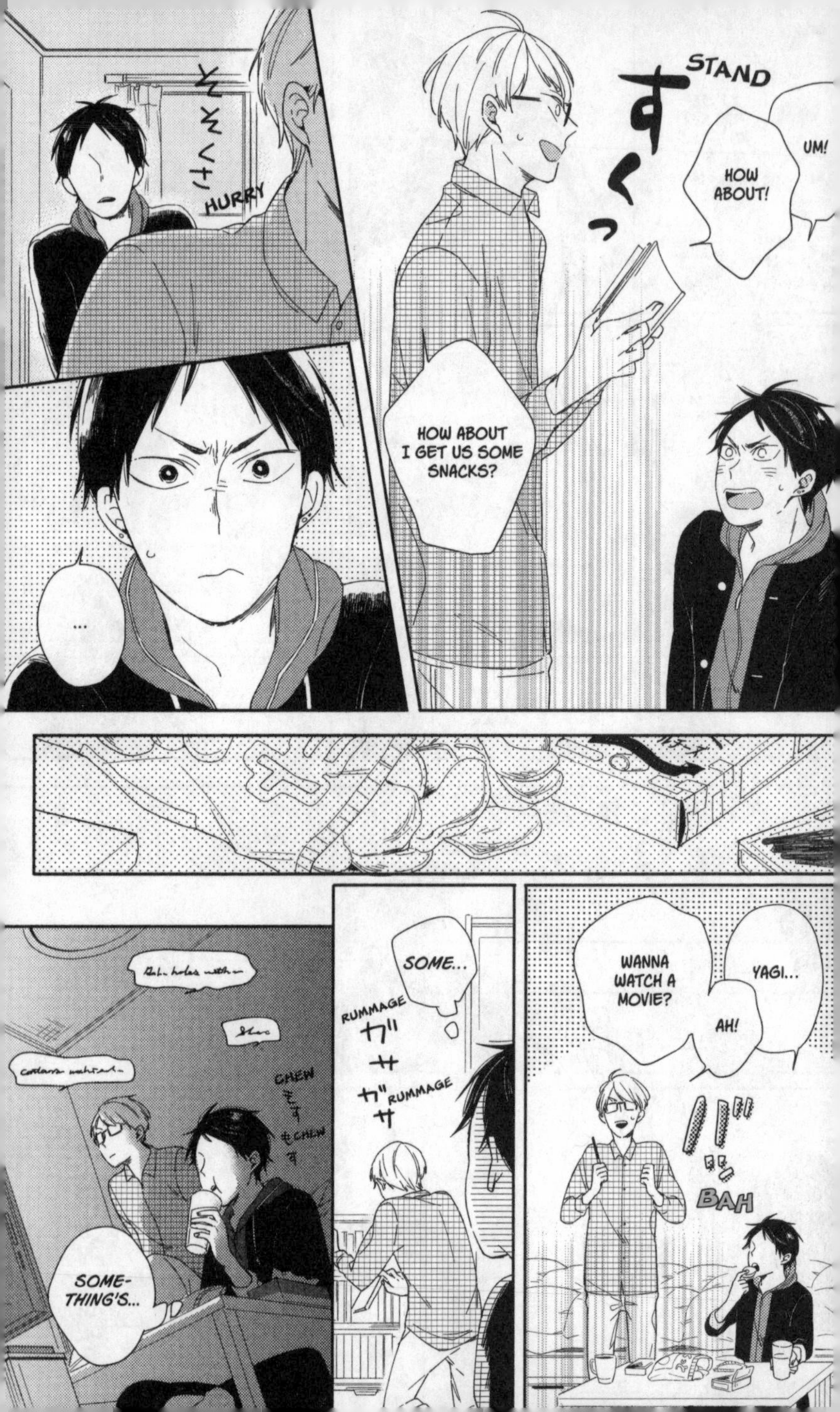
STAND
すくっ
UM!
HOW ABOUT!
HOW ABOUT I GET US SOME SNACKS?
そそくさ
HURRY
...
YAGI...
AH!
WANNA WATCH A MOVIE?
BAH
SOME...
RUMMAGE
ガサ
ガサ
RUMMAGE
CHEW
CHEW
SOME-THING'S...

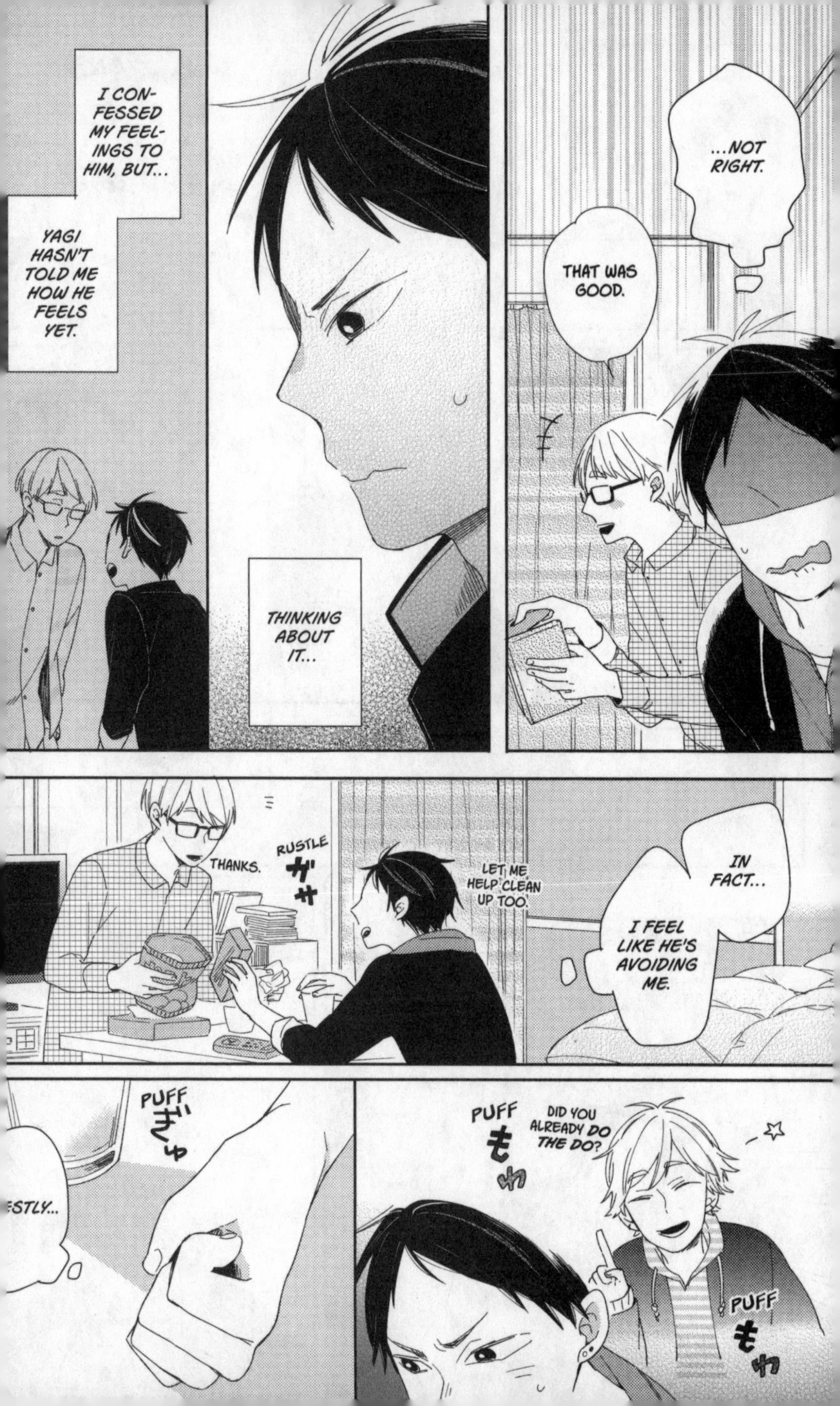
…NOT RIGHT.
THAT WAS GOOD.
THINKING ABOUT IT…
I CONFESSED MY FEELINGS TO HIM, BUT…
YAGI HASN'T TOLD ME HOW HE FEELS YET.
IN FACT…
I FEEL LIKE HE'S AVOIDING ME.
LET ME HELP CLEAN UP TOO.
RUSTLE
ザサ
THANKS.
DID YOU ALREADY DO THE DO?
PUFF
もゎ
PUFF
もゎ
PUFF
ぎゅ
ESTLY...

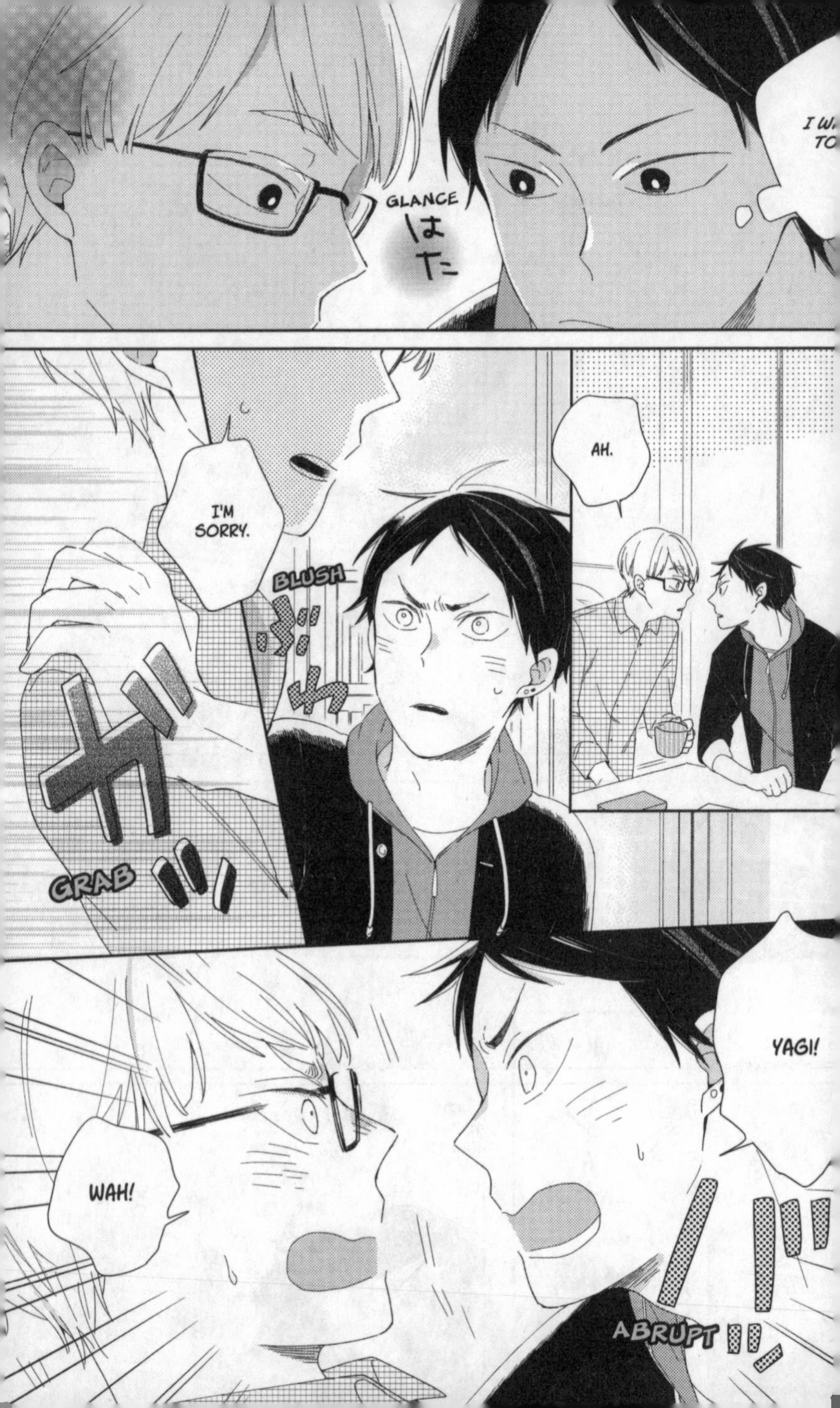

GLANCE
AH.
I'M SORRY.
BLUSH
GRAB
YAGI!
ABRUPT
WAH!

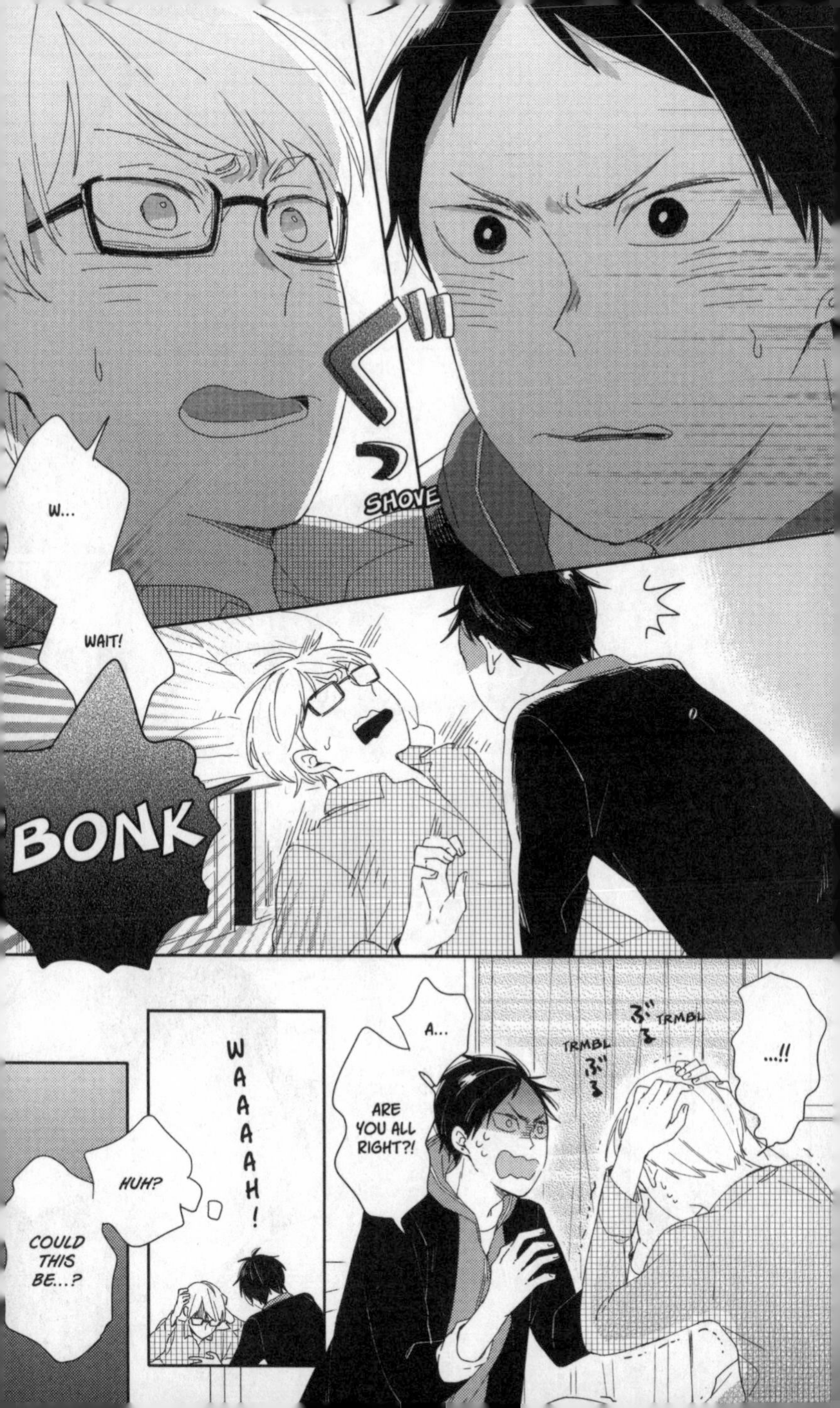

SHOVE
W...
WAIT!
BONK
...!!
ぶる TRMBL
TRMBL ぶる
A...
ARE YOU ALL RIGHT?!
WAAAAAH!
HUH?
COULD THIS BE...?

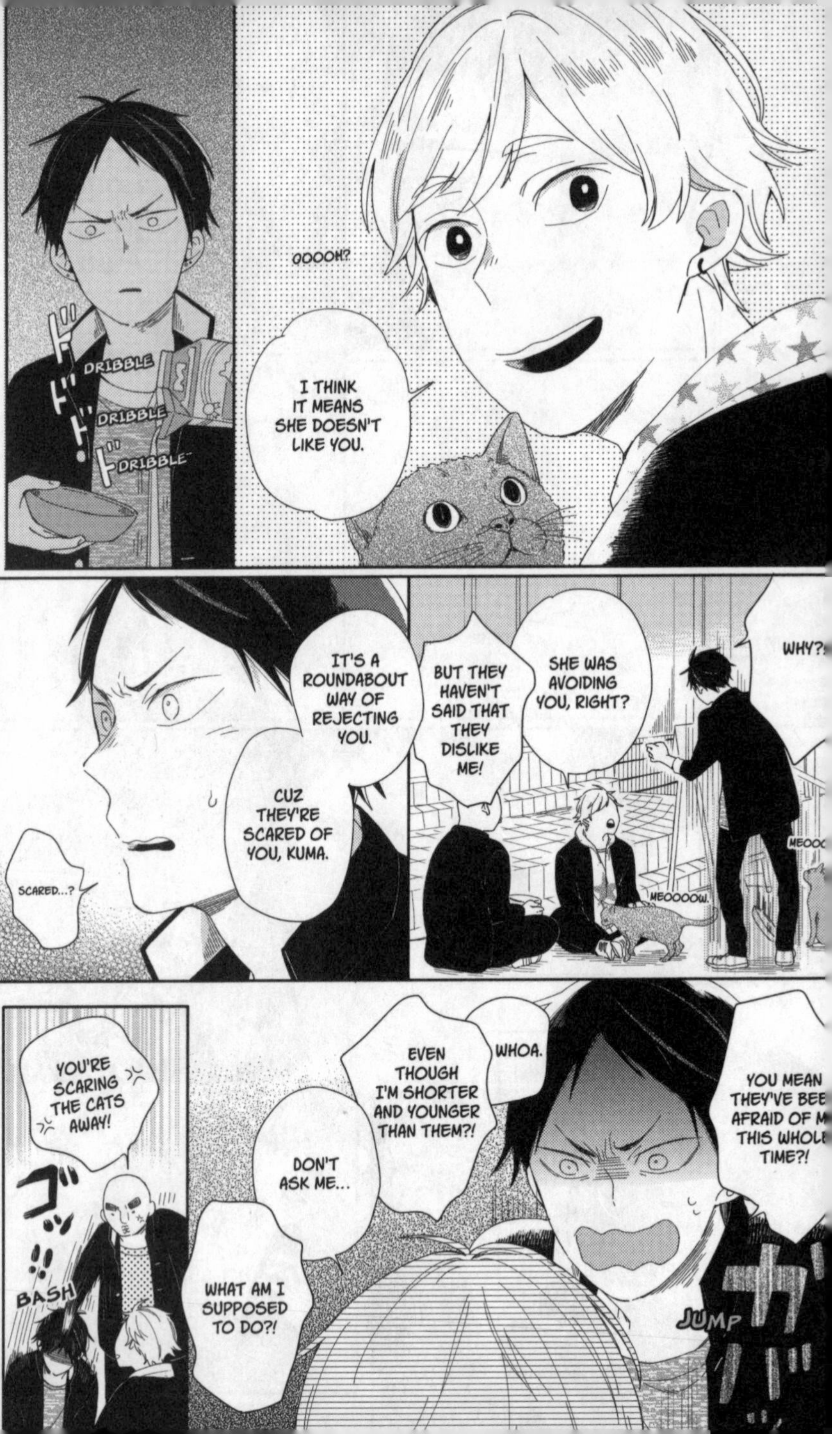
OOOOH?
I THINK IT MEANS SHE DOESN'T LIKE YOU.
DRIBBLE
DRIBBLE
DRIBBLE
WHY?!
SHE WAS AVOIDING YOU, RIGHT?
BUT THEY HAVEN'T SAID THAT THEY DISLIKE ME!
MEOOO
MEOOOOW.
IT'S A ROUNDABOUT WAY OF REJECTING YOU.
CUZ THEY'RE SCARED OF YOU, KUMA.
SCARED...?
YOU MEAN THEY'VE BEE AFRAID OF M THIS WHOL TIME?!
JUMP
WHOA.
EVEN THOUGH I'M SHORTER AND YOUNGER THAN THEM?!
DON'T ASK ME...
WHAT AM I SUPPOSED TO DO?!
YOU'RE SCARING THE CATS AWAY!
BASH

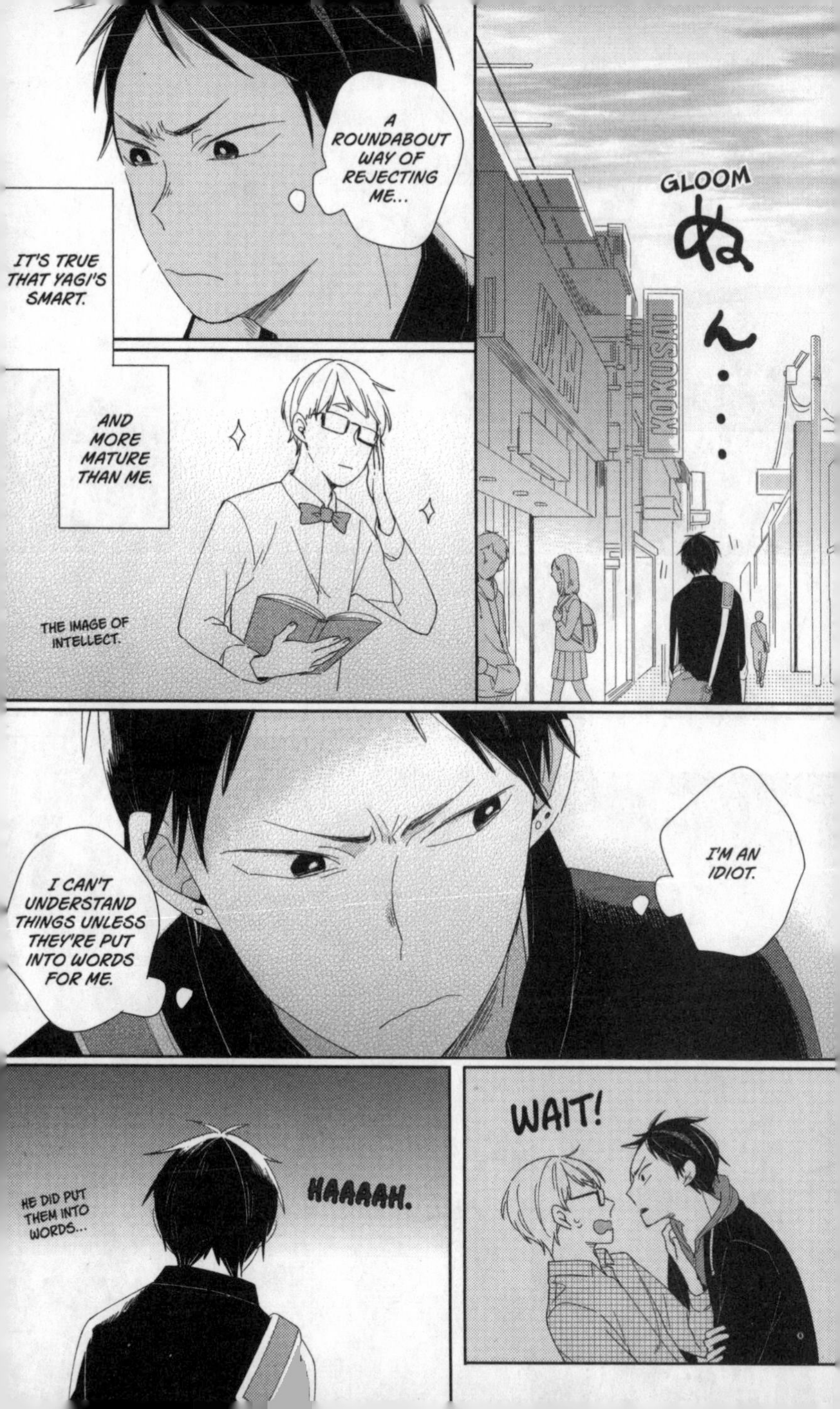
GLOOM
ぬん・・・
A ROUNDABOUT WAY OF REJECTING ME...
IT'S TRUE THAT YAGI'S SMART.
AND MORE MATURE THAN ME.
THE IMAGE OF INTELLECT.
KOKUSAI
I'M AN IDIOT.
I CAN'T UNDERSTAND THINGS UNLESS THEY'RE PUT INTO WORDS FOR ME.
WAIT!
HAAAAH.
HE DID PUT THEM INTO WORDS...

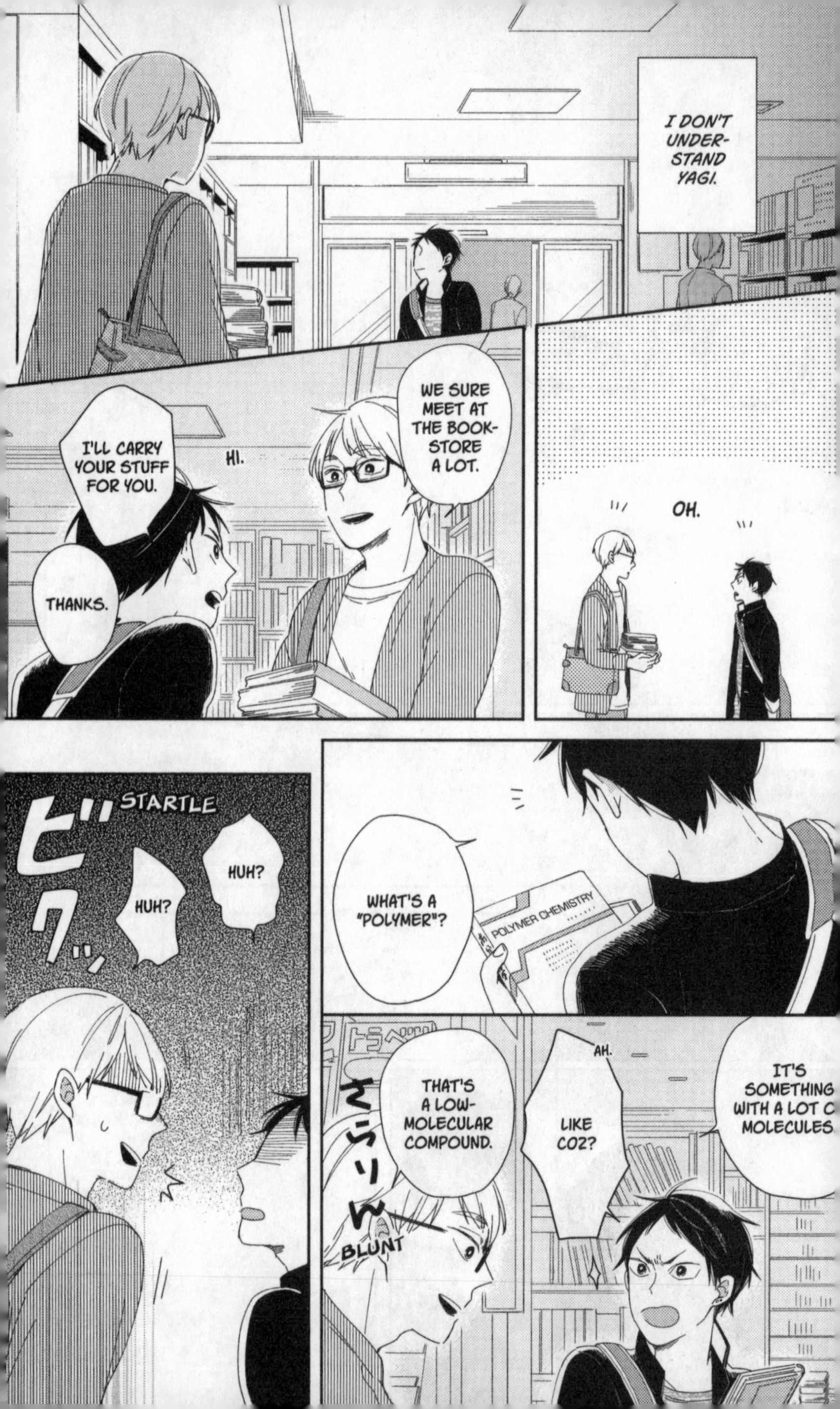
I DON'T UNDER-STAND YAGI.
OH.
WE SURE MEET AT THE BOOK-STORE A LOT.
HI.
I'LL CARRY YOUR STUFF FOR YOU.
THANKS.
WHAT'S A "POLYMER"?
POLYMER CHEMISTRY
IT'S SOMETHING WITH A LOT O MOLECULES
AH.
LIKE CO2?
THAT'S A LOW-MOLECULAR COMPOUND.
さらりん
BLUNT
ビクッ
STARTLE
HUH?
HUH?

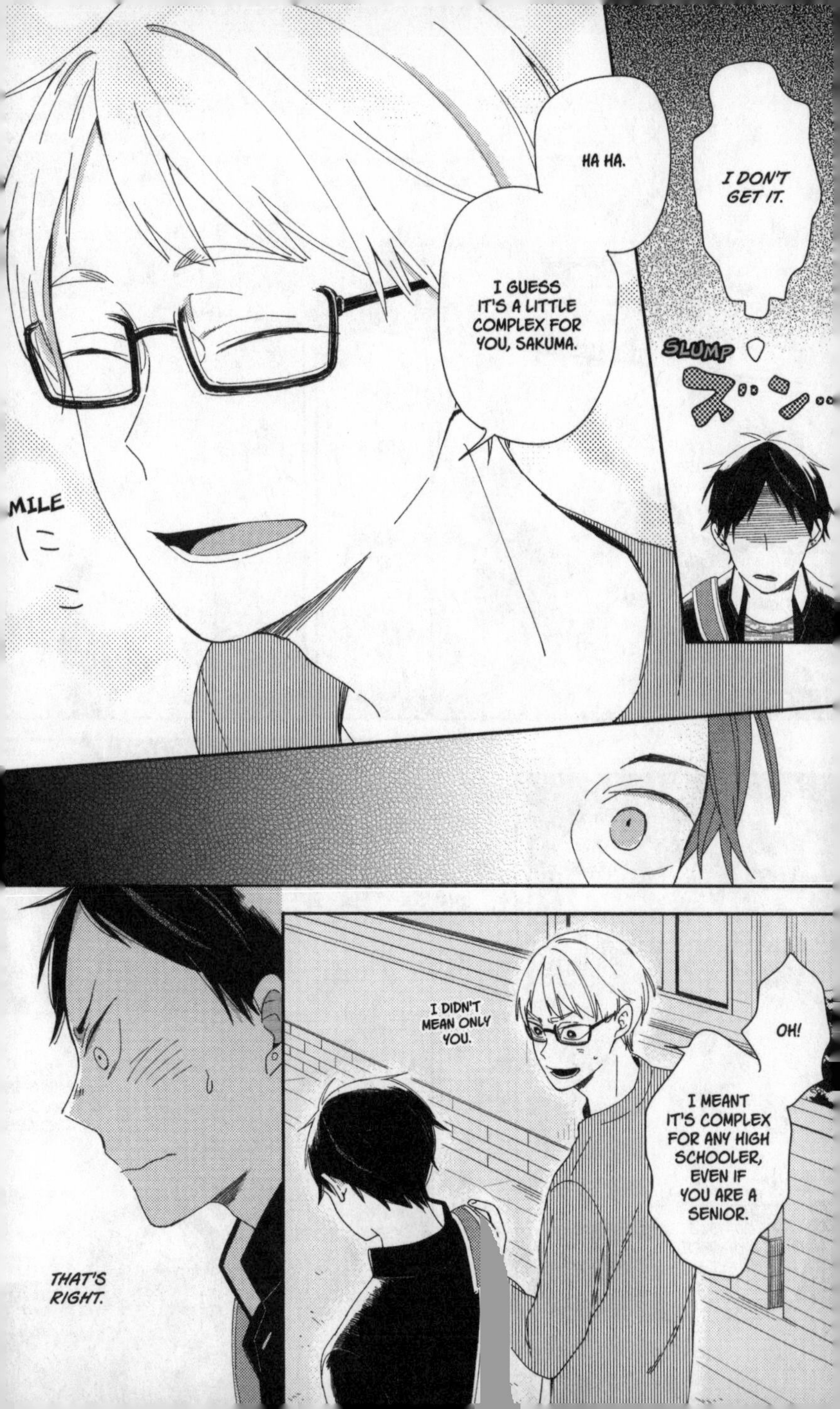
I DON'T GET IT.
SLUMP
HA HA.
I GUESS IT'S A LITTLE COMPLEX FOR YOU, SAKUMA.
MILE
OH!
I MEANT IT'S COMPLEX FOR ANY HIGH SCHOOLER, EVEN IF YOU ARE A SENIOR.
I DIDN'T MEAN ONLY YOU.
THAT'S RIGHT.

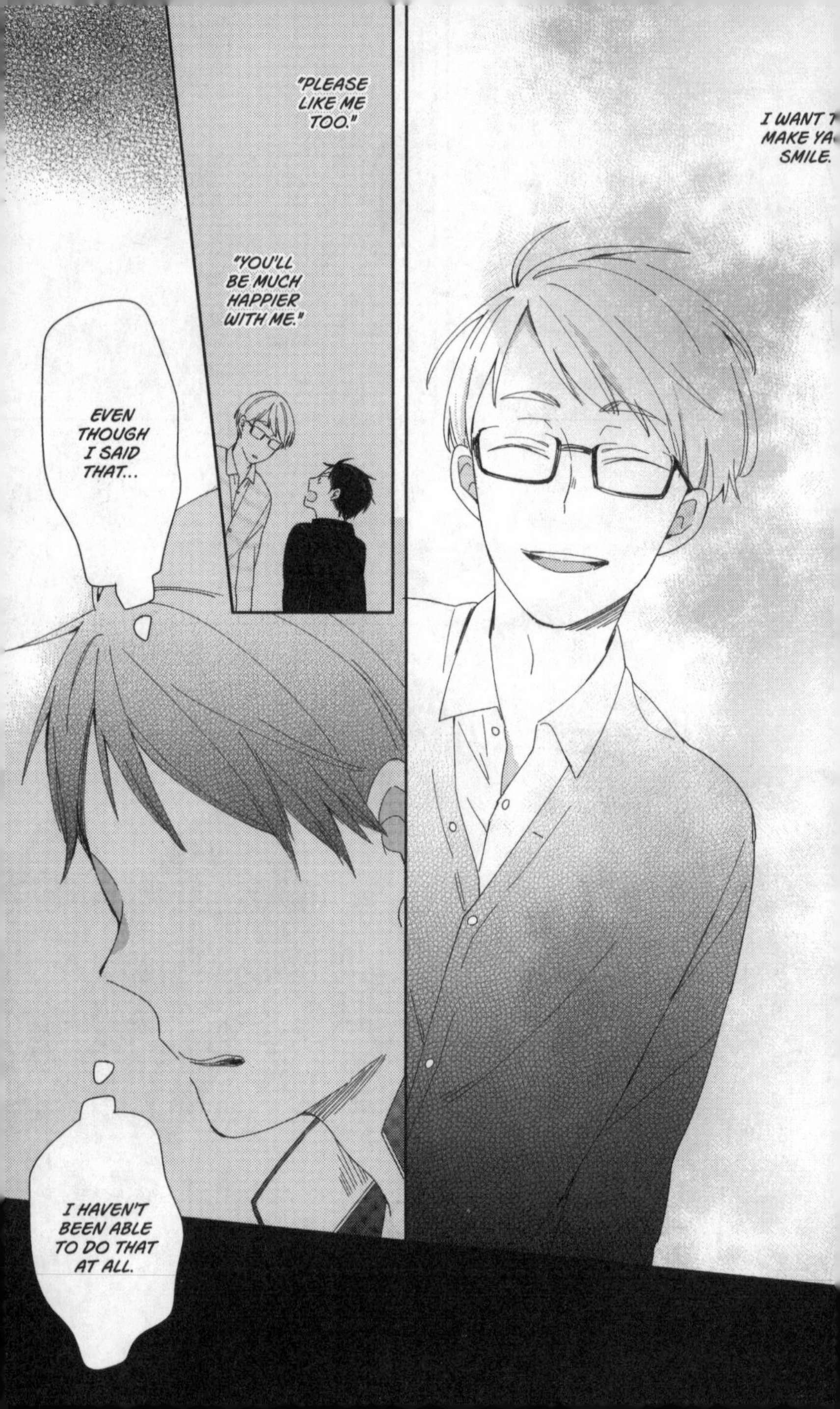
I WANT T MAKE YA SMILE.
"PLEASE LIKE ME TOO."
"YOU'LL BE MUCH HAPPIER WITH ME."
EVEN THOUGH I SAID THAT...
I HAVEN'T BEEN ABLE TO DO THAT AT ALL.

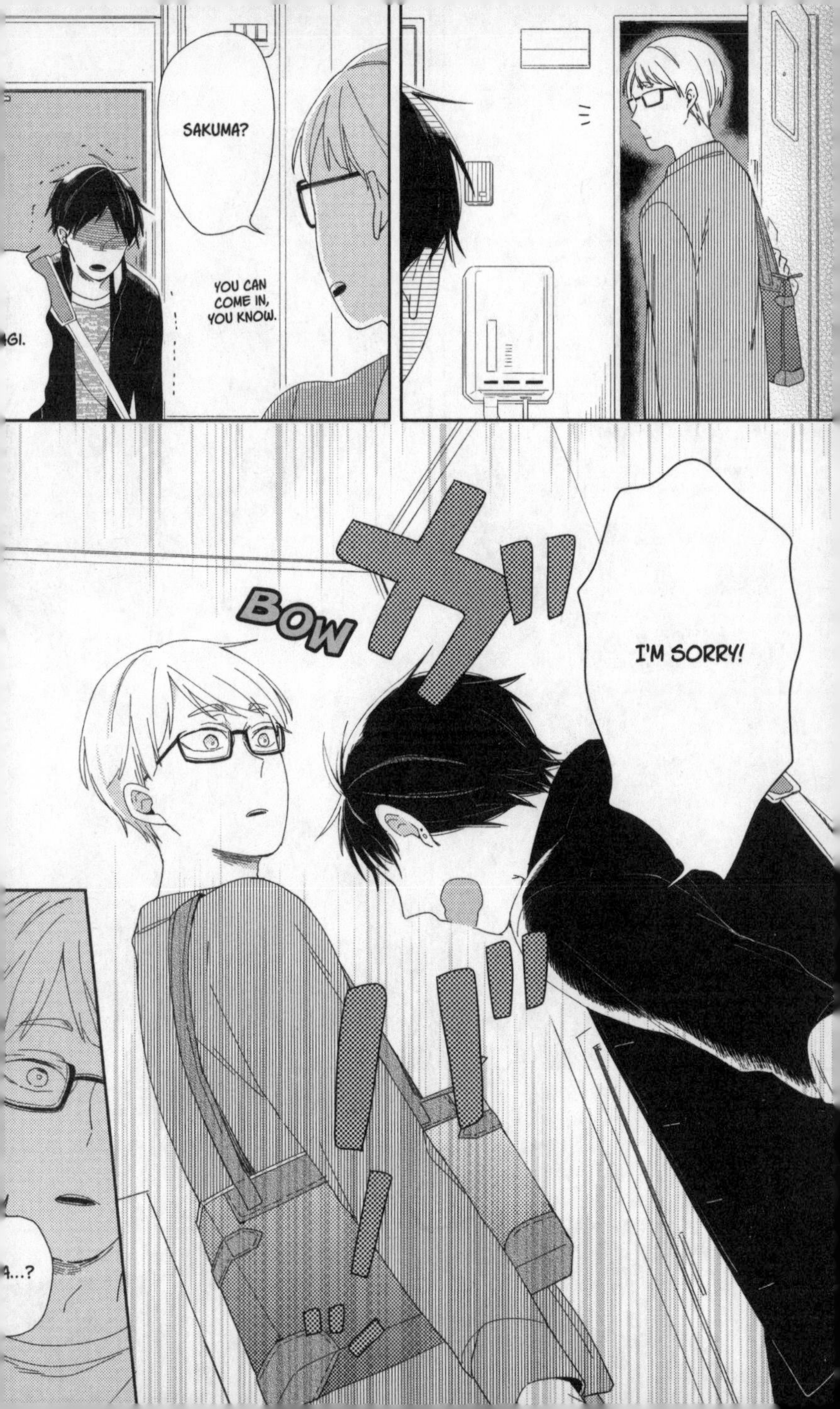
SAKUMA?
YOU CAN COME IN, YOU KNOW.
I'M SORRY!
BOW

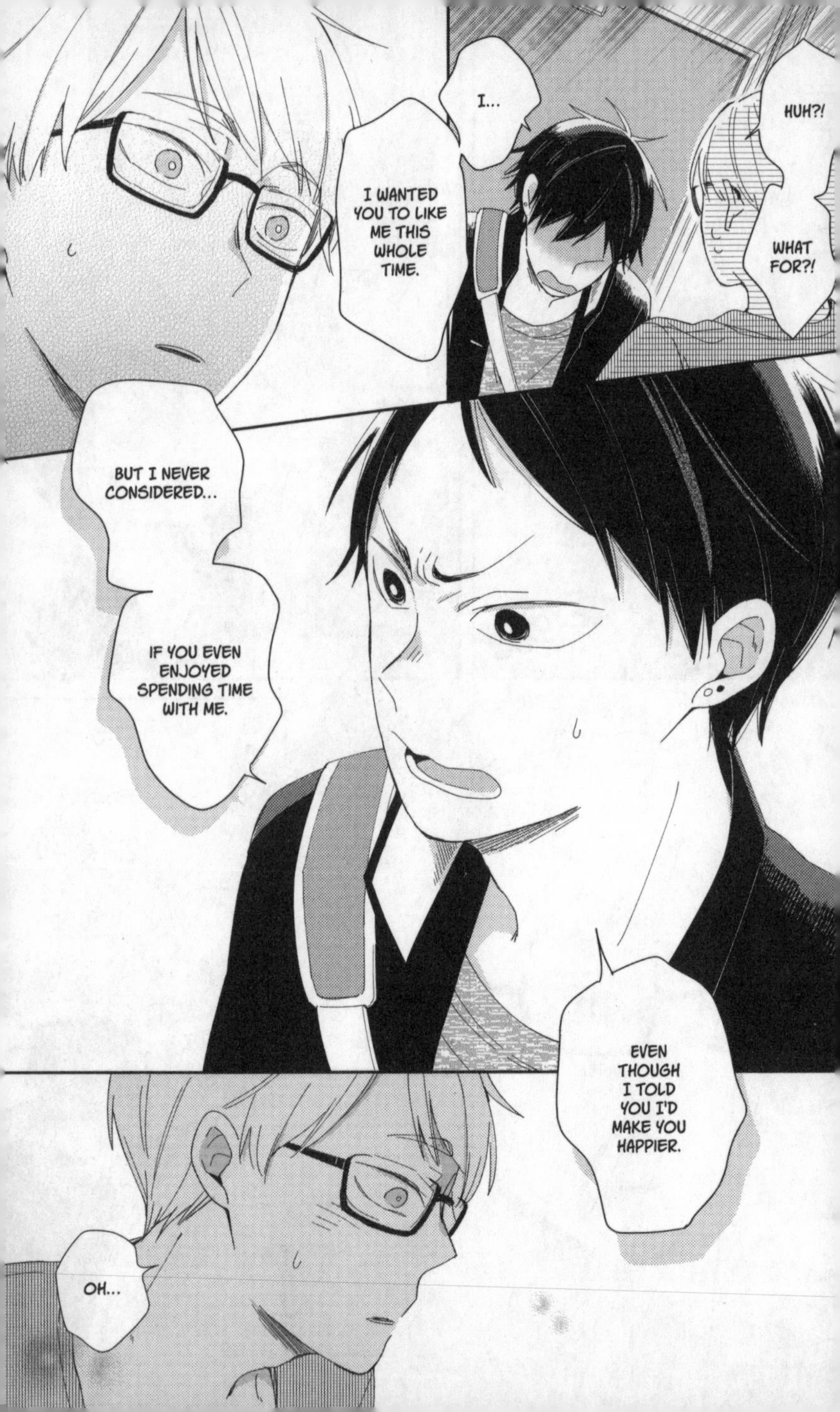
HUH?!
WHAT FOR?!
I...
I WANTED YOU TO LIKE ME THIS WHOLE TIME.
BUT I NEVER CONSIDERED...
IF YOU EVEN ENJOYED SPENDING TIME WITH ME.
EVEN THOUGH I TOLD YOU I'D MAKE YOU HAPPIER.
OH...

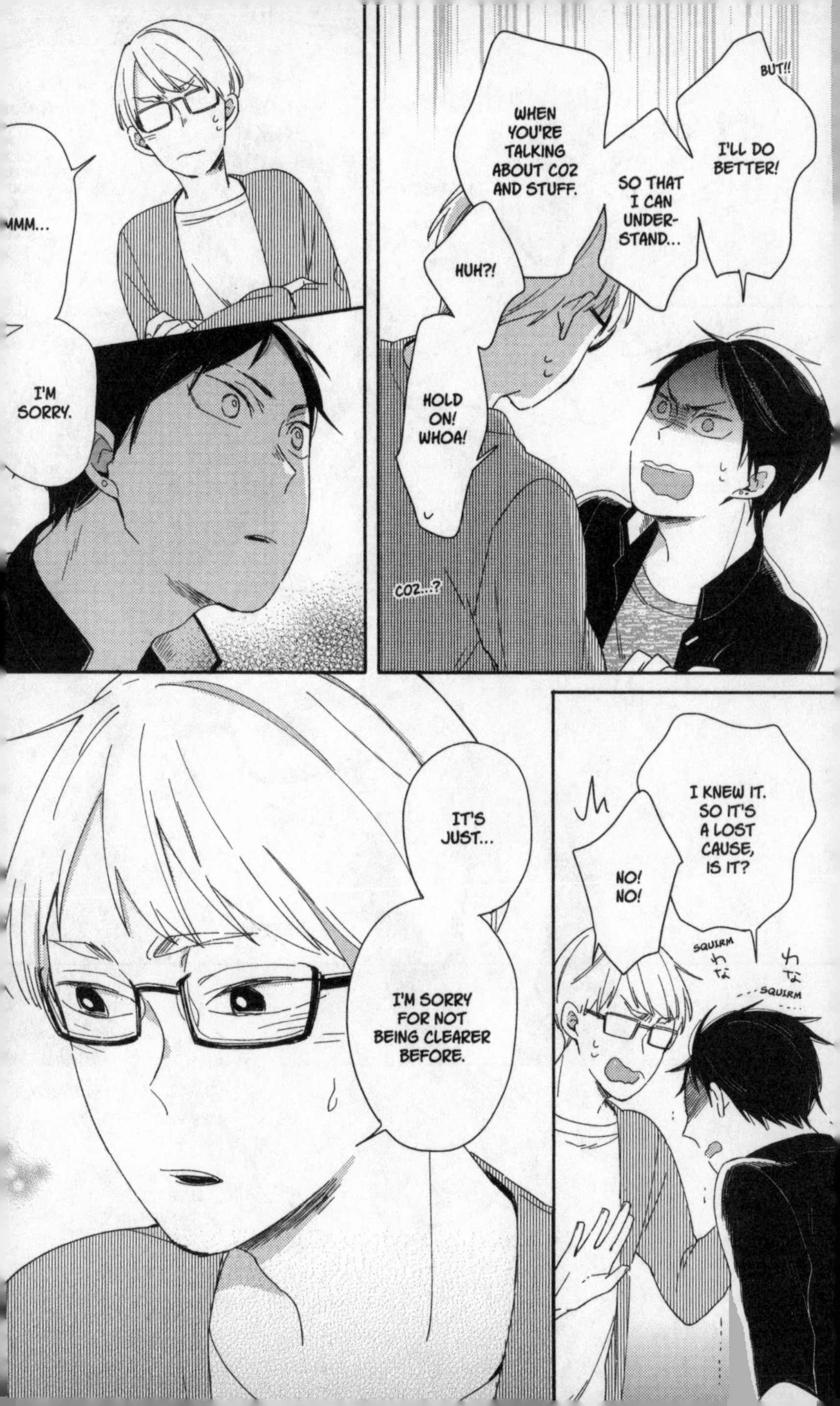
BUT!! I'LL DO BETTER!
SO THAT I CAN UNDERSTAND...
WHEN YOU'RE TALKING ABOUT COZ AND STUFF.
HUH?!
HOLD ON! WHOA!
COZ...?
MMM...
I'M SORRY.
I KNEW IT. SO IT'S A LOST CAUSE, IS IT?
NO! NO!
SQUIRM
SQUIRM
IT'S JUST...
I'M SORRY FOR NOT BEING CLEARER BEFORE.

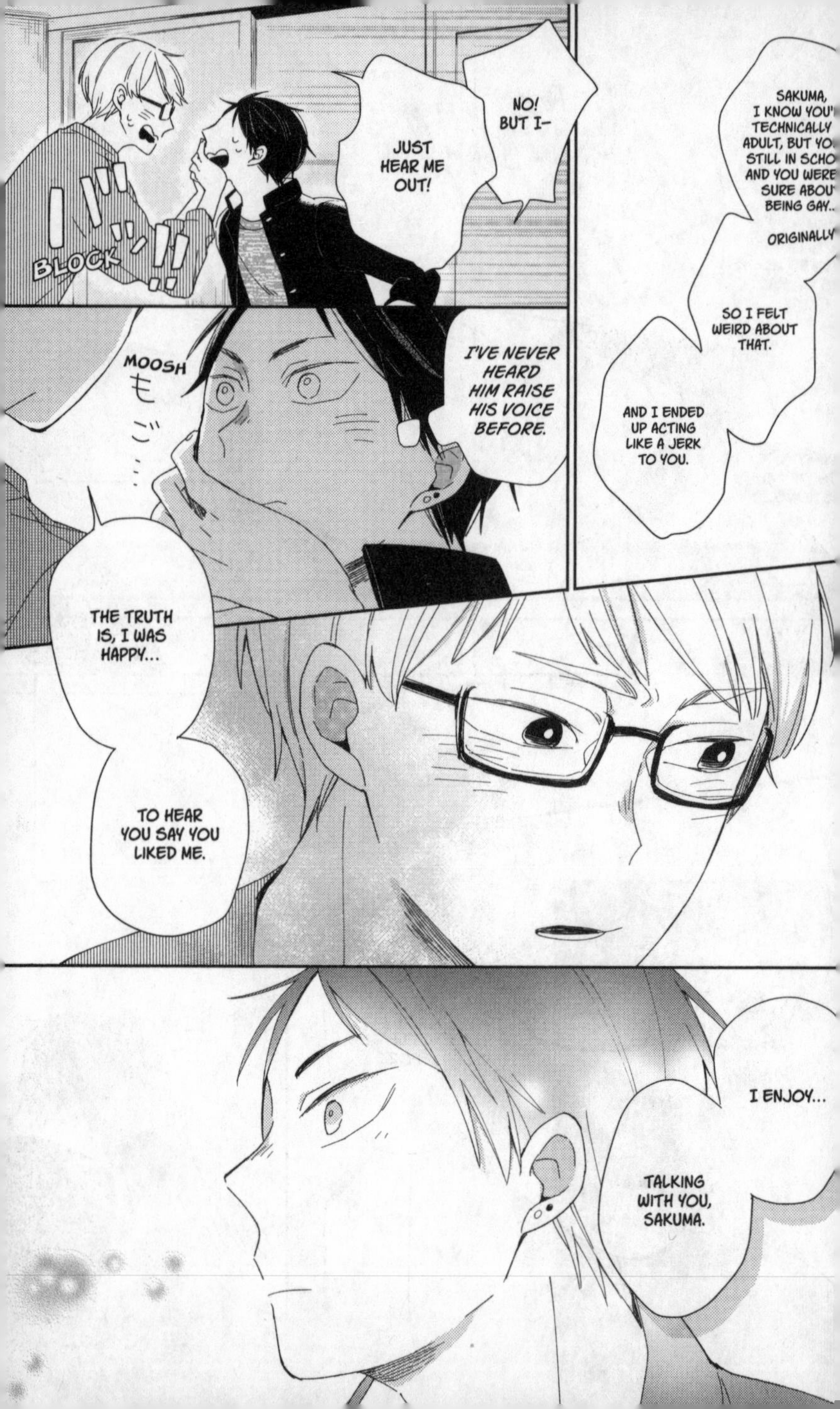

SAKUMA, I KNOW YOU' TECHNICALLY ADULT, BUT YO STILL IN SCHO AND YOU WERE SURE ABOU BEING GAY..
ORIGINALLY
SO I FELT WEIRD ABOUT THAT.
AND I ENDED UP ACTING LIKE A JERK TO YOU.
NO! BUT I-
JUST HEAR ME OUT!
BLOCK
I'VE NEVER HEARD HIM RAISE HIS VOICE BEFORE.
MOOSH
THE TRUTH IS, I WAS HAPPY...
TO HEAR YOU SAY YOU LIKED ME.
I ENJOY...
TALKING WITH YOU, SAKUMA.

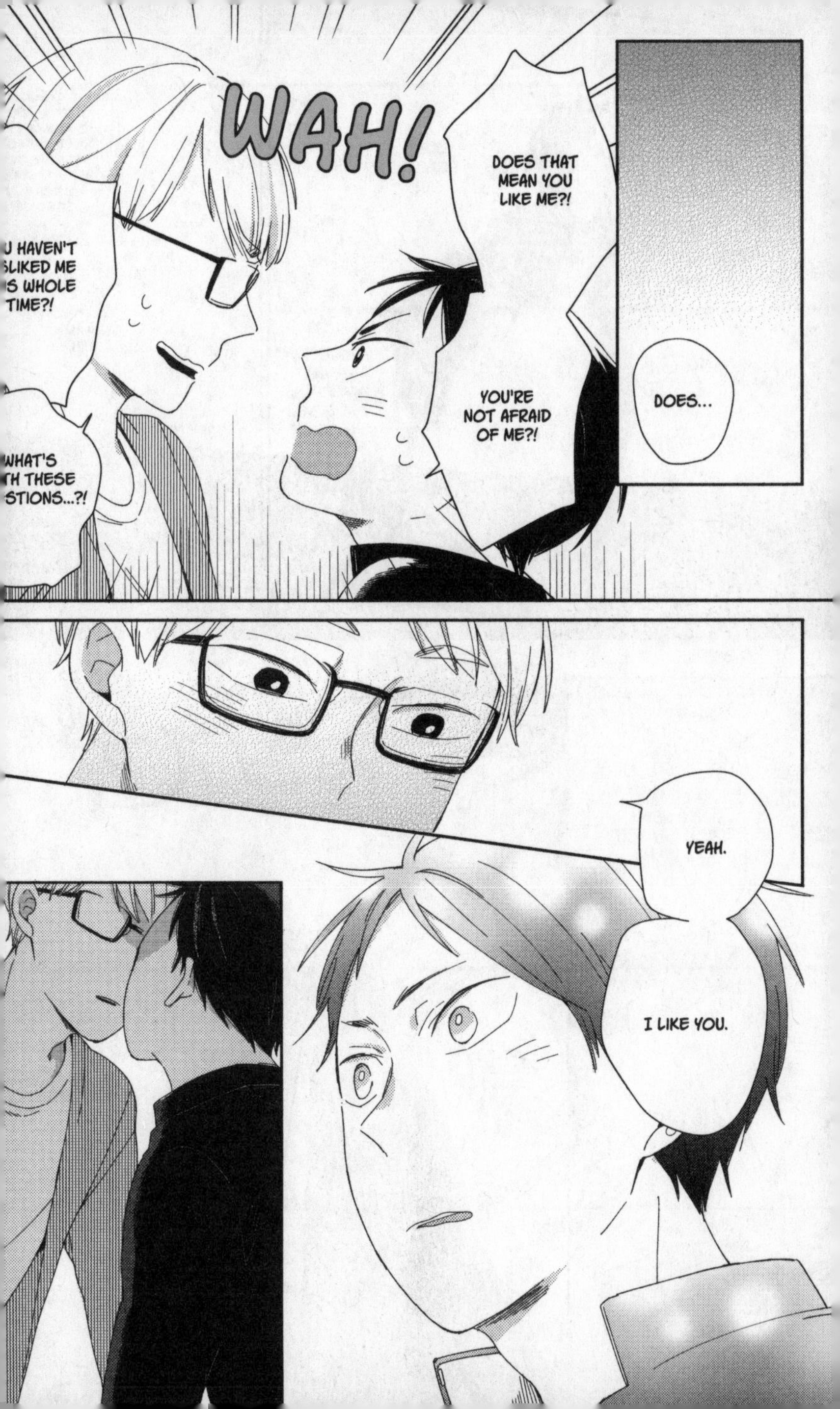
DOES...
DOES THAT MEAN YOU LIKE ME?!
YOU'RE NOT AFRAID OF ME?!
WAH!
U HAVEN'T SLIKED ME S WHOLE TIME?!
WHAT'S TH THESE STIONS...?!
YEAH.
I LIKE YOU.

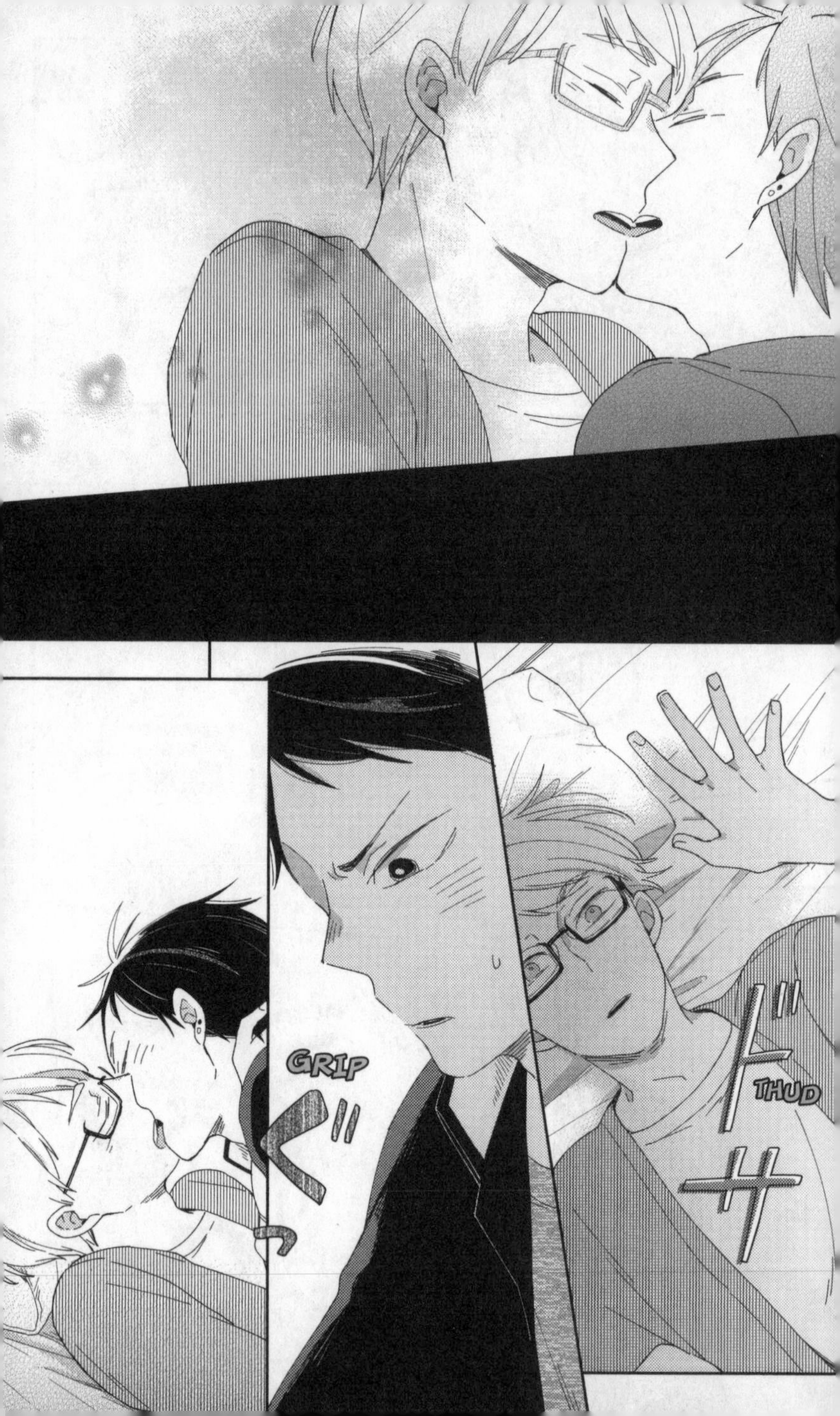
THUD
GRIP

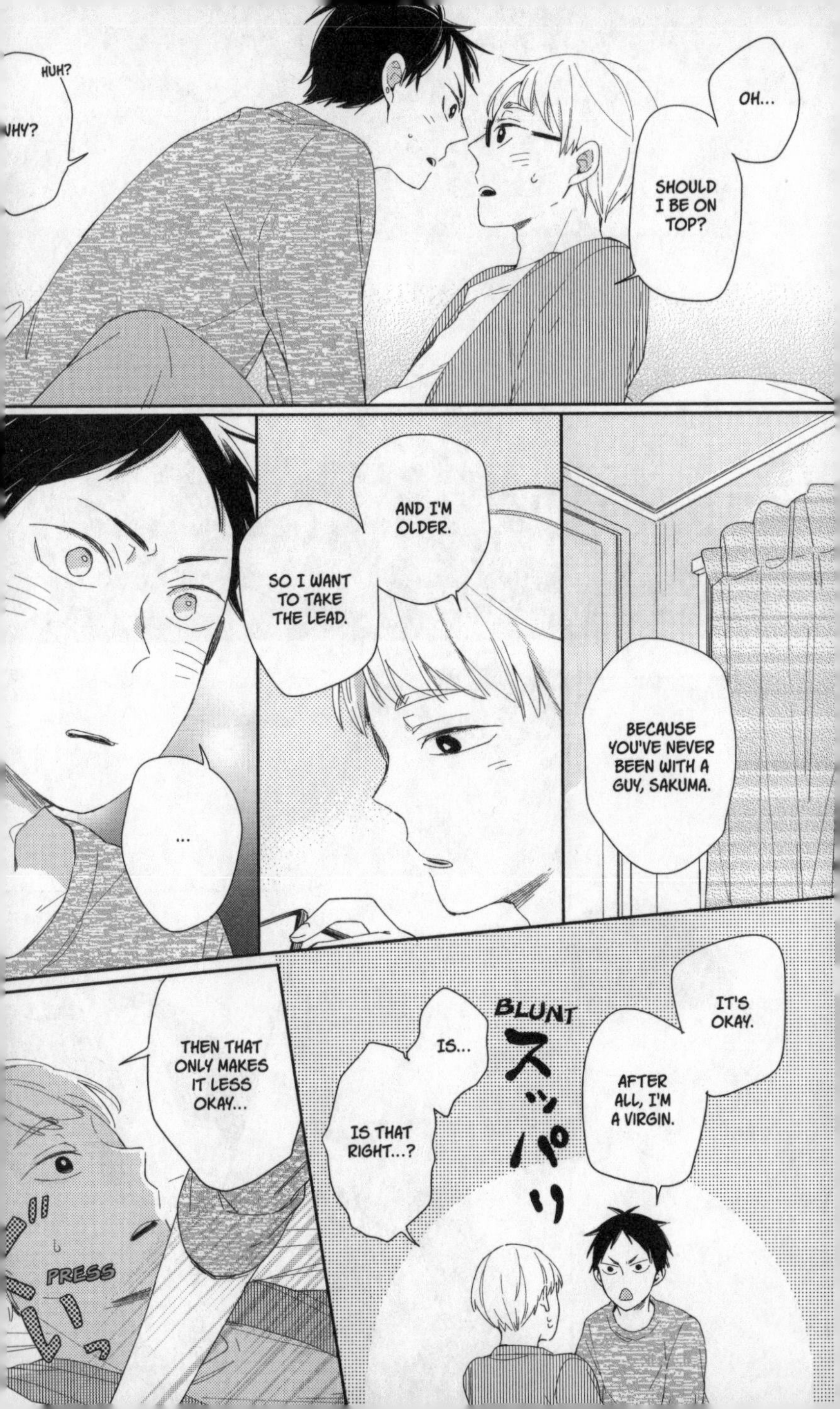
OH...
SHOULD I BE ON TOP?
HUH?
WHY?
BECAUSE YOU'VE NEVER BEEN WITH A GUY, SAKUMA.
AND I'M OLDER.
SO I WANT TO TAKE THE LEAD.
...
IT'S OKAY.
AFTER ALL, I'M A VIRGIN.
BLUNT
スッパリ
IS...
IS THAT RIGHT...?
THEN THAT ONLY MAKES IT LESS OKAY...
PRESS

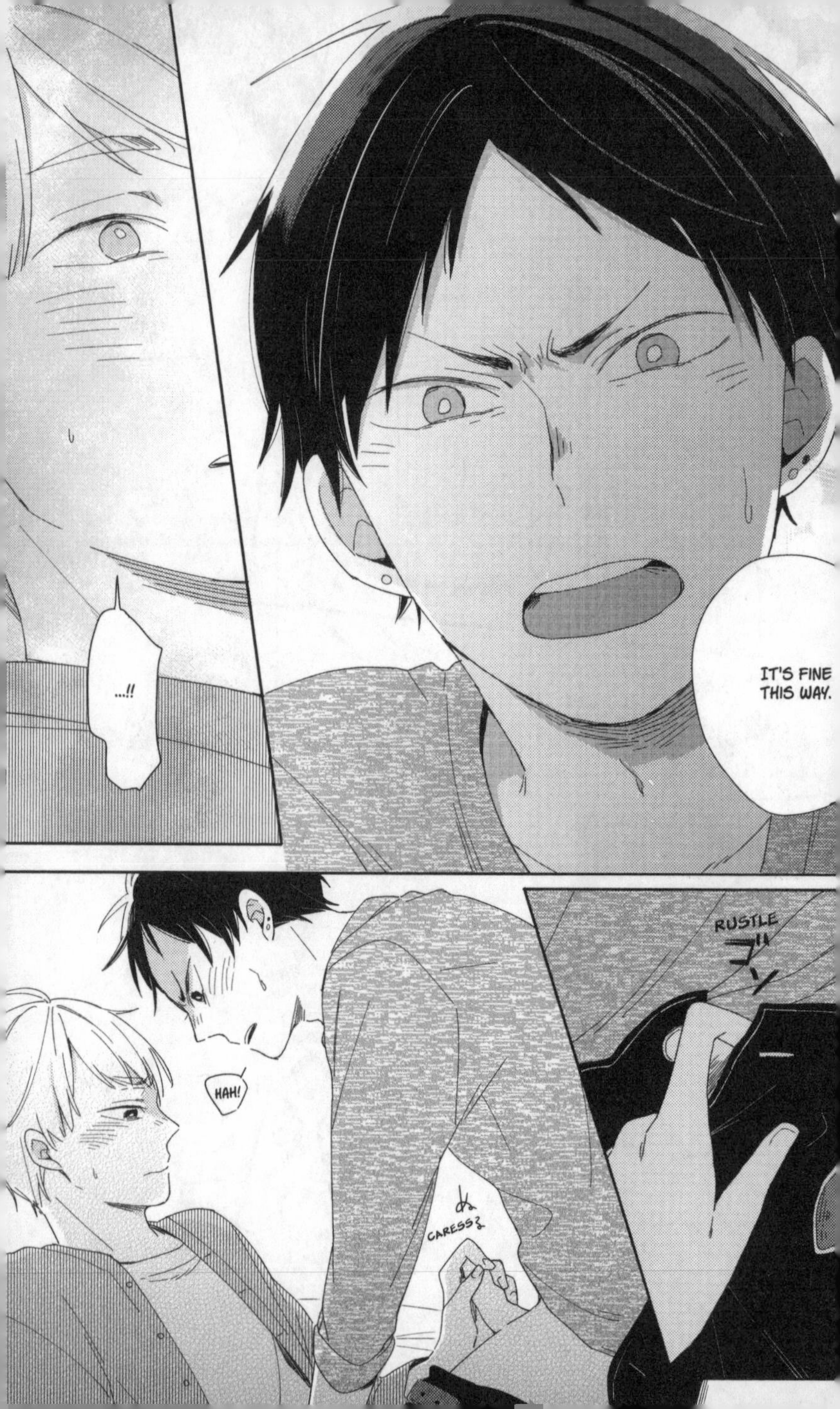

IT'S FINE THIS WAY.
...!!
RUSTLE
HAH!
CARESS

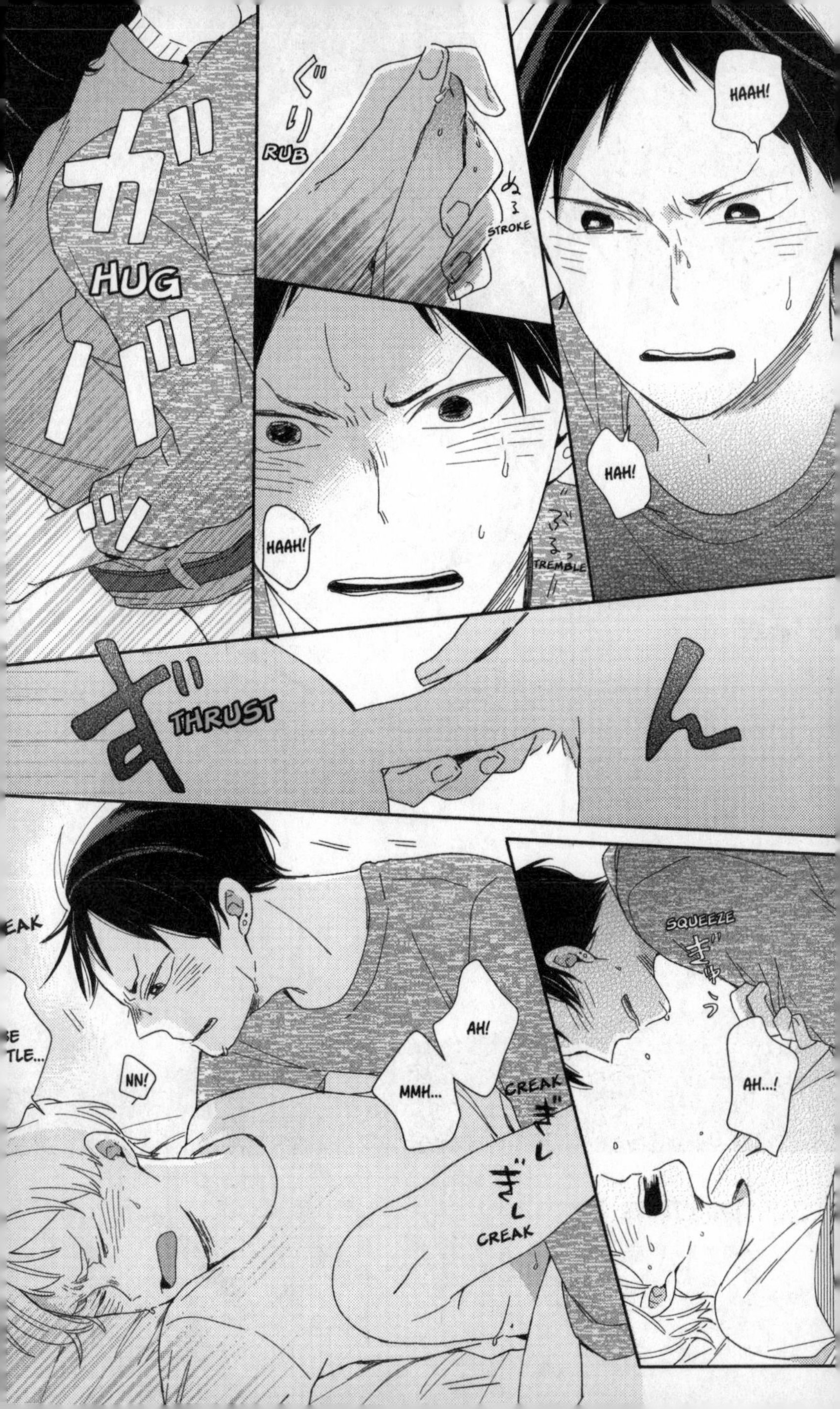
HAAH!
HAH!
ぐり
RUB
ぬる
STROKE
ぶる
TREMBLE
HAAH!
ガバ
HUG
ず
THRUST
ん
SQUEEZE
ぎゅう
AH...!
CREAK
ぎし
AH!
MMH...
NN!
ぎし
CREAK
EAK
BE
TLE...

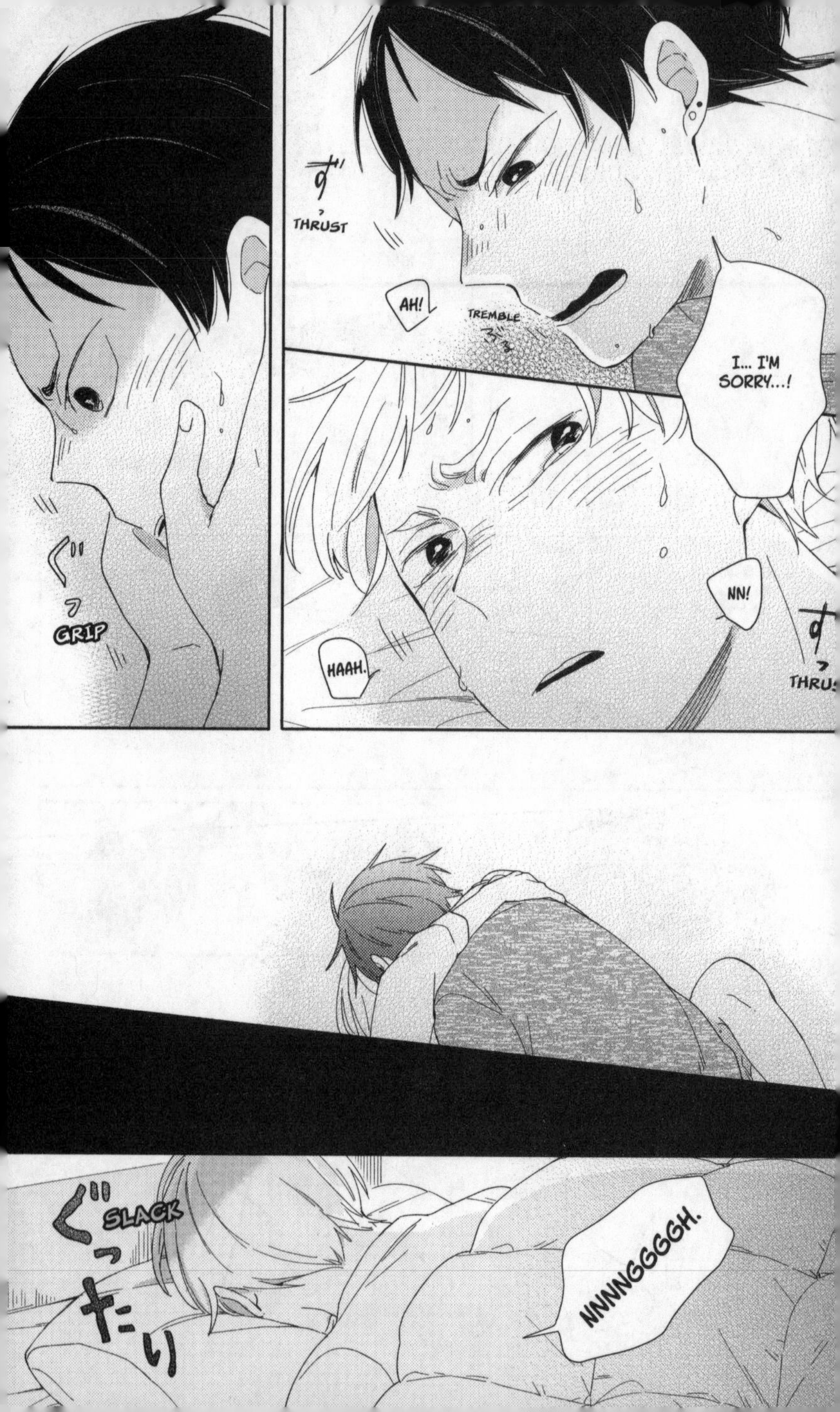
THRUST
AH!
TREMBLE
I... I'M SORRY...!
NN!
THRUS
HAAH.
GRIP
NNNNGGGGH.
SLACK

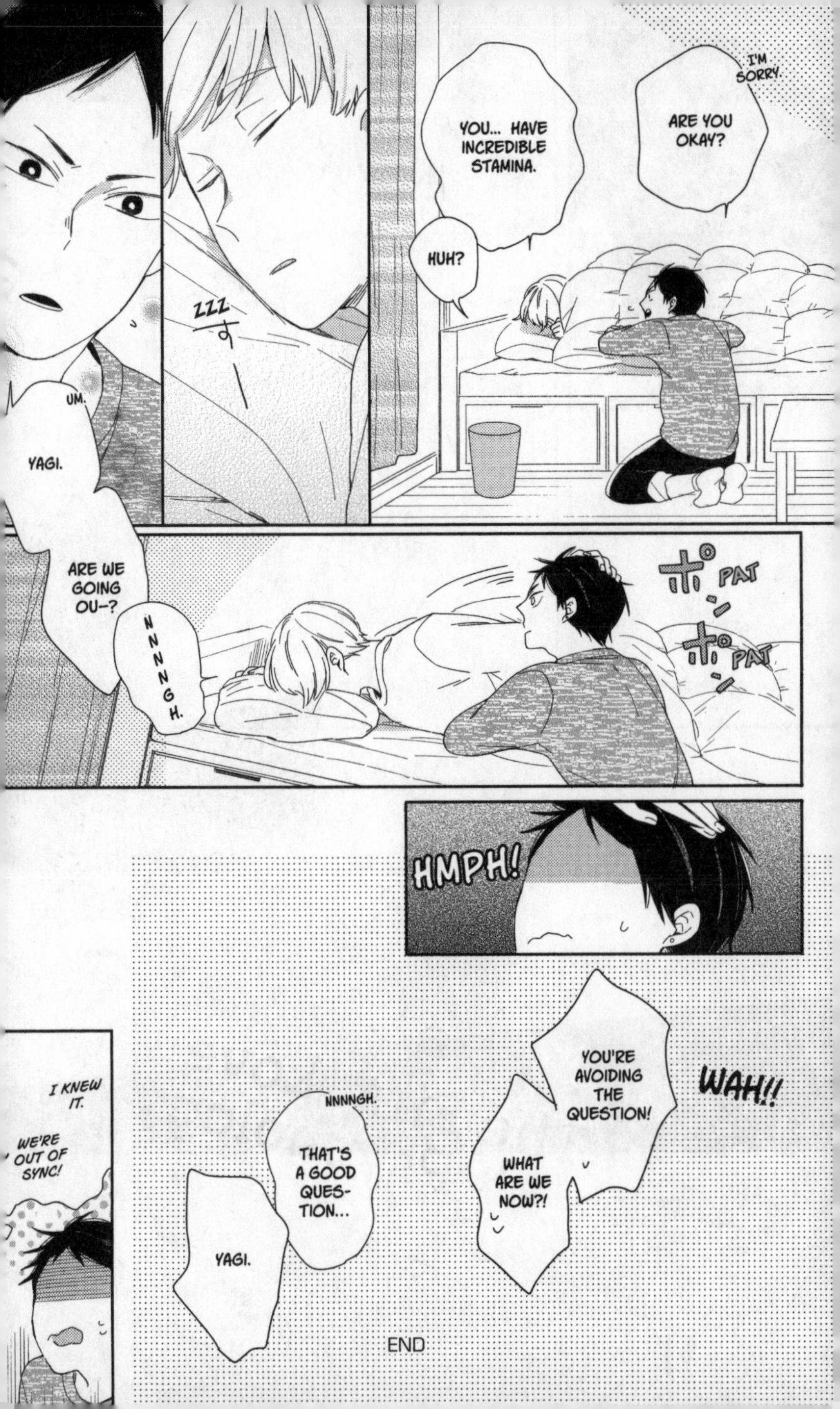
I'M SORRY.
ARE YOU OKAY?
YOU... HAVE INCREDIBLE STAMINA.
HUH?
ZZZ
UM.
YAGI.
ARE WE GOING OU-?
PAT
PAT
NNNNGH.
HMPH!
WAH!!
YOU'RE AVOIDING THE QUESTION!
WHAT ARE WE NOW?!
NNNNGH.
THAT'S A GOOD QUES-TION...
YAGI.
I KNEW IT.
WE'RE OUT OF SYNC!
END

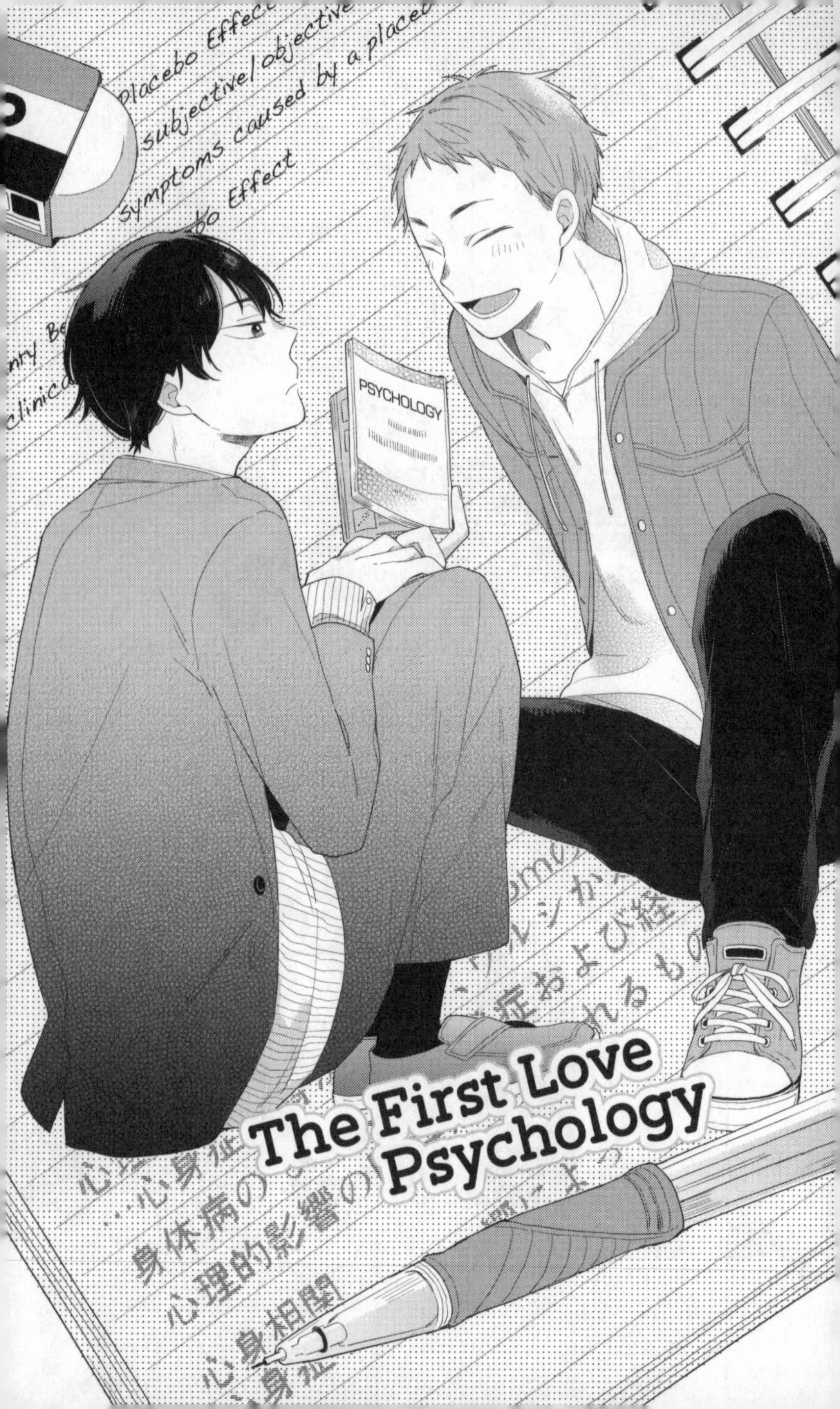

subjective/objective
PSYCHOLOGY
心理的影響の
心身相関
The First Love Psychology

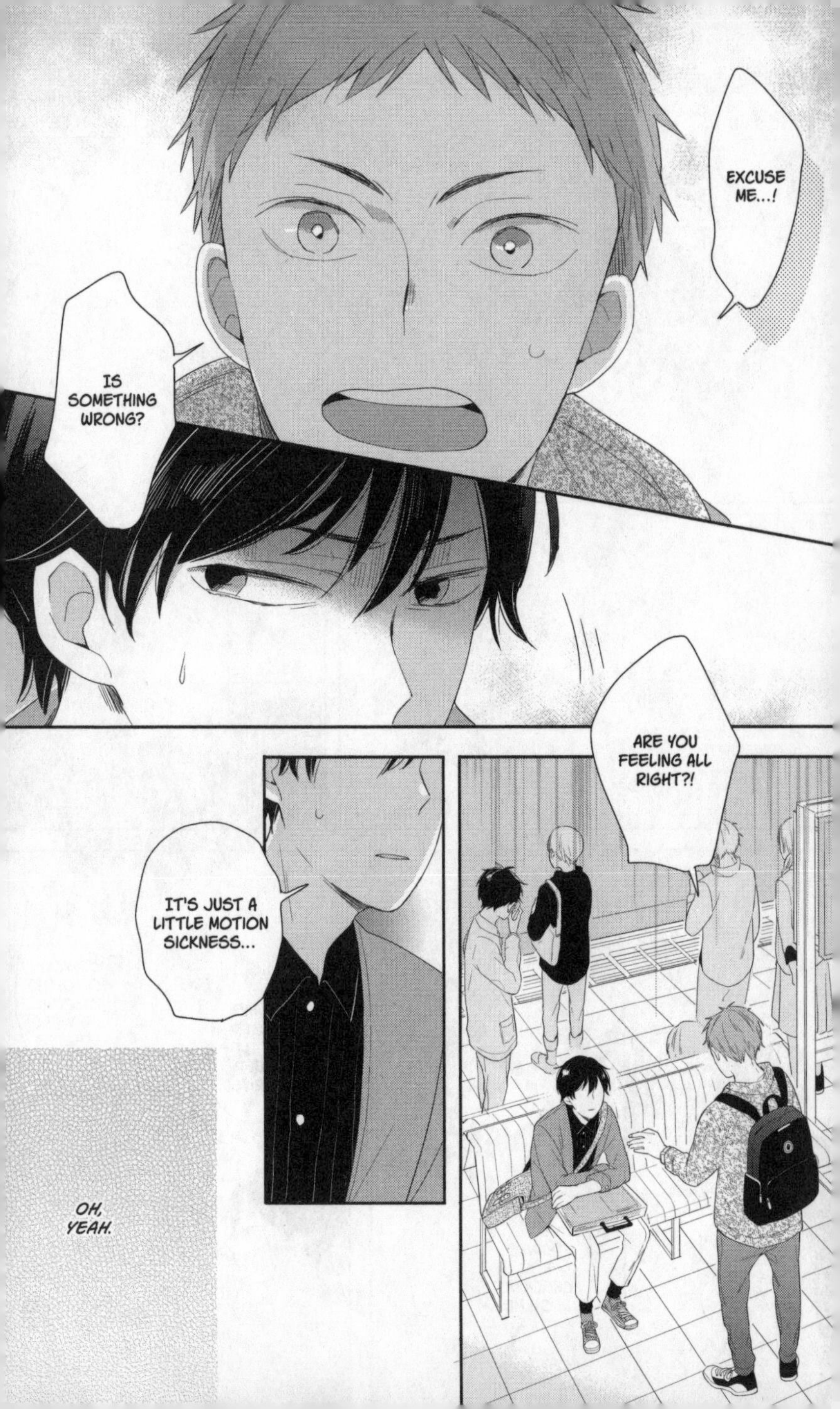
EXCUSE ME...!
IS SOMETHING WRONG?
ARE YOU FEELING ALL RIGHT?!
IT'S JUST A LITTLE MOTION SICKNESS...
OH, YEAH.

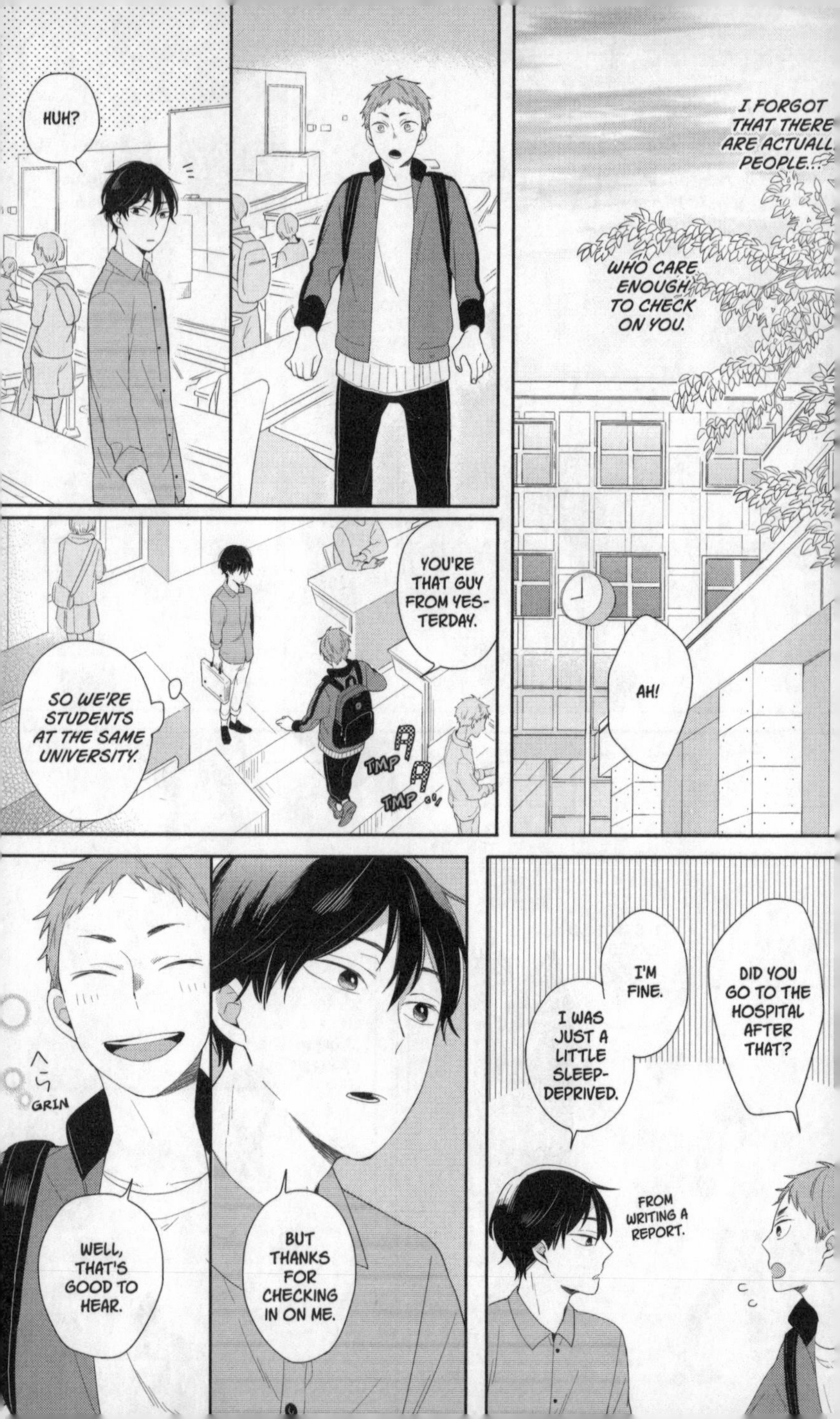
I FORGOT THAT THERE ARE ACTUALL PEOPLE...
WHO CARE ENOUGH TO CHECK ON YOU.
AH!
HUH?
YOU'RE THAT GUY FROM YES-TERDAY.
SO WE'RE STUDENTS AT THE SAME UNIVERSITY.
TMP
TMP
DID YOU GO TO THE HOSPITAL AFTER THAT?
I'M FINE.
I WAS JUST A LITTLE SLEEP-DEPRIVED.
FROM WRITING A REPORT.
BUT THANKS FOR CHECKING IN ON ME.
GRIN
WELL, THAT'S GOOD TO HEAR.

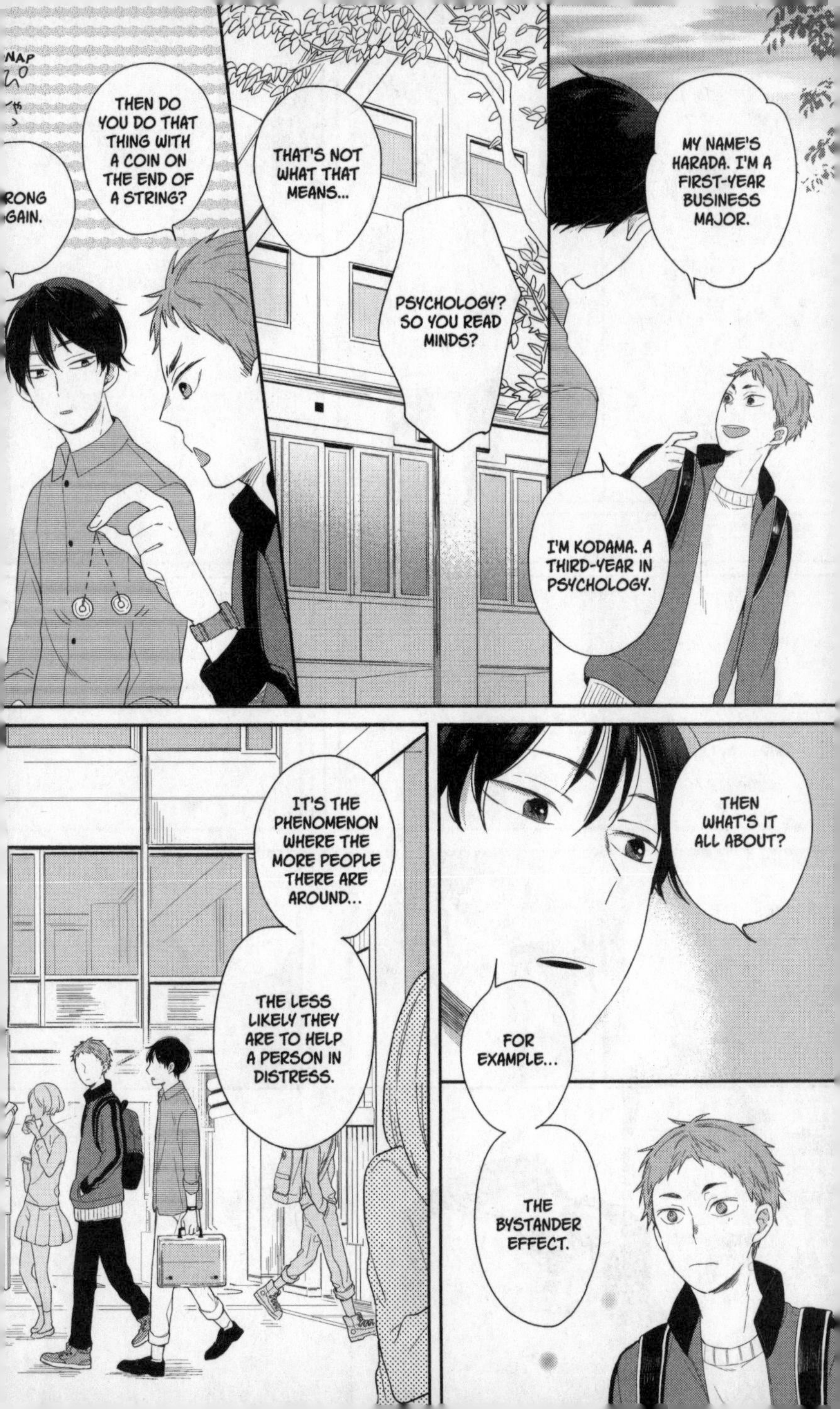
MY NAME'S HARADA. I'M A FIRST-YEAR BUSINESS MAJOR.
I'M KODAMA. A THIRD-YEAR IN PSYCHOLOGY.
PSYCHOLOGY? SO YOU READ MINDS?
THAT'S NOT WHAT THAT MEANS...
THEN DO YOU DO THAT THING WITH A COIN ON THE END OF A STRING?
NAP
RONG
GAIN.
THEN WHAT'S IT ALL ABOUT?
FOR EXAMPLE...
THE BYSTANDER EFFECT.
IT'S THE PHENOMENON WHERE THE MORE PEOPLE THERE ARE AROUND...
THE LESS LIKELY THEY ARE TO HELP A PERSON IN DISTRESS.

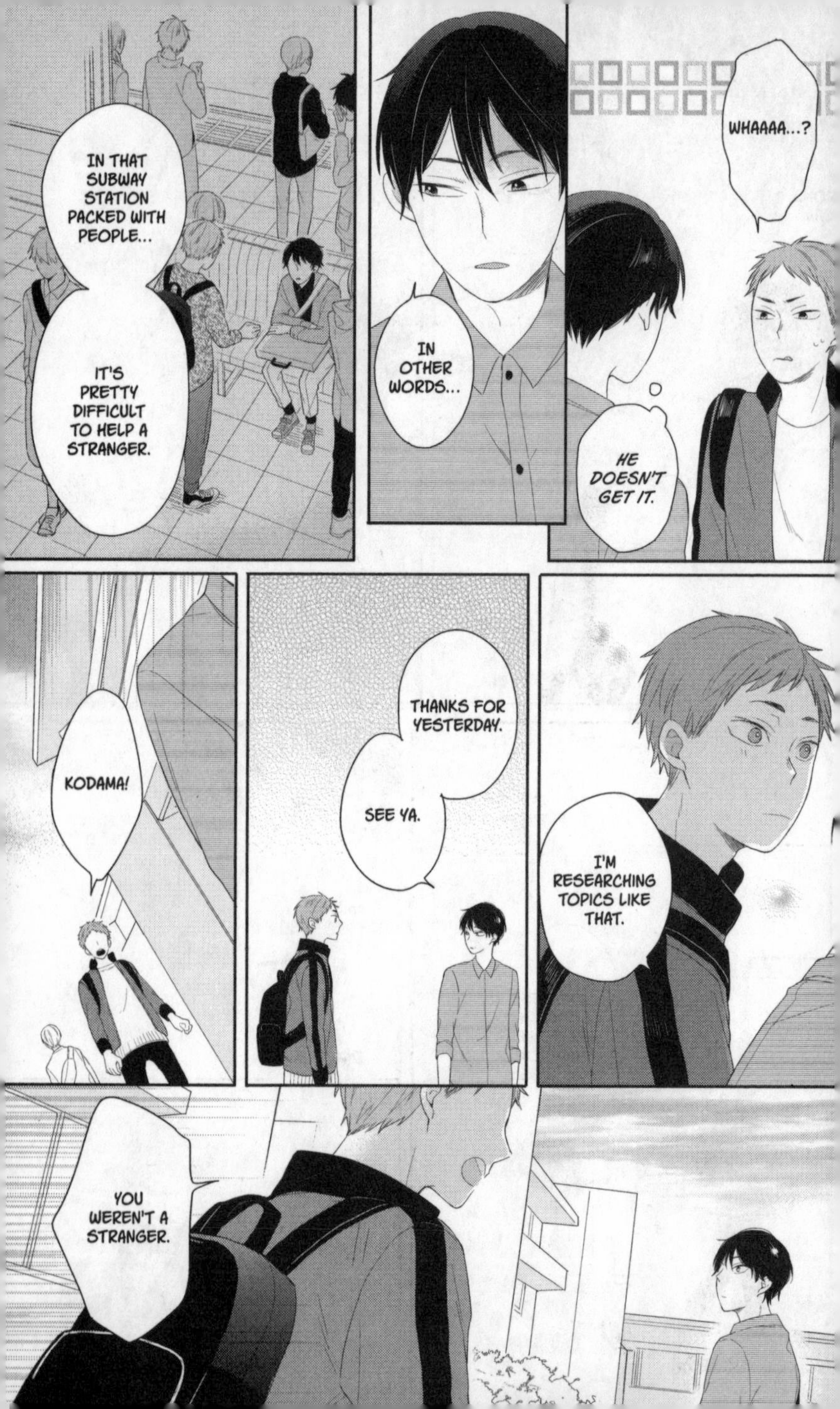
WHAAAA...?
HE DOESN'T GET IT.
IN OTHER WORDS...
IN THAT SUBWAY STATION PACKED WITH PEOPLE...
IT'S PRETTY DIFFICULT TO HELP A STRANGER.
I'M RESEARCHING TOPICS LIKE THAT.
THANKS FOR YESTERDAY.
SEE YA.
KODAMA!
YOU WEREN'T A STRANGER.

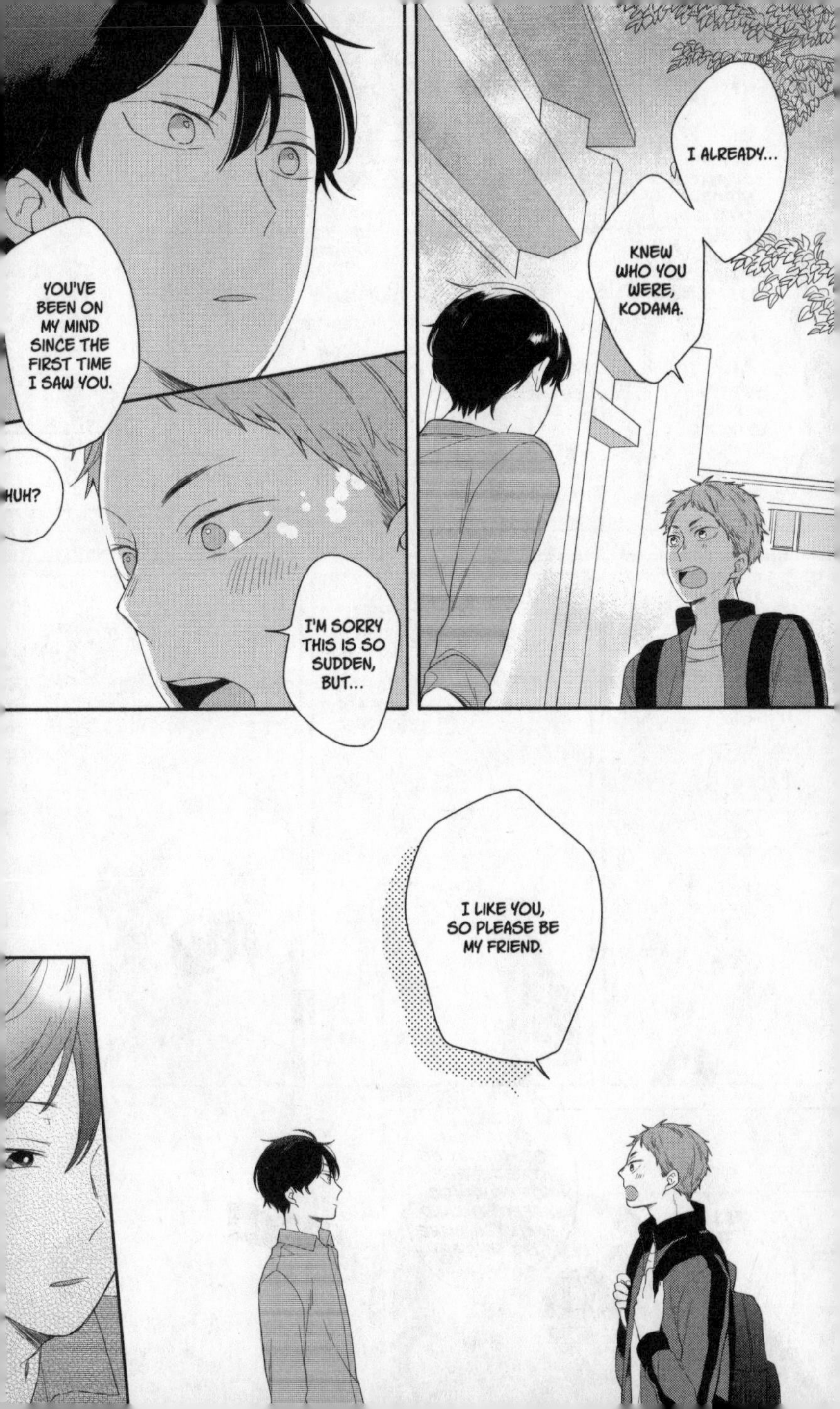
I ALREADY...
KNEW WHO YOU WERE, KODAMA.
YOU'VE BEEN ON MY MIND SINCE THE FIRST TIME I SAW YOU.
HUH?
I'M SORRY THIS IS SO SUDDEN, BUT...
I LIKE YOU, SO PLEASE BE MY FRIEND.

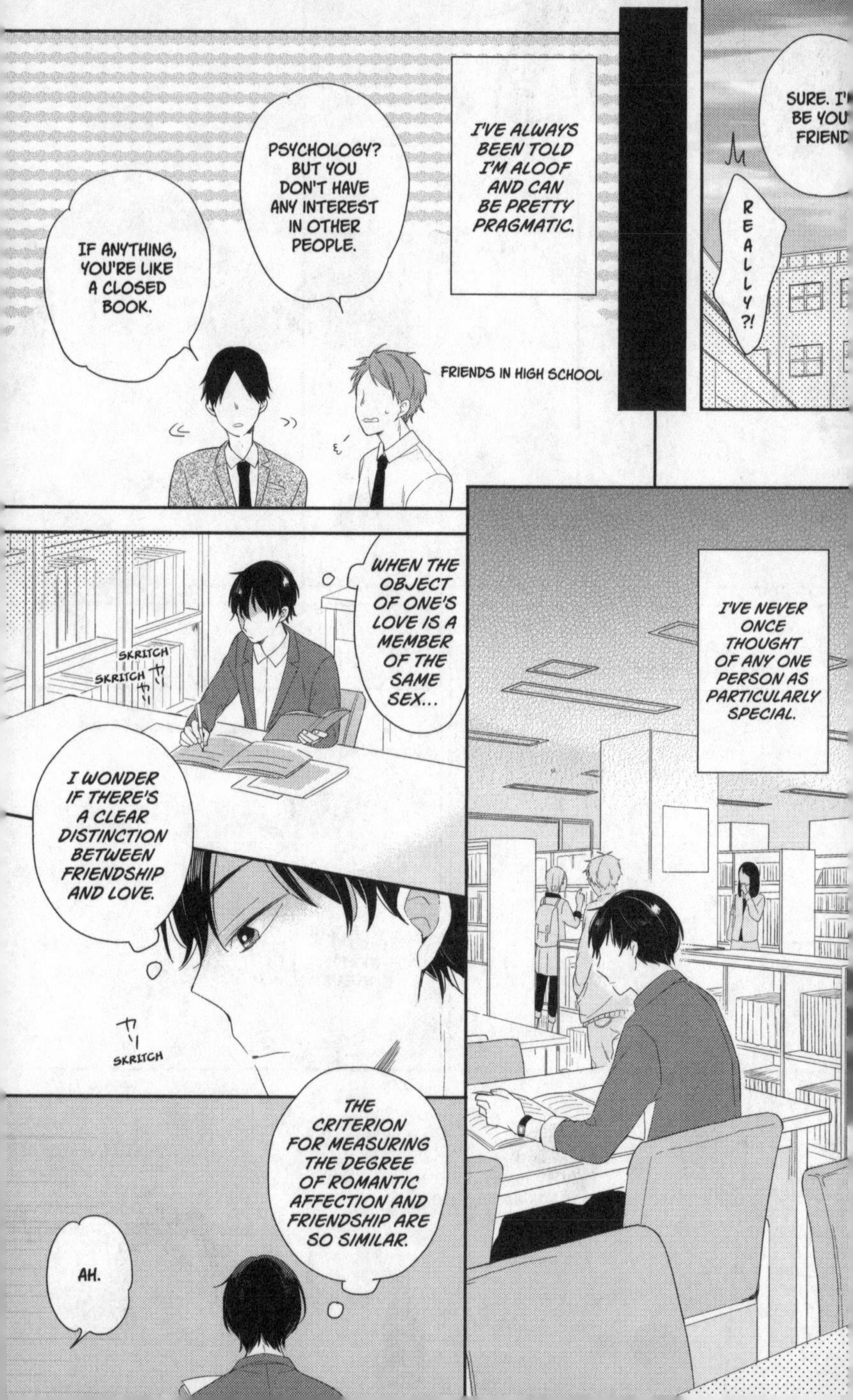

SURE. I'
BE YOU
FRIEND
REALLY?!
I'VE ALWAYS BEEN TOLD I'M ALOOF AND CAN BE PRETTY PRAGMATIC.
PSYCHOLOGY? BUT YOU DON'T HAVE ANY INTEREST IN OTHER PEOPLE.
IF ANYTHING, YOU'RE LIKE A CLOSED BOOK.
FRIENDS IN HIGH SCHOOL
I'VE NEVER ONCE THOUGHT OF ANY ONE PERSON AS PARTICULARLY SPECIAL.
WHEN THE OBJECT OF ONE'S LOVE IS A MEMBER OF THE SAME SEX...
SKRITCH
SKRITCH
I WONDER IF THERE'S A CLEAR DISTINCTION BETWEEN FRIENDSHIP AND LOVE.
SKRITCH
THE CRITERION FOR MEASURING THE DEGREE OF ROMANTIC AFFECTION AND FRIENDSHIP ARE SO SIMILAR.
AH.

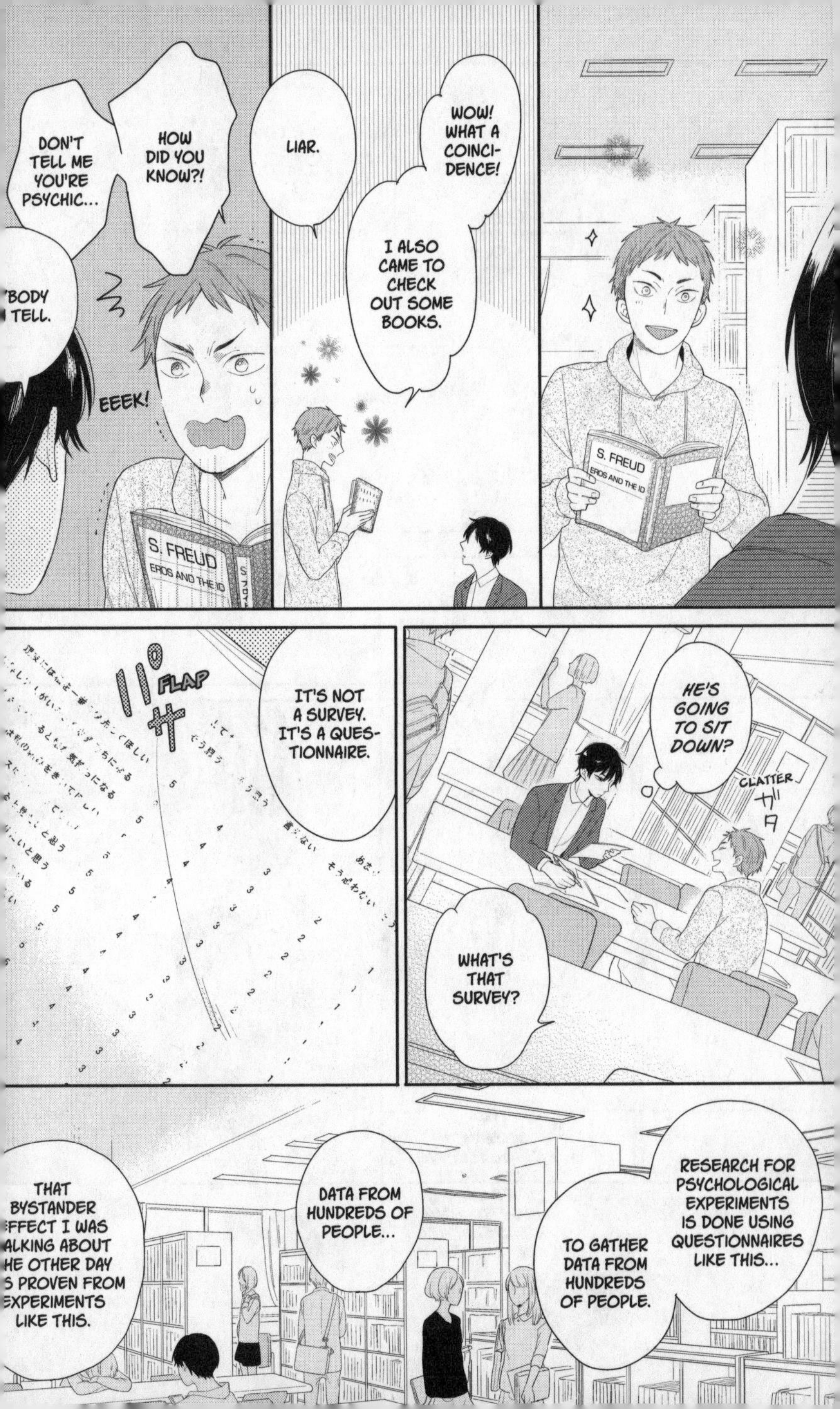

WOW! WHAT A COINCIDENCE!
I ALSO CAME TO CHECK OUT SOME BOOKS.
S. FREUD
EROS AND THE ID
LIAR.
HOW DID YOU KNOW?!
DON'T TELL ME YOU'RE PSYCHIC...
'BODY TELL.
EEEK!
S. FREUD
EROS AND THE ID
HE'S GOING TO SIT DOWN?
CLATTER
ガタ
WHAT'S THAT SURVEY?
IT'S NOT A SURVEY. IT'S A QUESTIONNAIRE.
パサ
FLAP
RESEARCH FOR PSYCHOLOGICAL EXPERIMENTS IS DONE USING QUESTIONNAIRES LIKE THIS...
TO GATHER DATA FROM HUNDREDS OF PEOPLE.
DATA FROM HUNDREDS OF PEOPLE...
THAT BYSTANDER EFFECT I WAS ALKING ABOUT HE OTHER DAY S PROVEN FROM EXPERIMENTS LIKE THIS.

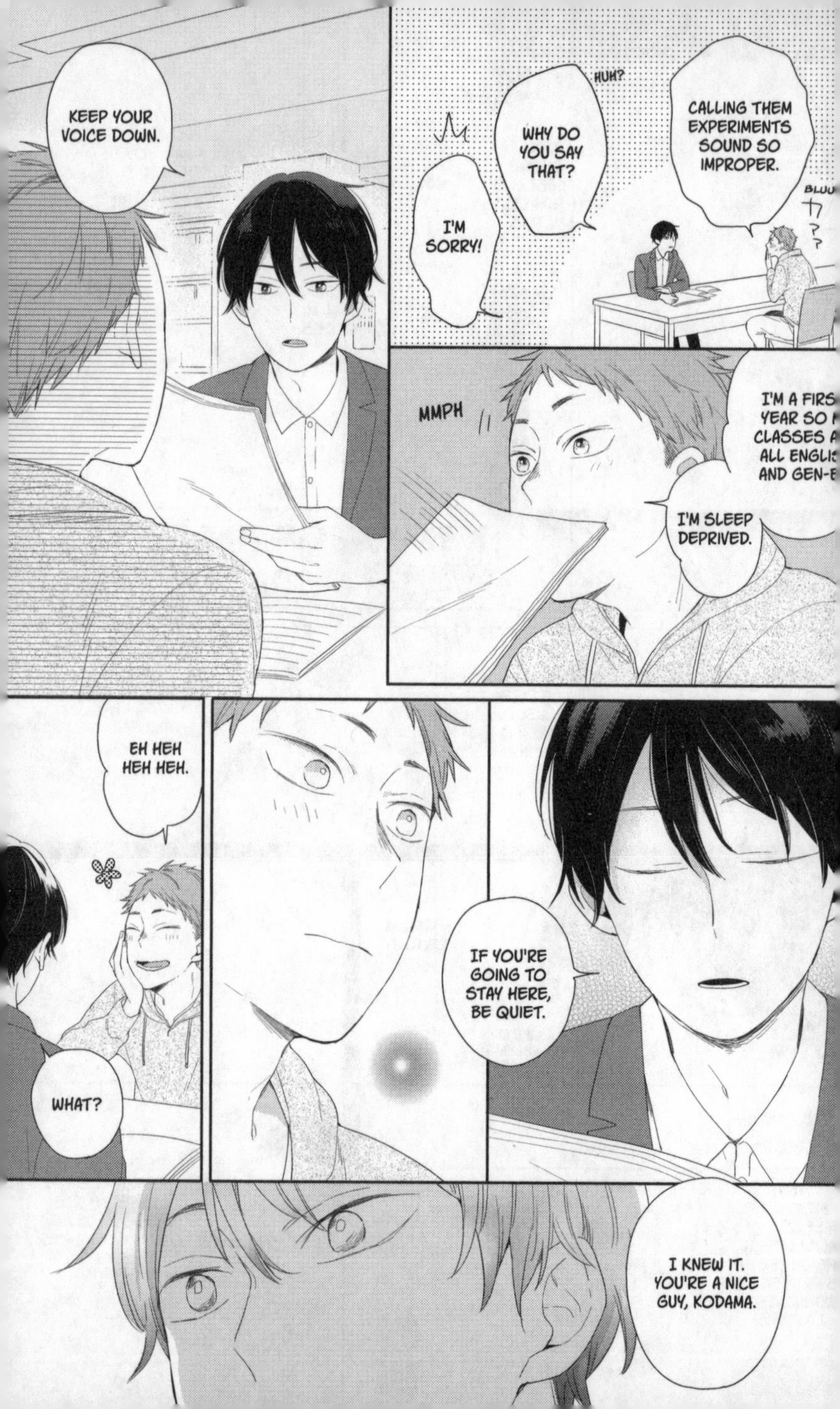
CALLING THEM EXPERIMENTS SOUND SO IMPROPER.
BLUU
HUH?
WHY DO YOU SAY THAT?
I'M SORRY!
I'M A FIRS YEAR SO CLASSES A ALL ENGLIS AND GEN-E
I'M SLEEP DEPRIVED.
MMPH
KEEP YOUR VOICE DOWN.
IF YOU'RE GOING TO STAY HERE, BE QUIET.
EH HEH HEH HEH.
WHAT?
I KNEW IT. YOU'RE A NICE GUY, KODAMA.

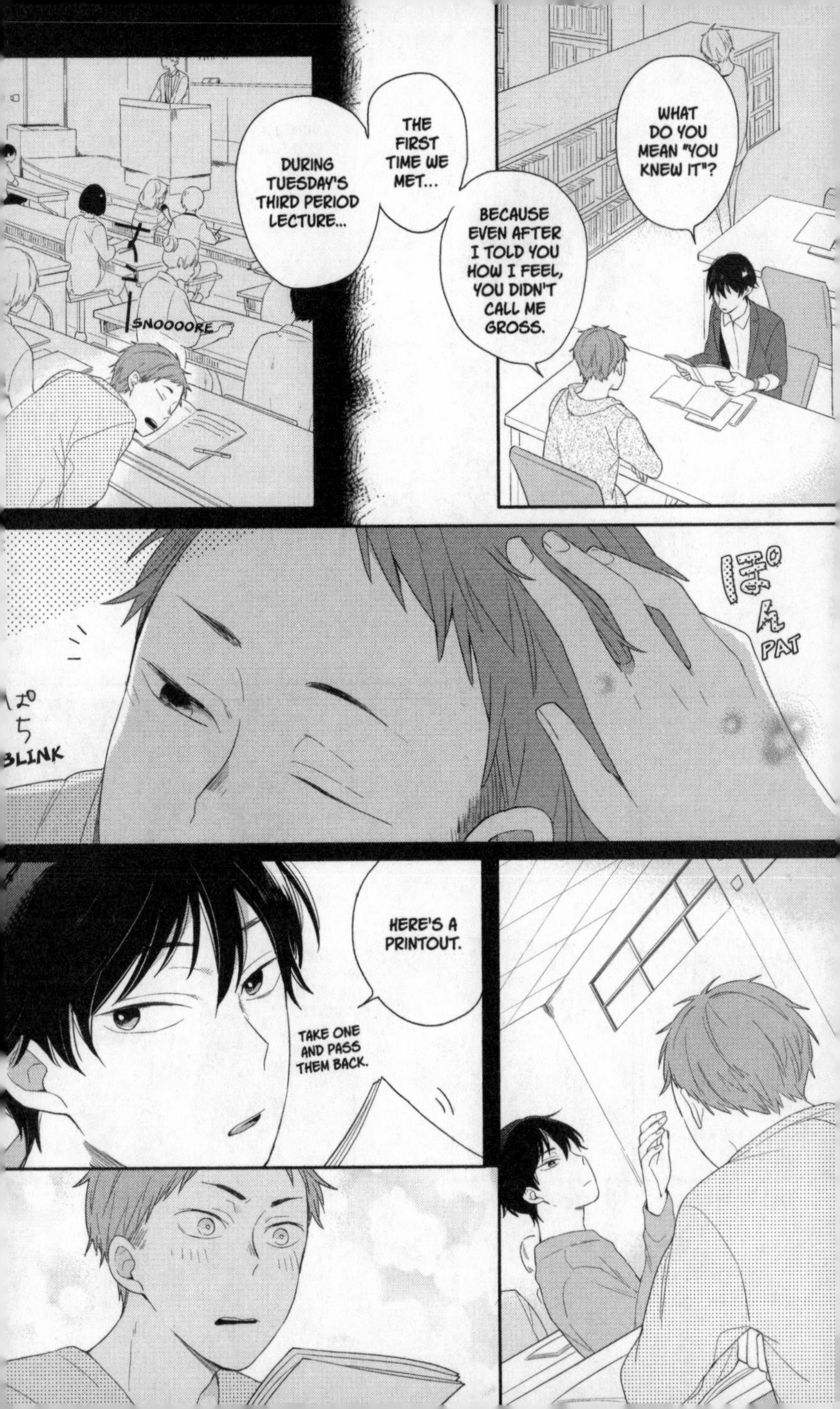
WHAT DO YOU MEAN "YOU KNEW IT"?
BECAUSE EVEN AFTER I TOLD YOU HOW I FEEL, YOU DIDN'T CALL ME GROSS.
THE FIRST TIME WE MET...
DURING TUESDAY'S THIRD PERIOD LECTURE...
SNOOOORE
ぽん
PAT
BLINK
HERE'S A PRINTOUT.
TAKE ONE AND PASS THEM BACK.

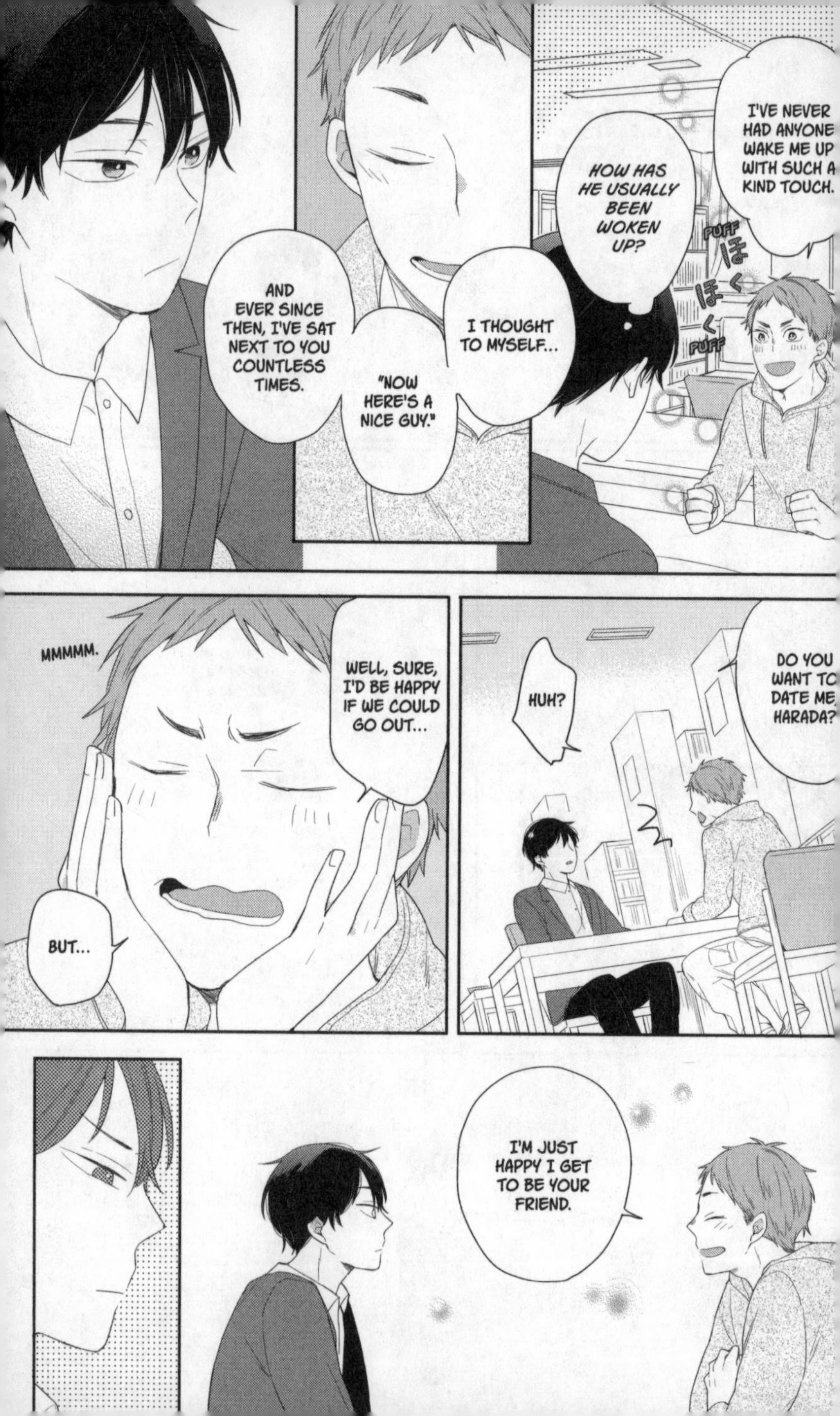
I'VE NEVER HAD ANYONE WAKE ME UP WITH SUCH A KIND TOUCH.
HOW HAS HE USUALLY BEEN WOKEN UP?
ほく PUFF
ほく PUFF
I THOUGHT TO MYSELF...
"NOW HERE'S A NICE GUY."
AND EVER SINCE THEN, I'VE SAT NEXT TO YOU COUNTLESS TIMES.
DO YOU WANT TO DATE ME, HARADA?
HUH?
WELL, SURE, I'D BE HAPPY IF WE COULD GO OUT...
MMMMM.
BUT...
I'M JUST HAPPY I GET TO BE YOUR FRIEND.

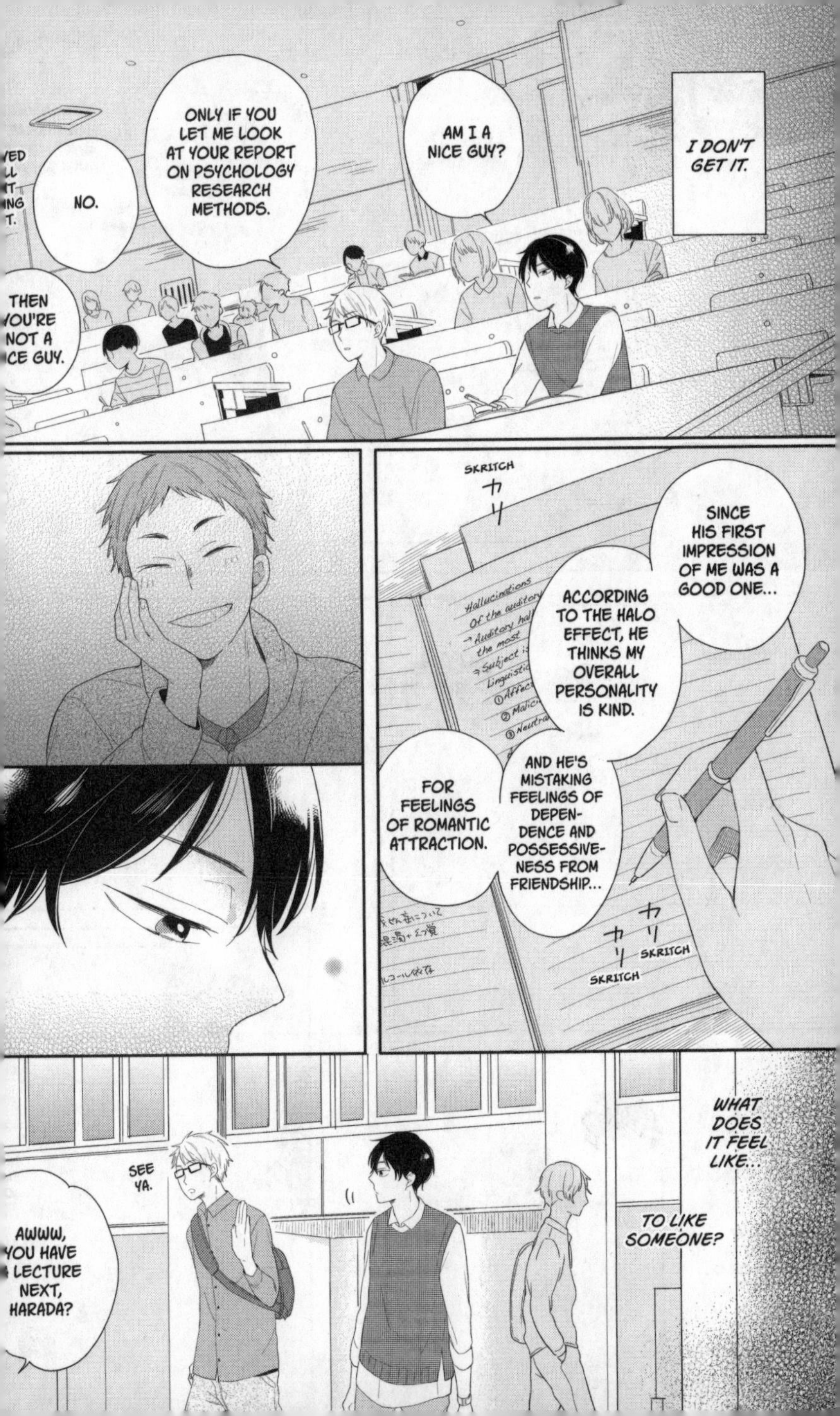
I DON'T GET IT.
AM I A NICE GUY?
ONLY IF YOU LET ME LOOK AT YOUR REPORT ON PSYCHOLOGY RESEARCH METHODS.
NO.
THEN OU'RE NOT A CE GUY.
SKRITCH
カリ
SINCE HIS FIRST IMPRESSION OF ME WAS A GOOD ONE...
ACCORDING TO THE HALO EFFECT, HE THINKS MY OVERALL PERSONALITY IS KIND.
AND HE'S MISTAKING FEELINGS OF DEPENDENCE AND POSSESSIVENESS FROM FRIENDSHIP...
FOR FEELINGS OF ROMANTIC ATTRACTION.
カリ SKRITCH
カリ SKRITCH
WHAT DOES IT FEEL LIKE...
TO LIKE SOMEONE?
SEE YA.
AWWW, YOU HAVE LECTURE NEXT, HARADA?

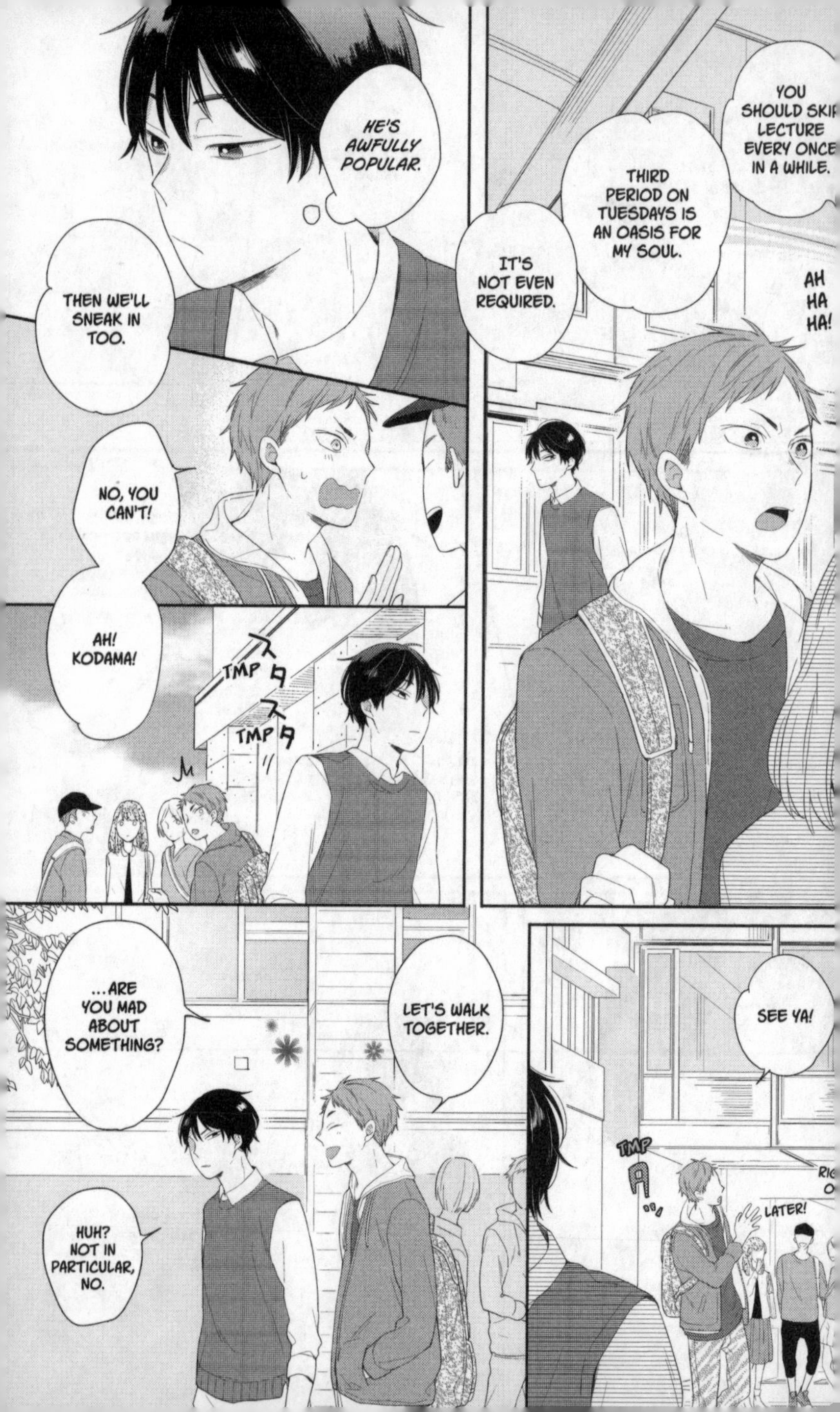
YOU SHOULD SKI LECTURE EVERY ONCE IN A WHILE.
THIRD PERIOD ON TUESDAYS IS AN OASIS FOR MY SOUL.
IT'S NOT EVEN REQUIRED.
AH HA HA!
HE'S AWFULLY POPULAR.
THEN WE'LL SNEAK IN TOO.
NO, YOU CAN'T!
AH! KODAMA!
TMP
TMP
SEE YA!
TMP
LATER!
LET'S WALK TOGETHER.
...ARE YOU MAD ABOUT SOMETHING?
HUH? NOT IN PARTICULAR, NO.

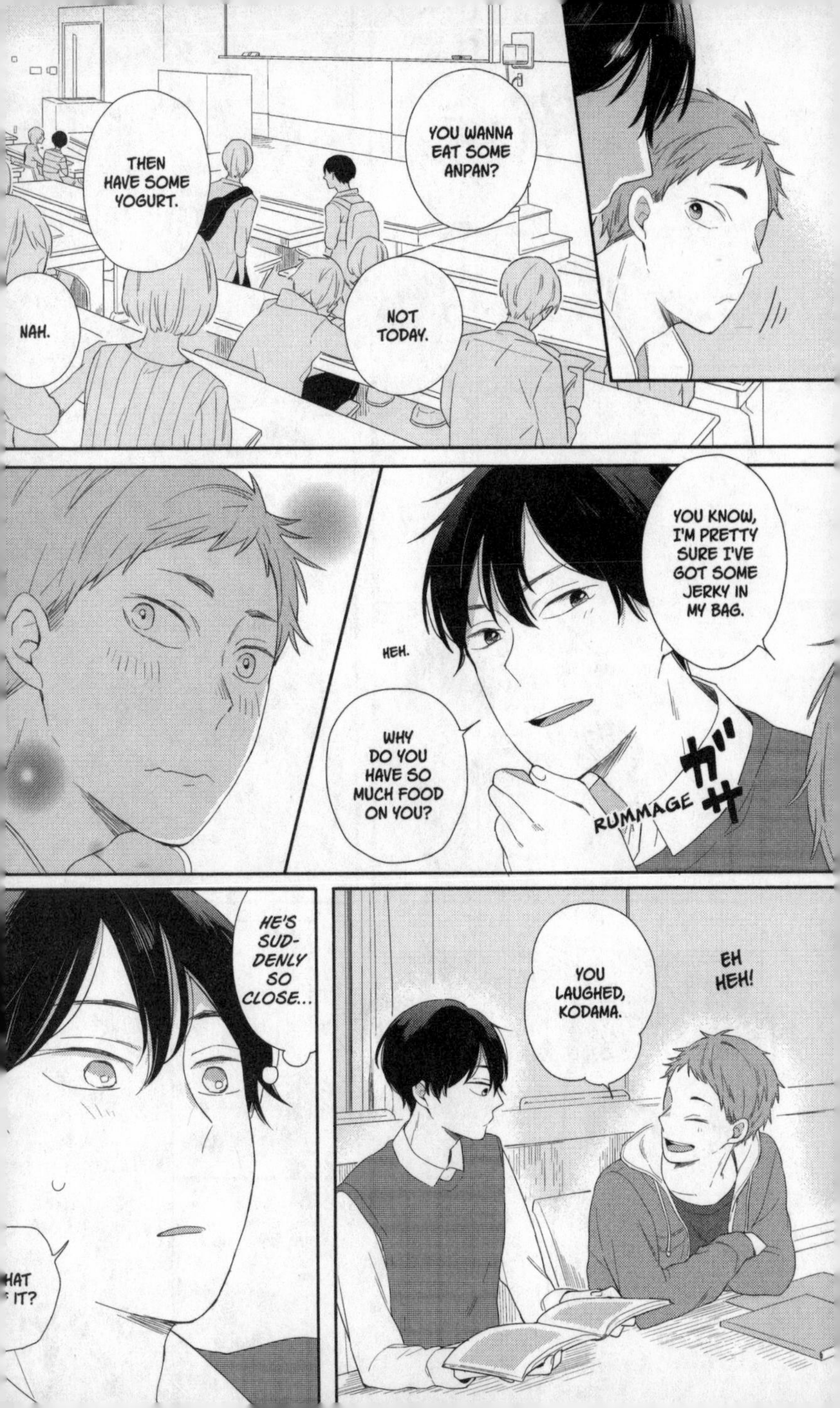
YOU WANNA EAT SOME ANPAN?
NOT TODAY.
THEN HAVE SOME YOGURT.
NAH.
YOU KNOW, I'M PRETTY SURE I'VE GOT SOME JERKY IN MY BAG.
HEH.
WHY DO YOU HAVE SO MUCH FOOD ON YOU?
RUMMAGE
EH HEH!
YOU LAUGHED, KODAMA.
HE'S SUD-DENLY SO CLOSE...
HAT IT?

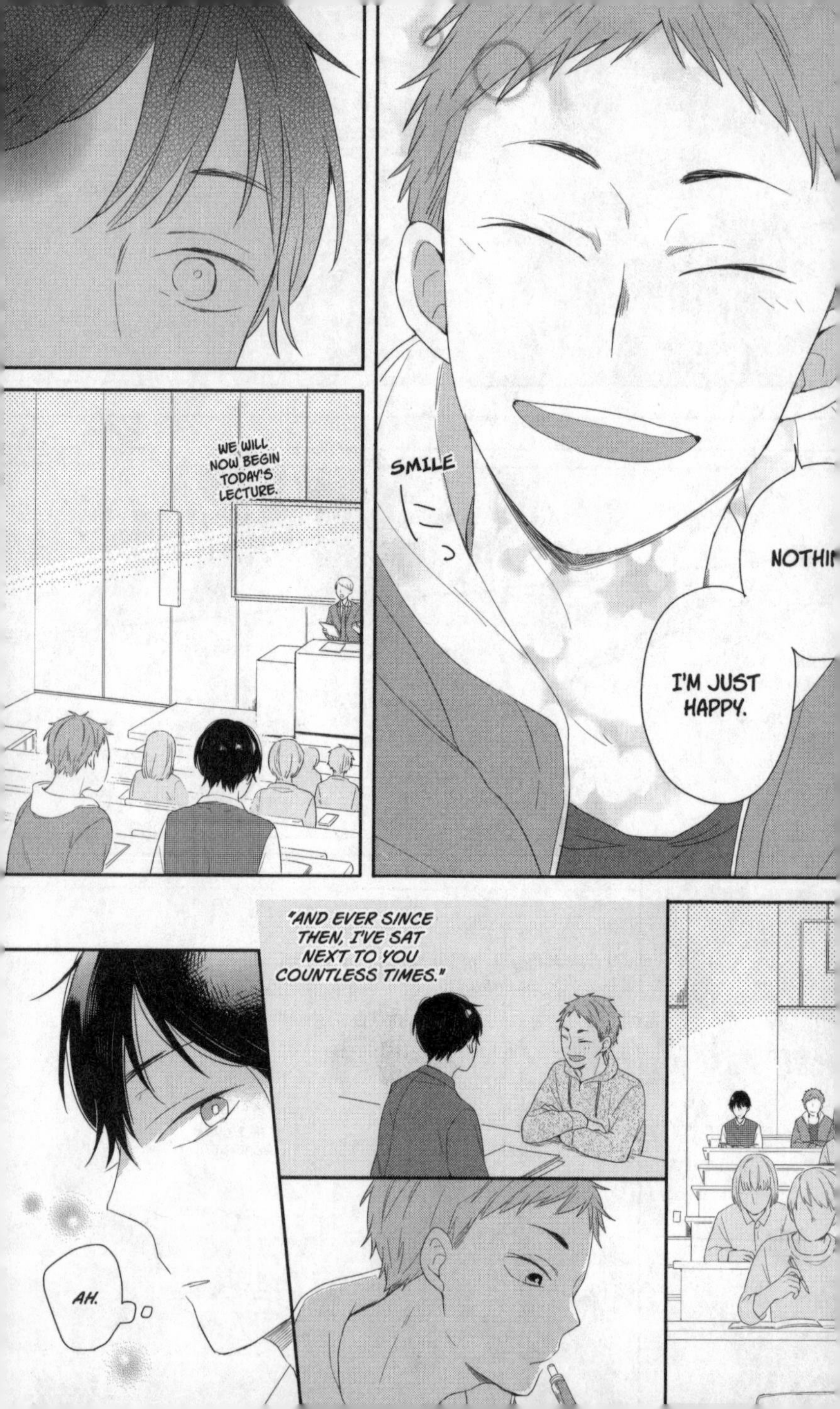
NOTHI
I'M JUST HAPPY.
SMILE
WE WILL NOW BEGIN TODAY'S LECTURE.
"AND EVER SINCE THEN, I'VE SAT NEXT TO YOU COUNTLESS TIMES."
AH.

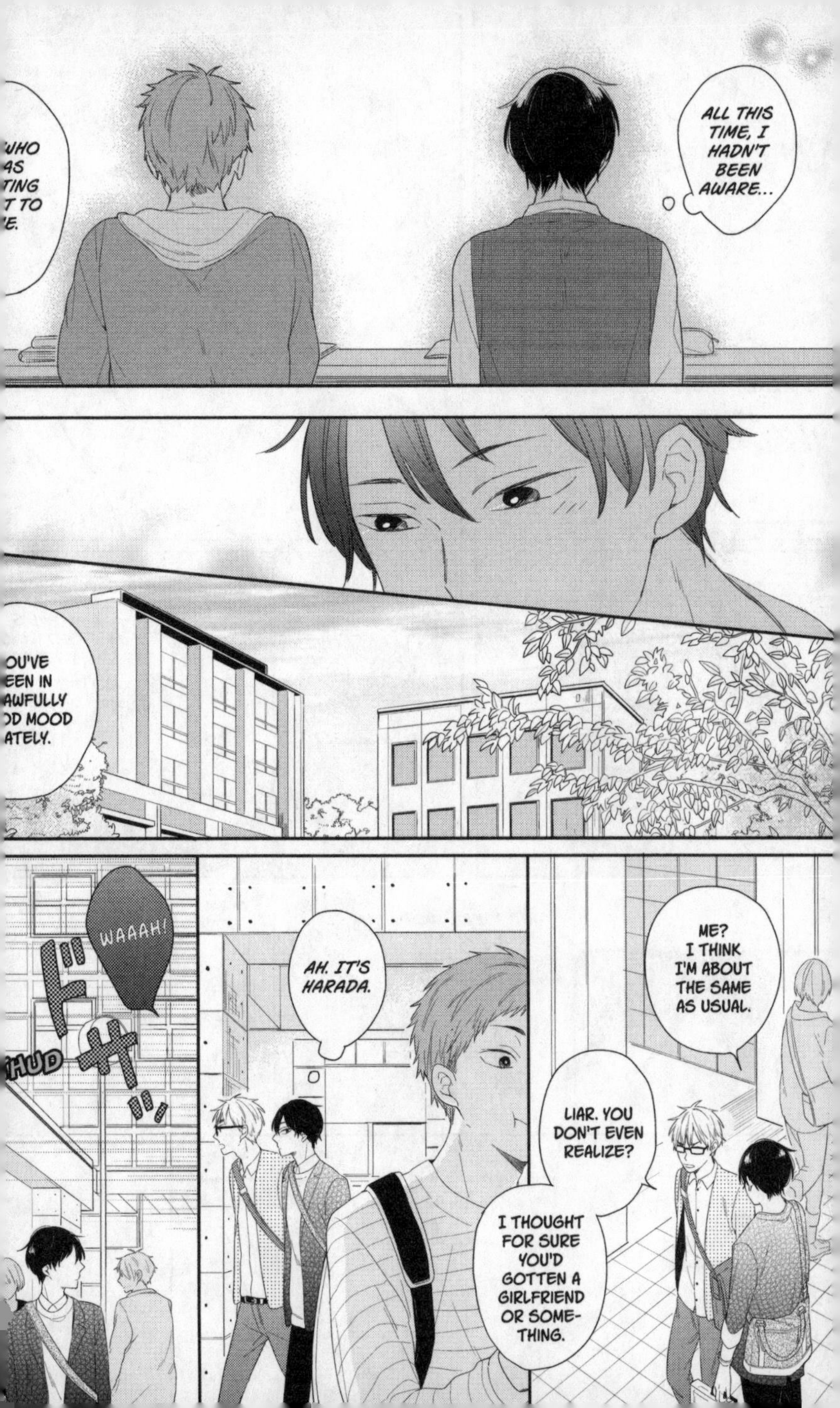
ALL THIS TIME, I HADN'T BEEN AWARE...
WHO AS TING T TO E.
OU'VE EEN IN AWFULLY OD MOOD ATELY.
ME? I THINK I'M ABOUT THE SAME AS USUAL.
LIAR. YOU DON'T EVEN REALIZE?
I THOUGHT FOR SURE YOU'D GOTTEN A GIRLFRIEND OR SOME-THING.
AH. IT'S HARADA.
WAAAH!
ドサッ
THUD

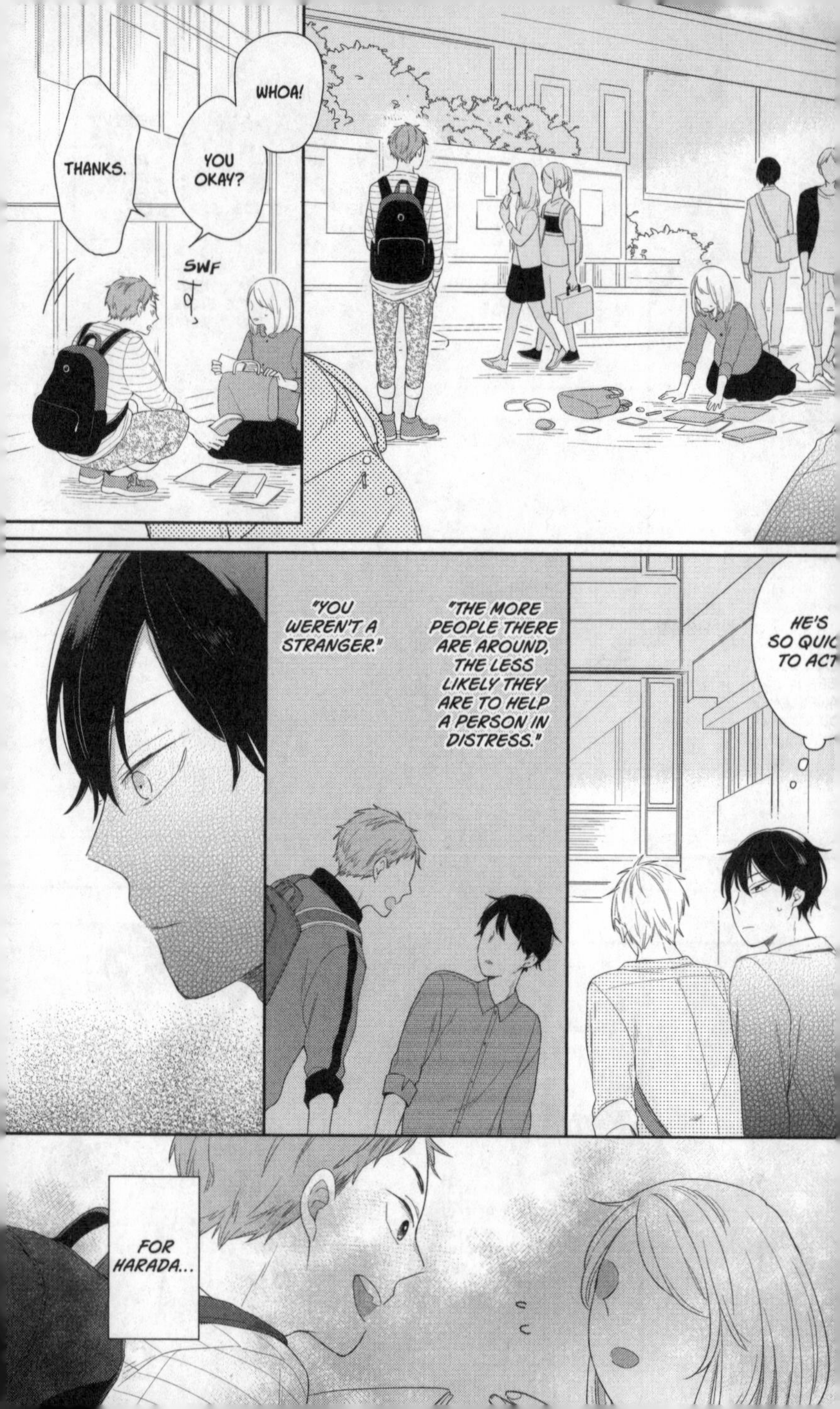

WHOA!
YOU OKAY?
THANKS.
SWF
HE'S SO QUIC TO ACT
"THE MORE PEOPLE THERE ARE AROUND, THE LESS LIKELY THEY ARE TO HELP A PERSON IN DISTRESS."
"YOU WEREN'T A STRANGER."
FOR HARADA...

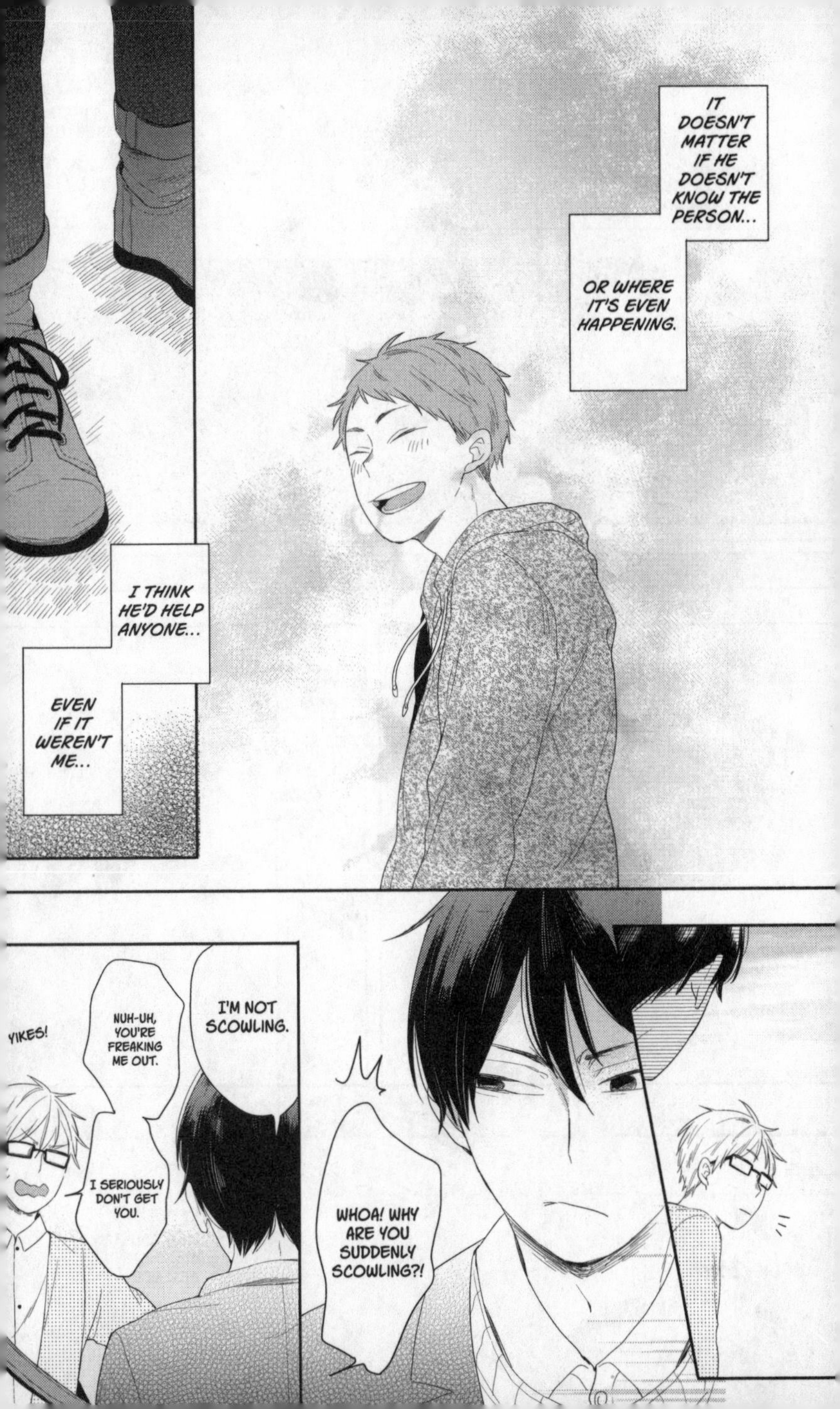
IT DOESN'T MATTER IF HE DOESN'T KNOW THE PERSON...
OR WHERE IT'S EVEN HAPPENING.
I THINK HE'D HELP ANYONE...
EVEN IF IT WEREN'T ME...
WHOA! WHY ARE YOU SUDDENLY SCOWLING?!
I'M NOT SCOWLING.
NUH-UH, YOU'RE FREAKING ME OUT.
YIKES!
I SERIOUSLY DON'T GET YOU.

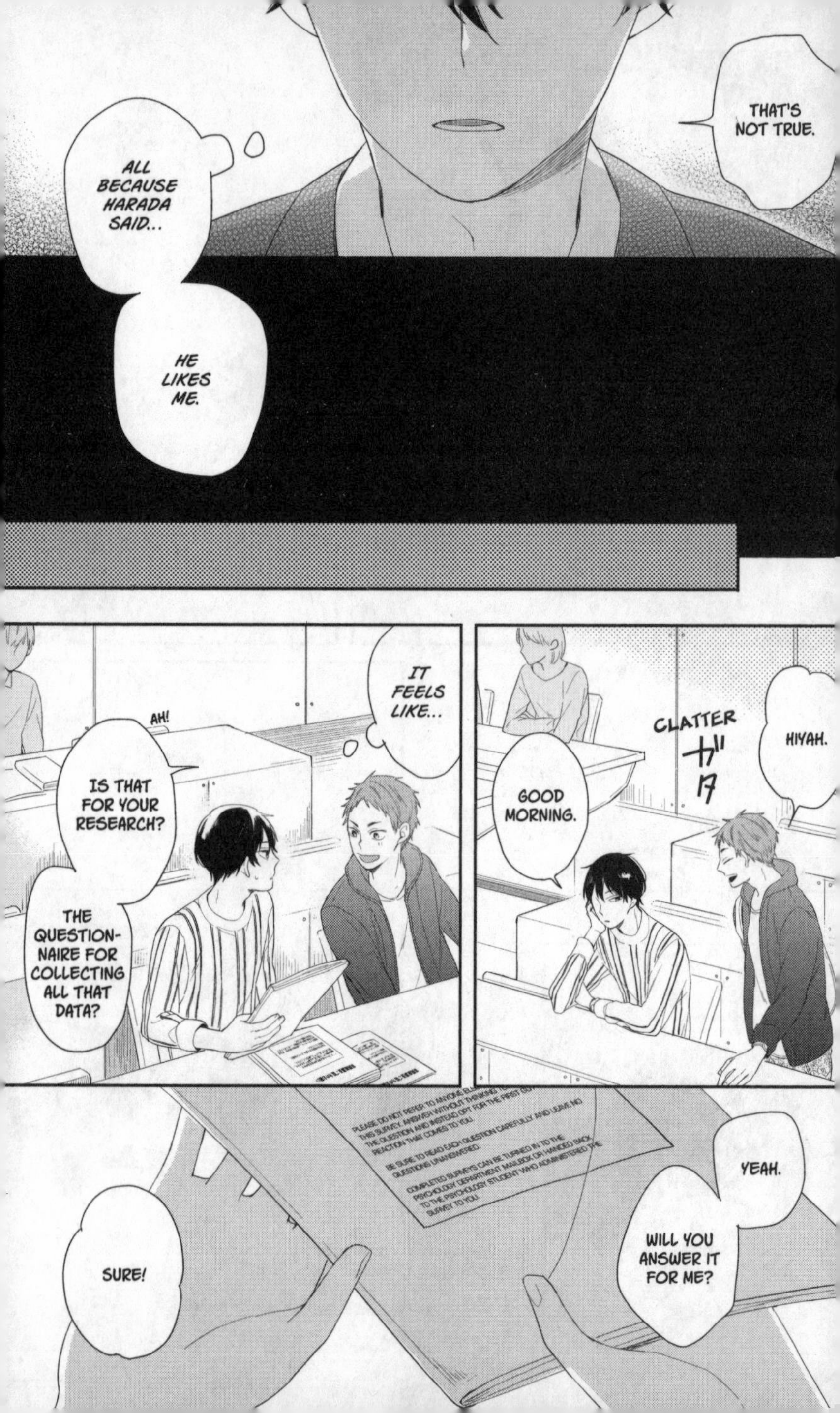
THAT'S NOT TRUE.
ALL BECAUSE HARADA SAID...
HE LIKES ME.
HIYAH.
CLATTER
GOOD MORNING.
IT FEELS LIKE...
AH!
IS THAT FOR YOUR RESEARCH?
THE QUESTION-NAIRE FOR COLLECTING ALL THAT DATA?
BE SURE TO READ EACH QUESTION CAREFULLY AND LEAVE NO QUESTIONS UNANSWERED.
COMPLETED SURVEYS CAN BE TURNED IN TO THE PSYCHOLOGY DEPARTMENT MAILBOX OR HANDED BACK TO THE PSYCHOLOGY STUDENT WHO ADMINISTERED THE SURVEY TO YOU.
YEAH.
WILL YOU ANSWER IT FOR ME?
SURE!

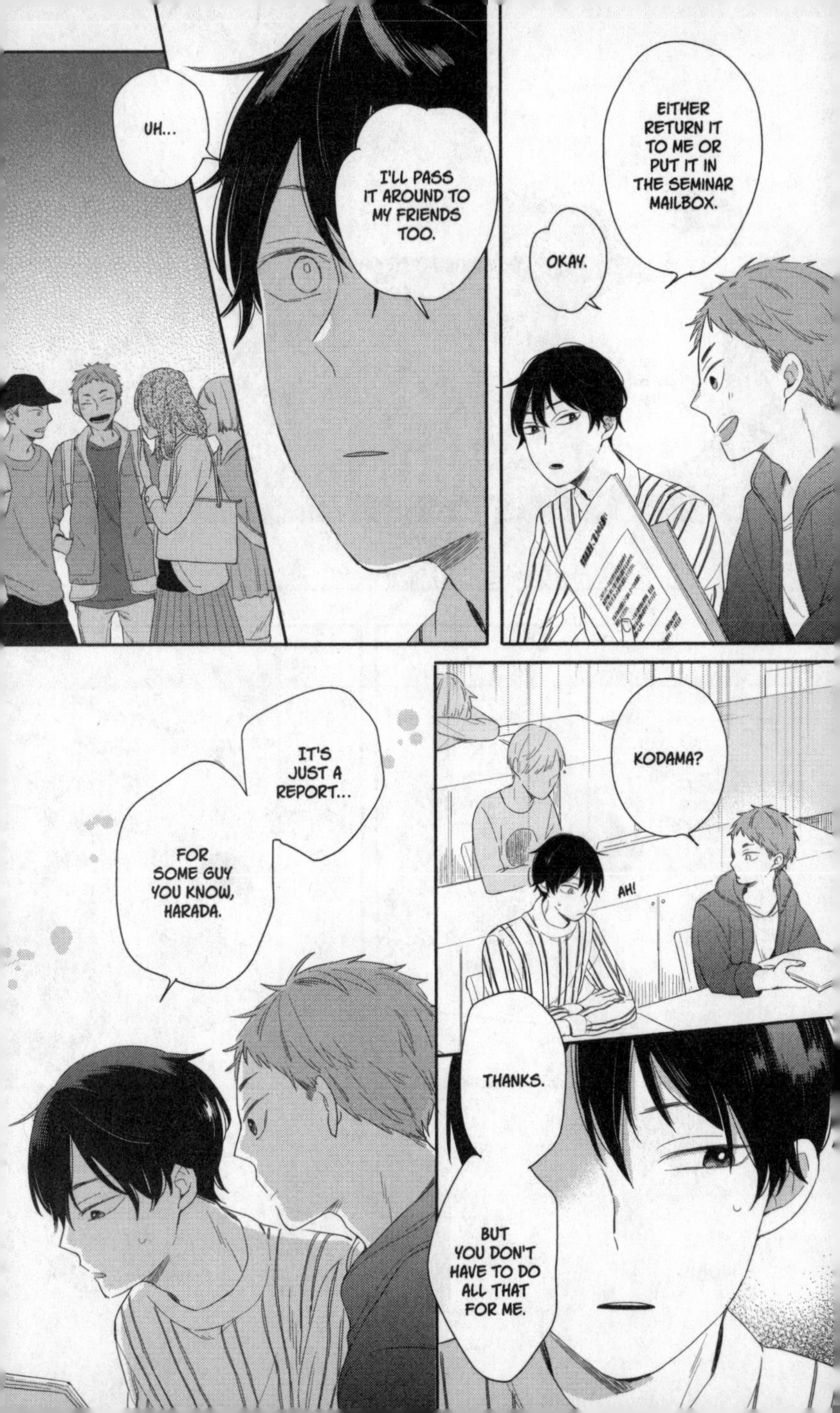
EITHER RETURN IT TO ME OR PUT IT IN THE SEMINAR MAILBOX.
OKAY.
I'LL PASS IT AROUND TO MY FRIENDS TOO.
UH...
KODAMA?
AH!
THANKS.
BUT YOU DON'T HAVE TO DO ALL THAT FOR ME.
IT'S JUST A REPORT...
FOR SOME GUY YOU KNOW, HARADA.

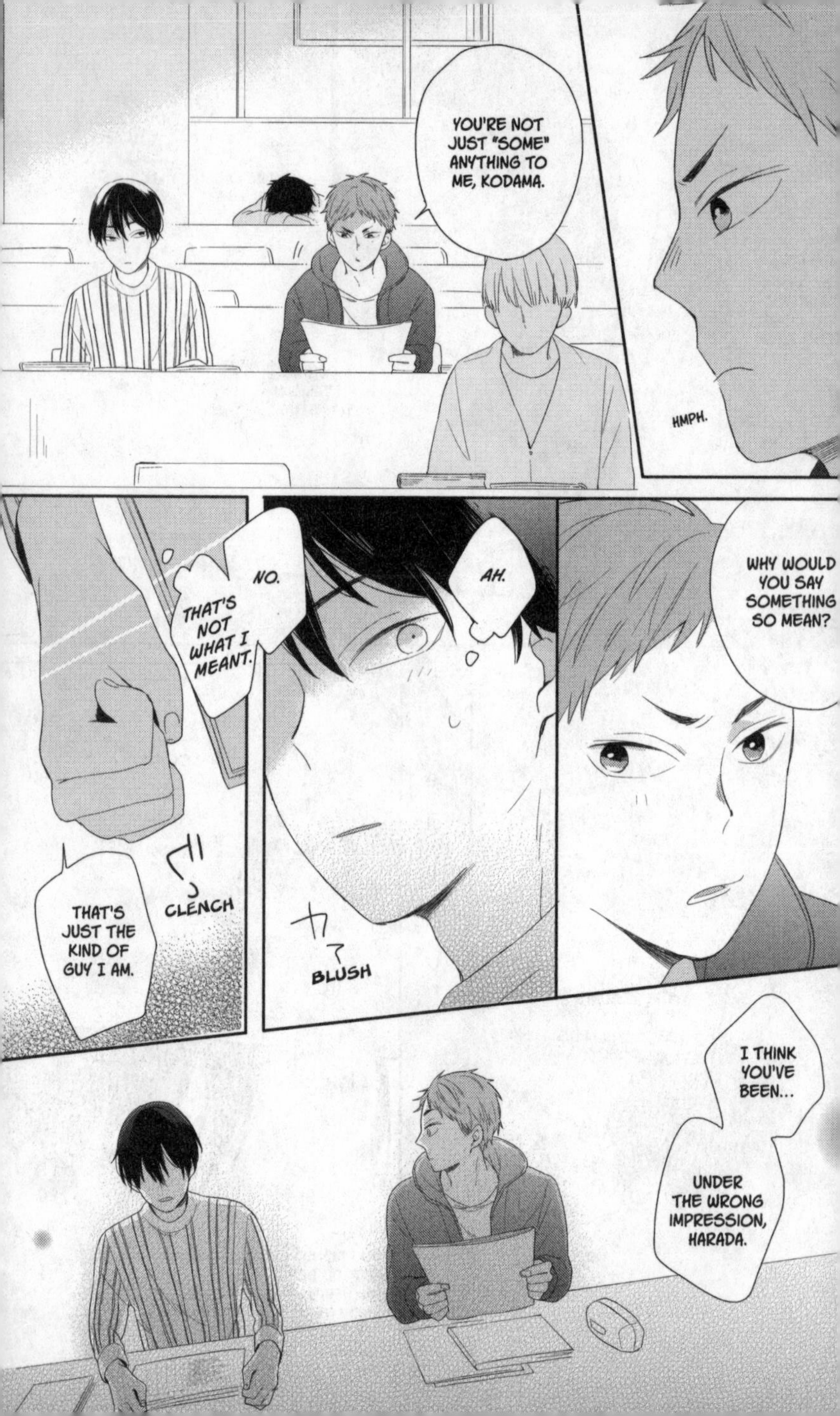
HMPH.
YOU'RE NOT JUST "SOME" ANYTHING TO ME, KODAMA.
WHY WOULD YOU SAY SOMETHING SO MEAN?
AH.
BLUSH
NO.
THAT'S NOT WHAT I MEANT.
CLENCH
THAT'S JUST THE KIND OF GUY I AM.
I THINK YOU'VE BEEN...
UNDER THE WRONG IMPRESSION, HARADA.

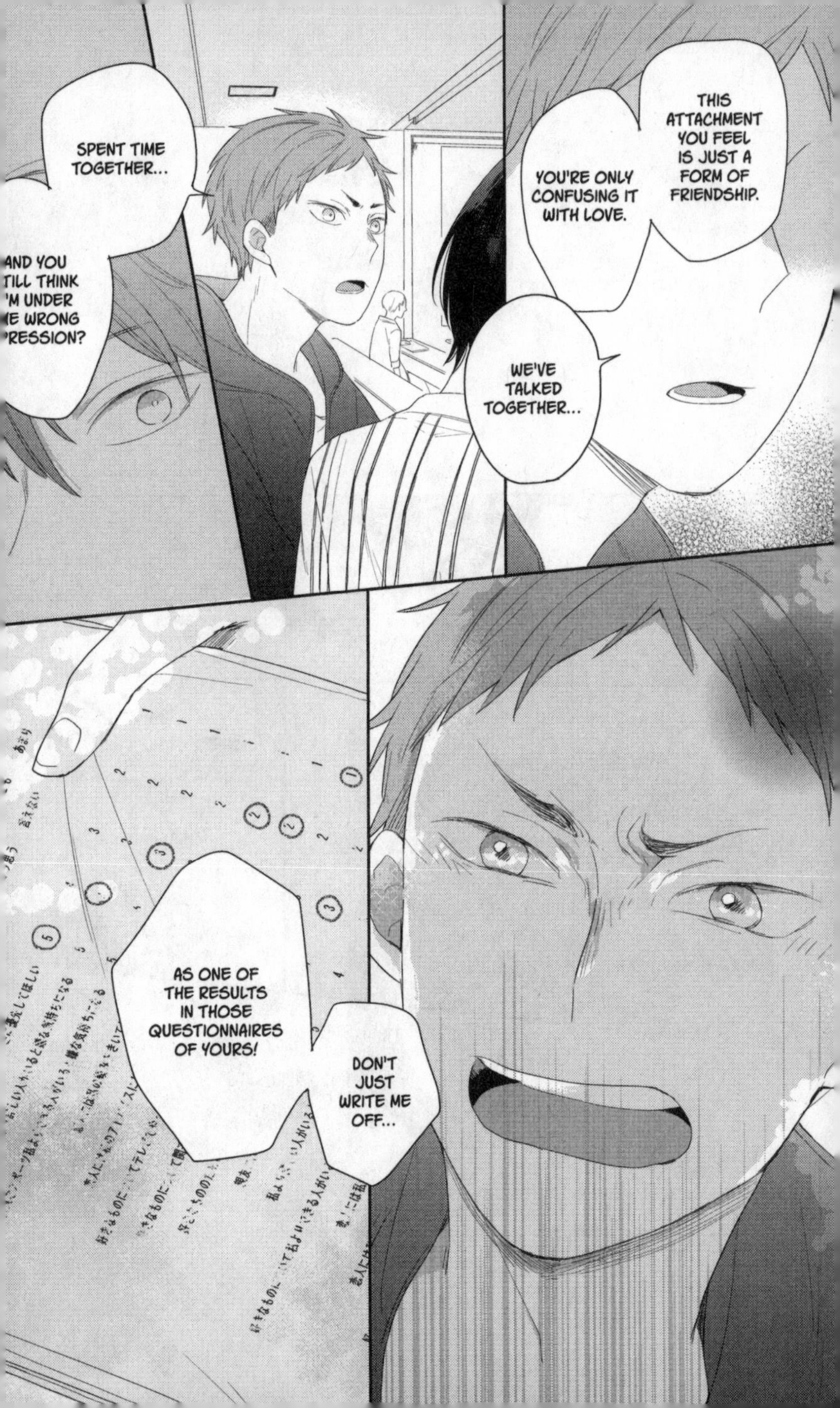
THIS ATTACHMENT YOU FEEL IS JUST A FORM OF FRIENDSHIP.
YOU'RE ONLY CONFUSING IT WITH LOVE.
WE'VE TALKED TOGETHER...
SPENT TIME TOGETHER...
AND YOU TILL THINK 'M UNDER E WRONG 'RESSION?
DON'T JUST WRITE ME OFF...
AS ONE OF THE RESULTS IN THOSE QUESTIONNAIRES OF YOURS!

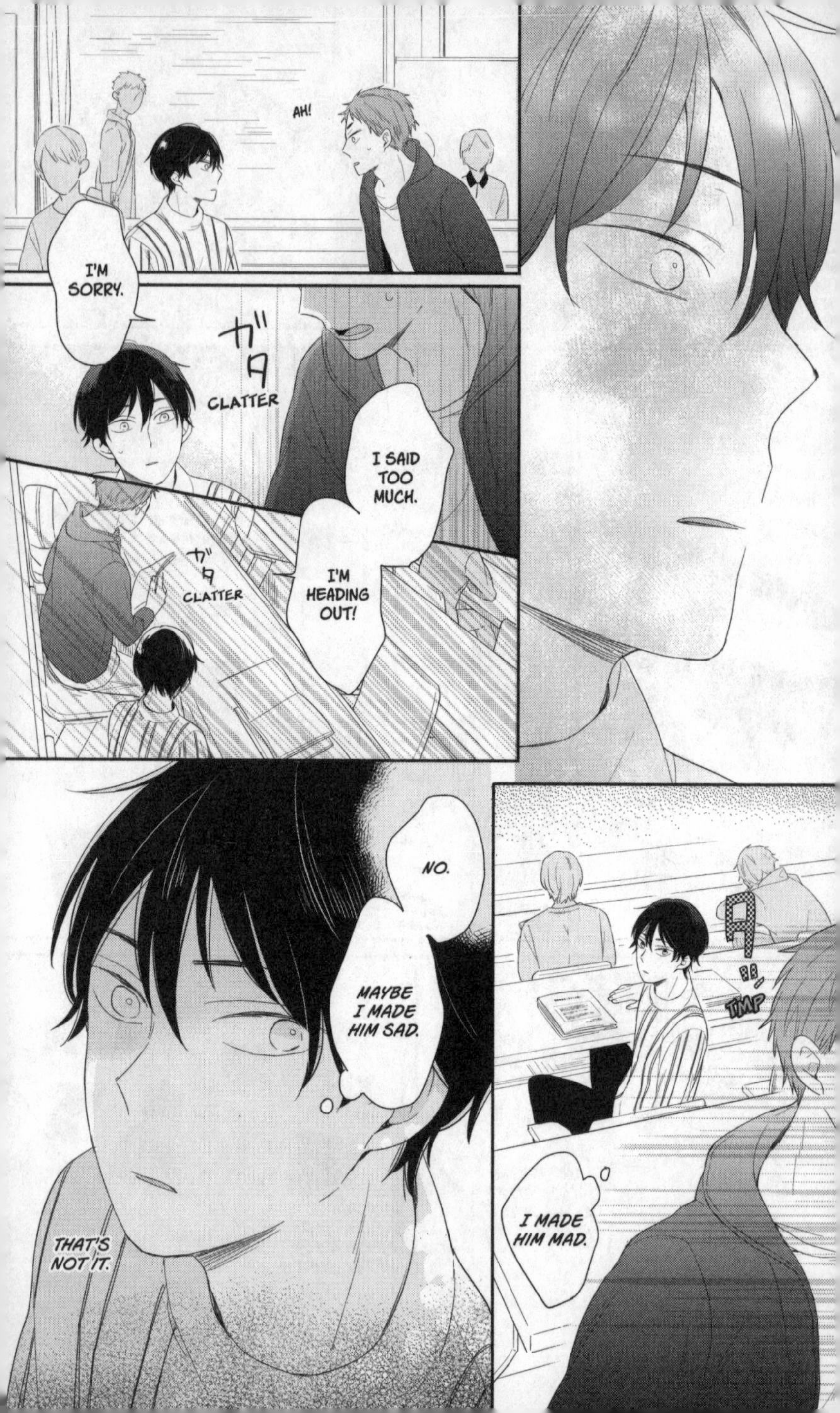
AH!
I'M SORRY.
ガタ
CLATTER
I SAID TOO MUCH.
ガタ
CLATTER
I'M HEADING OUT!
TMP
I MADE HIM MAD.
NO.
MAYBE I MADE HIM SAD.
THAT'S NOT IT.

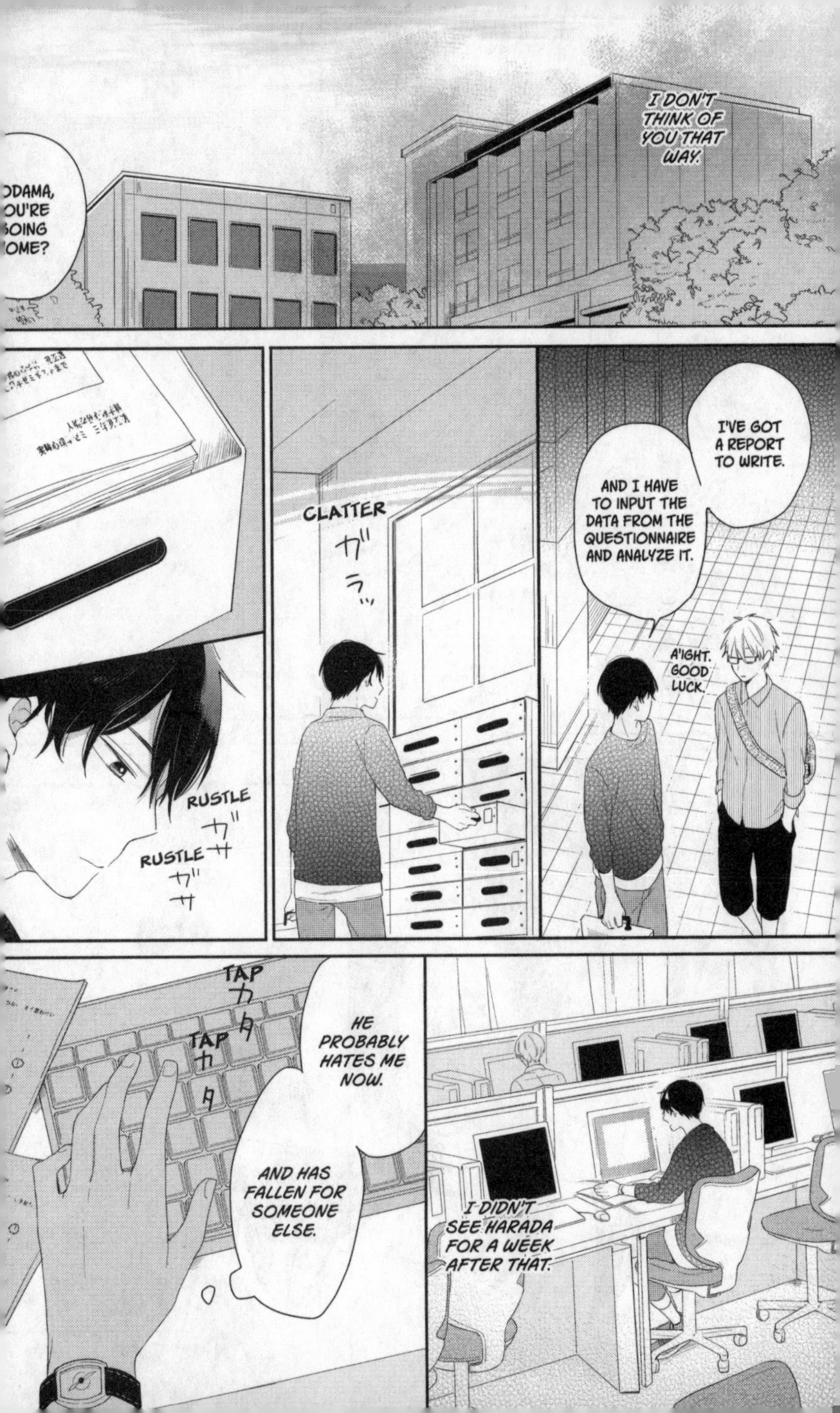
I DON'T THINK OF YOU THAT WAY.
ODAMA, OU'RE GOING OME?
I'VE GOT A REPORT TO WRITE.
AND I HAVE TO INPUT THE DATA FROM THE QUESTIONNAIRE AND ANALYZE IT.
A'IGHT. GOOD LUCK.
CLATTER
ガラッ
RUSTLE
ガサ
RUSTLE
ガサ
I DIDN'T SEE HARADA FOR A WEEK AFTER THAT.
HE PROBABLY HATES ME NOW.
AND HAS FALLEN FOR SOMEONE ELSE.
TAP
カタ
TAP
カタ

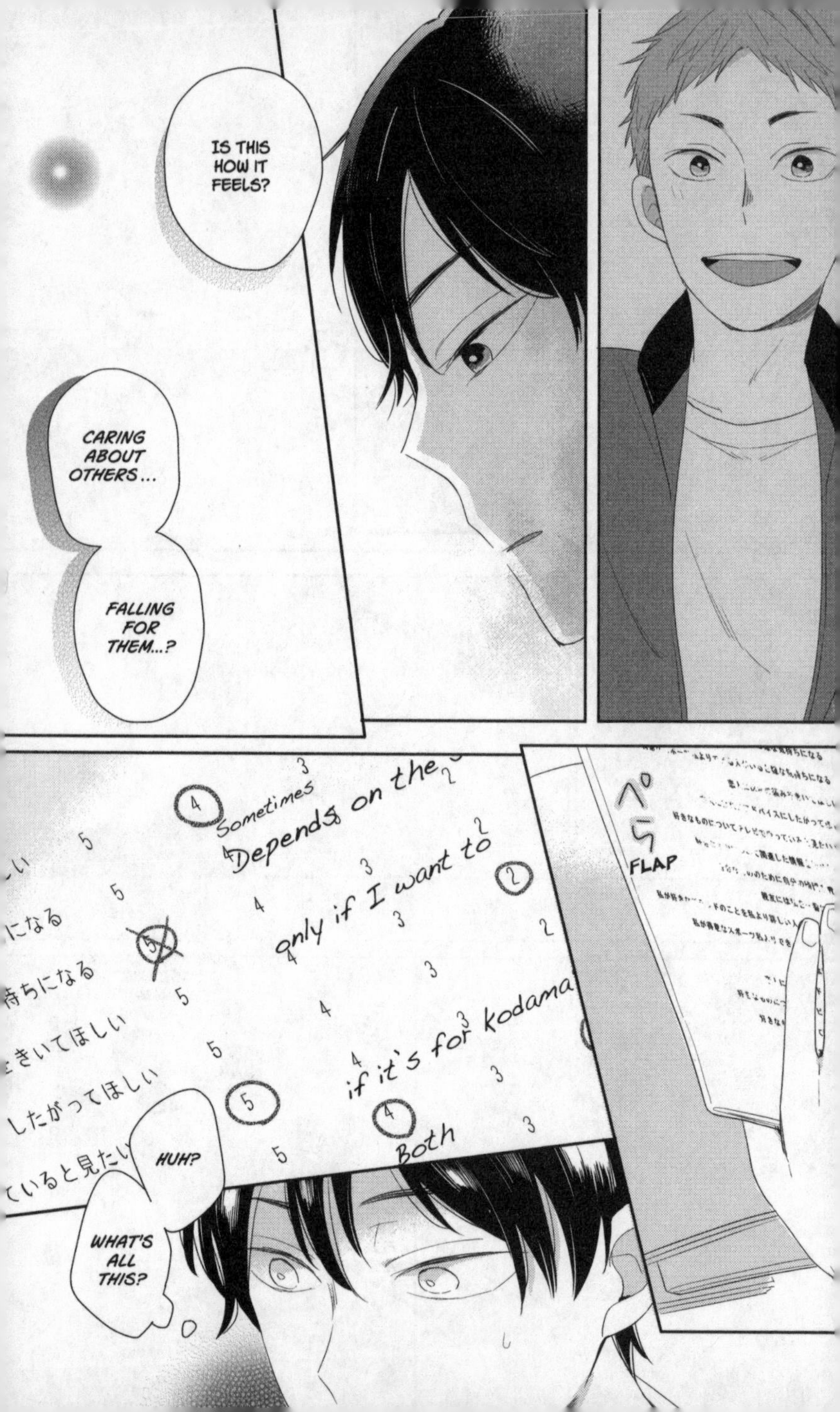
IS THIS HOW IT FEELS?
CARING ABOUT OTHERS...
FALLING FOR THEM...?
ぺら
FLAP
Sometimes
Depends on the
only if I want to
if it's for kodama
Both
になる
持ちになる
きいてほしい
したがってほしい
ていると見たい
HUH?
WHAT'S ALL THIS?

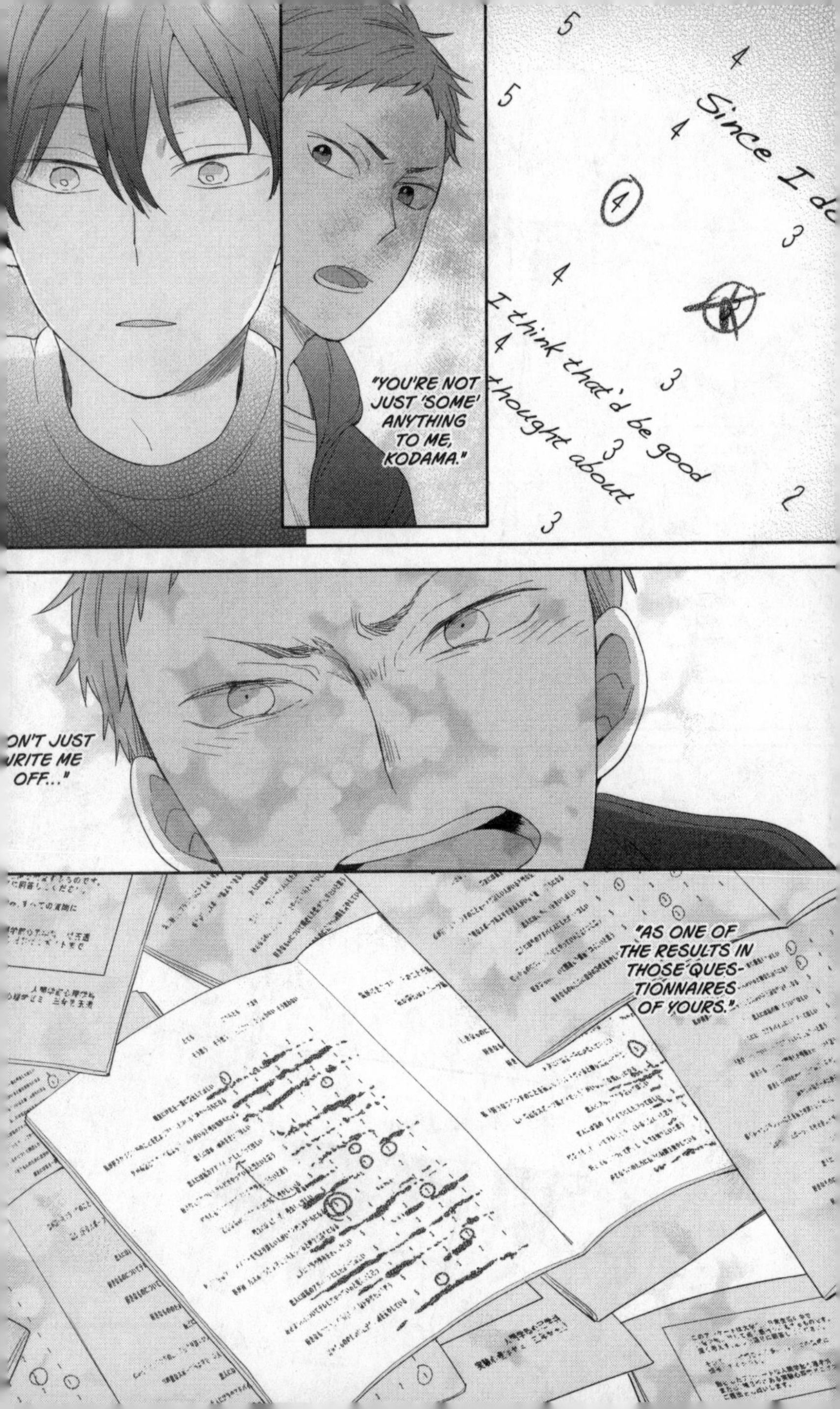

Since I do
I think that'd be good
thought about
"YOU'RE NOT JUST 'SOME' ANYTHING TO ME, KODAMA."
ON'T JUST WRITE ME OFF..."
"AS ONE OF THE RESULTS IN THOSE QUES-TIONNAIRES OF YOURS."

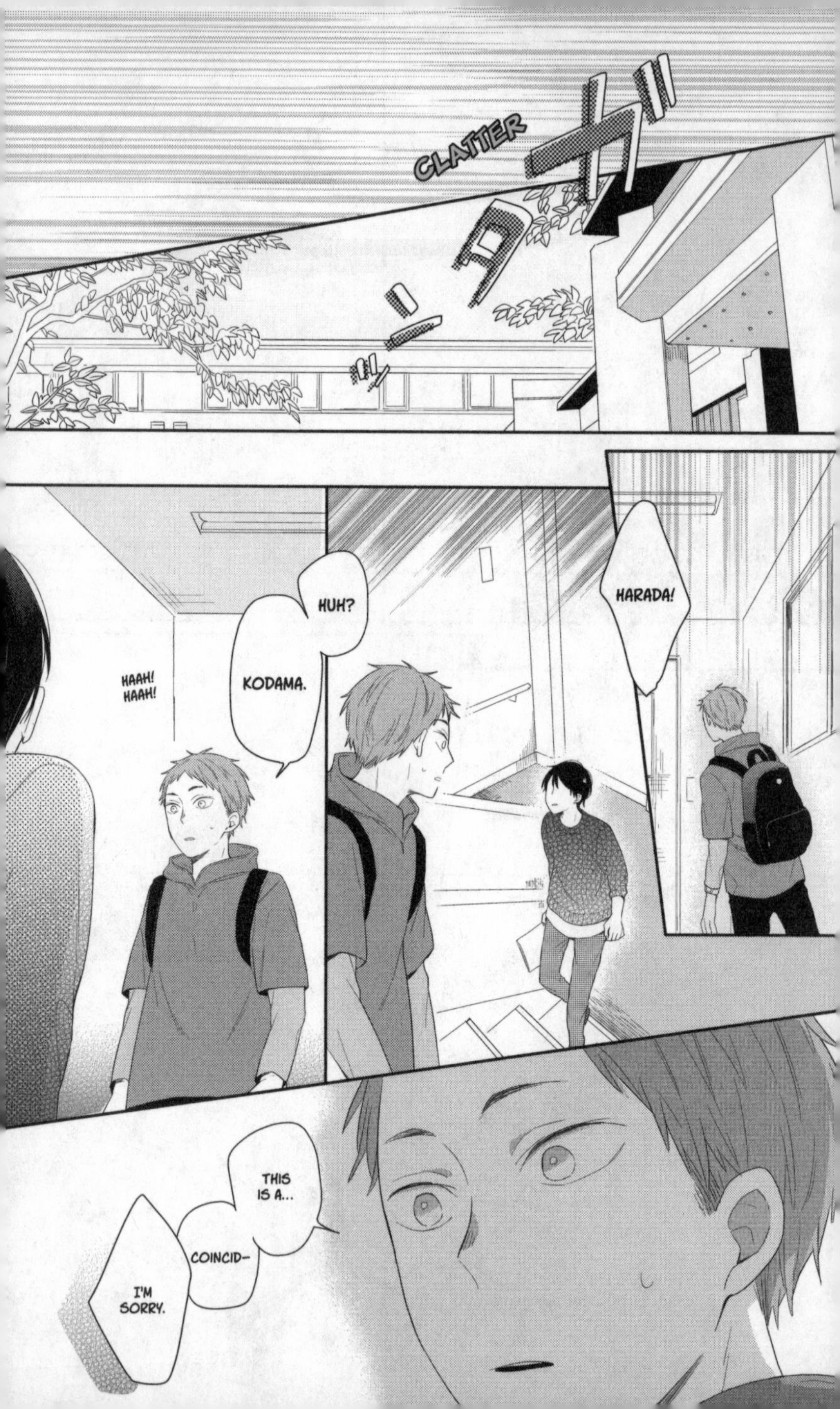
CLATTER
HARADA!
HUH?
KODAMA.
HAAH! HAAH!
THIS IS A...
COINCID-
I'M SORRY.

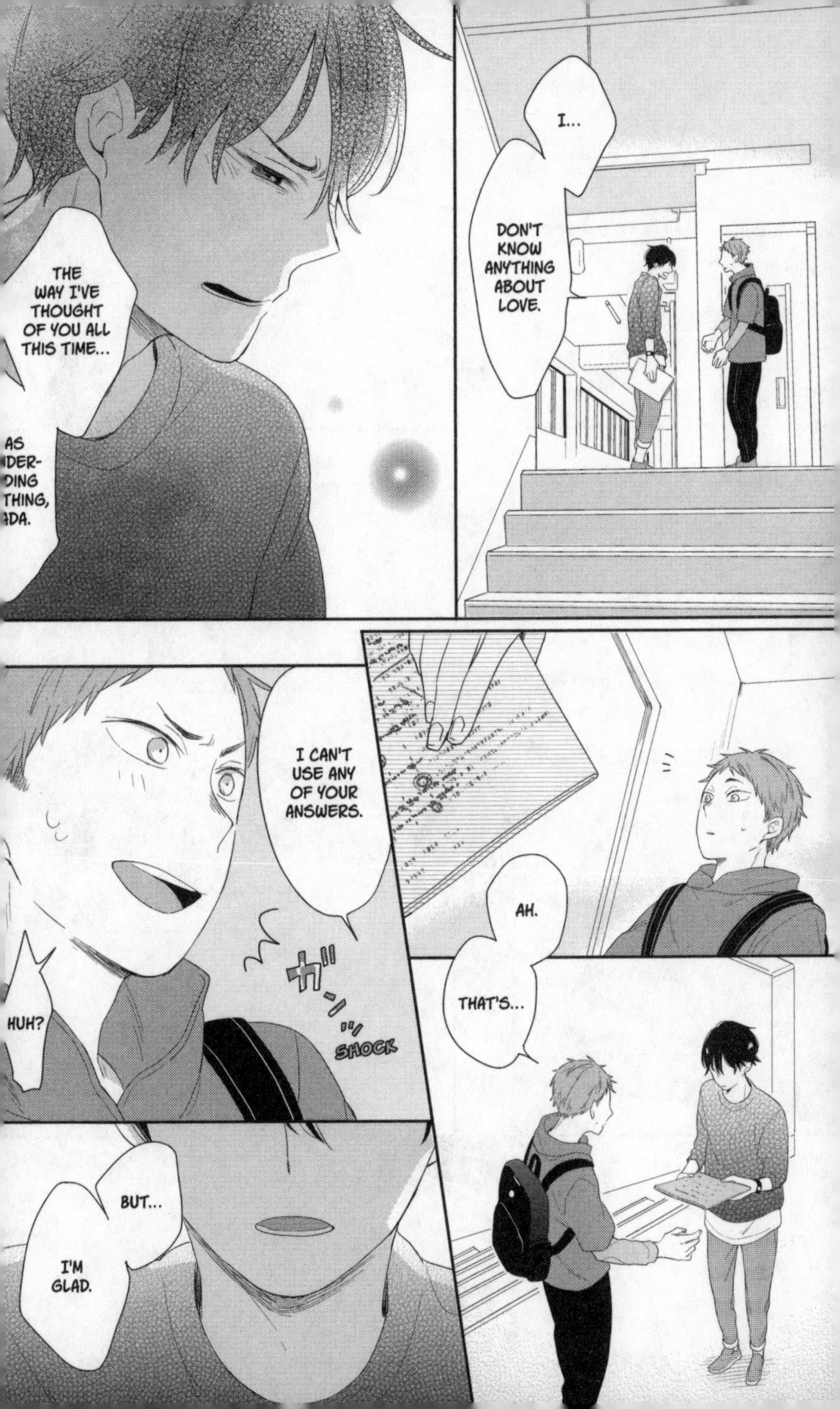
I...
DON'T KNOW ANYTHING ABOUT LOVE.
THE WAY I'VE THOUGHT OF YOU ALL THIS TIME...
AH.
I CAN'T USE ANY OF YOUR ANSWERS.
HUH?
SHOCK
THAT'S...
BUT...
I'M GLAD.

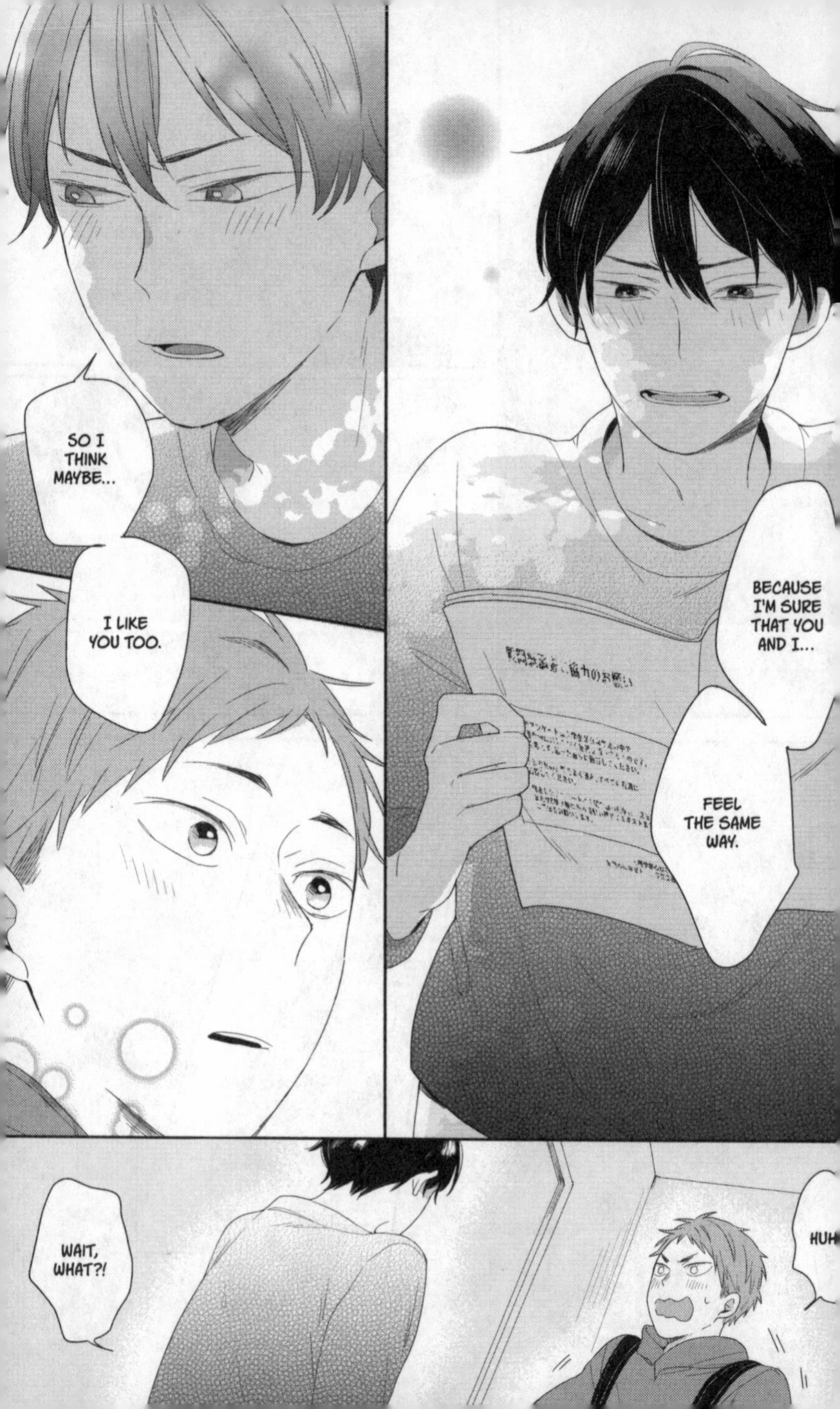
BECAUSE I'M SURE THAT YOU AND I...
FEEL THE SAME WAY.
SO I THINK MAYBE...
I LIKE YOU TOO.
HUH
WAIT, WHAT?!

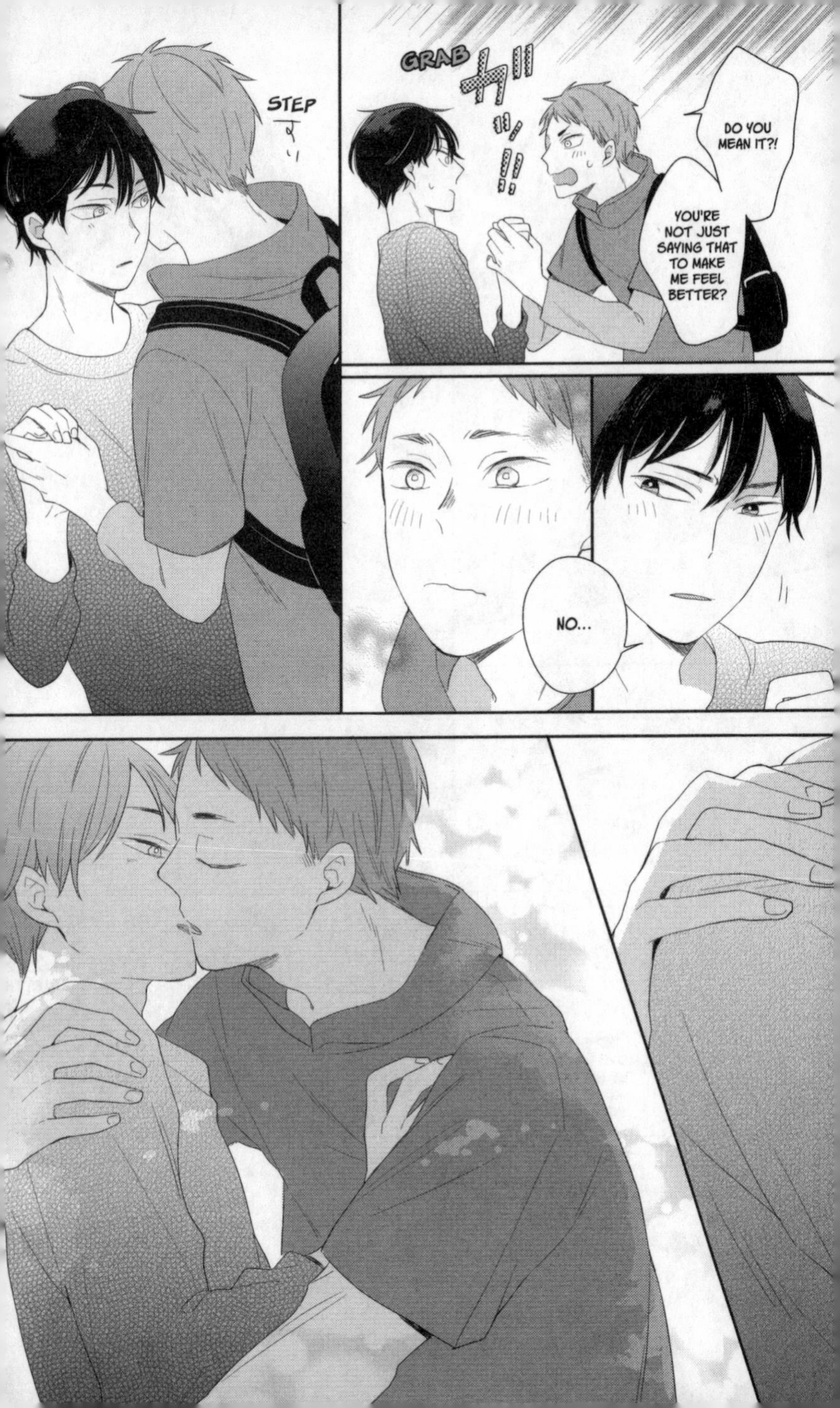
GRAB
DO YOU MEAN IT?!
YOU'RE NOT JUST SAYING THAT TO MAKE ME FEEL BETTER?
NO...
STEP

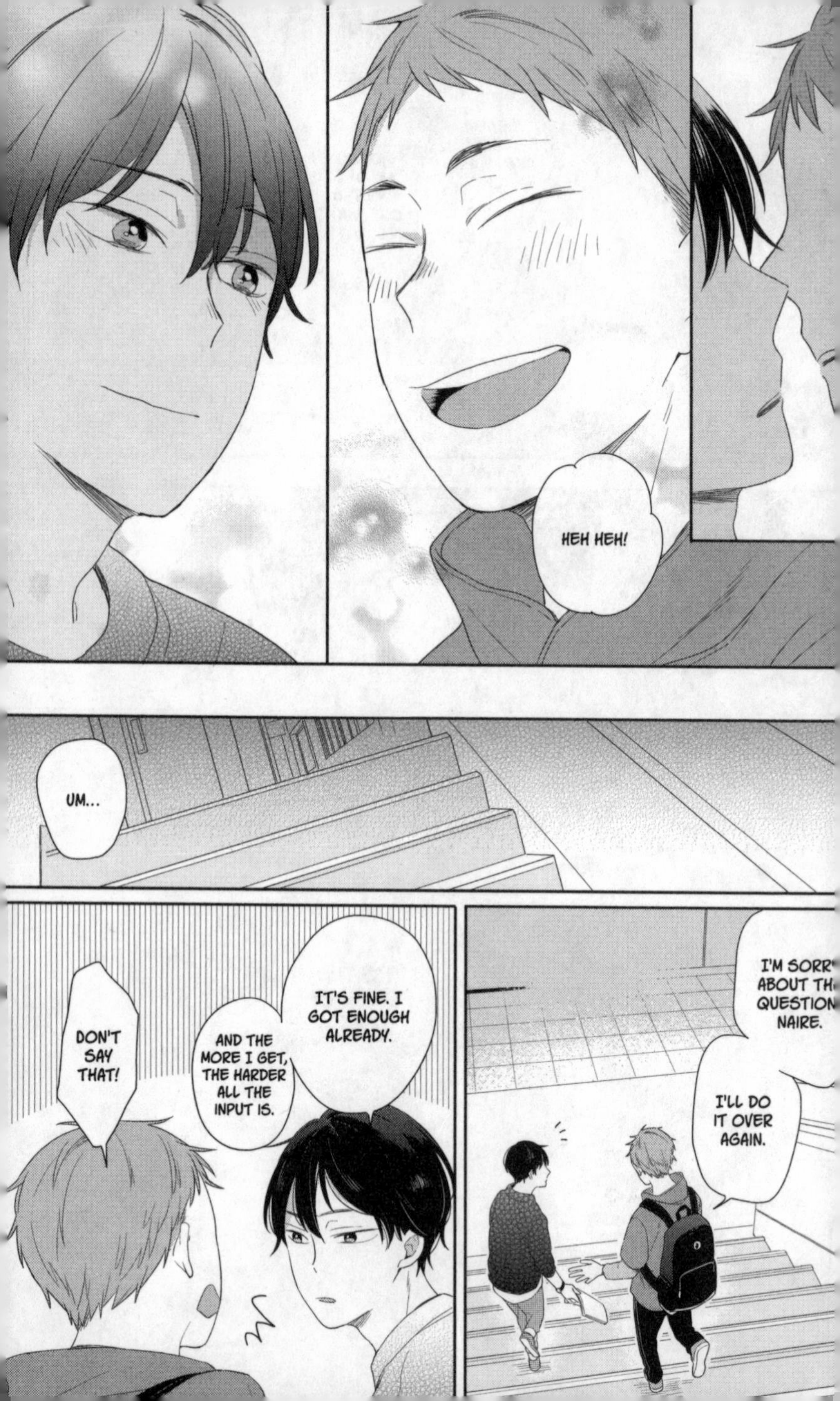
HEH HEH!
UM...
I'M SORR ABOUT TH QUESTION NAIRE.
I'LL DO IT OVER AGAIN.
IT'S FINE. I GOT ENOUGH ALREADY.
AND THE MORE I GET, THE HARDER ALL THE INPUT IS.
DON'T SAY THAT!

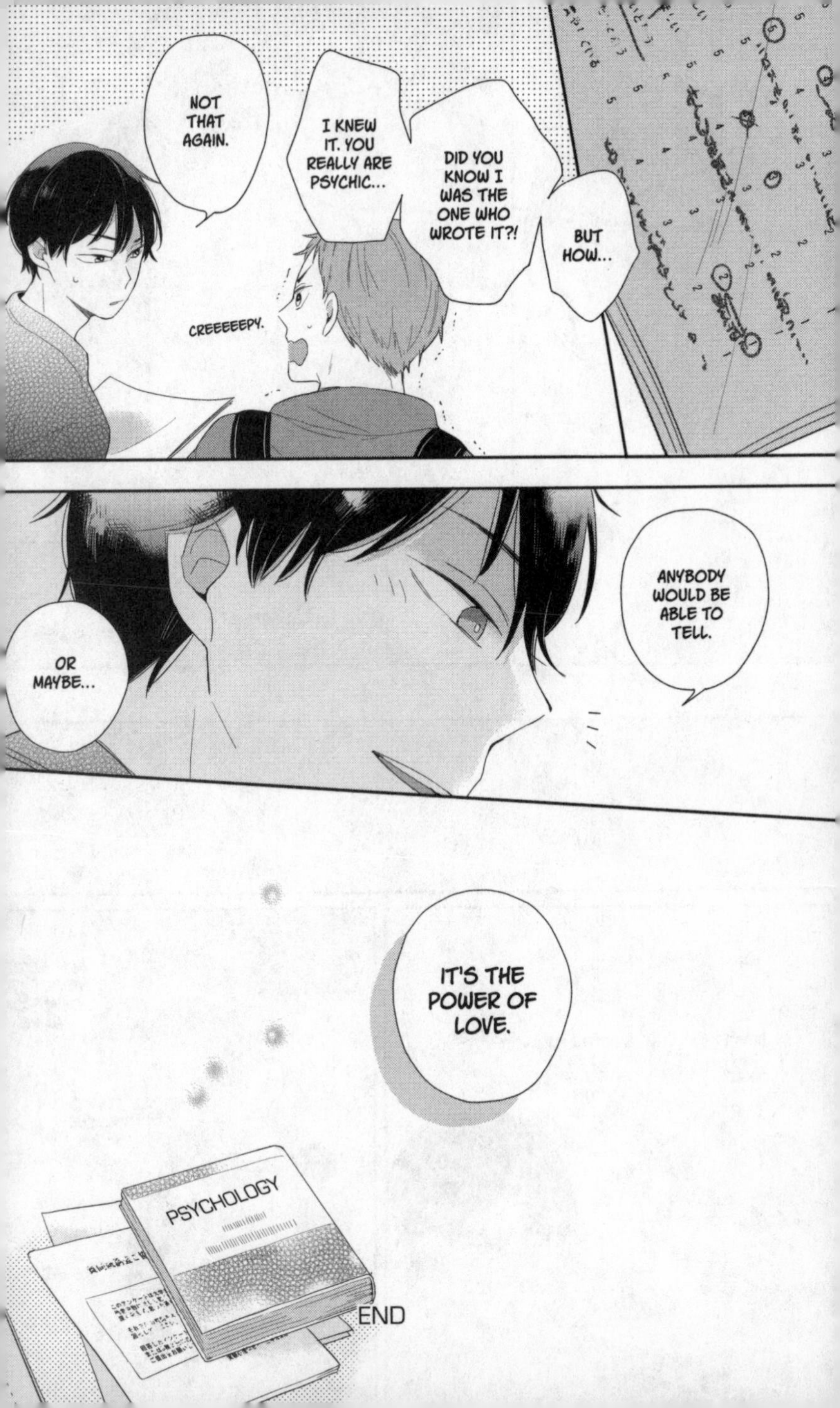
BUT HOW...
DID YOU KNOW I WAS THE ONE WHO WROTE IT?!
I KNEW IT. YOU REALLY ARE PSYCHIC...
CREEEEEPY.
NOT THAT AGAIN.
ANYBODY WOULD BE ABLE TO TELL.
OR MAYBE...
IT'S THE POWER OF LOVE.
PSYCHOLOGY
END

Would you like

to be a family?

Would you like

to be a family?

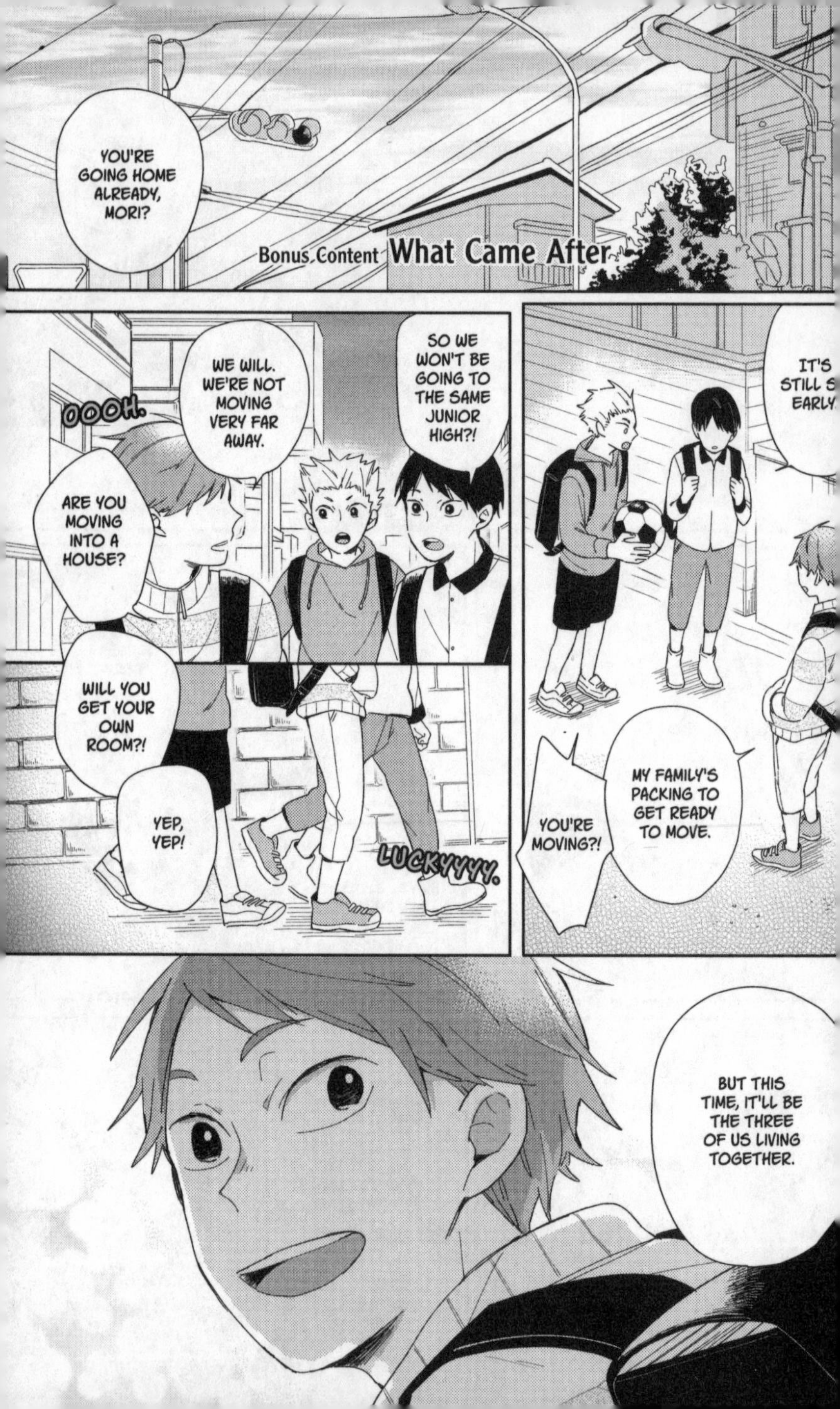
YOU'RE GOING HOME ALREADY, MORI?
Bonus Content What Came After
IT'S STILL S EARLY
MY FAMILY'S PACKING TO GET READY TO MOVE.
YOU'RE MOVING?!
SO WE WON'T BE GOING TO THE SAME JUNIOR HIGH?!
WE WILL. WE'RE NOT MOVING VERY FAR AWAY.
OOOH.
ARE YOU MOVING INTO A HOUSE?
WILL YOU GET YOUR OWN ROOM?!
YEP, YEP!
LUCKYYYY.
BUT THIS TIME, IT'LL BE THE THREE OF US LIVING TOGETHER.

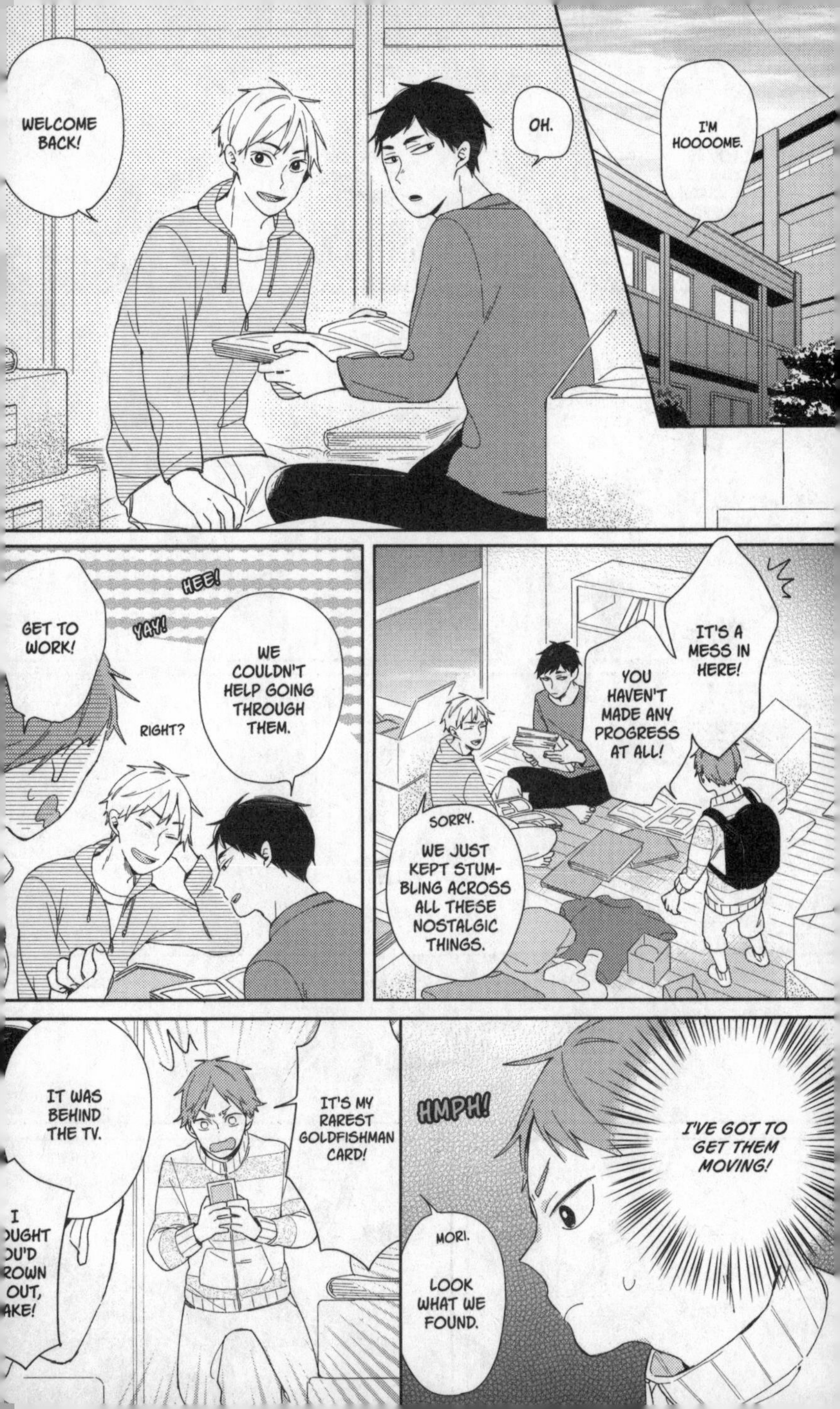
I'M HOOOOME.
OH.
WELCOME BACK!
IT'S A MESS IN HERE!
YOU HAVEN'T MADE ANY PROGRESS AT ALL!
SORRY.
WE JUST KEPT STUMBLING ACROSS ALL THESE NOSTALGIC THINGS.
HEE!
WE COULDN'T HELP GOING THROUGH THEM.
YAY!
RIGHT?
GET TO WORK!
HMPH!
I'VE GOT TO GET THEM MOVING!
MORI.
LOOK WHAT WE FOUND.
IT'S MY RAREST GOLDFISHMAN CARD!
IT WAS BEHIND THE TV.
I OUGHT OU'D ROWN OUT, AKE!

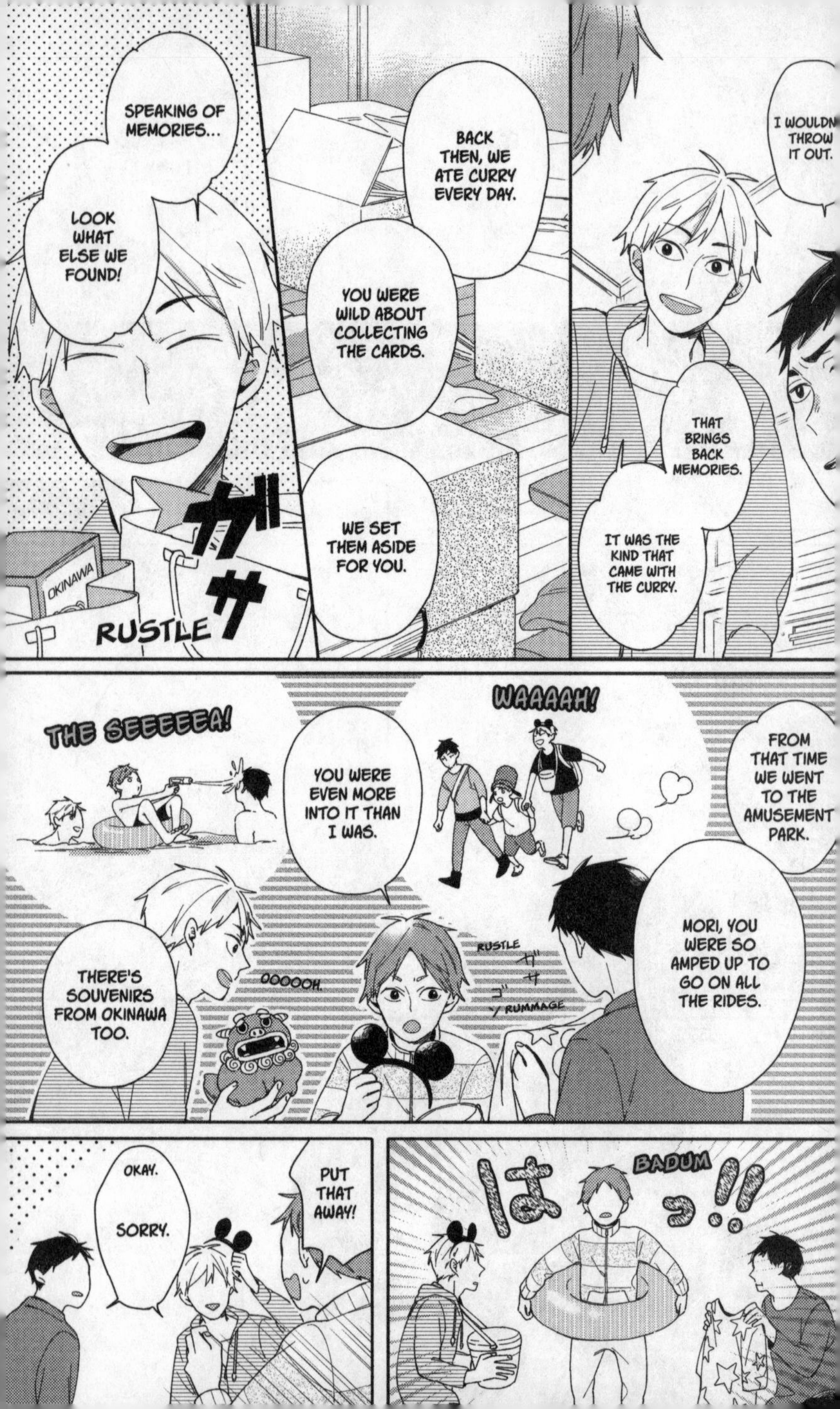
I WOULDN THROW IT OUT.
THAT BRINGS BACK MEMORIES.
IT WAS THE KIND THAT CAME WITH THE CURRY.
BACK THEN, WE ATE CURRY EVERY DAY.
YOU WERE WILD ABOUT COLLECTING THE CARDS.
WE SET THEM ASIDE FOR YOU.
SPEAKING OF MEMORIES...
LOOK WHAT ELSE WE FOUND!
ガサ
RUSTLE
OKINAWA
FROM THAT TIME WE WENT TO THE AMUSEMENT PARK.
WAAAAH!
MORI, YOU WERE SO AMPED UP TO GO ON ALL THE RIDES.
RUSTLE
ガサ
ゴソ
RUMMAGE
YOU WERE EVEN MORE INTO IT THAN I WAS.
THE SEEEEEA!
THERE'S SOUVENIRS FROM OKINAWA TOO.
OOOOOH.
BADUM
はっ!!
PUT THAT AWAY!
OKAY.
SORRY.

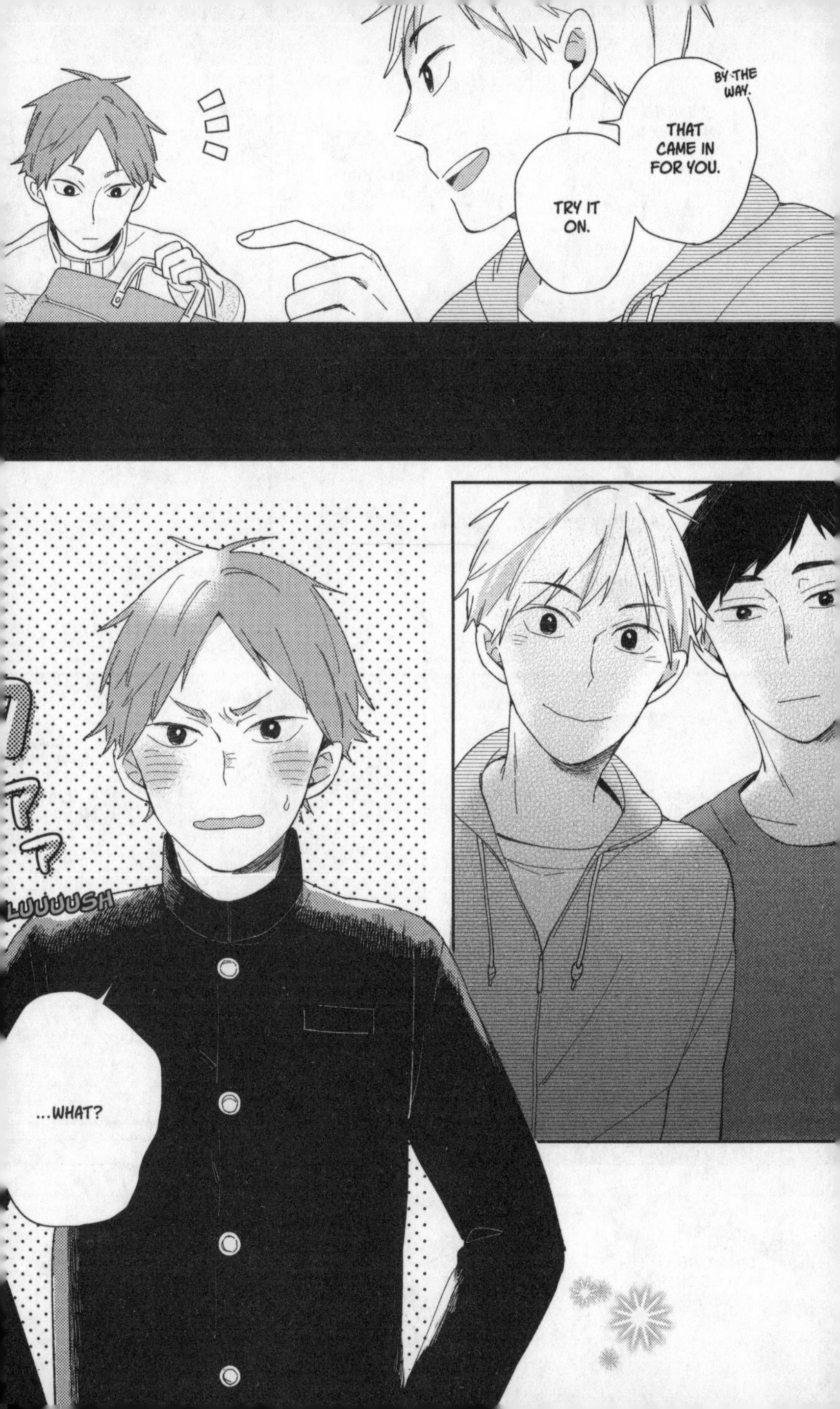
BY THE WAY.
THAT CAME IN FOR YOU.
TRY IT ON.
LUUUUSH
...WHAT?

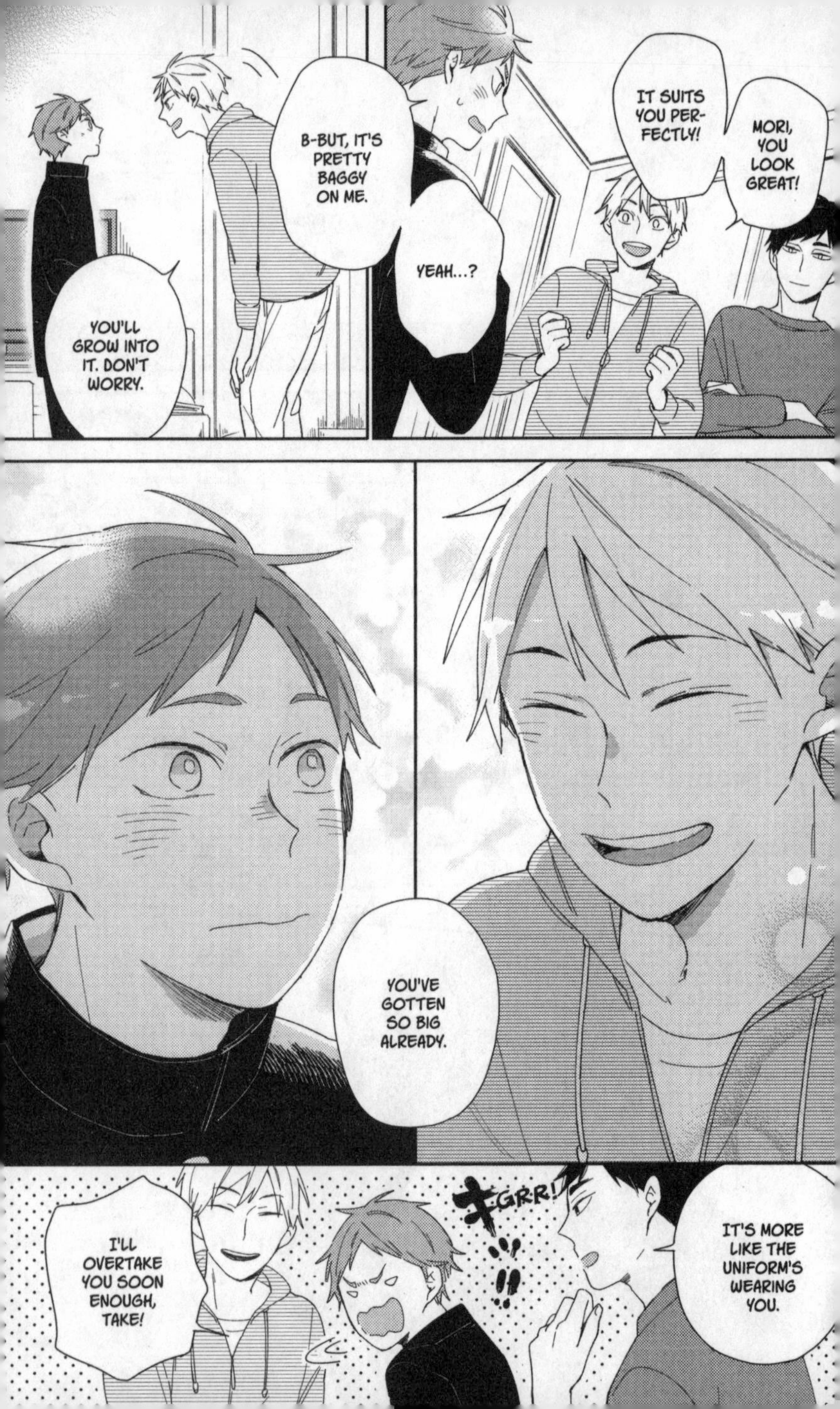
MORI, YOU LOOK GREAT!
IT SUITS YOU PER-FECTLY!
YEAH...?
B-BUT, IT'S PRETTY BAGGY ON ME.
YOU'LL GROW INTO IT. DON'T WORRY.
YOU'VE GOTTEN SO BIG ALREADY.
IT'S MORE LIKE THE UNIFORM'S WEARING YOU.
GRR!
I'LL OVERTAKE YOU SOON ENOUGH, TAKE!

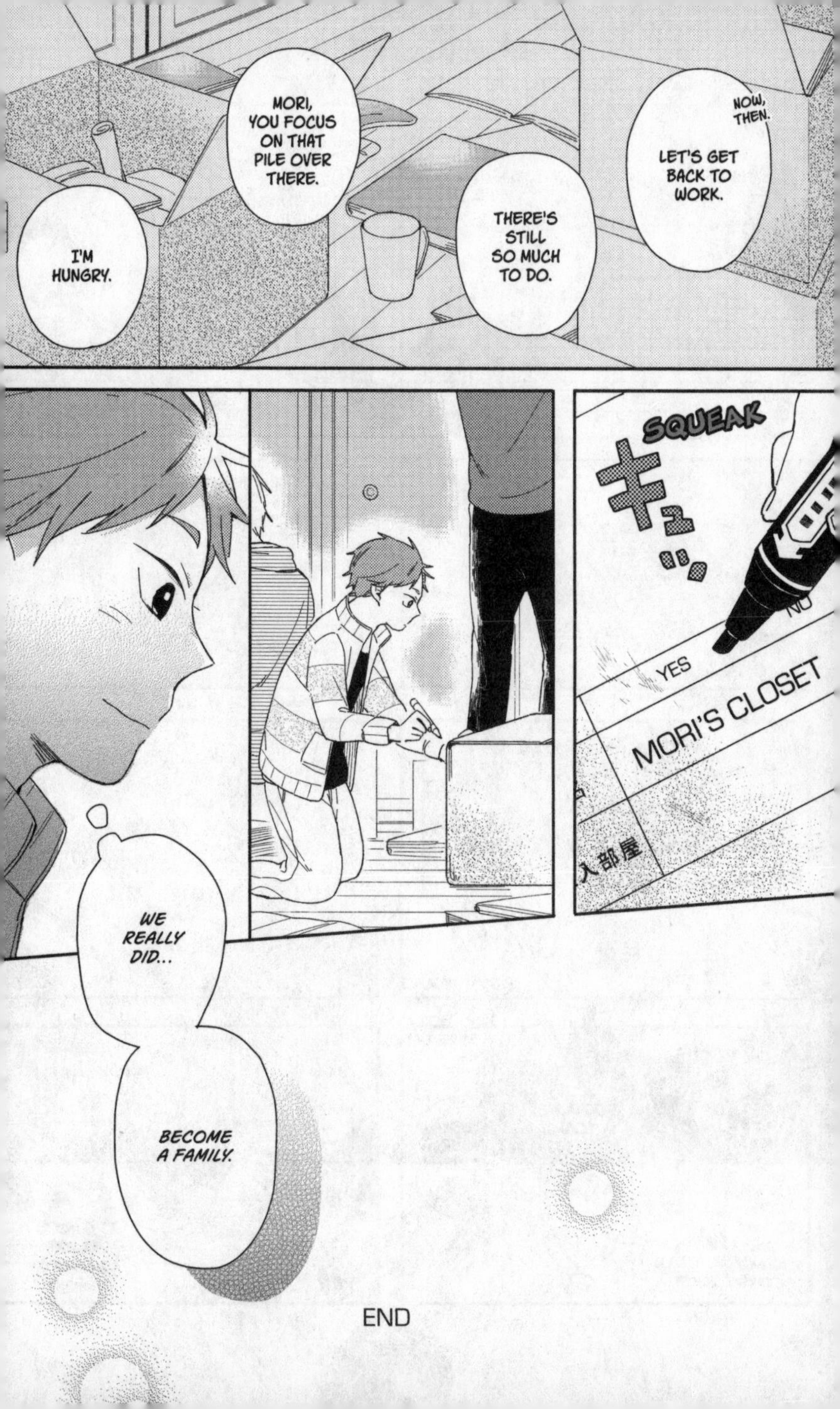
NOW, THEN.
LET'S GET BACK TO WORK.
THERE'S STILL SO MUCH TO DO.
MORI, YOU FOCUS ON THAT PILE OVER THERE.
I'M HUNGRY.
SQUEAK
キュッ
NO
YES
MORI'S CLOSET
WE REALLY DID...
BECOME A FAMILY.
END

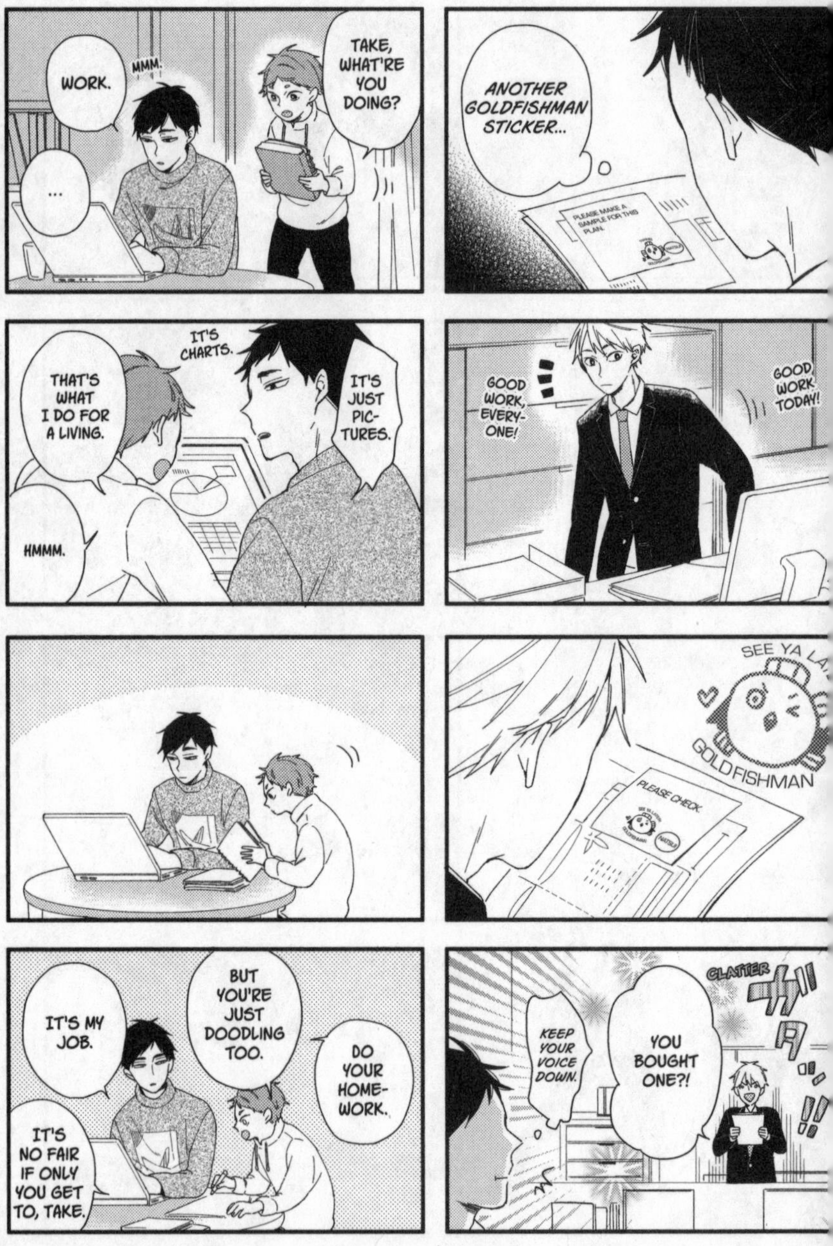
ANOTHER GOLDFISHMAN STICKER...
PLEASE MAKE A SAMPLE FOR THIS PLAN.
GOOD WORK TODAY!
GOOD WORK, EVERY-ONE!
SEE YA LA
GOLDFISHMAN
PLEASE CHECK.
CLATTER
YOU BOUGHT ONE?!
KEEP YOUR VOICE DOWN.
TAKE, WHAT'RE YOU DOING?
MMM.
WORK.
...
IT'S JUST PIC-TURES.
IT'S CHARTS.
THAT'S WHAT I DO FOR A LIVING.
HMMM.
DO YOUR HOME-WORK.
BUT YOU'RE JUST DOODLING TOO.
IT'S MY JOB.
IT'S NO FAIR IF ONLY YOU GET TO, TAKE.

ZZZ
スコー
ZZZ
すー
HOW CUTE!!
LET ME JOIN TOO!
HERE I COME!
10 MIN-UTES LATER
MOOSH
もみくちゃ…
NNNNGH.
NONE OF THEM SLEPT WELL.
NNNNGH.

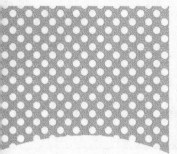

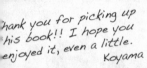

Thank you for picking up this book!! I hope you enjoyed it, even a little.

Koyama

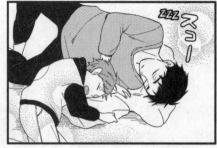

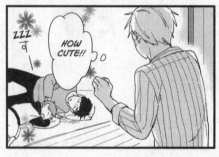

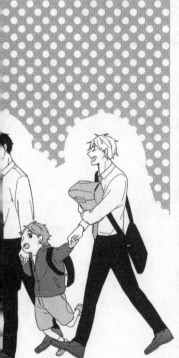

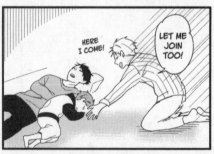

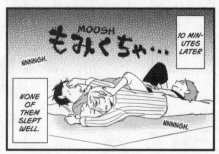

Would you like
to be a family?

REPLAY
Saki Tsukahara

SAKI TSUKAHARA

MATURE 18+

Yuta and Ritsu have been playing baseball together since they were children, but after being defeated in a local tournament over the summer, they must retire from the high school team to study for university entrance exams. Still, Yuta finds himself unable to give up his lingering attachment to baseball. The one person who can truly understand him is Ritsu, who has been acting worryingly distant since they quit the team.

But there's something Yuta himself doesn't understand... Does he think of Ritsu as his partner in the way that a teammate would, or is the affection between them something stronger?

Super serious Asahi Suzumura and laidback, easygoing Mitsuki Sayama might seem like an odd couple, but they made a deal; they'll vacation around the world and when they get back to Japan, they'll get married. As they travel from country to country, the different people, cultures and cuisine they encounter begin to bring them closer together. After all they're not just learning about the world, but about themselves too.

KOIMONOGATARI: LOVE STORIES, VOLUME 1

Tohru Tagura

♂LOVE-x-LOVE♂

When Yuiji accidentally overhears his classmate Yamato confessing to another friend that he's gay, his perspective shifts. Seeing Yamato in a new light, Yuiji does his best not to let prejudice color his view, but he still finds himself overthinking his classmates' interactions now. He especially notices the way Yamato looks at one particular boy: Yuiji's own best friend. Even though he tells himself he shouldn't get involved, Yuiji finds he just can't help it; watching Yamato's one-sided love draws him in a way he never expected. At first, it's empathy, knowing that the boy Yamato has his sights on is definitely straight and has no idea. But as his own friendship with Yamato develops and the two of them grow closer through a mutual study group, Yuiji comes to truly care about Yamato as a person, regardless of his sexuality. He only wants Yamato to be happy, and to be able to express his true self.

DEKOBOKO SUGAR DAYS

Atsuko Yusen

MATURE 18+ ♂LOVE-x-LOVE♂

Yuujirou Matsukaze has been close friends with Rui Hanamine since the two of them were children. Back then, Yuujirou was the one who stood up for and took care of his adorable, soft-hearted friend. But as it turns out, Yuujirou's childhood dreams end up growing a little too big to handle — or, rather, too tall! At over six feet in height, the cheerful and happy-go-lucky Rui towers over his would-be protector... and still has no idea Yuujirou's had a crush on him since they were kids!

THIS WONDERFUL SEASON WITH YOU

Atsuko Yusen

this **Wonderful season** with **you**

ATSUKO YUSEN

δLOVE-x-LOVEδ   MATURE 18+

Enoki is practically the poster-boy for what a typical nerd looks like: short and slight, complete with big round glasses and social awkwardness. His main hobby is making video games, and he's used to not having many friends at school. Then, he meets Shirataki, a former member of the baseball club and his exact opposite; tall, muscular and sporty. Despite their many differences, the spark of friendship between the two boys begins to grow into something more...

TOKYOPOP

DON'T CALL ME DADDY
Gorou Kanbe

Don't Call
Me Daddy.

GOROU KANBE

§LOVE-x-LOVE§

Long before the events of *Don't Call Me Dirty*, Hanao Kaji and Ryuuji Mita were close friends...
When Ryuuji is left to raise his son Shouji as a single father, Hanao steps up to help him out. At
first, their family life is happy and content, but Hanao's true feelings for Ryuuji become more and
more difficult for him to ignore. The pressure of staying closeted eventually becomes too much
to bear; Hanao leaves, choosing to run from his feelings and his fears of somehow "messing
up" Shouji's life when he starts getting teased at school for having two dads. Years later, when
he comes home to care for his aging father and ends up advising Shouji on his blossoming
relationship with Hama, Hanao realizes it's time to face his own past... and his future.

THE ANATOMIST

Esa Parr

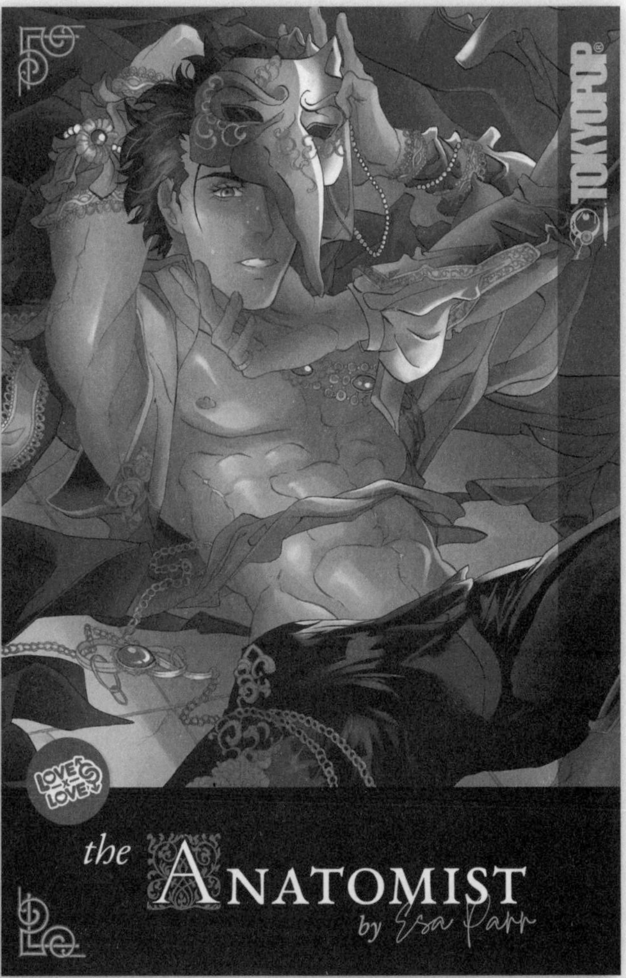

TOKYOPOP
LOVE x LOVE
the ANATOMIST
by Esa Parr

LOVE-x-LOVE MATURE 18+

Venice, 1549 — the height of the Renaissance in Italy, a time of incredible advancement in the arts, technology and science. Giorgio is an anatomist, passionate about studying the human body and advancing the field of medicine. For this, he's willing to take steps as drastic as necessary, and doesn't hesitate to experiment even on living people. In the name of science, he makes the beautiful Belfore his guinea pig, keeping him around as a subject and a lover. But having studied Belfore for years, Giorgio's ability to gain new knowledge from him plateaus. That's when he meets the angelic, strikingly gorgeous Harlow during Carnival. Harlow's unique physiology as an intersex individual sparks new interest for Giorgio's research. However, he did not expect the delicate feelings that Harlow seems to be developing for Belfore...

TOKYOPOP

KATAKOI LAMP
Kyohei Azumi

ᵟLOVE-x-LOVEᵟ

Kazuto Muronoi runs a cute little coffee shop, where many people enjoy doing some work or writing papers for school. Among his coffee shop's regulars is a college student named Jun, who often studies there. It was love at first sight for Kazuto! Will Kazuto be able to find the courage to confess his crush before Jun graduates college and stops frequenting the shop? And to make matters even more complicated... it seems Jun has his sights set on another worker at the café!

THE CAT PROPOSED

Dento Hayane

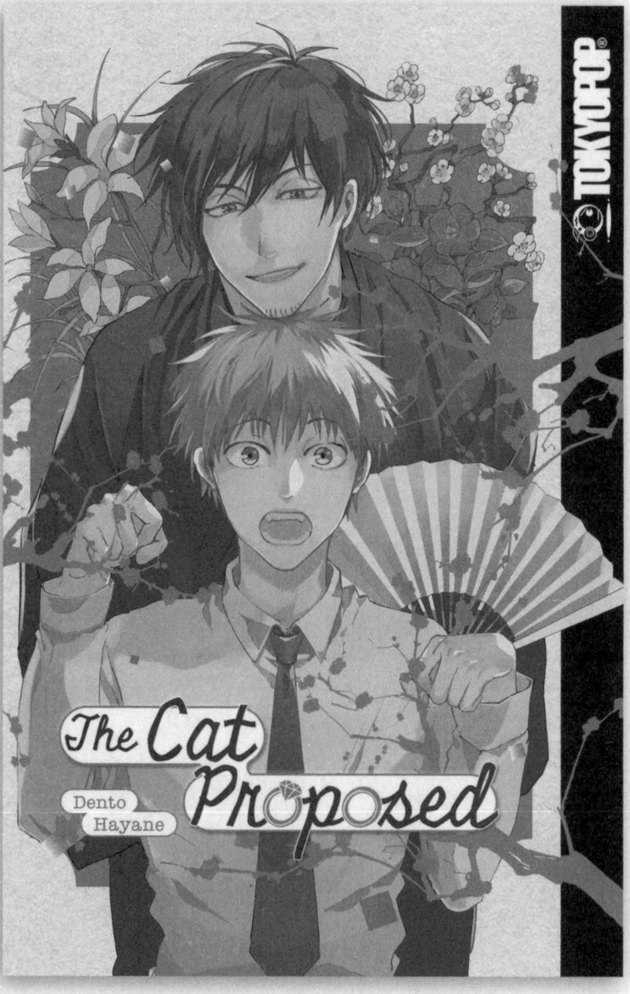
TOKYOPOP
The Cat Proposed
Dento Hayane

LOVE-x-LOVE

Matoi Souta is an overworked office worker tired of his life. Then, on his way home from a long day of work one day, he decides to watch a traditional Japanese play. But something strange happens. He could have sworn he saw one of the actors has cat ears. It turns out that the man is actually a bakeneko — a shapeshifting cat from Japanese folklore. And then, the cat speaks: "From now on, you will be my mate."

THE GOD AND THE FLIGHTLESS MESSENGER

Hagi

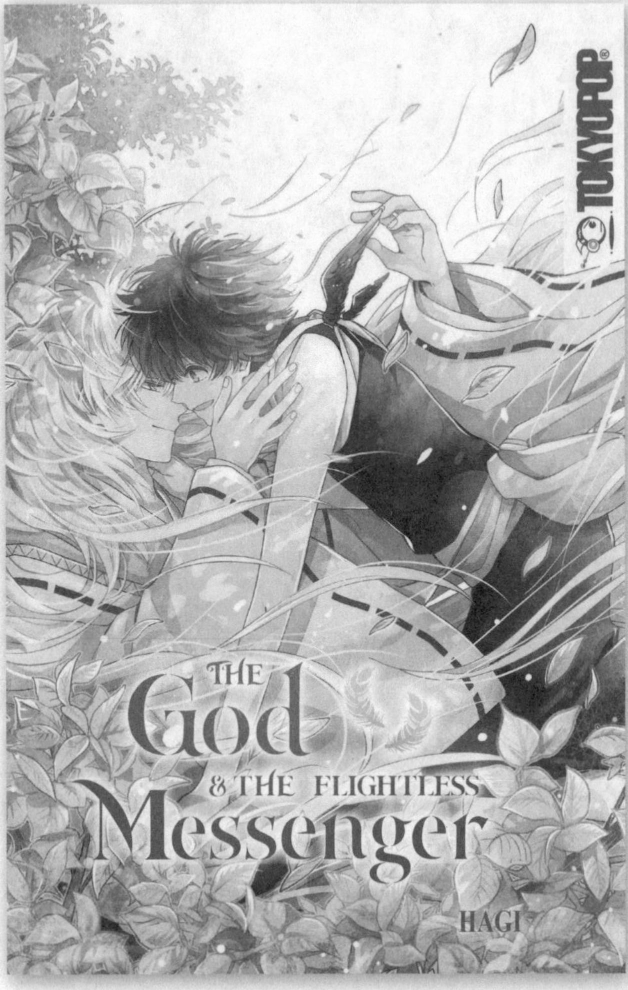
TOKYOPOP
THE
God
& THE FLIGHTLESS
Messenger
HAGI

LOVE-x-LOVE

A messenger's duty is to care for and protect the god they've been assigned to. In order to complete these tasks, such messengers require wings. Shin, however, can't fly. His tiny, useless wings make him the target of ridicule and scorn among the other messengers and have kept him from being able to serve a god... until now. Determined to prove himself as a capable messenger despite his flightlessness, Shin accepts his assignment to a mysterious being on one of the nearby mountains. At first, it seems an easy task to keep his charge safe and happy — especially when the deity in question is just a cute, fluffy ball of fur. But things aren't always what they seem. Recently, messengers flying over the strange god's mountain have been disappearing. Even as suspicion mounts against his deity, Shin just can't bring himself to think that such a gentle god could have a dark side. It's strange, but for some reason... the mysterious, fluffy being feels so familiar to him.

TOKYOPOP

LAUGHING UNDER THE CLOUDS, VOLUME 1

KarakaraKemuri

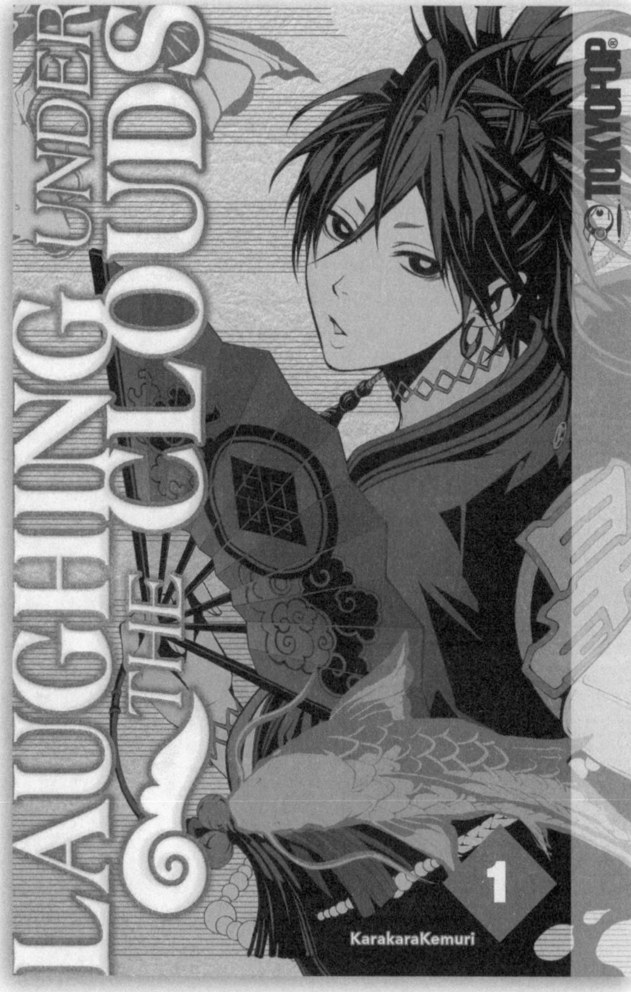
LAUGHING UNDER THE CLOUDS
TOKYOPOP
1
KarakaraKemuri

FANTASY

Under the curse of Orochi, the great demon serpent reborn every 300 years, Japan has been shrouded in clouds for as long as anyone can remember... The era of the samurai is at an end, and carrying swords has been outlawed. To combat the rising crime rates, an inescapable prison was built in the middle of Lake Biwa. When brothers Tenka, Soramaru and Chutaro Kumo are hired to capture and transport offenders to their final lodgings in this prison, they unexpectedly find themselves faced with a greater destiny than any of them could have imagined.

TOKYOPOP

A Gentle Noble's
VACATION
RECOMMENDATION

MISAKI • MOMOCHI • SANDO

1

ISEKAI

When Lizel mysteriously finds himself in a city that bears odd similarities to his own but clearly isn't, he quickly comes to terms with the unlikely truth: this is an entirely different world. Even so, laid-back Lizel isn't the type to panic. He immediately sets out to learn more about this strange place, and to help him do so, hires a seasoned adventurer named Gil as his tour guide and protector. Until he's able to find a way home, Lizel figures this is a perfect opportunity to explore a new way of life adventuring as part of a guild. After all, he's sure he'll go home eventually... might as well enjoy the otherworldly vacation for now!

Would You Like to Be a Family?
Manga by Koyama

Editor - Lena Atanassova
Marketing Associate - Kae Winters
Translator - Christine Dashiell
Copy Editor - Tina Tseng
Designer - Sol DeLeo
Editorial Associate - Janae Young
QC - Massiel Gutierrez
Licensing Specialist - Arika Yanaka
Cover Design - Sol DeLeo
Retouching and Lettering - Vibrraant Publishing Studio
Editor-in-Chief & Publisher - Stu Levy

A  Manga

TOKYOPOP inc.
5200 W Century Blvd
Suite 705
Los Angeles, CA 90045 USA

E-mail: info@TOKYOPOP.com
Come visit us online at www.TOKYOPOP.com

www.facebook.com/TOKYOPOP
www.twitter.com/TOKYOPOP
www.pinterest.com/TOKYOPOP
www.instagram.com/TOKYOPOP

ISBN: 978-1-4278-6845-9

First TOKYOPOP Printing: July 2021
Printed in CANADA

STOP

THIS IS THE BACK OF THE BOOK!

How do you read manga-style? It's simple! Let's practice -- just start in the top right panel and follow the numbers below!

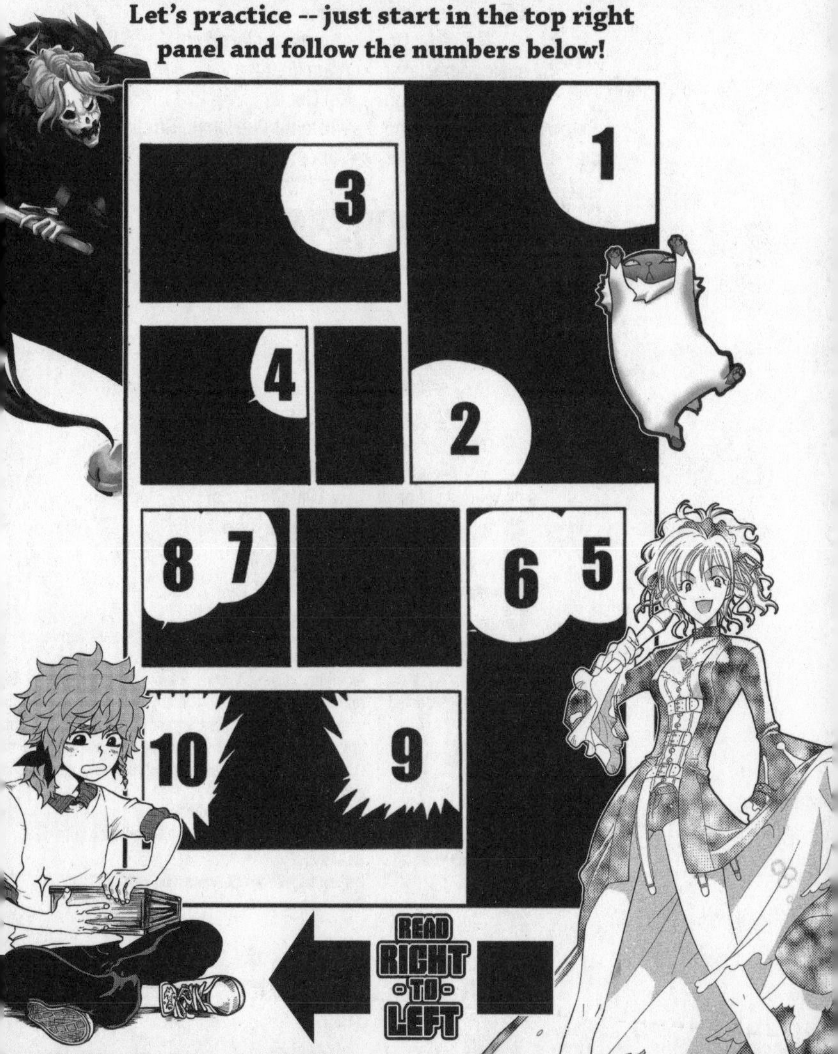
1
2
3
4
5
6
7
8
9
10
READ
RIGHT
-TO-
LEFT

rimson from ***Kamo*** / Fairy Cat from ***Grimms Manga Tales***
lorrey from ***Goldfisch*** / Princess Ai from ***Princess Ai***

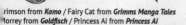